THE LEONARDO ALMANAC

International Resources
in Art, Science, and Technology

Edited by Craig Harris

The MIT Press
Cambridge, Massachusetts
London, England

DEDICATION

This book is dedicated to the individuals and organizations represented in *The Leonardo Almanac*. Their work as individuals reflects the creative force within the human spirit, and their efforts in collaboration establish opportunities to realize their vision.

Some of the items in the "Words on Works" chapter of this book are reprinted from other issues of *Leonardo*: *Leonardo* 24, Nos. 1&2 (1991); *Leonardo* 25, Nos. 1&2 (1991); *Leonardo* 26, No. 1 (1991).

This book was typeset by Craig Johnson and Chris Lippert and was printed and bound in the United States of America.

Library of Congress Cataloging-in-Publication Data

The Leonardo almanac : international resources in art, science, and technology / edited by Craig Harris.
    p.   cm. — (Leonardo books)
  Includes bibliographical references and index.
  ISBN 0-262-58125-6
  1. International Society for the Arts, Sciences and Technology. 2. Arts, Modern—20th century.
I. Harris, Craig, 1953 Mar. 08 II. Series
NX21.2.I59L46 1993
700'.1'05—dc20
                                              93-29033
                                                CIP

THE
LEONARDO
ALMANAC

CONTENTS

SERIES FOREWORD

Craig Harris
Series Editor

Many years of exploration in art, science and technology have brought us such fields as computer graphics, computer animation and music, scientific visualization and multimedia design—all of which are having a tremendous impact in the artistic, educational, research and commercial communities. The Leonardo Book Series is designed to provide comprehensive resources for orientation in and navigation through the fields in which art, science and technology converge. The series includes detailed perspectives on selected topics and on the areas where these topics intersect—with a healthy balance among philosophical, theoretical and historical perspectives and the practical applications of new ideas. The content of the series extends naturally from the long history of the journal *Leonardo* and from the activities of Leonardo, the International Society for the Arts, Sciences and Technology (Leonardo/ISAST). The goal of the series is to provide a guide through a complicated set of intersecting fields, reflecting the depth and scope of activities that will carry contemporary human perspective into the future.

Roger F. Malina
Chairman of the Board,
Leonardo/ISAST

We live in a world inevitably affected by developments in science and technology. Our knowledge of ourselves expands as discoveries in biology, neurobiology, psychology and the other sciences of living organisms are made. Technologies provide us with new tools for personal expression, but also provide a context for our existence. The linking of modern communications systems and networks places us in possible contact with a global community. Yet, within these advances, inequalities in the quality of life and access to the benefits of science and technology create human and social crises. The growing world population and the increasing burden of a technological society now leads to unacceptable burdens on the biosphere. In this changing world, the work of artists changes. Leonardo/ISAST seeks through its activities to document and communicate the work of artists who are cognisant of these changes—truly contemporary artists, who today are frequently also scientists or engineers.

INTRODUCTION

The Leonardo Almanac: International Resources in Art, Science, and Technology has been created to provide global orientation on a wide set of topics intersecting in the realm where art, science and technology converge. The publication demonstrates the interests and concerns evident in contemporary life, and reflects human expression and interaction at the cusp of another millennium. It further exemplifies how we apply scientific principles and develop technological resources to manifest our deepest perceptions about life. The *Leonardo Almanac,* and the resource project which forms the foundation for the book, are designed to be an ongoing data collection and dissemination activity, helping to document and acknowledge existing innovative work, to facilitate the creation of new work by providing improved information and communication networks, and to assist in maintaining a clarity of vision which makes it possible to evolve consciously and with purpose.

Many years of exploration and specialization in the art, science and technology domains has created a need for developing a comprehensive perspective. The requisites for maneuvering among a complex set of intersecting fields include collaboration with other individuals, in concert with the organizations and structures that individuals create to facilitate their work. The *Leonardo Almanac* strives to bridge traditional disciplinary and cultural boundaries and to promote the sharing of knowledge and resources between organizations and individuals on a global scale. Individuals seeking opportunities for artistic and educational development, or for contact with individuals and organizations with similar interests but different resources and areas of expertise, will find concrete information that can facilitate their search and provide insight into how others have responded to similar challenges. Organizations seeking collaborators to complete a project, or looking for artists who work in specific media for exhibits or events, have access to an international network of individuals and organizations to guide them to the most effective use of their resources. The goal remains to maximize human potential and to contribute to the consolidation of resources.

The origin for the *Leonardo Almanac* can be traced to several sources. Leonardo/ISAST began publishing in electronic media in 1988 with the establishment of *FineArt Forum* and the *Fine Art Science and Technology Database and Bulletin Board.*[1] Work on this project included the development of an organizations database, which was published by Leonardo/ISAST as a hardcopy index and directory of art, science and technology organizations, and was installed in electronic medium on the WELL and MCI systems.[2] This project was initiated in response to a recognized need for improved communication networks between individuals and organizations. This same need to facilitate communication and the exchange of knowledge prompted the development of a resource project within the International Computer Music Association, resulting in a publication coedited with Stephen Pope in 1987, entitled *Computer Music Association Source Book—Activities and Resources in Computer Music.*[3] The latter publication provided profiles of education and research facilities, tabulated a variety of details regarding technological resources, and included references to 15 years of proceedings and concerts from the association's international conferences. The orientation of the source book—presenting multiple perspectives on a complex and evolving universe—provides the model for this publication. Much is revealed about creative activity through close examination of existing education and resource programs, the resources present at institutions and at individual studios, and the art and writings of the individuals creating in these environments. It serves to document the work, and to provide greater access to the human, information, and technological resources which comprise the contemporary world. Another model for the *Leonardo Almanac* is the annual resource publication produced by the Center for Computer Assisted Research in the Humanities (CCARH), *Computing in Musicology*.[4] Each volume of the CCARH publication presents contemporary activity in musicological research from a variety of perspectives, including bibliographic references, surveys of software programs, directory information, and feature articles.

The *Leonardo Almanac* provides a variety of perspectives of current activities in art, science and technology. The title originates in the reference to a publication comprised of a collection of lists, tables, charts, and other useful information of interest to a disparate audience. More than a single image, or even a collection of still images or snapshot views of international activity, the *Leonardo Almanac* offers multiple intersecting views of the same world. The analogy is that of a kaleidoscope pointed at the globe, where each section of the publication presents a new cross section of the global community after altering the parameters for filtering and viewing the information. Each transformation of the kaleidoscope offers new opportunities for perusing a dynamic environment. The return to a previous state would be impossible, if only because one's perception has evolved in the process. The premier edition of the *Leonardo Almanac* includes the following perspectives:

The "Organization Profiles" chapter presents summaries and detailed reports, covering a wide range of activities at 50 organizations around the world. There is information about education programs, research projects, artist-in-residence programs, archive and resource projects, performance and gallery opportunities, and standards development activities.

Judy Malloy compiled 60 statements by artists in "Words on Works". These descriptions offer insights into how scientific principles and technological resources merge with personal perspectives to create specific works of art.

The "Leonardo Award Winners" chapter features individuals who have demonstrated exceptional work in the artistic and theoretical domains, and includes samples of work, bibliographic references and personal statements about their art and contemporary society.

"Leonardo Speakers' Network" provides an international presentation network comprised of artists, scientists and technologists working in a variety of fields. In addition to facilitating communication between organizations and individuals, the topics and bibliographies provide additional insights into contemporary issues and personal approaches.

"Disciplines, Activities and Resources" presents a data matrix identifying fields of interest, the nature of the activities performed by individuals and organizations, and technological resources applied.

As is the case with the "Leonardo Speakers' Network", the "Bibliographies" reflect the authors' perspectives and approaches as much as they provide pathways into a variety of contemporary topics of interest.

A set of Appendices and Indexes complete the volume, providing multiple pathways through the data.

Wherever possible, individuals and organizations are represented by the words they use to describe their own work, demonstrating the substance and depth of their activities. The *Leonardo Almanac* is a manifestation of current trends and interests in the fields which comprise the focus of the publication. The value of the information presented is a function of the quality and detail of the information solicited and supplied, and the vision which governs its presentation.

Readers are encouraged to pursue the hidden revelations and underlying threads which permeate the *Leonardo Almanac*, probing beyond task orientation, into the regions where the source of human creativity is revealed. It is in that realm where we can carry on a constructive exploration of the factors that define the quality of contemporary life, and consciously set on the course that our activities today will impose on the future.

---

[1] R. Malina, "Fineart Forum and F.A.S.T.: Experiments in Electronic Publishing in the Arts", *Leonardo* **24**:2 (Oxford, UK: Pergamon Press, 1991).

[2] E. Crumley, *International Opportunities for Artists: Grants, Fellowships, Funds, Artist-in-Residencies* (Oxford, UK: Pergamon Press, 1988).

[3] C. Harris and S. Pope, eds., *Computer Music Association Source Book—Activities and Resources in Computer Music* (San Francisco, CA: International Computer Music Association, 1987).

[4] W. Hewlett and E. Selfridge-Field, *Computing in Musicology* (Menlo Park, CA: Center for Computer Assisted Research in the Humanities).

ACKNOWLEDGMENTS

A publication of this nature could not be produced in a timely fashion without the efforts of many people. This book represents the dedicated work of the entire Leonardo/ISAST staff, both in the initial development of content previously published in the journal *Leonardo* and in the electronic publications, and in the preparation of the information for the *Leonardo Almanac*. Annie Lewis provided invaluable advice and assistance in activities ranging from data solicitation, collection and data entry to publication design and indexing. Judy Malloy's contributions in compiling the "Words on Works" and the "Bibliographies" chapters represent three years of work cultivating each section to provide a wide range of perspectives. Nancy Nelson's work developing *FineArt Forum*, *Leonardo Electronic News* and the *Fine Art, Science and Technology Database and Archive* was instrumental in preparing the foundation for the system which made the *Leonardo Almanac* possible. Zara Santos spent countless hours entering mountains of survey information and massaging the bibliographies. Pat Bentson and Pam Grant-Ryan have been extremely helpful in a variety of production issues.

Leonardo/ISAST implemented a student intern program with Steve Wilson's Art and Telecommunications students at San Francisco State University. Michelle Devine and Amy Wulfing from the class at San Francisco State University, and Gordon Terry, a visiting student from the Rhode Island School of Design were deeply involved in pouring through five years of data, assisting in the process of incorporating the information into a comprehensive, integrated resource. These students' assistance is greatly appreciated, and we hope that their experience working on this project was valuable in providing insight into the world of art, science and technology. Finally, I would like to acknowledge Beverly Reiser and Trudy Myrrh Reagan of YLEM: Artists Using Science and Technology for distributing our survey to their membership. This widened the scope of the data solicitation, increasing the value of the information represented in the book.

Craig Harris
San Francisco, California
July 1993

ORGANIZATION PROFILES

INTRODUCTION

The patterns of interaction are evolving among organizations operating in the realm where art, science and technology converges, forging creative partnerships and methods for developing human and technological resources. The activities of the organizations featured in this chapter demonstrate the vitality of the international community, and the intense focus directed towards exploring these diverse fields, and life in contemporary society. The profiles are further indication of the global interest in building bridges across traditional field distinctions and cultural boundaries. The interdisciplinary orientation and the collaborative efforts contribute to a synthesis of knowledge acquired from many years of specialization into a more comprehensive understanding about human activity.

This chapter provides information about education programs, research projects, artist-in-residence and arts funding programs, archive and resource projects, performance and gallery opportunities, and standards development activities. There are summaries and detailed reports, covering a wide range of activities around the world. Organizations that operate at the local level are included with those that operate in the national and international arenas, demonstrating the many ways that the activities of organizations and individuals intersect. Contributions to the section were supplied by the organizations in response to solicitation for the *Leonardo Almanac*, and during the course of Leonardo/ISAST's other publishing and society activities. Organizations are invited to submit information about their activities to be incorporated into the database, and for use in future publications.

ART & SCIENCE COLLABORATIONS, INC. (ASCI)

Cynthia Pannucci
PO Box 040496
Staten Island, NY 10304-0009 USA
Tel: (718) 816-9796

The primary mission of ASCI is to champion interactive, kinetic and technology-based art and to encourage collaborations between the art and science communities. To support this effort, ASCI is devoted to providing access to information and resources, to creating opportunities for artists, and to building public awareness and appreciation for members' art and collaborative projects.

ASCI achieves these objectives through monthly meetings, a monthly bulletin, public exhibitions and publications. The monthly meetings have come to represent the backbone of the organization in terms of opening a dialogue between members and building the supportive community necessary for collaboration to sprout and grow. ASCI's guest speaker roster began with artist member, Eric Staller, who has been building interactive, techno-performance sculpture for the past 15 years. In his work Staller has incorporated a Volkswagon Bug embedded with several thousand small Christmas tree bulbs, a fiber-optic bubble boat, and a circular bicycle-for-four. Recently he and his architect wife have produced two large-scale kinetic sculptures for corporate atrium spaces in Japan. Other artist members to make presentations have included: Gerald Marks, who produced a 3D video for the Rolling Stones; Steven s'Soreff, who creates post-conceptual "art of the future"; Sydney Cash, who works with opto-kinetic glass sculpture; Tom Klinkowstein, who develops fax and telecommunications projects; and Doris Vila, whose new work links video holograms from her residency in Cologne, Germany.

In order to increase members' access to technical information, guest speakers on alternating months come from local service organizations, industries representing new materials or technologies or are professional consultants. Karen Helmerson, Deputy Director of FILM/VIDEO ARTS in Manhattan, New York City, NY, described their programs and services for artists; Carl Machover, President of international computer graphics consulting firm MAC, Inc. brought ASCI members up-to-speed on Virtual Reality technologies; Theresa Bell, product manager at Rosco Labs, Inc., demonstrated 3-M's "light-piping" film and Rosco's dichroic glass filters; and Fred M. Wilf, Esq. of Elman and Wilf spoke to the group about issues of non-disclosure agreements, and how to protect intellectual property. Some of the monthly meetings are spent visiting a different artist member's studio. The closer look at the work, equipment, tools and studio set-ups is a big success because of the relaxed and personal aspects of the situation.

ART COM

Carl Loeffler
PO Box 193123 Rincon Annex
San Francisco, CA 94119-3123 USA
Tel: (415) 431-7524
Fax: (415) 431-7841
Email: artcomtv@well.sf.ca.us

Founded in 1975, Art Com is a San Francisco-based cultural organization specializing in the interface of contemporary art and new communication technology. Select projects include:

Art Com Electronic Network (ACEN)
Available on the Whole Earth 'Lectronic Link (WELL), ACEN is an on-line information service and bulletin board, featuring discussion groups, publications, global projects, electronic galleries and more. Art Com is also available as alt.artcom, a news group distributed internationally by USENET.

Art Com Magazine
Since 1975 Art Com magazine has served as an artist-based chronicle of contemporary art activities. The publication is now released monthly and is available free of charge.

Art Com Distribution
The Art Com organization publishes an annual *Media Distribution Catalog*, and releases periodic updates.

Art Com Television
The Art Com organization maintains an independent video distribution service which operates in 14 countries, providing programming for broadcast and cable television. Art Com also organizes touring video programming for educators and festivals.

Contemporary Art Press
The Art Com organization maintains Contemporary Arts Press, publishers and distributors of books on contemporary art, specializing in post modernism, video, computer and performance art.

ART RESEARCH CENTER (ARC)

PO Box 30098
Kansas City, MO 64112 USA
Tel: (816) 531-7799

ARC's 25-year history has established its international orientation on aesthetics and experimental art making, with a focus on scientific, technical and social interrelationships. For its members, associates and colleagues, ARC provides exhibition opportunities, stimulation of its theoretical concepts, its worldwide alliances and its special cooperation with others of many disciplines.

ARTS WIRE

Anne Focke
811 First Avenue, #403
Seattle, WA 98104 USA
Tel: (206) 343-0769
Email: afocke@tmn.com

Anna Couey
1077 Treat Avenue
San Francisco, CA 94110 USA
Tel: (415) 826-6743
Email: couey@tmn.com

Arts Wire is an on-line computer-based network service providing immediate access to news, facts, information and dialogue on the social, economic, philosophical, intellectual and political conditions affecting the arts and artists today. Available to artists, crafts people, arts organizations, and interested individuals, Arts Wire provides access to local, regional, and national perspectives through the use of a personal computer, connected via a modem to existing telephone lines.

Arts Wire aims to increase dialogue among its users, encouraging them to interact more extensively to share information. Arts Wire is committed to providing a forum for the free expression of ideas among the many diverse communities and individuals that comprise the United States arts community.

Arts Wire is a program of the New York Foundation for the Arts in collaboration with many individuals and organizations around the country. From the outset, Arts Wire has involved artists in its planning and design, and is committed to keeping artists' voices at the heart of the service.

Information on Arts Wire is organized into Interest Groups, established by people who gather and disseminate arts-related news and ideas. Interest Groups currently in formation are: AMCOL (American Music Center On-line); American Indian Telecommunication; Association of Hispanic Arts; Association of Independent Video and Film Makers; Coalition of Community Cultural Centers, Chicago; a consortium of arts magazines; CraftNet; Grantmakers in the Arts; Greater Philadelphia Cultural Alliance; Literary Network; Middle Passage/Regional Educational and Arts Computer Network; National Alliance of Artists' Communities; NAAO (National Association of Artists Organizations); National Campaign for Freedom of Expression; National Institute of Arts & Disabilities; National Performance Network; NewMusNet; A New York statewide Interest Group; Public Partners (an Interest Group of the state and regional arts agencies); Visual AIDS and the AIDS Working Group.

AUSTRALIAN NETWORK FOR ART AND TECHNOLOGY (ANAT)

Lion Arts Center
PO Box 8029
Hindley Street
Adelaide 500 Australia
Tel: 61-8-2319037
Fax: 61-8-2117323
Email: anat@peg.pegasus.oz.au

ANAT undertakes a wide range of activities including training programs, funding of artist's projects, maintenance of a relevant database, curatorial advice and conference organization. ANAT was the host organization for the Third International Symposium for Electronic Art (1992), the most significant art and technology event held in Australia.

THE BANFF CENTRE FOR THE ARTS

Douglas MacLeod, Sara Diamond, Kevin Elliott
PO Box 1020
Banff, Alberta T0L 0C0 Canada
Tel: (403) 762-6309
Email: kelliott@acs.ucalgary.ca

The Banff Centre for the Arts is a year-round facility providing a wide range of opportunities for professional artists to develop and expand their creativity. The Centre provides a supportive environment and the means to acquire new conceptual and technical skills. Artists are encouraged to explore traditions, forms, media, and practices in a community of peers. As well, artists are encouraged to explore the connections between art-making and critical thought in the broader context of culture and society.

The mandate of the Centre for the Arts is to develop and expand the creativity of the individual artist. Recognizing the continuing needs of mature artists for transformative growth in their professional lives, the Centre offers programs specifically designed to help such individuals acquire the conceptual and technical skills to create new work. At the same time, the Centre aims to act as a catalyst in relation to the larger world of culture and society, playing a leadership role in promoting the health of the arts and in defending a progressive conception of the arts as living culture.

Artists are involved in programs and projects in many ways and often return at successive stages of their careers. The artistic community is mixed in age, gender, nationality, media, and cultural history. The faculty at the Centre are working artists who commit a significant part of their professional lives to shaping program concepts and processes. Through their expertise and leadership, they help to implement the intent of the Centre for the Arts.

Programs of the Centre include Media Arts (Television & Video, Audio, Computer Applications & Research, New Media Research); Visual Arts (Art Studio, Ceramics, Photography, Walter Phillips Gallery); Music (Chamber Music, Master Classes, Long- and Short-Term Residencies, Jazz Workshop); Theatre Arts (Dance, Music Theatre, Opera, Singing, Drama); Literary Arts (Writing, Radio Drama, Screenwriters' Workshop, Publishing, Playwrights' Colony, Arts Journalism); and the Leighton Studios (all disciplines). In addition, the Centre supports thematic residencies across programs and disciplines (1993/94 "Nomad"); and special conferences (1993 "The Tuning of the World", the First International Conference on Acoustic Ecology).

The Banff Centre overlooks the town of Banff, Alberta, located in the Canadian Rocky Mountains. The Centre provides full accommodation services to artists on a shared basis. Rooms are furnished and equipped with bath or shower. A few one-bedroom suites are available during the fall and winter period. Artists bringing families to Banff may find accommodations in the towns of Banff or Canmore. Dining room service is provided for breakfast, lunch and dinner. A community services office provides referrals, medical and counseling services, travel and visa assistance, and other information and support for artists in residence.

The Banff Centre awards financial aid to artists based primarily on artistic merit. In most cases and for most programs, acceptance to the program is accompanied by financial aid. Such aid will vary by program and applicant, and may cover the costs of program fee, room, and meal plan. Stipends are not normally available.

Focus on Media Arts

The Banff Centre was founded in 1933 as a theatre summer school. Over the decades it has expanded and grown to encompass the whole spectrum of artistic disciplines, and established an international reputation for the quality of its programs in the service of professional artists in career transition.

The newest division of the Centre is Media Arts, established in 1990. Media Arts provides production and technical support to artists working with a wide range of mediums, including television, video, interactive multimedia, telecommunications, audio, electroacoustics, digital imaging, animation, and virtual environments. It consists of three connected programs which share facilities, equipment, and staff. The three programs are Computer Applications and Research; Audio; and Television &

Video. Interested applicants are free to make project proposals to a single program or to any combination of the three.

As well, Media Arts has recently (1992) begun a significant applied research initiative, funded by the Canadian Department of Communications, to develop new computer-based tools for artists producing work in the context of the emerging digital culture.

The programs of Media Arts offer project-based residencies for artists, both long- and short-term; associate residencies for technical practitioners working in the artistic context (stipend provided); workshops, seminars and colloquia in the theory and practice of electronic mediums; concerts, performances and installations; and access to electronic tools for artists working in related programs of the Centre. Much of the work produced in Media Arts is disseminated internationally through exhibition, electronic and print publications, video, broadcast television and radio, and compact disc.

Highlights of 1992

The Television & Video program completed production of *Travelogue Four: Coming From the Wrong Side* by Belgian artist Stefaan Decostere. The video premiered at The Banff Centre July 10, and was broadcast later in the year on the Belgian Radio Television Network, the Access Network in Alberta, the Knowledge Network in British Columbia, and the Saskatchewan Television Network. It was also screened at the Montreal Festival of New Cinema. Meena Nanji completed *Voices of the Morning*, and it subsequently won the Juror's award from the Black Maria Festival, and it was scheduled for screening at the National Asian American TV Festival, Women in the Director's Chair, and the American Film Institute Festival.

Other video work produced in Media Arts during 1992 included Paul Wong's *Chinaman's Peak: Walking the Mountain*, which premiered at the IMAGE and NATION Festival in Montreal and was shown at the Contemporary Art Gallery in Vancouver; and pieces by Shani Mooto (working with Shona Bahari) and Gita Saxena (*New View, New Eyes*). Critic Zainub Verjee wrote about the work of these resident artists, and many of the artists participated in the Art Studio's *Instability of the Feminist Subject* residency.

During 1992, the Audio program was active in a range of projects including recordings of chamber music (Howard Bashaw, Steve Reich, Robert Rosen, Jacques Diennet, Talivaldis Kenins, Jean Coulthard, Anton Kuerti, Graciane Finzi, Moshe Denburg), jazz (Bill Frisell, Orange Then Blue, Kenny Wheeler), electroacoustics (Daniel Scheidt, Maryann Amacher, Roger Doyle, Wende Bartley, Dennis Smalley, Peter Nelson, Michael Matthews), and opera (Michael Maguire); sound/mixed-media installations (David Felder, Margo Kane, Phillip Djwa, Gudrun Gut, Pauline Cummins); radio and radiophonics (Francis Dyson, Dick Higgins, Hildegard Westerkamp, Dan Lander, Hank Bull); and TV/video soundtracks (John Oswald, Brian Ales, Maria Luisa Mendosa, Paul Wong, Meena Nanji).

Computer Applications and Research began the first pieces in the Art and Virtual Environments Project, working with artists including Michael Naimark, Michael Scroggins, Ron Kuivila, Pauline Cummins, Michael Mackenzie and Toni Dove. This project provides artists with access to virtual reality equipment and technologists for the purposes of artistic creation. Lawrence Paul's virtual reality project *Inherent Rights, Inherent*

Visions premiered at the National Gallery of Canada in September. This is the first virtual reality piece to be shown in the National Gallery, and the exhibition led to requests for showings in Finland, Poland, France, Korea and Japan. Marcos Novak, Diane Gromala and Yacov Sharir created a video of their multimedia work, *The Virtual Dervish*. This work includes dance, theatre, interactive music, projects and virtual reality. And Perry Hoberman (Brooklyn, NY) completed the planning and preliminary work on his virtual reality conference. Computer Applications & Research also presented work at the Digital World Conference in Los Angeles, at the SIGGRAPH Computer Graphics Conference in Chicago, and at the Medienbiennale in Leipzig.

Media Arts presented a range of interactive, sound-based work developed at the Banff Centre in the exhibition *Machine-Mind-Music*, curated by audio program director Kevin Elliott, at the 1992 Glenn Gould Conference in Toronto. The event featured an extended concert of interactive live music, mostly developed at the Centre, by composers Daniel Scheidt, Michael Century, John Oliver, Keith Hamel, Wende Bartley, David Eagle, and Jocelyn Robert; the virtual environment composition *Babel Project* (excerpt), by Roger Doyle and Dorota Blaszczak; a hypermedia display including the Centre's *Glenn Gould Profile*; and *North Revisited*, a work by Kevin Elliott and Rick Bidlack, using virtual sound production techniques developed at the Centre.

BAY AREA CENTER FOR ART & TECHNOLOGY (BACAT)

1095 Market Street, Suite 209
San Francisco, CA 94103 USA
Tel: (415) 626-2979

BACAT was founded in 1985 to facilitate explorations into art and technology, and the unique synergy between these two broad areas of human endeavor. Art represents the creative impulse within all humans, an impulse thwarted as often as not by the dictates of *responsibility*. Technology is often the fruit of creative impulses applied to practical problems. But technology comes to embody the dominant priorities of the society in which it develops, and only through concerted effort can it be made to serve creative ends.

BACAT promotes explorations into lost or diminished subjective sensibilities. The hope is that this activity will tear the thin veneer of dulled acceptance of the intimate realities of daily life. Foremost in this effort is developing creative uses of new communication technologies, and artistic uses of older ones. Revealing the nitty-gritty details of daily life in a meaningful way requires above all a reassertion of public space and of public discourse, validating the perceptions and experiences of average citizens.

THE CADRE INSTITUTE: COMPUTERS IN ART AND DESIGN/ RESEARCH AND EDUCATION

Joel Slayton
School of Art and Design
San José State University
One Washington Square
San José, California 95192 USA
Tel: (408) 924-4368
Email: slayton@sjsuvm1.bitnet.edu

The CADRE Institute of the School of Art and Design at San José State University is an interdisciplinary academic program dedicated to experimental applications of computer graphics, interactive media and electroacoustics. CADRE faculty and students are actively engaged in research, testing and exploration of new computer-based media in the visual arts, design, music, installation, performance and education.

The CADRE Institute evolved from a 1981 recommendation by the California Arts Council. The council resolved that industry, as well as the public, needed to be made more aware and become more supportive of the arts and their relationship to new technology. The objective was to establish an interdisciplinary educational center for the exploration of computer media in Silicon Valley.

As a catalyst to this objective, The CADRE Conference was sponsored in 1984 by San José State University. This festival-like event engaged the entire region in a series of exhibitions, concerts, performances, industry tours, technology workshops and symposia on the latest in computer visualization and acoustics. Building on the interest stemming from this conference the School of Art and Design at San José State University initiated The CADRE Institute for the research and exploration of emerging media technology.

The School of Art and Design offers professional programs in the visual and three dimensional arts, photography, graphic design, illustration, interior design, industrial design, art education, and art history. The CADRE Institute offers advanced computer-based instruction in each of these disciplines, as well as specialized undergraduate and graduate programs in computer graphics and interactive media. The Electro-Acoustic Studio, a sister program in the Music Department, offers opportunities for digital composition and performance. Additional adjunct programs in Theater Arts, Engineering and Computer Science provide opportunities for interdisciplinary study.

Industry Sponsors
Corporations involved in sponsored project support and in providing educational opportunities include: Alias Research, Apple Computer Inc., Asanti Technologies, Caliber Tech, Inc., Compression Labs, Inc., E-mu Systems, Ford Motor Company, IBM, OpCode, Pacific Bell, RasterOps Corp., Riverview Systems Group, Panasonic Corp., Silicon Graphics Inc., Software Systems Inc., Sun Micro Systems, and VideoMedia Inc..

Conferences
The CADRE Institute is the home of the 1986 Silicon Valley Festival of Electronic Arts, The 1989 National Computer Graphics Association Arts Conference: *The Dimensions of Interactivity*, the 1992 International Computer Music Conference hosted by the Electro-Acoustic Studio, and the 1992 International Industrial Design Conference.

Educational Programs

Bachelor of Arts with Emphasis in Computer Arts
An interdisciplinary undergraduate degree program requiring inter-departmental and university study.

Master of Arts in Multimedia Computing
Professional research and applications development involving interactive multimedia.

Master of Fine Arts in Computers and Electronic Arts
Terminal degree program for creative investigation in computer visualization, installation, performance, interactive systems, electroacoustics and digital video technology.

Project Descriptions

■ Digital Media and Interactive Systems
Joel Slayton, CADRE Institute Director

DoWhatDo, A Site Specific Experimental Theatrical Work
DoWhatDo was sponsored by the San José Institute of Contemporary Art with support from the National Endowment for the Arts and the City of San José, California. The premiere took place on October 16, 1992 at the International Computer Music Conference.

DoWhatDo introduced the next generation *techno-urban drive-in* as a principal means of social interaction. The top floor of the city of San José's public parking facility was transformed into a hi-tech, multimedia drive-in, drive-through interactive movie. The dynamic transformational character of the site enabled electronic creation of environments specific to the cultural disposition of the performers and audience. *DoWhatDo* involved the collaboration of over 200 interdisciplinary artists, musicians and performers with technologists encompassing computer graphics, engineering, interactive systems, video, networking, telecommunications and electroacoustics.

Virtual Reality Pedestal Display System
This is a prototype *stand-alone* interactive stereo viewer developed in collaboration with Professor An Nygun (Engineering and Robotics). The pedestal design enables users to interact, navigate and control scenes.

■ Interactive Multimedia for Education
Kathy Cohen, Art History

IBM Partnership Project: Multimedia for Multicultural Learning
The Multimedia for Multicultural Learning project is sponsored by IBM, the California Department of Education and the California State University system. Development of four interactive multimedia modules which introduce students to a variety of cultures using local architecture as the metaphor.

Library of the Future & The Knowledge Network
This project is based on the development of a prototype for the Library of the Future in conjunction with Bellcore, the research division of Pacific Bell. It involves the distribution of images, sound and text using a variety of interactive communication devices. These resources facilitate the exploration of multicultural, multimedia database design for distribution over university networks.

■ Interface Design and Multimedia
Patricia Coleman, Studio Art

Think A Thought
Think a Thought is a visual animation and multimedia demonstration created for Apple Computer for the Hypercard 2.0 product introduction at the World Wide Developers Conference and MacWorld in San Francisco.

Exploring Architecture
The Learning Station is an interactive multimedia project produced for the Frank LLoyd Wright Exhibition: *In Realm of Ideas* for the County of Marin and San Diego Museum of Modern Art.

HyperDodgson
An interactive kiosk created for the George Coates Performance Works for the production *Right Mind*, commissioned by the American Conservatory Theater (ACT) of San Francisco. A multimedia kiosk was installed in the ACT lobby.

■ Experimental Vehicle Design
Del Coates, Transportation Design

Concept Vehicle Design
The project explores three-dimensional modeling and rendering techniques for vehicle design, and is sponsored by Ford Motor Company.

There is an emphasis on surface rendering capabilities for articulated visualization.

Quantification of Empirical Aesthetics
This is an interactive multimedia project for aesthetic analysis, evaluation and research relating to product design criteria.

■ Telepresence and Robotics
Kelvin Chan, Technical Coordinator

Mini Telepresent Robots
Mini-Telepresent Robots incorporates designs for gathering and transmission of visual and acoustic information. Robots respond to stimulus such as motion, color and sound, enabling independent navigation and communications among robots for collective interactions and behavior.

Children's Technology Workshop
The Children's Technology Workshop is sponsored by the Pacific Science Center in Seattle, Washington, in conjunction with the University of Washington Human Interface Technology Lab. It consists of an eight-week program introducing virtual reality, robotics and automation, computer graphics and animation, interactive multimedia and electroacoustics to students aged 7-17.

■ Information Systems and Networking
Don Tanner, Assistant Director of University Computing

Distributed Communications
This project develops audio and video applications for distribution over interactive data networks. The focus is on developing multi-user educational and entertainment systems involving satellite, microwave, T1, ISDN, ATM and Internet communications.

■ Computer Music Composition and Performance
Allen Strange, Co-Director, Electro-Acoustic Studio

Cygnus
Cygnus is a collaborative site-specific installation created with microwave sculptor Mike Heively. Topographic data is translated into MIDI sound scores, providing a music map that is converted to microwave for deep space transmission of sonic forms. The installation includes specific configuration of sculpture antennae based on astronomy.

Interactive Compositions for Computer and Violin
Live performance of electronic music and traditional string instrumentation.

■ Digital Recording and Orchestration
Dan Wyman

Film Scoring
Feature works include *Halloween*, *The Fog*, *Hellnight*, *Missing*, the *Lawnmower Man* and the experimental electronic work, *XHERONE*, commissioned by the Stuttgart Tage fur Neue Musik.

■ Electronic Mural Project
Judith Mayer

Global Interactive Art Network
A global tele-interactive art network enables artists from different locations to draw and create together as if they were in the same room work-

ing on the same canvass. The *Electronic Mural Project* links geographically and culturally diverse communities through computer and telecommunication networks.

■ Conversational Systems
Steve Durie

Association Engine
This project involves computer-to-computer dialog for dynamic temporal control of image and sound retrieval, referencing, sequencing, editing, composition and performance. Conversational simulation techniques provide models for machine association and user interface design.

■ Video and Animation
John Bender, Jason Challas, Cassandra Lehman

Digital Visualization System
The Digital Visualization System is based on the development of computer-controlled access, manipulation, editing and image synthesis for integrated recording of image processing, computer animation, digital and analog video and audio.

CAPP STREET PROJECT

270 14th Street
San Francisco, CA 94103 USA
Tel: (415) 626-7747
Fax: (415) 626-7991

Capp Street wishes to serve a larger audience through outreach to diverse audiences and the expansion of programs presented.

The Residency Program supports artistic research and development by providing multi-disciplinary artists with living, studio and exhibition space as well as funding and administrative support.

The Experimental Projects Program challenges traditional exhibition practices and encourages interdisciplinary collaboration between the arts, sciences, and humanities. This program is open exclusively to San Francisco Bay Area artists.

The Off-Site Installation Program provides opportunities for artists to create temporary installations in response to specific public sites in the San Francisco Bay Area. Capp Street assists artists in site selection, covering materials expenses and paying direct artist fees.

Capp Street Project continues to expand its Educational Programs as well. They have opened up the creative process to a larger community through:

- Artists workshops that assist artists in resolving career issues and identifying available community resources.
- SITE SPECIFICS: Forums on Contemporary Culture that examine current issues in contemporary art, particularly as they relate to site-specific installation work.
- The Archive on Installation Art includes over 500 artists and organizations currently working in the field and is open to the public. The archive is a unique resource for artists, curators, and scholars. It features catalogs, résumés, bibliographies and documentation of artists' projects.

THE CENTER FOR ARTS & TECHNOLOGY AT CONNECTICUT COLLEGE

Noel Zahler
Connecticut College
270 Mohegan Avenue, Box 5632
New London, CT 06320 USA
Tel: (203) 439-2001
Fax: (203) 439-2700
Email: nbzah@mvax.cc.conncoll.edu

The Center for Arts & Technology at Connecticut College is the primary site on campus for the introduction, adaptation and dissemination of new technologies to the college community. In addition to offering research facilities and expertise, the Center is involved in a number of on-going activities that demonstrate a broad range of interdisciplinary interests, including the fields of theater, music, art, dance, physics, psychology, literature/linguistics, mathematics, child development and education.

The Center sponsors biennial arts & technology symposia, which have attracted great interest from the international science and art communities. The symposia have brought the latest and most innovative research applications to the campus. The 1993 Fourth Biennial Symposium on the Arts & Technology featured 72 presentations, with topics covering the fields of art, music, medicine and education.

The symposia are organized to present a balanced representation of the technical and aesthetic forces determining the computer arts. These are opportunities for experiencing the merging of music, art, technology, dance, poetry, theater, scientific visualization, cognitive psychology, film studies, physics, and other relevant topics. In addition to four days of presentations by artists, scientists, and technology experts, there are concerts, panel discussions and exhibitions of computer art and design.

In addition to national corporate support, the Center has established relationships with several local high technology firms that have demonstrated their interest in the Center. Specifically, the Center is providing needed expertise and access to new fields for defense-dependent firms seeking avenues for diversification. The Center is building long-term ties with corporations for both endowment building and research partnership. Connecticut College students play a vital role in these partnerships.

The college is in a unique position to supply the Center's corporate sponsors with the brightest young minds in the region to work as student interns. Student internships are available during the winter and summer breaks at local high technology firms.

The diversity of research pursuits of the faculty Fellows adds another component to the activities of the Center. Research grants are supported by local Corporate Partners, making possible a rich assortment of on-going projects. Proposals which have been funded include: Structure of Language; Referential Dependencies of Natural Language and Theoretical Apparatus; Interactive Wayfinding; Use of Cues by Men and Women; Computational Analysis of Metal Binding Modes in Bleomycin; Digital Sound Acquisition; and 3D Computer Animation and Sound.

In addition to the biennial symposia, the Center sponsors a regular schedule of colloquia, which brings to campus recognized leaders in specific areas of interest to the Fellows. Recent speakers have included Antonio Camurri, Professor of Informational Technology in the Department of Information Systems and Technology at the University of Genoa, Italy, and Volker Nolte, Provincial Rowing Coach of Ontario, Canada.

The Center has been involved most recently in two projects which demonstrate the collaboration of the arts and technology. Two of the Fellows developed AICP software which allows a computer to substitute for another musician or an entire orchestra. Also, in the summer of 1992 the Center co-produced with the International Sculpture Center in Washington, D.C. a 60-minute video on the computer and sculpture. The video, which has received wide distribution, features 40 international sculptors who use computers in their work.

CENTER FOR EXPERIMENTS IN ART, INFORMATION AND TECHNOLOGY AT THE CALIFORNIA INSTITUTE OF THE ARTS (CEAIT)

David Rosenboom, Mark Coniglio,
Morton Subotnick
School of Music,
California Institute of the Arts
24700 McBean Parkway
Valencia, CA 91355 USA
Tel: (805) 253-7816
Fax: (805) 254-8352
Email: davidr@calarts.edu
markc@calarts.edu
morts@calarts.edu

CalArts' Center for Experiments in Art, Information and Technology (CEAIT) was founded in 1988-89 to encourage and nurture the development of applications for new technology in the performing arts and to assist in the development of new works of art which, by their innovative nature, direct the evolution of these media in the service of new aesthetic goals. CEAIT is intended to serve as a focal point for interdisciplinary collaboration in the arts. At present, these emphasize the potential manifested by recent developments in computer technology for creating working environments in which the artist user can interact spontaneously with artistic material in real-time and the computer's ability to respond in complex ways to subtle features contained in performance gestures. In addition, these media enable artists to interact with very large databases for the purpose of creating images, making music, doing research, simulating theatrical situations, creating art through telecommunications and the manipulation of information.

Though CEAIT originated from activities in CalArts' School of Music, it benefits from a board of advisors within the Institute which represents the Schools of Art, Music, Dance, Theater, and Film/Video. CEAIT is presently planning projects that involve all these areas in a three-tiered program of activities:

1. An ongoing foundation to support technical and artistic development activities, fostering a stimulating learning environment and producing tools needed for artistic projects.

2. A program of residencies for artist-developers, workshops for invited participants, working conferences focused on specific development issues. This part of the program provides a testing environment for art works in their final stages of development and for products of the art technology and education industries.

3. A program of public presentations to include demonstrations of new developments, reports on work accomplished, performances of works in progress and high-profile productions of major artistic works that employ interactive media.

It is the intention of CEAIT to foster the development of affordable and accessible technologies which can help the artistic community participate in the evolution of the emerging global culture. Support for CEAIT is provided from the Peter Norton Family Foundation, the AT&T Foundation, Yamaha Corporation of America, and the National Endowment for the Arts.

Projects

Composition Software for Children
A major recent project has focused on developing computer-assisted teaching software designed to introduce children from ages 8 through 12 to specific notions about composition. A new program, the *Electronic Music Canvas*, presents the child with a blank canvas onto which distinct musical gestures may be entered using either a MIDI keyboard or a mouse. Gestures can be easily moved along the two axes of the canvas, pitch and time, allowing the child to organize gestures as they desire. Musical operations can also be performed on gestures, (e.g. inversions,

Fig. 1. Graduate Composer Becky Allen performing with the VideoHarp and *Interactor* software developed by Mark Coniglio and Morton Subotnick, in a CEAIT event at the Electronic Café International in Santa Monica. (Photo: Steven Gunther)

changes of tempo). Used in this way, one might describe the activity as *musical finger painting.*

Upon observing children from three area schools using the software, it was determined that more direction was needed to move the children toward the notions of composition mentioned above. To this end, an interactive scripting language was added. The scripting language is similar in style to that used in Hypercard, offering ease of use for those who do not generally write computer programs. This language allows manipulation of the materials created by the user. This means that the computer can generate examples (an ABA form, for example), from music created by the youngsters. This is done one step at a time, with each step offering the child an opportunity to make decisions about the example as it is created. Later trials with the children showed this to be a more effective and challenging method of leading them toward specific learning goals. CEAIT is currently working in collaboration with a teachers' college at Bowling Green State University to develop a complete curriculum for use with the software. In so doing, it is expected to place the software in several local classrooms.

Body Movement Sensors

CEAIT is developing a set of sensors to measure the movement of a performer's body, based on the extension of a device created by Mark Coniglio called MidiDancer. This device measures the movement of a dancer at primary limb joints and sends that information to a computer for use in generating music. The sensors used in the original MidiDancer were bulky and crude, consisting simply of a potentiometer attached to the limb to be measured. The new device uses flat plastic strips that can measure bending of a body part with better analog to digital conversion. A glove has been built that uses these flex sensors with great success.

The final goal is to create a suit or unitard with several sensors that can be slipped on by any performer. Once the hardware has been completed, software will be developed that can learn to recognize gestures made by the performer so that gestures can control output devices.

Interactive software - music cognition

Projects inspired by work in music cognition and neural information processing have just begun. These are focused on creating interactive software, designs for musical input structures, audio and graphics computation and real-time digital signal processing. One result is the program HFG (Hierarchical Form Generator), by David Rosenboom. HFG is a software package for parsing real-time musical inputs into musically meaningful sub-groupings, such as phrases or gestures, for the purpose of extending the formal possibilities of interactive performance. It includes a parsing algorithm based on a partial model of musical perception emphasizing analysis of musical contours in several parameters.

Interactive access to large-scale musical databases

Several projects in this area have been conceived and are underway. One is based on a collaboration with now-deceased composer John Cage and the Los Angeles Museum of Contemporary Art to create a mobile, museum sound installation in which audience members can use composing strategies based on chance procedures to assemble customized audio compositions that draw from material contained in very large-scale sound and image databases. The contents of these databases would relate to the life and work of John Cage and related artists and musicians.

Other large-scale musical database projects involve the creation of interactive displays on the future of the recording media with the National Academy of Recording Arts and Sciences (NARAS) and several on contemporary world music, music and the brain, and an introduction to experimental composition with La Cité de la Musique in Paris.

Experimental animation, hyper-media and music
Another project involves the integration and linking of studios and software in CalArts' computer music, hyper-media and experimental animation facilities. The current plan calls for this to be based on high-level, RISC computing platforms to create a system that can support serious, collaborative art work within the Institute.

CD-ROM Project
CEAIT is actively exploring the CD-ROM as a medium for new artworks. At present, a course in new media has been launched in which students produce CD-ROM works with assistance from The Voyager Company. Artists drawn from several disciplines, including composers, animators, graphic designers and film makers are being invited to create works that will extend this medium.

Public Programs and Residencies

Public technology demonstrations
CEAIT has produced an ongoing series of demonstrations and performances in collaboration with the Electronic Café in Santa Monica, aimed at familiarizing the public with emerging applications (Figure 1). Each of these has included demonstrations of new work from CEAIT, demonstrations by guest artist/developers, and a telecommunications link, including video and audio, with artists or developers at another center in which related work is going on. Audience members have been able to interact with both the presenters and the technology at each of these events. One highlight included two simultaneous concerts linked through this medium, one in Santa Monica, California and one in Nice, France. Real-time performance interaction was facilitated by transmission of MIDI data over satellites. David Rosenboom in California and Terry Riley in France performed a long-distance duet work with two MIDI keyboards and Yamaha Disklaviers.

Performances and Residencies
CEAIT is currently sponsoring showcase performances in the Los Angeles area. In each case, these involve presentations of music and art work that makes use of new, technological media or has grown through related developments. Some of these have included short or long-term residencies during which development work has been carried out by these artists at CEAIT. Some highlights have included Trimpin, Robert Ashley and his performance company, Tod Machover, Salvatore Martirano, and a computer-extended trio with David Rosenboom, Charlie Haden and Trichy Sankaran.

Facilities

CEAIT has recently established a Development Laboratory within the computer music studios in the School of Music at CalArts. The Lab is devoted to explorations of new media and is intended to support primarily development work. As results emerge from this work, they are immediately applied in the rich, interdisciplinary art-making context that Cal-

Arts offers. Much useful feedback to developers is provided in this way. These results are also integrated into the CalArts curriculum as appropriate.

Integrating Technology at CalArts
One of CalArts' great strengths is its interdisciplinary environment. From the beginning it has been CEAIT 's intention to grow into a leading role in the integration and coordination of technology within the Institute.

CENTRO RICERCHE MUSICALI (CRM)

Laura Bianchini,
Michelangelo Lupone
via Lamarmora, 18-1
00185 Rome, Italy

The Centro Ricerche Musicali (CRM) of Rome pursues the goal of constant interaction between the language of music and that of science by means of flexible experimentation with algorithms and systems for musical composition adapted to the demands of the expression of contemporary music. Monteverdi, while proposing the particular conditions for the advancement of *style*, specified that the evolution of technology and of compositional thought should coincide and be integrated within the musician. While it is not the intention to combine humanistic thought with scientific thought, nor the culture of the *immeasurable* with experimental tradition, the view that a rapport between these two types of thought is indispensable for a conscious culture. Such a rapport might render them capable of verifying, promoting and comprehending the need for the advancement of each other. From this view emerges the figure of a musician conscious of scientific implications and, conversely, the figure of a scientist culturally aware of contemporary artistic reality. This is a preliminary condition that lays the foundation for a common creative and speculative laboratory. CRM strives to satisfy the goals of a center of musical research, in addition to promoting a collaboration that is dynamic and coherent with progress in the realms of both humanistic and scientific thought.

At CRM, the two kinds of activities, artistic and scientific, directed by Michelangelo Lupone and the engineer Antonio Pellecchia, bring together the contributions of musicians and researchers with the characteristics described above. The results encourage the belief that the approach of CRM can prove useful in creating a more active exchange between the two cultures. In particular, CRM, the organizational direction of which is entrusted to Laura Bianchini, identifies itself with research and musical productions that, despite their typical technical complexity, have demonstrated themselves flexible and congenial to many diverse compositions. The inherent flexibility of the methods utilized at CRM has permitted CRM, in the past year, to deepen and dedicate ample space for psychoacoustic research. Considerations regarding research activities are coordinated by Fiammetta D'Emilio, a musician-anthropologist who is engaged in projects of exchange with the Consiglio Nazionale delle Ricerche (CNR).

Scientific research at CRM avails itself, above all, for the realization of computer music's environmental setting—hardware and software. The Centre collaborates with Alessandra De Vitis (physicist), whose expertise in the field of music permits a more immediate informative exchange on questions that are also technological. CRM also avails itself, for high-level programming, of the expertise of composer-mathematician Teo Usuelli and of some students at the University of Rome.

CONCEPTUAL DESIGN AND INFORMATION ARTS AT SAN FRANCISCO STATE UNIVERSITY

Steve Wilson
Art Department/School
of Creative Arts
1600 Holloway Avenue
San Francisco, CA 94132 USA
Tel: (415) 338-2291
Email: swilson@sfsuvax1.sfsu.edu

DANISH INSTITUTE OF ELECTROACOUSTIC MUSIC (DIEM)

Wayne Siegel
The Concert Hall Aarhus
Thomas Jensens Alle
DK-8000 Aarhus C, Denmark
Tel: (45) 86 20 21 33
Fax: (45) 86 19 43 86
Email: wsiegel@daimi.aau.dk

The SF State Conceptual Design and Information Arts program focuses on contemporary art explorations in non-traditional media that integrate the information bases, work styles, and perspectives of disciplines outside the arts. The program stresses integration of intuitive processes typical of the arts with structured processes of research, planning and problem solving more characteristic of other disciplines such as the humanities, science and technology. It promotes non-conventional art media, new media and the movement of artists into non-art contexts. The Conceptual Design and Information Arts program teaches students concrete skills related to contemporary theory and technology such as structured problem solving, analysis of biological systems, computers, telecommunications, interactive media, and the electronic synthesis of image, text, and sound, and explores the integration of these technologies into performance and installation. The program places emphasis on the perspectives of critical analysis of cultural systems, language and media.

DIEM is Denmark's national center for electroacoustic music. DIEM is an independent, non-profit organization funded by the Danish Ministry of Culture, whose purpose it is to assist in the production, teaching, research and performance of all styles and forms of electroacoustic music in Denmark. DIEM is a central cultural institution in Denmark with strong international relationships. The institution is housed in the concert center of Denmark's second largest city, Aarhus.

The DIEM studio consists of two rooms, 60 meters each, which were designed and constructed as a recording studio and control room when the concert hall was built in 1982. Equipment includes several Macintosh-based hard disk and sampling systems, a NeXT cube computer, and a wide range of commercially available MIDI equipment and software. The main hard disk recording system currently in use is an Audio Frame digital audio workstation. Studio time is made available at no charge to composers of all types of electroacoustic music, regardless of their artistic background or stylistic orientation. For most projects an audio technician is provided. The studio is used for tape music productions, and also provides studio time and technical and financial assistance for projects involving live and interactive computer systems.

Although DIEM is a non-affiliated independent organization, it works in close cooperation with other Danish institutions. The studio has been made available to The Royal Academy of Music in Aarhus and to The University of Aarhus for research projects and classes in electroacoustic music. DIEM has sponsored several concerts and festivals since 1988, including the NUMUS festival in Aarhus in 1988, the first Aarhus Computer Music Festival in 1989, and the 2nd NEMO Festival in 1992. Composers and performers such as Clarence Barlow, Michel Waisvisz, Alvin Lucier, George Lewis, Magnus Lindberg, Trevor Wishart, Paul Lansky, Stephen Montague, and Kaija Saariaho have been featured. A wide variety of activities have been presented, including a concert for symphony orchestra and computer. DIEM has been selected to host the 1994 International Computer Music Conference.

DO WHILE STUDIO

Jennifer Hall
273 Summer Street
Boston, MA 02210 USA
Tel: (617) 338-9129

Do While Studio is a collective of fine artists who use electronic tools and techniques to explore new avenues for their art. Do While provides access to evolving and established forms of computer technology for painters, sculptors, designers, photographers, animators, videographers, sound and performance artists. Organized to serve artists, Do While furnishes a technologically creative environment with facilities rarely found outside of academic settings or expensive video production houses. Do While's workshops, seminars and tutorials offer artists extensive and inexpensive opportunities for learning, research, experimentation and collaboration.

EDUCATION COUNCIL OF THE GRAPHIC ARTS INDUSTRY, INC.

1899 Preston White Drive
Reston, VA 22091-4367 USA
Tel: (703) 648-1768
Fax: (703) 620-0994

The mission of the Education Council is to coordinate the programs of its members and industry organizations in areas of career awareness/recruitment, education/training and industry image, and to take a leadership role in addressing unmet needs in these areas. In fulfilling its mission, the Council has the following goals:

- To coordinate and facilitate development and distribution of information about activities and materials which promote a broader understanding of careers in the modern graphic arts industry
- To coordinate, promote and facilitate a national effort to develop a positive and professional image of the graphic arts within the industry and in the general public
- To promote activities which relate to education, training and recruitment for the graphics arts industry
- To serve as a resource center for information on graphic arts education, training and recruitment
- To coordinate, encourage and recognize the improvement of quality programs and projects in graphic arts education, training and recruitment
- To identify unmet needs in education, training and recruitment and to encourage the development of programs to meet these needs.

GROUPE DE RESEARCHES MUSICALES (GRM/IRA)

Hugues Vinet, Daniel Teruggi
116, av du President Denney
75786 Paris 16 France
Tel: (33-1) 42 30 21 82
Fax: (33-1) 42 30 49 88

GRM was founded by Pierre Schaeffer more than 30 years ago and is directed by Francois Bayle. Today it remains a very active center of contemporary musical creation. The GRM, Department of the INA (National Institute of Audiovisual) since 1975, is located in the Maison de Radio France, and is well-integrated in the French audiovisual institution. Current activities include:
- research in creation tools
- research in musical sciences
- music and radio production
- training courses
- concerts
- publishing

THE HUMANITIES COMPUTING FACILITY AT THE UNIVERSITY OF CALIFORNIA AT SANTA BARBARA (HCF)

University of California, Santa Barbara
Santa Barbara, CA 93106-3170 USA
Tel: (805) 893-2208
Email: HCF1DAHL@ucsbuxa.bitnet
        HCF1DAHL@ucsbuxa.ucsb.edu

The Humanities Computing Facility at the University of California at Santa Barbara was established to provide faculty members and graduate students in the humanities and fine arts at UCSB with access to advanced computer equipment and software suitable for research and instructional purposes in their disciplines. Among its present high end equipment, HCF has a Kurzweil scanner, two multimedia configurations, one for the Macintosh and one for the IBM, and several machines with very large hard disks for text analysis purposes.

The HCF conducts seminars on topics of interest to computing humanists, such as Email, uses of the Internet, electronic text, and multimedia instructional applications. It publishes the newsletter REACH, Research and Educational Applications of Computers in the Humanities. The HCF's Executive Director, Eric Dahlin, is also the current editor of the ACH Newsletter, the newsletter of the Association for Computers and the Humanities.

INDEPENDENT MEDIA DISTRIBUTORS ALLIANCE (IMDA)

c/o Fanlight Productions
47 Halifax Street
Boston, MA 02130 USA
Tel: (617) 524-0980
Fax: (617) 524-8838

IMDA is a national network of independent commercial and noncommercial film and video distributors, united in a commitment to create and expand audiences for new messages and new voices reflecting the political, cultural and artistic diversity of American life. IMDA represents a broad range of independent film and video programming—works which are innovative in form, style, and subject matter; work which challenges our usual assumptions; and works which give voice and visibility to people and experience often absent from mass market media. IMDA is dedicated to creative integrity and to the economic survival of the producers whose work they distribute. IMDA is further dedicated to a multiplicity of voices, and to encouraging cultural and artistic diversity in all aspects of their endeavors, including the full and active participation of people of color, women, and others traditionally under-represented in the media.

They are equally committed to understanding and meeting the needs of the communities and audiences who use their programming, as well as educating and developing new audiences for independent work. IMDA seeks to strengthen the field of independent distribution through:
- Networking and resource sharing
- Developing common strategies for audience development and expansion
- Exploring new technologies and approaches to distribution
- Advocating for the interests of independent producers, distributors, and their audiences.

INTEGRATED ELECTRONIC ARTS RENSSELAER (IEAR) STUDIOS

Neil Rolnick
Department of the Arts
Rensselaer Polytechnic Institute,
DCC 135
Troy, NY 12180-3590 USA
Tel: (518) 276-4784
Fax: (518) 276-4780
Email: rolnick@iear.arts.rpi.edu

The iEAR Studios is a center for the creation of time-based electronic art, including combinations of music, video, imaging and animation, installation and performance. As part of the Department of the Arts at Rensselaer Polytechnic Institute, the iEAR Studios offer a unique Masters of Fine Arts degree in the Electronic Arts. Based on the model of an art school in a sophisticated technological environment, the MFA program is focused on the integration of the various artistic disciplines which use computers and electronic technology as their primary tools. Each semester the studios serve up to 200 undergraduate non-majors and 16 full time graduate students in the MFA program, as well as faculty, staff and visiting artists.

The studio facilities at iEAR, as of December 1992, include:
- The *Integrated Studio*, an on-line video editing room with Grass Valley editing, switching, digital effect, and character generation, supporting

SVHS, Hi8 and Umatic-SP formats, and including 8 channels of Pro-Tools hard disk-based sound recording and editing, and a full Macintosh-based MIDI system

- Two off-line video editing rooms
- The *Computer Music Studio*, including 4 channels of Pro-Tools and a full Macintosh-based MIDI system
- Two graphic workstation studios including 4 channels of Pro-Tools and a full Macintosh-based MIDI system
- Two graphics workstation studios including Amiga and Macintosh platforms for imaging and animation
- The *Electronic Arts Workstation Center*, including 4 SVHS video editing stations and 3 Macintosh-based music workstations, primarily for use by undergraduate students
- The *iEAR Space*, a multipurpose blackbox studio for audio and video production, public lectures, small scale performances, installations and rehearsals.

In addition to its academic and educational mission, iEAR also functions as a major venue for the exhibition and public performance of experimental and electronic art and music in the Capital District of New York State. The Studios produce more than 30 public lectures, exhibitions, and concerts annually, often featuring internationally recognized musicians, video artists, and media theorists, as well as showcasing and promoting locally-based talent. The Studios also produce a weekly cable program, *hOUR iEAR*, which is broadcast throughout the Capital District to a potential audience of 250,000. 1993 will see the inauguration of a series of live satellite broadcasts from iEAR, and work on a major public installation linking the Rensselaer campus with the center of Troy, New York.

The final component of activity at the iEAR Studios is comprised of an active artist-in-residence program, often including close work with graduate student assistants. Other organizations which have collaborated with iEAR, or which are currently exploring collaborative projects include Composers Forum in New York City, the Banff Centre for the Arts, the Media Lab at MIT, the Albany Symphony Orchestra, and the Center for Performance Studies at Arizona State University.

iEAR WORKS

The primary focus at iEAR is the making of art with technology, rather than on the research and development of new technology. Graduate students and faculty come from backgrounds in music composition, painting, sculpture, film making, photography, graphic design and video art. Regardless of their individual backgrounds, everyone working at iEAR is encouraged to become familiar with all of the technologies available to them. This approach is based on the concept that the similarities in the tools for the different electronic media effectively break down barriers between the various disciplines, and that artistic thought and practice function similarly, regardless of media. The result is a community of artists, including faculty, students, and visitors, who are learning to conceive of work in the electronic media in a coherent way, encompassing interactions between the artists, the technology, and the audience.

Activity at iEAR can be divided into two general areas: presentation and outreach activities and the creation of new works in a variety of media. The umbrella under which the bulk of the public presentation takes place is the *Electronic Arts Performance Series (EAPS)*. This series includes 12-16 evening concerts or exhibitions annually, featuring work by an international array of musical and media artists as well as work by iEAR faculty and students. EAPS also includes approximately 10 mid-day lectures in the *Out to Lunch* series each year. There is also an on-going video exhibition in the *Vertical Gallery*, the main stairway of the central campus library. The iEAR graduate students, under the supervision of faculty artist Brandy Miller, also curate and produce *hOUR iEAR*. Beginning in 1993-94, with funding from an NEA Visual Artists' Forums Grant, iEAR will begin live satellite broadcast of *In A Word: With Technology*, a series of programs in which visiting artists will show their work and discuss it with an in-studio audience, and with audiences at selected sites around the country. Artists involved in the *EAPS* and *Out to Lunch* series have included composers Carl Stone, Pamela Z, Larry Polansky, Warren Burt and Nick Didkovsky; media artists such as Antonio Muntadas, Sara Diamond, Shu Lea Cheang and Ellen Spiro; and curators such as Kate Horsfield and John Hanhardt.

Creative work in the studio is produced by faculty and students, as well as through a number of visiting artist programs. These programs provide a means for artists to use iEAR's studio facilities to produce new works, sometimes over the course of an entire semester, and sometimes over a few intensive weeks. Visiting artists who have produced new work in the studios include composers Robert Ashley, Tod Machover, Joseph Celli and Jin Hi Kim, and media artist Dieter Froese.

The iEAR faculty includes: Kevin Daniel, computer imaging and electronic sculpture; Brandy Miller, Media Arts; Richard Povall, computer music and intermedia; Miroslaw Rogala, computer imaging and multimedia installation; and Neil B. Rolnick, computer music and performance. Some current projects by faculty members include:

- compact disk recordings of music by Neil Rolnick, featuring the composer with the New York New Music Ensemble, Robert Dick, George Lewis and Gordon Gottlieb, funded by grants from the Cary Trust and the National Endowment for the Arts, and released on the Bridge, O.O. Discs and Centaur labels.

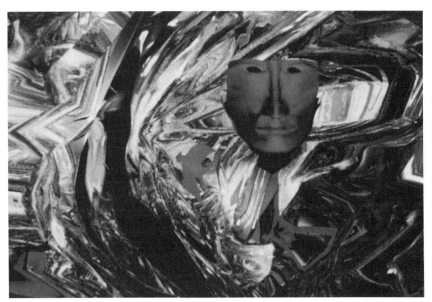

Fig. 2. Joseph L. Giroux, *Isolation Sketch #3*, 1992. **This work is a study of rendered 3D images for use in a performance which includes video and live recitation of Giroux's original poetry. (Photo: J. Giroux)**

- *The Last Garden*, an interactive multimedia performance project using dancer-triggered video motion-sensing systems to control computer music and laser disc video systems by Richard Povall, in collaboration with John Mitchell and choreographer Kathleen Smith at the Institute for Studio in the Arts at the Arizona State University.
- *Revisiting the Birthplace of the American Industrial Revolution*, funded by the National Endowment for the Arts Art in Public Places Grant, which explores the human and architectural implications of the decay of a northeastern industrial center
- *Yugoslavia Requiem*, a multimedia music and performance piece by Neil Rolnick with student video artist Patricia Abt, funded by the New York State Council on the Arts.

Student work similarly spans traditional boundaries between media, including graphics and animation, music, video, installation and performance-oriented work. Joseph L. Giroux's Isolation Sketch #3 is a study of rendered 3D images for use in a performance which includes video and live recitation of Giroux's original poetry (Figure 2).

INTERACTIVE MULTIMEDIA ASSOCIATION (IMA)

Jenifer Fox, Pam Briggs
3 Church Circle, Suite 800
Annapolis, MD 21401-1933 USA
Tel: (410) 626-1380
Fax: (410) 263-0590

The Interactive Multimedia Association is an international trade association representing the full spectrum of the multimedia industry: applications developers; suppliers of hardware and software; system integrators, publishers and distributors; educators and users. The IMA mission is to promote the development of interactive multimedia applications and reduce barriers to the wide-spread use of multimedia technology.

Established in 1988 as the Interactive Video Industry Association, the IMA now has 250 corporate, institutional and individual members who share a common interest in the production, delivery, and use of multimedia technology. The IMA serves as a forum for the open exchange of views, opinions, and technical proposals within the dynamic and rapidly expanding multimedia community. IMA's members are encouraged to become involved in the association's programs and projects, where they can play an active role in shaping the future of multimedia computing by working with others to advance the industry and to establish a strong and profitable marketplace.

Compatibility Project

Four years ago, the IMA board of directors authorized the creation of the Compatibility Project to provide a forum for industry members to develop technical solutions to the cross-platform compatibility problem. The Project's first publication, Recommended Practices for Multimedia Portability, provided guidelines for manufacturers and application developers of interactive video systems. More recently, a *Request for Technology* process was developed that will permit rapid adoption of multi-media standards based on a detailed set of requirements developed by the IMA.

In March 1992, the IMA announced that Intel Corporation has agreed to open the details of its RTV 2.0 (Real Time Video) video algorithm, which is used to create motion video images on computer, and make them available to the IMA. In another development, the Compatibility Project's Digital Audio Technical Working Group delivered the findings of the IMA's first industry recommendation to multimedia developers for cross-platform compatibility. This newly-released document specifies standard digital audio interchange formats.

In addition to these and other technical documents, the Compatibility Project publishes a quarterly *Proceedings* of the activities of its technical working and focus groups. Participation from all segments of the multimedia industry is encouraged in the activities of the Compatibility Project.

THE INTERNATIONAL COMPUTER MUSIC ASSOCIATION (ICMA)

Larry Austin
2040 Polk Street, Suite 330
San Francisco, CA 94109 USA
Tel: (817) 566-2235
Fax: (817) 565-4919
Email: icma@cube.cemi.unt.edu

IMA Membership

Membership in the IMA is open to any corporation, institution, organization, or individual actively involved in the production or use of multimedia technology, applications and services.

The ICMA is an international affiliation of individuals and institutions involved in the technical, creative and performance aspects of music. It serves composers, computer software and hardware developers, researchers, and musicians who are interested in the integration of music and technology. ICMA functions include:

- Presenting the annual International Computer Music Conference
- Professional Networking
- Specialized Publications and Recordings
- Sponsored Research
- ICMA Commission Awards

The ICMA co-sponsors the annual International Computer Music Conference (ICMC), which, since its inception in 1974, has become the preeminent yearly gathering of computer music practitioners from around the world. The ICMC's unique interleaving of professional paper presentations and concerts of new computer music compositions—referreed by ICMA-approved international panels—creates a vital synthesis of science, technology, and the art of music.

Networking

The ICMA and the ICMC represent unique opportunities to interact with others concerned with the cross-influence of the creative and technological in computer music and related fields (applications in composition, musicology, music theory, music printing, music instruction). The ICMA Membership Directory lists names, addresses, and telephone numbers for all members. In many cases Email addresses and Fax numbers are provided as well.

Publications and Recordings

Since its inception in 1979 as a non-profit corporation, ICMA has provided a centralized base of information dissemination for the computer music community through its quarterly newsletter *ARRAY*, back-issue sales of ICMC Proceedings, the ICMA Membership Directory, the ICMA Video Review and the forthcoming ICMC Proceedings Anthology Series and the ICMA Recording Series.

Research

In 1988 ICMA became the official secretariat of the American National Standards Institute (ANSI) Standard Music Representation Language project. This ongoing project is charged with creating a standard language description and storage and interchange format for all forms of musical communication — sonic as well as graphic. This standard is intended for automated processing in music printing, cataloging and storage, multimedia presentations, teaching and research, and creative activities in all computer music media. ICMA's participation is consistent with the association's mission to serve as a nexus of information. ICMA is expanding its research sponsorship to include partnerships with non-profit and corporate institutions to establish ICMA Resident Research Fellowships to sustain independent projects and creative activity in all aspects of computer music.

Commission Awards

In 1991, the first International Computer Music Association Commission Awards were presented to three composers to compose computer music compositions for premiere performances during the 1992 ICMC. Each composer received a $1,000 commission award from the ICMA Commission Awards Fund plus travel expenses to attend and participate in preparations for the premiere performance.

Membership

Membership is open to individuals and institutions and entitles the member to democratic participation in the professional concerns of the organization, including the election of the ICMA Board of Directors, participation in the annual membership meeting, and the right to influence the administration, goals, and actions of the ICMA. Officers and elected members of the Board of Directors are accountable to each member of the organization. The most important reason for joining the ICMA is to support its continuing efforts to promote the standards of excellence all practitioners of computer music expect for their field of research and creative activity.

THE INTERNATIONAL DIGITAL ELECTROACOUSTIC MUSIC ARCHIVE (IDEAMA)

Marcia Bauman
Center for Computer Research in Music and Acoustics (CCRMA)
Stanford University
Stanford, CA 94305 USA
Email: bau@ccrma.stanford.edu
Tel: (415) 723-4971
Fax: (415) 723-8468

Background and History

The International Digital ElectroAcoustic Music Archive (IDEAMA) is dedicated to collecting, preserving and disseminating internationally renowned electroacoustic music. Co-founded in December 1990 by Stanford University's Center for Computer Research in Music and Acoustics (CCRMA), and the Center for Arts and Media Technology (ZKM), in Karlsruhe, Germany, the IDEAMA's initial goal is to create a target collection of early electroacoustic music composed during the period 1940-1965. Much of this music now resides on deteriorating analog tape. In an effort to preserve this music, it will be transferred to digital storage media, using CD standards. A wide range of information about the music will be entered into the IDEAMA catalog database.

For its broadest possible accessibility, the database will conform to existing library cataloging standards and authority control by use of MARC format. Every effort will be made to design the database in such a way that libraries and other scholarly institutions will be able to integrate it into their existing on-line catalogs. As a "paperless" archive, the IDEAMA will store all materials entirely in digital form. Once digitized, all materials are returned to their owners.

Although a large number of important electroacoustic works are currently accessible on analog tapes at the centers where they were produced, access to them is limited. The same is true for important works which are available through the private collections of individuals. Thus, one of the main challenges in developing the IDEAMA target collection is to identify and locate the desired materials so that an international collection of important electroacoustic music repertoire can be accessible at one location.

Organization

Founding Institutions

The two IDEAMA founding institutions, CCRMA and ZKM, are jointly responsible for collecting archive materials on a regional basis. ZKM focuses on European electroacoustic music, while CCRMA is responsible for music from the Americas, Asia and Australia.

Both founding institutions will provide each other with the materials they collect so that the complete target collection will be available at each location. Stanford University will house the IDEAMA at the Braun Music Center Archive of Recorded Sound. In Karlsruhe, the IDEAMA will be the core of the music section at ZKM's Mediathek, a media library where different art forms and technology converge to create vital new relationships.

Boards

To identify, locate and choose materials for inclusion in the target collection, each founding institution has formed a selection committee comprised of eminent composers, musicologists and other individuals who are well-versed and active in the field. In addition, internationally renowned composers and researchers form an overall international advisory board which establishes the international scope and reputation of the archive.

IDEAMA Branches

Two other categories of IDEAMA institutions have been defined. A partner institution has a collaborative relationship with the founding institutions, contributing materials to the target collection and/or participating in research for the catalog database. Partner institutions will also house the target collection and the catalog. After the target collection has been established and the catalog database implemented at the founding and partner institutions, an organization may become an affiliate branch by housing the target collection and integrating the archive database into its existing format.

Presently, there are five formally designated partner institutions: the New York Public Library (NYPL); the National Center for Science Information Systems (NACSIS), in Tokyo; the Institut de Recherche et de Coordination Acoustique/Musique (IRCAM) in Paris; the Groupe de Recherches Musicales de l'Institut National de l'Audiovisuel (INA/GRM); and the Groupe de Musique Experimentale de Bourges (GMEB).

The NYPL is planning an overall electroacoustic music collection. IDEAMA activities will take place within this context. Initial efforts are being made to digitize the works of such composers as Paul Lansky, Pauline Oliveros and Charles Dodge. NYPL will contribute to IDEAMA these and other works more readily available to NYPL on the East Coast.

In Japan, NACSIS serves as the nucleus for the nationwide comprehensive Science Information System, which covers the natural and social sciences, and the humanities. NACSIS links university libraries, computer centers, information processing centers and national university research institutions via computer and telecommunication networks. Research and development is carried out at NACSIS to compile databases and to create information systems.

The NACSIS collaboration involves acquisition of electroacoustic music by Japanese composers as well as the development of the catalog database. A list of approximately 160 Japanese works has been compiled at NACSIS, with bibliographic data in MARC format. Osaka University and Kunitachi College will support NACSIS in the dissemination of the IDEAMA.

INA/GRM, formerly the Groupe de Musique Concrète at Radio-diffusion-Television Française, was the first major location in the world for electroacoustic music production. Approximately 125 European works will be provided by INA/GRM.

IRCAM is one of the four components of the Centre National d'Art de Culture Georges Pompidou, together with the French National Museum of Modern Art, the Public Information Library, and the Industrial Design Centre. It is an internationally renowned center for interdisciplinary research in the areas of computer technology, acoustics, digital sound synthesis, real-time digital signal processing, psychoacoustics, and computer music composition. In addition, IRCAM produces concerts, and its pedagogy department offers a series of educational symposia, seminars, courses and workshops for the public. IRCAM will provide access to European electroacoustic music and house the IDEAMA target collection and database.

GMEB was founded in 1972. Over the past 20 years, GMEB has sponsored an internationally acclaimed electroacoustic music festival and competition. Prize-winning works from GMEB have been broadcast in the "Le Chant du Monde" series and performed all over the world. Both IRCAM and GMEB will provide access to more recently composed European electroacoustic music.

The Target Collection
The original analog tapes for targeted works exist in a number of libraries, archives, radio stations, studios and private collections. Each founding institution has formulated a list of works based on their availability through these sources and upon the recommendation of each institution's selection committee. Approximately 800 works are presently being sought.

ZKM Selections
The European selection committee held its first official meeting at ZKM in May, 1992. At that time, committee members collectively recommended approximately 400 European works composed between 1930 and 1970. The two main criteria for selecting a work were its historical significance, and the urgency precipitated by the deterioration of the original analog tape on which it resides. Sources for the European works include major centers such as INA/GRM; Westdeutschen Rundfunks, Koln (WDR); and the Studio di Fonologia Musicale presso la sede RAI-TV, Milan. In addition, works from smaller private and studio collections, and from the estates of Hermann Heiss and Joerg Mager will be included. The committee also decided to include, where possible, multiple versions of selected works and sound source materials, and later, film music, experimental radio plays and multi-media works.

CCRMA Selections
Several major centers have been contacted and arrangements are being made to digitize approximately 400 works and auxiliary materials. These centers include the Mills College Tape Music Center and the University of California, San Diego, which hold many of the pieces produced at the San Francisco Tape Music Center. Other centers include Columbia University's historic Electronic Music Center and the Library of Congress. The Library of Congress will provide works by Vladimir Ussachevsky which were moved there from Columbia University. A number of significant works by Canadian composers such as Hugh Le Caine and Istvan Anhalt are available through the National Library of Canada. The Laboratoris de Investigacion y Produccion Musical (LIPM), the first major center for Latin American electroacoustic music, has digitized approximately 30 works for the target collection.

The personal collections of Max Mathews and Gordon Mumma provide a wealth of historically significant electroacoustic music for the IDEAMA. Mathews has contributed tapes of the earliest computer sound and music developed at Bell Laboratories. Gordon Mumma's collection includes taped performances by the ONCE Theater Group. CCRMA will contribute other early computer generated works. Works by composers who were not necessarily associated with major centers, but whose contributions are no less significant, will also be included.

NACSIS is researching and acquiring Japanese works, while research at CCRMA has been initiated to identify Australian works for the target collection. Works by Australian composer Tristram Cary have been digitized, and a search for other Australian early electroacoustic music has been initiated in the publication "Sounds Australian."

Once the target collection is completed, more recently composed works will be added in order to represent the field from its inception to the present day. In the meantime, both founding institutions are faced with the complicated task of researching the copyright ownership for each targeted work. Permission is requested to copy and distribute materials for the purposes of preservation, private research, classroom lectures/presentations and IDEAMA-sponsored performances.

Database and Cataloging

Several categories of information have been established for a more comprehensive study of cataloged electroacoustic works. In addition to the basic details (e.g., titles, dates, durations), there will be information regarding multiple versions of works, studio production techniques, equipment, sound source materials, and performance history. Every effort will be made to include as much information as possible within the given MARC format data fields. The text information and computer-scanned images (e.g., scores), will be stored and retrieved on CD. A user interface will be developed to activate sound playback media such as CD players and jukeboxes.

Acknowledgements

At Stanford University, the International Digital ElectroAcoustic Music Archive is supported by the Andrew W. Mellon Foundation and the National Endowment for the Arts. At ZKM support comes from the state of Baden-Wuerttemberg and the city of Karlsruhe.

INTERNATIONAL DIRECTORY OF DESIGN 1993

Ray Lauzzana
Penrose Press
PO Box 470925
San Francisco, CA 94147 USA
Tel: (415) 567-4157
Fax: (415) 896-1512
Email: lauzzana@netcom.com

Penrose Press has published the second edition of the *International Directory of Design*, describing over 2000 design programs and schools, presenting the diversity of international design. The directory was created as a guide to international design education. A multimedia version of the directory, entitled the *Interactive International Directory of Design*, is expected to be available in the Fall of 1993.

The directory is indexed across a broad spectrum of disciplines, including architecture & building, advertising & media, ceramics & glass, costume & theatrical, fashion & clothing, film & video, furniture & furnishings, graphics & printing, interior & decorating, jewelry & metalwork, landscape & urban, ornament & decor, product & industrial, textile & fabric, vehicle & transport.

INTERNATIONAL DIRECTORY OF ELECTRONIC ARTS (IDEA)

Annick Bureaud
CHAOS
57, rue Falguiere
75015 Paris, France
Tel: 33-1-43-20-92-23
Fax: 33-1-43-22-11-24
Email: bureaud@altern.com

INTERNATIONAL SCULPTURE CENTER (ISC)

David Furchgott
1050 17th Street NW, Suite 250
Washington, DC 20036 USA
Tel: (202) 785-1144
Fax: (202) 785-0810

THE INTERNATIONAL SOCIETY OF COPIER ARTISTS (ISCA)

Louise Neaderland
800 West End Avenue
New York City, NY 10025 USA
Tel: (212) 662-5533

IDEA is an ongoing directory project covering the whole range of activities in the fields of art and technology, including computer art, computer animation, video, interactive art, networking, holography, laser, computer music, sound works, space/sky art, performing art, computer literature and poetry, robotic art, and virtual reality. The second edition is bilingual, in French and English, and contains more than 2800 addresses world-wide concerning organizations (festivals, galleries, museums, art centers, schools and universities, centers for research and creation, production companies, resource centers, non-profit organizations), artists, and other individuals (theoriticians, critics, researchers, curators) and periodicals. A bibliography and four indexes complete IDEA.

The International Sculpture Center is a non-profit membership organization devoted to the advancement of contemporary sculpture. Activities of the ISC include: sculpture conferences; symposia and workshops; a computerized artists registry and referral service entitled *Sculpture Source*; *Sculpture* magazine; exhibitions; and various other member services.

TECHshops
TECHshops are four-day intensive hands-on workshops, designed to enhance the technical skills and career development of sculptors. The ISC has brought together professionals from across the United States, offering TECHshops participants the best possible instruction in each discipline. Over 450 artists from around the world have learned invaluable techniques from their experience in the TECHshops program. The workshops take place in an intimate workshop setting, providing individual attention. Participants gain valuable technical skills, and have opportunities to network with other artists taking part in the workshops.

Lifetime Achievement Award in Contemporary Sculpture
In 1991 the ISC's International Board of Directors voted to establish an annual award recognizing the lifetime achievements and contributions of an outstanding individual to contemporary sculpture. The board established a committee of leading arts professionals to select a distinguished artist. He or she receives the award and is recognized by the ISC at a gala event in Washington, D.C. Louise Bourgeois and George Segal were selected as the first two recipients of this annual award, in 1991 and 1992 respectively.

The ISCA is a non-profit organization founded in 1982 to promote the use of the photocopier as a creative tool. To this end the society publishes the *ISCA Quarterly*, a collection of original xerographic works, as well as a newsletter. It also maintains an extensive slide archive and circulates two major traveling exhibitions of xerographic prints, bookworks and postal art.

THE INTERNATIONAL SOCIETY FOR THE ARTS, SCIENCES AND TECHNOLOGY (LEONARDO/ISAST)

Craig Harris, Roger Malina
Leonardo/ISAST
672 South Van Ness Avenue
San Francisco, CA 94110 USA
Tel: (415) 431-7414
Fax: (415) 431-5737
Email: isast@garnet.berkeley.edu
　　　 fast@garnet.berkeley.edu
　　　 craig@well.sf.ca.us
　　　 rfm@cea.berkeley.edu

Leonardo/ISAST has been a publisher and facilitator in the art, science and technology communities for twenty five years. The journal Leonardo was founded in 1968 in Paris by kinetic artist and astronautical pioneer Frank Malina. Malina saw the need for a journal that would serve as an international channel of communication between artists, with an emphasis on the writings of artists who use science and developing technologies in their work. Following Frank Malina's death in 1981, *Leonardo* was moved to California by his son Roger F. Malina, an astrophysicist at the University of California at Berkeley. With the support of founding board member Frank Oppenheimer, the International Society for the Arts, Sciences and Technology (Leonardo/ISAST) was formed in 1982 to address the rapidly expanding needs of the art, science and technology community. Leonardo achieves these goals through a variety of regional and international activities, including publishing in hard copy and electronic media, facilitating in conferences and festivals, conducting an awards program, and managing networking projects.

The emphasis on integration of these diverse fields provides a foundation for all of the society's activities. The interdisciplinary and international nature of this domain, and the cross-fertilization which takes place between areas of expertise among related fields creates a need for the unique perspective which Leonardo/ISAST brings to the community. Helping to build a fruitful relationship among artists, developers, educators, students, and audience is a fundamental goal of the society. The society fosters communication across cultural and economic borders by offering opportunities to individuals who generally find it difficult to get their work out in public view.

Leonardo/ISAST Publications

Leonardo/ISAST publications include the journal *Leonardo*, *Leonardo Music Journal*, the hardcopy newsletter *Leonardo Currents*, the electronic newsletters *Leonardo Electronic News* and *FineArt Forum*, the *Leonardo Book Publications Series*, the *Leonardo Fine Art Science Technology (FAST) Database and Archive*, multimedia publications, and monographs. The content is comprised of a wide variety of related material, including perspectives from artists, scientists, developers, educators, historians and philosophers; reviews of books, audio recordings, multimedia products; notification and reviews regarding concerts, conferences, exhibitions; and profiles about educational programs, industry developments, foundation activities, residency programs, museum/gallery and performance opportunities. Leonardo/ISAST directs its publishing activities with a perspective which incorporates all material into its existing and projected publications in a way which is sensitive to their unique content, scheduling and technological requisites.

■ *Leonardo* Journal

For twenty five years the journal *Leonardo* has provided a unique and valuable forum for artists, scientists, engineers, philosophers, educators and others to offer their perspectives on artistic activity and the impact of scientific and technological development. The journal's reputation as an important publication is widespread, covering over 50 countries. *Leonardo* features peer-reviewed articles by artists about their own work, and places no restriction on artistic tendency, content or medium. *Leonardo* includes discussions of new concepts, materials and techniques, and covers subjects of general artistic interest. In addition to regularly publishing issues which span a variety of related topics, Leonardo/ISAST has produced special issues dedicated to covering specific fields, such as *Art and Interactive Telecommunications*, *Visual Mathematics*, and *The Archives of Holography*. Leonardo/ISAST collaborated with SIGGRAPH in publication of its 1989 and 1990 *Art Show Catalogs*.

■ *Leonardo Music Journal*

In 1991 Leonardo/ISAST established the *Leonardo Music Journal* (LMJ), a companion issue of Leonardo dedicated to music and the sonic arts, distributed with an audio CD. *LMJ* publishes peer-reviewed writings by composers, sound artists, researchers, musicians, instrument builders and musical theorists about their own work. The focus of the publication is on experimental aesthetics and technologies as they relate to cultural, social, historical and political musical contexts. The journal is especially committed to providing a forum for the international community of independent artists and scholars whose work extends the boundaries of musical and artistic disciplines in new and provocative ways.

■ Leonardo/MIT Press Book Series

MIT Press is joining Leonardo/ISAST in the production of the Leonardo Book Series, which highlights topics related to art, science and developing technologies. The first two volumes, published in 1993, include the *Leonardo Almanac: International Resources in Art, Science, and Technology*, edited by Craig Harris, and *The Visual Mind: Art and Mathematics*, edited by Michele Emmer. See the Series Introduction of the *Leonardo Almanac* for further information.

■ Electronic Publishing

Leonardo/ISAST has been involved in the development of electronic publishing since 1988. This aspect of the activities of Leonardo/ISAST was established as a response to the expanding need for orientation among a complex set of fields and issues, and for connectivity between individuals and among institutions. The availability of emerging and increasingly-accessible electronic network facilities around the world offers new opportunities to reach a wider audience and to attract content contributions from new sectors of the international art/science/technology community. The content covers all applications of science and technology to the arts. Activities in this arena include electronic newsletters, the *Leonardo Fine Art Science Technology (FAST) Database and Archive*, and multimedia publications.

Leonardo Electronic News
Leonardo Electronic News is a monthly electronic newsletter distributed gratis on the Internet electronic network. The editorial focus consists of artists' *Words on Works*, short feature articles, bibliographies, publication reviews, Leonardo/ISAST Member News, calls for papers, conferences, symposia and festivals, notices about competitions, news of *FAST Database* updates, and calendar items.

FineArt Forum
Leonardo/ISAST began publishing the electronic newsletter *FineArt Forum* in 1988. The content areas intersect with *Leonardo Electronic News*, with a focus on timely announcements of new activities and calls for submissions and participation. Leonardo/ISAST now distibutes *FineArt Forum* monthly, on behalf and the Art Science Technology Network. This

publication is currently edited by Paul Brown, and is published by Mississippi State University and the National Science Foundation Engineering Research Center.

Fine Art Science Technology Database and Archive

The *Fine Art Science Technology (FAST) Database and Archive* is the repository for information collected through all of its publishing activities. Information developed for the journals and the electronic newsletters is incorporated into the database and archive on an ongoing basis, along with relevant information from surveys and other data collection solicitations. The *FAST Database and Archive* is a comprehensive collection of information, including information about artist-in-residence opportunities, educational programs, research projects, and funding organizations. There is an extensive database of individuals and organizations working in the realm where art, science and technology converge, including names, telephone numbers, postal and electronic addresses, discipline orientation and technology used. The archives in the system provide in-depth profiles of both individuals and organizations, artists' perspectives on their own work, bibliographies, glossaries, publication reviews, and examples of work. This forms the foundation for the *Leonardo Almanac.*

Multimedia Publications

In the Spring of 1993, Leonardo collaborated with Quanta Press for a Compact Disc-Read Only Memory (CD-ROM) publication on the topic of art and mathematics, *Chaos: Fractals and Magic.* Other multimedia publications in conjunction with the MIT Press are in the planning stages, including a CD-ROM based on the *Leonardo Almanac.*

Conference/Festival/Symposium Activities

Leonardo/ISAST participates in the development of conferences, festivals, and symposia as part of its outreach activities. At a regional level the organization cooperates with the organization YLEM/Artists Using Science and Technology. In the national and international arenas Leonardo/ISAST has worked with the Inter-Society for Electronic Arts (ISEA), the Arts Science Technology Network (ASTN), SIGGRAPH, the CyberArts International Conference and Exposition, the Australian Network for Arts and Technology (ANAT), the Canadian Electroacoustic Community (CEC), the International Computer Music Association, and Ars Electronica. The society's collaboration takes many forms, with its representatives serving on program selection committees, awards and advisory committees, artist-in-residence advisory committees, and a variety of other organizations' boards of directors. Leonardo/ISAST creates special presentation sessions for events, such as the session entitled *Creative Environments of the Future*, developed for the 1992 CyberArts International Conference and Exposition. The Leonardo/ISAST publishing activities provide additional opportunities for collaboration, resulting in such publications as the 1989 and 1990 SIGGRAPH Art Show Catalogs, and the *Electronic Art* supplemental issue of the journal *Leonardo*, based on the First International Symposium on Electronic Arts (FISEA) held in Holland in 1988.

Leonardo/ISAST Awards

The Leonardo/ISAST award program is dedicated to recognizing significant work by contemporary artists and to acknowledging exemplary contributions made by individuals toward the synthesis of contemporary art, science and technology. See the Leonardo Award Winners chapter of the *Leonardo Almanac* for details.

Speakers' Network
The goal of the *Leonardo Speakers' Network* is to facilitate speaking and presentation engagements for artists, researchers, scholars and technology developers with interested groups and organizations. The program offers a platform from which artists, scientists and technologists can make their work known. See the Speakers' Network chapter of the *Leonardo Almanac* for details.

THE INTER-SOCIETY FOR THE ELECTRONIC ARTS (ISEA)

Theo Hesper, Wim van der Plas
C. Kouwenbergzoom 107
3065 KC Rotterdam
The Netherlands
Tel: 31-79-612930 or 31-10-2020850
Fax: 31-79-611737
Fax Newsletter: 31-75-701906
Email: isea@mbr.frg.eur.nl
        isea@sara.nl

ISEA was founded in 1990 to act as an umbrella organization for institutions, organizations and individuals active in the field of the electronic arts. The aims are to further communication between artists and scientists in all related disciplines, and to develop a more structured approach towards the problems and potentials of electronic art. ISEA helps to develop electronic art projects, and coordinates the continuation of the International Symposia on Electronic Art:

1988, Utrecht, First International Symposium on Electronic Art (FISEA)
1990, Groningen, Second International Symposium on Electronic Art (SISEA)
1992, Sydney, Third International Symposium on Electronic Art (TISEA)
1993, Minneapolis, Fourth International Symposium on Electronic Art (FISEA93)
1994, Helsinki, Fifth International Symposium on Electronic Art (ISEA 94)
1995, Montreal, Sixth International Symposium on Electronic Art (ISEA 95)

ISEA Members receive a monthly Newsletter in either electronic or hardcopy format. Associate membership is free of charge for two years for those that cannot afford the membership fee.

LABORATORIO DE INFORMÁTICA Y ELECTRÓNICA MUSICAL (LIEM)

Adolfo Núñez, Carlos Cester
Santa Isabel 51
28012 Madrid, Spain
Tel: (34) (9) 468 23 10
Fax: (34) (9) 530 83 21

The Laboratorio de Informática y Electrónica Musical (LIEM) belongs to the Centro para la Difusión de la Música Contemporánea (CDMC). This institution is part of the Ministry of Culture and is a focal point in the promotion and stimulus of contemporary music in Spain. The LIEM opened in 1989 and has been extremely active, mainly due to a strong interest in electronic and computer music in Spain. The LIEM is mainly an instrument for composers to develop and produce their compositions for tape, or to research the possibilities of real time electronics.

MICRO GALLERY: COMPUTER INFORMATION ROOM

The National Gallery
Trafalgar Square
London WC2N 5DN United Kingdom
Tel: 071-839-3321

The National Gallery houses one of the worlds finest collections of Western European painting. To help visitors find out more about it the Gallery has installed a new facility, The Micro Gallery. Sponsored by the American Express Foundation, this computerized information system contains background information on every painting in the Collection.

The Micro Gallery enables visitors to explore their individual areas of interest, whether it is a particular painting, artist, period, subject matter or genre. The information is presented on color touch screens which also provide the controls for the system. To operate, one only needs to touch the required 'button' control on the screen.

The heart of the system is a complete illustrated catalogue of the Collection, accessed through the four sections indicated below. Within any section one can select the catalogue entry for a given painting by touching a 'thumbnail' image of the painting.

The *Artists* section contains a biography and visual index of the works of all the artists represented in the collection.

The *General Reference* section contains entries and example paintings for key terms and subjects.

The *Picture Types* section provides a visual classification of the Collection by types of painting.

The *Historical Atlas* contains a series of maps and entries with example paintings, presenting the Collection by time and place.

The Micro Gallery contains 12 workstations, each providing a visual encyclopedia of the Collection. The system is very easy to use and requires no particular knowledge of computers or art history.

THE MILLS COLLEGE CENTER FOR CONTEMPORARY MUSIC (CCM)

Chris Brown, Maggi Payne
Mills College
5000 MacArthur Blvd.
Oakland, CA 94613 USA
Tel: (510) 430-2191

CCM offers programs in composition, electronic and computer music systems, and recording engineering to undergraduate women and graduate co-educational students. In the context of an experimental music composition program, the CCM provides hands-on training in computer music languages, software synthesis, multi-track recording and synchronization, MIDI instrumentation and control, and digital audio technologies. The Electronic Music emphasis is a track in the undergraduate Music major program at Mills, with courses also available to the student body at-large. Graduate-level courses are offered as part of the Master of Fine Arts in Electronic Music and Recording Media degree, as well as to students pursuing the Master of Arts degree in Composition. These are generally two-year programs.

MUSEUM FÜR FOTOKOPIE

Klaus Urbons
Postfach/Postbox 10 12 30
Kettwiger Strasse 33
D-4330 Mulheim a.d. Ruhr 1,
Germany
Tel/Fax: 0049 (0) 208 3 44 61

Klaus Urbons, one of the pioneers of Copy Art in Germany, founded the Museum für Fotokopie in the year 1985. The goal was to tie together the art of Electrography and the representation of its development with the research and documentation of the history of the photocopy. The museum intends to build a bridge across the previously isolated fields of copier-generated art and copying technique. On one hand it presents to the public recent works of international artists in the context of old copying machines, and on the other hand it offers the possibility to use these rare instruments for creative works. The assembly of a collection of international electrographic art was started to demonstrate the broad spectrum of this new form of art. In addition, a special library was compiled to provide artists and students access to rare publications on copier art and techniques. For Urbons the realization of this project is a continuation of his own work with photocopy art. The Museum für Fotokopie should, like a work of art, not only conserve the past and introduce the contemporary, but should also serve as a model to prospective developments of art in the age of science.

During the past six years, 20 exhibitions of international art from the field of Copy Art and Electrography have been shown. The museum has presented solo exhibitions, group and traveling shows, has organized a Copy Art Competition and has arranged courses to teach the artistic techniques of copier-generated art. The museum's art collection now includes nearly 500 works of art and continues to grow, thanks to the donations from artists all around the world.

The Museum für Fotokopie maintains alliances with other international copy art centers, especially the International Museum of Electrography in Cuenca (Spain) which is part of the University Castilla-La Mancha, the self-supporting Centre Copie Art in Montréal. Numerous artists in the international community also collaborate with the Museum.

The exploration of the photocopy, as well as the collection of historically important photocopying machines, prove to be projects that are still unique. Today this technical collection holds more than 200 copiers, including Edison's Mimeograph No. 1 (1887), the first xerographic photocopier from Haloid, and the portable universal copier of 1990, the Digital CopyCam. The museum also owns a unique archive about the development of the photocopy as an art medium and rare documents from the history of modern photocopying technology.

The Museum für Fotokopie is meant to be part of a museum of media in the future, providing services to artists as a workshop and laboratory, and presenting the symbiosis between art, science and technology to the public.

THE NATIONAL CENTER FOR SCIENCE INFORMATION SYSTEMS (NACSIS)

3-29-1 Otsuka
Bunkyo-Ku
Tokyo 112 Japan
Tel: 81-3-3942-2351
Fax: 81-3-3814-4931

NACSIS was founded in April 1986 as a center for joint use by universities in accordance with the National School Establishment Law. NACSIS is a central organ for promoting the services of national and comprehensive science information systems and it is carrying out the following work:

- Planning and coordinating the science information system.
- Performing comprehensive research and development work on science information and the science information system.
- Constructing and operating the Science Information Network.
- Offering cataloging information services for monographs and serials.
- Supplying secondary information, such as bibliographies, serials, abstracts, numerical values, images, and others.
- Promoting the database construction.
- Providing electronic mail and bulletin board services.
- Providing education and training, including training courses, lecture meetings and symposia.

The Center tries to achieve the fundamental function common to universities and related organizations across Japan, such as supplying science information and performing research and development work related to the distribution of science information. Work planning and other important items are decided by obtaining advice from the Board of Councilors and the Advisory Council. Professional items are reviewed and discussed by respective committees in such a manner that the opinions of universities across the nation can be reflected in the operation. The organization has a Director General and a Deputy Director General, and the internal organization consists of the Administrative, Operations, and Research and Development Departments.

NETWORKED VIRTUAL ART MUSEUM

Carl Eugene Loeffler
Studio for Creative Inquiry, Telecommunications and Virtual Reality
College of Fine Arts
Carnegie Mellon University
Forbes Avenue
Pittsburgh, PA 15213 USA
Tel: (412) 268-3452
Fax: (412) 268-2829
Email: cel@andrew.cmu.edu

The Networked Virtual Art Museum is a project directed by Carl Eugene Loeffler, Research Fellow at the Studio for Creative Inquiry, College of Fine Arts, Carnegie Mellon University (CMU). The project investigates telecommunications and virtual reality, and provides a basis for multiple users located in distant geographical locations to be conjoined in the same virtual, immersion environment. The project employs telecommunication hardware as well as hardware associated with virtual reality: data eyephones and multi-directional navigation devices.

The first technical demonstration was conducted on September 11 and 12, 1992 between CMU in Pittsburgh and the Expedition 92 conference in Munich, Germany. Users at the participating sites had independent viewpoints and ability to move objects within a shared immersion environment. The link was formed by employing 9600 BAUD modems and a telecommunication program developed by the project team. Update delay was imperceptible over standard voice grade lines.

The Networked Virtual Art Museum was presented at the Worldwide Design Conference, Ford Motor Company in Dearborn, Michigan on November 2, 1992. The Ford demonstration featured a technical demonstration of networked virtual reality as well as the presentation of two new applications designed by Loeffler:

- CAR, in which users navigate a Ford Festiva on two roadway courses: a winter night scene, with snow; and a day scene with an ocean view. Considerable attention is given to the ability to interact with the controls of the automobile: engine, wipers, lights, horn, radio, etc...
- DESIGN, in which users render and shape a virtual substance, employing special tools. This application is being presented as proof of concept for a functional NETWORKED VIRTUAL DESIGN STATION (tm), currently under development by the project team.

The project utilizes WorldToolKit, a virtual world development program, available from Sense8 Corporation; the Virtual Research head mounted display (HMD); the Ascension Technology 6D mouse (The Bird); and dual 486/50 compatibles, with DVI and MIDI.

PAULINE OLIVEROS FOUNDATION INC.

156 Hunter Street
Kingston, NY 12401 USA
Tel: (914) 338-5984
Fax: (914) 338-5986
or
89 Chambers Street
New York, NY 10007 USA
Tel: (212) 619-5726

Founded in 1985, The Pauline Oliveros Foundation is committed to the support of all aspects of the creative process for a worldwide community of artists. The foundation supports, presents and sponsors innovative artists. The following areas currently represent the ways in which the Foundation carries out this mission.

Programs
The Foundation presents and produces performances of emerging and established local, national and international composers, writers and performance artists. Local residencies are created for professional artists to create new works and technologies.

Publications/Projects
- Recordings include compact discs, cassettes and videos.
- A newsletter is a vehicle to enlist broader-based support for the Foundation's principles and programs.
- Scores from selected composers are made available to the public.
- A catalog with new works in all media by composers and sound artists is now available through the Foundation.

- Collaborations between the Foundation's artistic directors and American and foreign artists of international reputation result in the production of new musical and theater works.

Commissions
The Foundation commissions works from emerging and established artists for future performances, residencies and recording.

Development of software and hardware
This is an ongoing program which seeks to develop new technology for the advancement of the electronic media for use in performing, creating and non-profit business applications.

PUBLIC DOMAIN (PD)

Jim Demmers
PO Box 8899
Atlanta, GA 30332 USA
Tel: (404) 612-7529
Fax: (404) 894-7227
Email: pdomain@emory.edu
        jd21@prism.gatech.edu
        balder@gnu.ai.mit.edu

Public Domain (PD) began in the early 1980's as an anarchical group of performing musicians interested in alternative and experimental forms of music. In 1987 PD fashioned itself into a support group for multimedia and installation projects and in 1989 was incorporated as a non-profit organization. PD continues its support of non-traditional and experimental music through the sponsorship of the annual Destroy All Music Festival, and co-sponsorship, with the City of Atlanta's Bureau of Cultural Affairs, of the 1990 Montreaux—Atlanta Jazz and Music Festival. The organization began *Working Papers*, a series of presentations/performances by artists, writers, and theorists in which new work, and works in progress, could be presented and discussed.

Beginning in the Spring of 1991, PD again broadened its interests and activities to include the publication of a newsletter, *Noise*, and a quarterly journal of theory, art, and technology, *Perforations*. Concurrent with these efforts was an expansion of interests towards the consideration of computer networking and its potential as both a means and an end in the continuing efforts of the group to rethink art *after representation.*

With the acquisition of a Sun server in the Spring of 1992, PD now has the capability to provide computer network services to its own members as well as to designated representatives of other non-profit arts organizations. PD's existence as an Internet node has facilitated interaction between members, provided a means of contact with participants in *Working Papers*, and allowed artists and theorists from around the world to contribute to *Perforations* and to remain in communication with PD. The Internet has become the infrastucture necessary for Public Domain's self-design as a virtual organization and enables PD to interface and collaborate with other artists and arts groups world-wide who are also exploring computer networks as a potential medium for telematic art.

THE RESEARCH CENTER FOR MUSICAL ICONOGRAPHY (RCMI)

The City University of New York
33 West 42 Street
New York City, NY 10036 USA
Tel: (212) 692-2703

RCMI, the American national center and international headquarters of the Repertoire Internationale d'Iconographie Musical (RIdIM), is a project that catalogues artworks with musical subject matter for research purposes. Music iconography has been defined as the study of the representation of musical subjects (performers, performing sites, instruments, singers, musical scores) in the visual arts. Some recent definitions define it more loosely as the study of any artwork that contains a musical element in it, thus broadening the discipline's scope considerably. The sources constitute a rich body of evidence for the study of performing practice, social history, pictorial symbolism, and musical and art historical chronology, and are therefore of importance to scholars in many disciplines including art history, cultural history, sociology, and musicology (organology, acoustics, etc.).

A primary objective of RIdIM is to gain bibliographic control over this vast resource. Since it was founded in 1971, RIdIM has formulated cataloging rules endorsed by the International Association of Music Libraries, the International Musicological Society, and the International Council of Museums. In several countries, government-supported national centers or RIdIM maintains a staff that visits museums in their country to systematically catalogue artworks according to the international cataloguing rules. Several centers have almost completed catalogues of all the major museums in their countries. The RCMI collection at present includes some 1,200 items from 12 countries. RIdIM is a sister project of RISM (International Repertory of Musical Sources) and RILM (International Repertory of Music Literature).

SCIENCE AND ART

Marc Van Boom
Heldenstraat 35 Bus 2
2650 Edegem, Belgium
Tel: 03-458-26-74

The focus of Science and Art is to create a cooperation between creative persons with different skills and specializations for the purpose of realizing techno-art expositions. Collaborations include artists, decorators, astronomers, engineers, musicians and scientists. Technological and scientific realizations can be viewed as the "hardware" of modern society, with art in all of its forms and dimensions viewed as the "software". Science and Art brings the "hard and soft ware" together in a context which incorporates the visitors into the art work as active participants. The expositions created combine different human realizations and aims to create a form of consciousness called *multi-dimensional consciousness* (Figure 3).

Fig. 3. *Moon Crater,* **in the Planetarium within** *Space Art* **from Belgium origin. This manifestation of Science and Art's total techno-art concept included a computer-regulated light show. (Photo: L. Peeters)**

THE SOCIETY FOR THE HISTORY OF TECHNOLOGY

The University of Chicago Press
Journals Division
PO Box 37005
Chicago, IL 60637 USA

The Society for the History of Technology was formed in 1958 to encourage the study of technological development and its relationship with society and culture. The society is interdisciplinary, and in addition to a concern with the history of technological devices and processes, is also interested in the relationship of technology to politics, economics, labor, business, the environment, public policy, science and the arts. *Technology and Culture*, the official publication of the society, is included with membership. Membership is international, open to individuals, organizations, corporations, and institutions interested in the purposes and activities of the society. The society holds annual meetings, sometimes in collaboration with related organizations.

STANDARD MUSIC DESCRIPTION LANGUAGE/ HYTIME STANDARD

Charles Goldfarb, Steve Newcomb
International Computer Music
Association (ICMA)
ANSI X3V1.8M Secretariat
2040 Polk Street, Suite 330
San Francisco, CA 94109 USA
Tel: (817) 566-2235
Email: cma@dept.csci.unt.edu
        newcomb@techno.com

The ANSI X3V1.8M Standard Music Representation Language Work Group has been creating a standard music description language for adoption by the American National Standards Institute. This standard is intended as a storage and interchange format for musical ideas, and is expected to be used for automated processing in such areas as music printing, library cataloging and storage, multimedia presentations, teaching and research. After several years of developing the various aspects of this music description language, the committee has extracted a time model, now known as the ISO/IEX HyTime Hypermedia/Time-based Structuring Language, which is being proposed as a worldwide technical standard for integrated hypermedia. Hytime is an application of SGML (The Standard Generalized Markup Language—an internationally standardized language for document description) that effectively adds standardized mechanisms to SGML for identifying locations in SGML and non-SGML documents, establishing hyperlinks, and scheduling events in time and space.

THE STANFORD UNIVERSITY CENTER FOR COMPUTER RESEARCH IN MUSIC AND ACOUSTICS (CCRMA)

Patte Wood
CCRMA/Music Department
Stanford University
Stanford, CA 94305-8180 USA
Tel: (415) 725-3573
Fax: (415) 723-8468
Email: patte@ccrma.stanford.edu

CCRMA is an interdisciplinary facility where composers and researchers work together using computer-based technology as a new musical and artistic medium and as a research tool. Areas of ongoing interest at CCRMA include: Applications Hardware, Applications Software, Synthesis Techniques and Algorithms, Physical Modeling, Real-Time Controllers, Signal Processing, Digital Recording and Editing, Psychoacoustics and Musical Acoustics, Applied Pattern Recognition and Artificial Intelligence, Music Manuscripting by Computer, Composition, and Real-Time Applications with Small Systems.

CCRMA activities include academic courses, seminars, small interest group meetings, summer workshops and presentations. Concerts of computer music are presented several times each year with an annual outdoor computer music festival in July. In-house technical reports and recordings are available, and public demonstrations of ongoing work at CCRMA are held quarterly during the academic year.

TASK FORCE AND TECHNICAL COMMITTEE ON COMPUTER GENERATED MUSIC

Denis Baggi, Goffredo Haus
IEEE Computer Society
1730 Massachusetts Avenue
Washington, DC 20036-1903 USA
Email: baggi@berkeley.edu
music@imiucca.csi.unimi.it

The Task Force on Computer Generated Music is intended to be the preliminary form of a Technical Committee on Computer Generated Music. It is a constituent part of the IEEE Computer Society and operates under the rules and policies of that society. The IEEE Computer Society is a constituent society of the Institute of Electrical and Electronic Engineers (IEEE).

By Computer Generated Music the IEEE Computer Society and its members define an area from an interdisciplinary standpoint that lies between artistic creation at one extreme—such as music created with the help of computer technology - and engineering - e.g., sound synthesis and audio processing—at the other, without excluding the boundaries. Thus Computer Generated Music is meant to be a broad scientific area dedicated to, though not exclusively, research in music modeling, synthesis and analysis of music by computer and/or electronic means. An example of such an endeavor is the construction and definition of musical tools, methodologies and standards in software and hardware.

One important purpose of the Task Force is to place Computer Generated Music among those subjects generally accepted among academic disciplines by encouraging the creation of academic chairs, departments and organizational entities dedicated to Computer Generated Music within engineering academic establishments, research laboratories and government agencies. The Task Force will strive to make the results of the most advanced research in the field available to everybody and encourages experimentation by practitioners of the field. Material will be distributed in the form of books, CDs, possibly diskettes using audio, video and other media forms. The group recognizes the existence of other organizations dedicated to Computer Music and related applications of computer science to music and musicology, and actively seeks possible ways of collaboration. It will not duplicate efforts, projects or other organized activities by any other society, but will try instead to support existing activities. Due to the fact that this activity is part of a professional engineering society, it will be able to put some emphasis on those types of activities generally neglected by musical societies.

The Task Force will provide a forum for exchange of ideas among interested practitioners, researchers, developers, manufacturers, maintainers, users, students and creative people in the field of Computer Generated Music. It will further promote and facilitate the sharing of ideas, methods, techniques, tools, standards, and experiences between members for more effective use of Computer Generated Music technology. The Task Force gives great importance to contacts with organizations responsible for the definition of standards (e.g., the International MIDI Association) and with manufacturers of musical equipments. Its desire is not only to act as a reference point, testing laboratory and knowledge pool for the industry of instruments for Computer Generated Music, but also to actively participate in the definition and in the development of systems that may be of interest to the community of people active in Computer Generated Music. In this context, the Task Force is capable of lending its expertise both from an engineering as well as from an artistic standpoint.

TRANSIT

Wilhelm-Greil-Str-1
A-6020 Innsbruck, Austria
Tel: 0512 58 06 01
Fax: 0512 58 32 02

TRANSIT is a non-profit organization dedicated to the realization of artistic projects in the electronic space, especially in the field of the mass media radio and TV. TRANSIT is supported at regional and federal levels and by the ORF (Austrian Broadcasting Corp., Regional Studio Tirol). Artists, authors, composers and theoreticians from different fields, from Austria and abroad, are invited to submit project proposals or papers. The managing committee decides the financial and technical feasibility of the submitted projects and oversees realization of the selected projects. The managing committee is responsible for the selection and publication/distribution of the theoretical contributions. Final decisions may, in some cases, be delegated to expert juries.

TRANSIT

- is concerned with the theory and practice of art in electronic space, with special emphasis on the constantly changing role of the mass media TV and radio, particularly considering the development of new communications systems
- is organizing projects on this subject by Austrian and international artists, writers and composers
- is an initiative to promote a continuous confrontation with electronic space as the location, context and content of art
- provides access to production facilities (ORF - Austrian Radio and TV/artist workshops)
- searches for new forms for cultural events
- arranges colloquia and symposia on the arts in electronic space
- organizes the documentation of all TRANSIT projects by theoreticians who accompany a specific project from beginning to end
- is setting up a data-bank for the arts in electronic space
- is producing a publication on the history of art in the electronic space in Austria
- monitors existing art networks
- is establishing a multi-media work station in which artists, writers and composers will be able to explore new technology and communication systems

THE TYRONE GUTHRIE CENTER AT ANNAGHMAKERIGG, COUNTY MONAGHAN, IRELAND: A WORKPLACE FOR ARTISTS

Annaghmakerigg
Newbliss, County Monaghan
Ireland
Tel: 047 54003
Fax: 047 54380

The Tyrone Guthrie Center welcomes artists from Ireland and abroad to a unique working environment set in the midst of 400 acres of forested estate overlooking a large lake. Artists may stay for a period of time ranging from one week to three months in the Big House, which is run like a country hotel, or for up to a year at a time in one of the five new self-catering houses in the old farmyard.

Between the Big House and the two studio blocks, there are a variety of workspaces available, from the quite small for drawing and illustration to the very large for sculpture and painting. Each visual artist who comes has her or his own studio, suited to the work they intend to do. There is also a music room for composers and musicians, a large rehearsal and performance space for groups, and an extensive library. A photographic darkroom and print workshop are planned for 1993. At certain times of the year it is possible by special arrangement to accommodate groups of artists, theatre companies, sculpture symposiums, composers' master classes, writers' workshops and other such collaborations.

The Tyrone Guthrie Center is open to practitioners of all the arts, from the north and south of Ireland and from abroad. To qualify for residence it is necessary to show evidence of a significant level of achievement in the relevant fields. It is possible to apply by sending an up-to-date curriculum vitae, a few samples of recent work and an outline of the project to be undertaken at the Center. The center can also send a form for this purpose if necessary. People who have a clear idea of what they want to do there will get the most benefit from a stay at Annaghmakerrig.

Once accepted Irish artists are asked to contribute what they can afford towards the cost of their stay. The rest is make up by subsidies from the two Arts Councils in Ireland which are administered by the Center. Overseas artists are expected to pay the whole cost of their residency.

V2 ORGANIZATION

Alex Adriaansens, Joke Brouwer, Rik Delhaas
Muntelstraat 23
5211 PT's - Hertogenbosch, The Netherlands
Tel: 31-73-137958
Fax: 31-73-122238

The V2 Organization has been in operation as an artist collective for ten years. During the past six years, V2 has put an increasing emphasis on recent developments concerning the utilization of technology in art. The international *Manifestation for the unstable media* that has taken place annually since 1987 chooses a theme connected with the use of technology in art, and brings artists and scientists together.

Over the past five years the V2 Organization has manifested itself as an international media art center. In addition to media art presentations V2 organizes workshops for the production of media art, provides a video rental facility for art organizations and artists, and operates a distribution center for independently released books, magazines, records, compact discs, and video tapes.

THE VASARI PROJECT AT THE NATIONAL GALLERY

Trafalgar Square
London WC2N 5DN United Kingdom
Tel: 071-839-3321

The National Gallery, in collaboration with Birkbeck College, University of London, is developing equipment capable of making high quality electronic images of paintings. The result of this collaboration is VASARI: Visual Art Systems for Archiving and Retrieval of Images, a project funded by the European Community ESPRIT 11 scheme which has been in progress for the last three years. The project aims to show that it is feasible to make high resolution digital images with accurate color directly from paintings.

YLEM: ARTISTS USING SCIENCE AND TECHNOLOGY

Beverly Reiser, Trudy Myrrh Reagan
Box 749
Orinda, Ca 94563 USA
(510) 482-2483
Email: trudymyrrh@aol.com
       ylem@well.sf.ca.us

Ylem is an organization of artists and art lovers who look to science and technology for ideas and inspiration. That encompasses artists who work with videos, ionized gasses, computers, lasers, holograms, robotics and other new media. It also includes artists who use traditional media in new ways.

Ylem keeps its members informed about opportunities to show their work in upcoming exhibits, competitions, and conferences. It also brings members' work directly to the public through its own publications, events and exhibits. The membership includes many well-known figures in the arts and sciences, as well as collectors, educators, students, art agents, architects and engineers, physicists and mathematicians.

Diverse techno-aesthetic interests are demonstrated every other month at the Ylem Forums. They include presentations by scientists who appreciate the aesthetic values within their disciplines, and by artists who enjoy the science and technology that underlie art.

Ylem's feature annual publication is the *Directory of Artists Using and Science and Technology*. This is a directory of the over two hundred current members of Ylem. The directory brings these artists into contact with curators, art collectors, gallery owners, educators and other artists.

Ylem publishes a monthly newsletter that features short articles about and by members on the tech-art scene. The Ylem Newsletter lists the latest information on exhibits, openings, art opportunities, forums and networking events. This includes visits to studios of creative San Francisco Bay Area people working in the arts and sciences.

ZAKROS INTERARTS/ NEW MUSIC THEATRE

Randall Packer
614 York Street
San Francisco, CA 94110 USA
Tel: (415) 282-5497
Fax: (415) 282-4228

Zakros InterArts is a center for electronic music and media arts. Zakros InterArts offers courses and workshops taught by leading San Francisco Bay Area musicians and engineers who focus on electronic music and the integration with all forms of multimedia.

Zakros InterArts addresses the current crisis in the electronic media arts—the lack of information and training for incorporating high quality musical and sound resources into multimedia production. The organization offers professional instruction designed to enhance the musical skills of visual and media artists, as well as to open up new creative inroads for musicians already working with electronic music.

Zakros InterArts covers the broad spectrum of state-of-the-art computer music composition and production, with a special emphasis on interactive multimedia and live performance. Topics range from hard-disk recording to editing digital synthesizers, from composing with sequencers to the basics of MIDI, from QuickTime movies to multimedia performance. Classes are geared towards providing skills useful to both the musician and the multimedia artist at all levels of experience.

New Music Theatre is now in its fifth year, creating and presenting new music, music theater, and interdisciplinary performance in San Francisco. Led by Artistic Director Randall Packer and a core team of recognized interdisciplinary artists, New Music Theatre has established itself as an innovative company creating new performance works in the San Francisco Bay Area.

New Music Theatre is committed to a new form of live performance which dissolves the boundaries between the various art forms—music, theatre, visual arts, literature, electronic arts and dance. This exploration has led to the creation of multi-dimensional stage, visual and sound designs which bring about the new relationship between the audience, the performer, the theatrical environment, and the electronic media.

ZENTRUM FÜR KUNST UND MEDIENTECHNOLO- GIE KARLSRUHE (ZKM)

Heinrich Klotz
Kaiserstr. 64
D-76 131 Karlsruhe, Germany
Tel: (49) 721-93400
Fax: (49) 721-934019
Email: info@zkm.de
       music@zkm.de
       image@zkm.de

The Center for Art and Mediatechnology was established as a foundation by the city of Karlsruhe and the State of Baden-Wuerttemberg in 1989. The goal of the Foundation as a facility for research, dissemination of culture and training is to facilitate the all-embracing and wide-reaching exploration of art and mediatechnology, especially in the areas of visual images, music and word, and their interrelationships. Currently the Center's activities are spread over three different locations in the city of Karlsruhe. In 1996 the Center will move to a renovated factory site which will house all departments in a total area of 15,000 square meters. The investments will accumulate to $100 Million. In the current state, the two institutes for research and production are already functioning within the limits of a start-up operation. Two museums and an audio-visual library are being planned so they can open to the public in 1996.

■ Museum of Contemporary Art
Heinrich Klotz, Director

The collection of this museum is already now one of the largest collections of media-art. In contrast to traditional museums it will house contemporary art ranging from traditional media like oil paintings to video installations and interactive exhibits.

■ Media Museum
Hans-Peter Schwarz, Director

This museum will focus on how technology, art and perception influenced each other over the course of time. Hands-on experiments and interactive installations will expose the visitor to the manifold intertwinings of media technology and cultural changes.

■ Mediathek

The Mediathek is comprised of three sections: a library, a videotheque and an audiotheque. All collections will be publicly accessible in 1996. Already now, the videotheque (Dieter Daniels) aquired many artists' videos and the famous Infermental collection of experimental videos. The heart of the audiotheque (Thomas Gerwin) is the International Digital ElectroAcoustic Music Archive (IDEAMA), a joint undertaking between CCRMA, Stanford University, and ZKM. Partner institutions are GRM (Paris), IRCAM (Paris), GMEB (Bourges), NACIS (Tokyo), EMS (Stockholm), and the New York Public Library (NYPL).

■ Institute for Image Media
Jeffrey Shaw, Director

The Institute for Image Media focuses its practical research and production activities in the following areas: Video, Computer Graphics, Computer Animation, Digital Multimedia, Interactivity, Visualization, and Telecommunication. Through the accumulated activities of its resident artists and technicians, the institute will be able to develop specialized in-house hardware and software resources which will facilitate new and experimental forms of media art production.

■ Institute for Music and Acoustics
Johannes Goebel, Director

The work of the Institute centers around artistic production, scientific research and the development of tools for composition. Radio plays, works with live-electronics, tape-music, sound-installations and intermedia works are carried out in temporary work spaces. The new building will provide recording and rehearsal studios on a professional level.

General Statements
The Institutes do not offer educational programs. Specific workshops are offered for professionals. In general, artists can apply for residencies to work on defined projects, funded by third parties or, within limits, from the Center itself. Since 1989, the MultiMediale festival is staged bi-annually, presenting art installations, interactive exhibits, mixed media performances and concerts.

WORDS ON WORKS

ABOUT WORDS ON WORKS

Judy Malloy

Art/Science/Technology is a melting pot into which artists with widely different backgrounds and approaches are thrown together. Although diverse creators sometimes mingle uneasily in this late 20th century stew, their cohabitation can enrich our individual approaches. If we are on the verge of a new Renaissance, it is partially because, as is evident in *Words on Works*, we are eroding the barriers between (formerly) separate art worlds.

In the spirit of *Leonardo*, the statements in *Words on Works* are what the artists themselves have chosen to say about their own work. Taken as a whole these statements echo pervasive concerns of contemporary artists—multicultural sources, appropriation, narrative content that is sometimes fractured and/or distorted. In addition, they contain concerns of artists who have been working with contemporary technology for several decades—investigations into the nature of perception, humanization of technology, global communication. Weaving in and out of this collection of short, informal statements about new artworks in which art and technology coexist are the threads of interactivity and a related awareness of the changing role of the audience from that of static viewer to that of participant.

Artists in *Words on Works* range from environmental artist Melynda Reid (*Stake Out At Post Office Bay*) who lives in a trailer near the Apalachicola River in Florida to cyber artists Dale Nason and Troy Innocent who issue their *Cyber Dada Manifesto* from Footscray, Australia. The artists represented here live and make art all over the world—from Grenoble, France where Christiane Geoffroy examines biotechnology in her video installation *Geo-Genetic* to Columbus, Ohio where Collis Davis produced his interactive narrative *Elegba's Stratagem* that uses video and sound to combine elements from African mythology with the story of a contemporary African-American artist.

Art writing in *Words on Works* ranges from Fortner Anderson's concise one hundred word description of his collaboratively produced software *The Odyssey* to Sara Roberts' example laden ("Get your arm back in the car, do you want to lose it?") description of *Early Programming*, an interactive reservoir of maternal sayings. Ways of conveying the essence of the work range from Mary Jean Kenton's meaningful, visual prose about the Pennsylvania farm where she lives and works on her ongoing installation of horticulture, naturally occurring materials and paint to Michael Joyce's seductive, layered prose that echoes the polyphonic writing in his hypertextual novel *afternoon, a story*.

Like Lynn Hershman's *Longshot* (a videotape in which the "camera's surveillance of the subject is constant") the art in *Words on Works* may have narrative content that examines the society we live in. Or, like Aviva Rahmani's *Ghost Nets* (an environmental work located on Vinalhaven Island off the coast of Maine), it may focus on our relationship to the environment in which we live. Coexisting in this melting pot are artworks as radically different in conception and execution as conceptual artist Stephen Moore's *Seminal Chrono-Schema*, a long-term project that is based on ideas and information about the history of art, and computer artist Lynn Pocock-Williams' *A Certain Uncertainty*, an experimental music video that features The New York Guitar Project, and focuses "on the connections between the qualities of the sounds and visuals."

Approaches here range from the "marriage of acoustical and electronic sound worlds" that Neil Rolnick strives for in *ElectriCity* and *ReRebong* to Abbe Don's intimate interactive multimedia installation *We Make Memories* that she describes as revealing "how our family history has been constructed and passed down matrilinearly." Diverse mediums are represented here—from Eleanor Kent's *Five Knitted Fractals*, wall works that use the traditional craft of knitting to "make something tangible that I could hold in my hands while still working with computers" to David Gaw's and Ed Koch's technically complex, computer-controlled *The Sock*, a "coactive" sculpture that is engineered with thirteen electric motors controlled by a grid of switches hidden under a carpet to react to viewer position.

Some *Words on Works* contributors use ancient sources to throw light on contemporary culture. For instance, Ben Britton shows us the world the way our ancestors saw it in *Lascaux*, a virtual reality installation that uses elements derived from the prehistoric paintings in the French Lascaux caves. Displaying text electronically, Fred Forest integrates Biblical events with the 1991 Gulf War. In *From Osiris to Sinai*, a diazo print scroll, Sonya Rapoport, who has been using cross-cultural sources for decades, traces similarities between the ancient Egyptian *Book of the Dead* and the Ten Commandments. Through the eyes of a culture very different from our own, poet G.P. Skratz and composer Bob Davis look at the American fascination with outer space exploration. Accompanied by visual illustrations, by a cappella duets and by sounds produced by Davis (on unusual instruments such as large water bottles), Skratz describes the progress through China of the American artifact-laden *Nixon Bookmobile*. As a counterpoint, Valerie Soe shatters cultural stereotypes by showing us another side of Asian culture in her video installation *Diversity* that features Chan Cheong-Toon, "regularly seen at a traffic island at the corner of Broadway and Columbus in San Francisco's North Beach section, singing furiously in Chinese to whoever cares to listen."

Some contributors alter the perception of our uneasy, shifting, late twentieth century environments. *Point of Reference*, a video installation by Dutch artist Madelon Hooykaas and British artist Elsa Stansfield (who have been making collaborative video installations, video tapes, and photo works since 1975) is "visually like a dark rocky island in a sea of information." Interactive art pioneer Jeffrey Shaw's video sculpture *Anamorphoses of Memory* centers optically distorted erotic memories on the bed with which they are connected. Behavioral scientist Walter Siegfried's *Sound Tracks to Reality* uses unexpected sounds in a conventional "Walkman" tour in order to alter participants' experience of their environment and thus increase their awareness and involvement with the space that surrounds them.

In contrast, others clarify human links in information absorption and/or reinforce them by emphasizing communication. Sas Colby, for instance, builds a narrative with stamp-sized miniature photographs that look at ways in which our bodies absorb information, and Craig Harris explores human creativity and communication in *Configurable Space*, a multimedia work that "is directed towards the development of a balanced understanding about how we use the visual, aural, tactile, and configurable capabilities of digital technologies."

We bring "to an immediate situation a potential for sensually experiencing the significances of all past experiences," wrote Adelbert Ames, an early researcher into the relationships between art and technology, in his notes on the nature of human perception.[1] In these *Words on Works*, artists relate experience to perception in different ways, as they describe works that range from mixed media sculpture to video installation. "My work is derived from things as I see 'em" Kimberly Kelzer says as she explains why her jewelry box *Home on the Range* (made of materials that range from silicone rubber to neon) looks like a combination of a toy oven and a stereotypical California desert. Although, at the time, he "had no idea that this event could filter its way into my work", a London immolation protest that he read about in the media became the heart of Paul Sermon's hypermedia *Think About the People Now*—an interactive work that involves the user in choices that channel perception of the event. In Lynn Kirby's multimedia installation *Portraits in Common Time*, the viewer's perception of three characters is partially shaped by the way those characters (as set forth by the artist) have chosen to organize the visual elements of their living spaces.

"As the Cybernetic Art of this generation grows more intelligent and sensitive, the Greek obsession with 'living sculpture' will take on an undreamed reality," Jack Burnham wrote in 1968[2], but a decade and a half later, he titled a book chapter "Art and Technology: The Panacea that Failed"[3] having come to believe that the anthropomorphism he had formerly sought in art and technology had expressed itself instead in conceptual art, performance art, and video art. Art and technology had not successfully integrated in part because of the "sense of mastery, manipulation and 'otherness'" that technology fosters, he postulated.

However, in 1992, (a year when the most successful United States presidential debate was generally agreed to be the one in which the candidates interacted with the audience), it is apparent that, in combination with audience involvement/interaction artists are effectively integrating that very sense of mastery and manipulation to humanize art and technology. "The thing about hyperfictions is that, for art, they tend to be extremely lifelike. They move and shift, allowing everything, and so allow only that we find our own perspective," says Carolyn Guyer about her hyperfiction *Quibbling*. "The entire virtual world represents the human experience of flying dreams," Fred Truck writes about his *Flying Dream*. Created with the tools of virtual reality, it integrates Leonardo da Vinci's flying machine and contemporary airspace obstacles such as telephone poles.

In his *Palm Size Plastic Case Series*, Joe Rosen gives the viewer a feeling of physical control by providing hand held, artist designed controllers. "A primary goal in each was to incorporate a mind and body interplay between users and on-screen computer objects and images," he says. Deborah Whitman, whose *Deus ex Machina/Closet of Angels* integrates technology (super 8 film loops) with wooden sculptural structures in a film sculpture that she feels is completed by audience participation, describes her ongoing series of film sculptures as "allegorical machines

1. Adelbert Ames, *The Morning Notes of Adelbert Ames, Jr.*, Hadley Cantril, ed. (New Brunswick, NJ: Rutgers University Press, 1960) p. 3

2. Jack Burnham, *Beyond Modern Sculpture; The Effects of Science and Technology on the Sculpture of this Century* (New York, NY: G. Braziller, 1968)

3. Jack Burnham, "Art and Technology: The Panacea That Failed" in *Video Culture; A Critical Investigation*, John G. Hanhardt, ed. (Layton, Utah: G.M. Smith, Peregrine Smith Books in association with VSW Press, 1968) pp. 232-248

with whimsical features which involve the audience in poetic narratives." As Hazen Reed puts it when he talks about his interactive documentary *Portraits of People Living with AIDS,* "Understanding that viewers are part of the process of meaningful creation is an important notion in all communicative acts, be they face to face conversations with other human beings, interactions with the environment, or dialogue with an interactive computer system."

The merger of art, science and technology is not yet without visible, occasionally awkwardly sewn seams, but the emergence of ideas and content and the more than occasional work in which the artist's vision fuses seamlessly with the medium, signal the arrival of a mature art form. The following works and artists (not mentioned above) are no less important participants/contributors: Die Audio Gruppe, Lutz Bacher, Maria Blondeel and Guy De Bievre, Bill and Mary Buchen, Martin Cox, Robert Edgar, Richard Gess, Francesco Giomi, Reiko Goto, Michael Horwood, Christopher Janney, James Johnson, Steve Mann, Michael McNabb, Pauline Oliveros, Nancy Paterson, Paul Rutkovsky, Claude Schryer, Jill Scott, Stephen s'Soreff.

THE ODYSSEY

Fortner Anderson

Dromos Editions
4083 Clark
Montreal, Quebec H2W 1X1 Canada
Email: fortner@well.sf.ca.us

The Odyssey is a collaborative computer program written as a Hypercard application for the Apple Macintosh computer (Mac Plus, SE or II). *The Odyssey* traveled for 4 months, 15 March–14 July 1989. During its travels, all who encountered *The Odyssey* were asked to contribute texts, sounds or images to its collection of data. Contributors passed their work on to others so that the journey could continue.

After 14 July 1989, all copies of *The Odyssey* were asked to be returned home. Upon their return, we hoped to compile a modern-day Domesday book, an electronic picture of the time from the material that was received.

HUGE UTERUS

Lutz Bacher

1592 Euclid Avenue
Berkeley, California 94708 USA

Huge Uterus (1989) includes the 6-hour real-time video record of the recent operation on my uterus. During the video/operation, the surgeon writes exploratory notes such as that used here for the title: "Huge uterus . . . with many tumors . . . no cancer . . . the tissue is healthy except for tumors . . . remove tumors . . . the uterus is an organ that heals well naturally".

The other image/narrative component of this installation is a visualization/preparation-for-the-operation sound tape that plays on an autoreverse tape player with detachable remote speakers: "As the anaesthetic begins to make you even more relaxed, external words and sounds simply serve as a background murmur interpreted as signals to relax. They're not recorded. You will not respond to them. You are very relaxed and very calm".

These tapes play on equipment that is configured as body/monitor/hookup. All of the apparatus (monitor, decks, speakers, wires) are visible in the actual installation. The video cassette recorder and audio tape decks are mounted on adjoining walls; their electrical wiring hangs free and visible and is connected to the video monitors and speakers, which are placed on the floor side-by-side in front of their decks. The video monitor lies on its back on the floor.

Huge Uterus was exhibited in the Bay Area Conceptualism exhibition

(Hallwalls, Buffalo, NY, Fall 1989), at the Simon Watson Gallery (New York City, Jan–Feb 1990) and at L.A.C.E. (Los Angeles, CA, Feb–Apr 1990).

SAM WIL DAT MYRNA ALLES VERTELT OVER KELLY HARPER

Maria Blondeel, Guy De Bièvre

Kunstenaarstraat 51
B-9040 Gent, Belgium

Sam Wil Dat Myrna Alles Vertelt Over Kelly Harper (Sam Wants Myrna to Tell Him Everything about Kelly Harper) is an audiovisual work by Maria Blondeel (images and photography) and Guy De Bièvre (sound and music). It was commissioned by Het Muziek Lod for the third annual Vertelfestival (Festival of Narratives) in Gent, Belgium.

Sam Wil Dat Myrna is an attempt to use non-literary computer logic to obtain a narrative result. As it was a first try, we decided to use existing commercial software (dBASE) in a rather simple fashion. The data we used were résumés of American and Australian soap-series as they appeared weekly in a popular local TV-programs magazine. We chose this kind of literature because it consists mainly of condensed announcements of non-events (such as "Sam bought a new car") alternating with highly dramatic ones (such as "Lucy's father was murdered").

A dBASE Data Entry Form was made that allowed inputting one sentence at a time as well as up to four names and three keywords derived from that sentence. About 1,000 sentences were entered that had to be sifted down to a maximum of 320 sentences. The sentences from this dBASE file were indexed, and a prolog was derived. This prolog consisted of all the sentences that had the keyword *vertellen* (to narrate). The index grouped these sentences alphabetically. Then, for the story itself, all sentences that featured names beginning with *S*, *M* or *K*, or the pronouns he or she, were located and edited. They were also ordered alphabetically, which allowed us to title our chapters *A,B,C,D*, etc. (For instance, Chapter A has, in alphabetical order, all sentences beginning with *A*.)

This 'story' (which had some interesting, often funny, coincidental narrative qualities) was then used as a script for the audiovisual. We decided that the approach of the script should be linear, that each sentence was worth 3 seconds and that we would work separately (sound vs. image) according to that structure, without any other agreements. In the end we had 320 slides and 16 minutes of soundtrack. The slides and the soundtrack used elements from the story and were separate, complementary interpretations of the story. Occasionally, there were some surprising coincidences and narrative qualities.

The story is offered to the audience of the audiovisual, as a libretto. One of the interesting things is that, when translated (the original version is in Flemish), the alphabetical order changes here and there and so does the narration.

The work premiered on 7 December 1991 in Gent, during the third annual Festival of Narratives, in a 'living-room' setting, using a four-channel audio system and four digitally controlled slide projectors.

LASCAUX

Ben Britton

College of DAAP
Mail Location 16
University of Cincinnati
Cincinnati, Ohio 45221-0016 USA
Email:
bbritton@headcheese.daa.uc.edu

Lascaux is a virtual-reality installation (Fig. 1). Its purpose is to reflect humanity and inspire peace, respect and consideration.

In the gallery are two rooms: the Nave and the Sanctuary. The audience sits in the Nave and watches on video monitors through the eyes of the viewer who interacts in the Sanctuary.

The Sanctuary is a private room designed for one viewer at a time. It is a dark room. In this darkened room is a pool of light. In the light are a chair, a joystick and virtual-reality goggles.

The viewer enters the dark room, enters the pool of light, puts on the

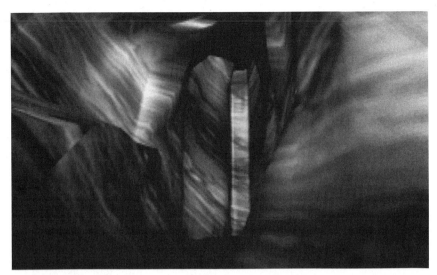

Fig. 1. Ben Britton, *Lascaux*, virtual-reality installation. Its purpose is to reflect humanity and inspire peace, respect and consideration.

virtual-reality goggles. A small stone lamp is visible in the niche on the wall. A red spot is painted on the wall. The viewer picks up the lamp and another dot becomes visible. He or she moves towards it, and a row of dots leads off into the darkness into the cave. Sometimes it is difficult to follow the trail of dots.

If the viewer follows far enough, he or she comes to a large lit hall where stone lamps on wall ledges illuminate giant paintings of animals. Side corridors lead off to other grottos. At the opposite end, the hall opens to a longer, wider tunnel, the ceilings and sides of which are painted with figures. At the end are three dots.

If the viewer stares at the paintings, they 'come to life' and reveal visions (through motion video and audio displayed in the goggles). If the viewer gazes on the fish, he or she comes underwater with fish all around, as if he or she were in the midst of a salmon run. If the viewer looks at a cow, he finds himself in a herd with mooing snouts, tails, hooves, flanks all around. Other events include sky, forest, waterfalls, lions, deer, bison, horse, bird and bear. After each vision, the viewer is returned to the cave.

Searching through the cave, the viewer finds interactive images hidden in niches that lead to other sequences. One of the hidden images is of a human being. When the viewer interacts with the image of the human, a figure appears in the cave initiating a secret, conveying a prophecy and greeting from real spirits. This experience is observed only in the Sanctuary—it is not perceived by those in the Nave.

Lascaux is related to our civilization. It celebrates innocence and examines human fault. It explores future, present and past. It speaks about love, fear and courage. It is a vessel of a message of peace.

GEO-SONIC

Bill Buchen and Mary Buchen

Sonic Architecture
PO Box 20873
Tompkins Square Station
New York City, New York 10009 USA
Tel/Fax: (212) 982-1743

GEO-SONIC (1988) is an artwork for computer that explores sound, language and geographics. It is a collage of sounds, speech and calligraphy from around the world that leads the participant in associative global dreams and journeys. Sounds sampled by the artists are digitized and played back, juxtaposed with on-screen visual imagery (by use of a track ball activated cursor). Visual elements include calligraphy from written language around the world and digitized historical and contemporary maps.

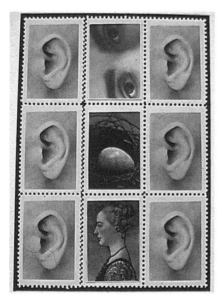

Fig. 2. Sas Colby, *Witness,* photo stamps, 4-x-3 in, 1986. A visual narrative was created with miniature photographs gummed and perforated like postage stamps.

PHOTO STAMPS/ WITNESS

Sas Colby

Box 794
El Prado, New Mexico 87529 USA
Tel: (505) 758-3966

GEO-SONIC equates geographic place with sound, language and symbols, and explores the relationship of sounds and visual symbols with people. It includes Aeolian pigeons from Bali (flutes attached to birds), the Brooklyn Bridge (before it was paved over), donkey caravans from Nepal, New York City fire sirens, Minnesota prairie tornado sirens, Thailand tribeswomen calling pigs, Indonesian frogs and Venice church bells.

In the *GEO-SONIC* system, data exists on three planes: the sonic plane (speech/sounds/music), the calligraphic plane (character as symbol) and the geographic plane (national or continental boundary as symbol). These planes exist as programming concepts and are not seen on the screen. The vertices where planes meet are interactive access points that can be entered or clicked on with a track ball to create interaction (a sound is heard or an image occurs on the screen).

For example, a link can be made along a plane or from one plane to another—Tokyo Bells/Venice Bells; a link can be made through the globe/ the transparent earth—Moscow USSR/Moscow Idaho; a link can be made through the atmosphere—rain in Bangkok/rain in Seattle (sonic plane); a link can be made through the oceans—sonar from the Atlantic Ocean to the Java Sea; a link can be made through a symbol along planes—Chinese symbol for lake (calligraphic plane)/sound of Lake Titicaca (sonic plane)/ outline of Lake Michigan (geographic plane).

During the years 1982–1989 I produced a series of miniature photographs that were printed in grids and gummed and perforated like postage stamps. I called them 'photo stamps', and thought of them as my visual vocabulary, using the images the way a writer uses words. Each was a kind of rebus. Compositions of stamps could be deciphered like puzzles.

Many stamps were produced from my original photographs and collages as well as from pictures appropriated from magazines. Occasionally a special stamp was designed to commemorate an event such as an exhibition or a person or alter ego. More often the stamps depicted ordinary subjects like road signs, moving cars, body parts, foods and animals. I also developed rubber-stamp cancellations that mimicked postal marks. In one, one of my pen names, "Serene Surrender", arched over "California, USA" with the date in the center of the circle.

The photographs were produced by a special piece of equipment in a photo lab in Florida. Unfortunately, the equipment has since been sold and the service is no longer available. Although I never saw the machine, I understand that it included a 'cluster lens' that made a grid of 25 identical images (color or black and white) the size of postage stamps on a 5-x-7-inch sheet. The sheet was then perforated around the edges and in the margins between the images to create the effect of stamps. The perforating machine was made of cast iron and was operated electrically by pressing a foot pedal.

Witness (1986, 4-x-3 inch), from my series of photo stamps, is about sensing and the way our bodies absorb information (Fig. 2). The image of an ear is repeated six times to emphasize its sensitivity and vulnerability as a point of entry into the body. Other images are eyes, classic windows to the soul; a blue egg in a nest, representing the seed of life; and a fifteenth-century Venetian silhouette depicting a long delicate neck, soft shoulders,

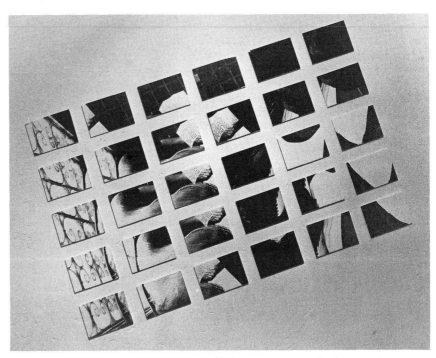

Fig. 3. Martin Cox, *Transaction: enough of its letters to make from Sydney interable,* 1989. 30 5-x-7 in. photographic grid, 33-x-52 in.

and breast—areas charged with erotic overtones. By commenting on each other, the pictures in *Witness* create a visual narrative that may be read as a story. Repetition is used for emphasis as a chorus is used in a song.

TRANSACTION

Martin Cox

1489 Avon Park Terrace
Los Angeles, California 90026 USA

Transaction (1989) was a process-oriented, site-specific installation (Fig. 3). It consisted of 160 black-and-white photographs.

I began by photographing four individuals in a series of staged events involving daily activities of contemporary Western life—walking up a staircase, shaking hands, getting out of a car, turning a key. Through this process of documentation, I amassed a large amount of detailed photographic evidence that formed the raw material for my work.

Using photographic printing techniques, I inverted, fractured and repeated the images. I then edited this material to produce sequences and groups of images to retell the events.

The subsequent installation at Intersection for the Arts, San Francisco, CA, was formed with these groups of images and with additional images produced when I photographed the inside gallery space. This meant that the walls, floor and ceiling of the gallery not only displayed the work but also became part of the imagery, providing a link between the viewer and the history of the events.

The exhibition was designed to be read as a single narrative, with the viewer detecting connections and incongruities from one sequence of images to the next by the juxtaposition of these images. In this way, *Transaction* explored the visual mystery and the apparent truth created by connecting isolated incidental evidence into a single narrative.

ELEGBA'S STRATAGEM

Collis Davis

Department of Theater
The Ohio State University
Haskett Hall, 156 West 19th Ave.
Columbus, Ohio 43210 USA
Tel: (614) 292-6637
Fax: (614) 292-3222
Email: davis.14@osu.edu

Elegba's Stratagem employs the computer as a tool for the design and presentation of branching narrative ideas and viewer mediation (Fig. 4). The basic equipment configuration consists of a personal computer (PC), three videodisk players that are controlled by the computer (via an interface card), a graphics overlay card that allows text and graphics originating from the PC to be combined with motion video from the videodisk players and a speech-recognition card for viewer input. The authoring system used creates the interactive program.

At the heart of this work is the projection of elements from the African orisha tradition—its pantheon of deities and their relationships—onto the story of a contemporary African-American artist who is in search of himself through his artwork. The connection between this tradition and the proposed interactive video is both metaphoric and symbolic.

Systematically, the screenwriter draws parallels between the role and function of Elegba (deity of the crossroads, or of karma in Eastern terms) and that of computer-program intelligence. As Elegba opens and closes doors of human destiny, so the computer governs the travel of data through a design of treelike structures. Factors determining which pathways will be open or closed at any given moment are largely a matter of the interaction between human behavior (viewer input) and the program, which represents the laws of the system—the values system.

Symbolically, the relationship is supported in terms of story, particularly through its major characters. They are seen as archetypal extensions of various important deities, all of whom are well known for their powers, personalities, behavior and domains of responsibility. In effect, these spiritual presences are manifested through their earthly hosts, who themselves are unaware of their possession by the archetypes.

The protagonist, Lazarus Wilder, named after his biblical namesake, encounters these characters in his everyday life and is creatively influenced by them. In the process, he discovers the key to his own paradoxical position within the orisha universe.

Fig. 4. Collis Davis, *Elegba's Stratagem,* an interactive narrative video production, features a speech recognition interface. (Photo: Robert Hutt)

WE MAKE MEMORIES

Abbe Don

618 Sanchez St.
San Francisco, CA 94114
USA
Tel: (415) 626-2334
Email: abbe@well.sf.ca.us

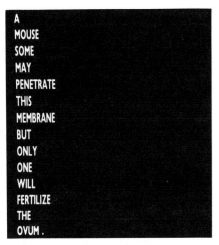

Fig. 5. Christiane Geoffroy, text from Géo-Genetic, videotape, 1989.

LIVING CINEMA

Robert Edgar

707 Continental Circle, #1412
Mountain View, California 94040
USA
Email: lull@well.sf.ca.us

As my great-grandmother told stories, she wove in and out of the past and present, the old country and America, English and Yiddish, business and family, changing voice from first person to direct address to third person. Each detail was part of the narrative continuum and was potentially linked to several other stories or digressions, some of them new, some of which I had heard before. However, both content and meaning were affected by the context: the presence of other visitors, whether we were baking together or looking at photos in her scrapbook, or if I interrupted the flow of the story to ask for more details. It was as if she had a chronological, topical and associative matrix that enabled her to generate stories in which content, structure and context were interdependent.

I have used my great-grandmother's storytelling style as a model to create an interactive multimedia installation that reveals how our family history has been constructed and passed down matrilinearly. A pictorial timeline of family photographs that date from 1890 to the present enables viewers to move through time on a Macintosh screen. By clicking on one of the head shots, viewers hear stories from my great-grandmother, my grandmother, my mother and me that weave in and out of the past and present, the old country and America, English and Yiddish, business and family.

We Make Memories is composed of a 9-megabyte Hypercard stack and a 30-minute videodisk. It requires a Macintosh II with at least 2 megabytes of random access memory (RAM) and a laser disc player with a serial port, ideally a Pioneer 4200, and a video monitor. *We Make Memories* is available as an environmental installation that recreates my great-grandmother's study, with a wooden desk covered with informal family snapshots tucked under a piece of plexiglass and formal family portraits hanging on the walls. The computer and video monitors as well as the mouse sit side-by-side atop the desk, and the rest of the video and computer equipment is hidden from view.

Living Cinema is a desktop video system that explores the montage of motion video, live video, cell/sprite animation, speech generation, videodisk audio, captured and manipulated images and image-manipulation routines in real time. *Living Cinema* combines the electronic manipulation of a video synthesizer with the formal strategies of cinema and the reorganizational capabilities of the computer: hypertonal montage. Composer Dutch Knotts works with audio samplers and synthesizers and parallels the processes I use with frame grabbers and image manipulation.

Living Cinema is built around the Truevision Targa 16 board, a speech synthesizer, MS-DOS computer, laser disc player, color video camera and monitor, and various storage devices and peripherals. The software was written in the C programming language.

In performance, the performer's relationship with the image goes beyond simply choosing the image—the performer builds and otherwise metamorphoses the image in real time. The pace of *Living Cinema* is not the pace of music videos; it is the speed of the aperceptual thought of the performers.

LA BIBLE ÉLECTRONIQUE ET LA GUERRE DU GOLFE

Fred Forest

Territoire Du M2
60540 Anserville, France

COACTIVE ART

David Gaw and Ed Koch

Coactive Aesthetics
PO Box 425967
San Francisco, California 94142
USA
Tel: (415) 626-5152
Fax: (415) 626-6320
Email: dgaw@coactive.com

GÉO-GENETIC

Christiane Geoffroy

6, rue d'Alma
38000 Grenoble, France

La Bible Électronique et La Guerre du Golfe (The Electronic Bible and the Gulf War) is a technological environment that I installed in the summer of 1991 at the Center of Contemporary Art La Basse in Paris, France. It is an electronic project/installation, occupying 150 square meters of floor space. Down in this 'hole'—specially prepared with perpendicular partitions equipped with mirrors and with 4 tons of sand—about 15 luminous 'journals' with electronic diodes are running. This configuration creates a luminous circulation of letters, words, sentences that is a very strange mixture of the purposes of the Bible and war. Nearby, cameras and television sets display high-speed transmissions about the Gulf war.

In this installation, I use technological means to integrate reality and events in the Bible. Differences between the speeds of the running sentences create a staggering dizziness and bring aesthetic pleasure.

Since 1988, we have been exploring a form of interactive art that we call *coactive art*. We use the term 'co-active', rather than 'interactive', to emphasize an aesthetic of the viewer-object interaction rather than an aesthetic of the object itself.

Our goal is to produce objects that permit viewers to perceive their influence on the objects without precisely knowing the nature of that influence. This implies that the objects must have a certain level of autonomy; their behavior must not be totally determined by environmental and/or sensory inputs.

We achieve this coupling of viewer and object through the use of computers, sensors and computer-controlled actuation devices such as motors, lights and video images. One such device, *The Sock*, is a 6-ft-tall monolithic form covered with a highly elastic material. Thirteen electric motors cause the shape to change and deform in various ways. Speed and direction of the motors, and thus the shape of the object, are controlled by input from a 10-×-12-ft grid of switches, hidden under a carpet, that determines the positions of viewers in the room. The sculpture is dynamic and changes its shape based on the presence of viewers.

Emotion Pictures, another project we are developing, is the next step in interactive video. Over the last few years psychophysiologists have developed techniques that allow one to crudely determine a person's emotional state or 'emotion estimate' based on basic physiological signs (skin temperature, pulse rate, skin conductance). The *Emotion Pictures* system captures and processes these signals, using the emotion estimate to control the sequence of images shown according to rules defined by the artist. For example, a rule might instruct, "if fear is increasing then show image-sequence y, otherwise show image-sequence z".

My work is about genetics—reproduction and manipulation. *Géo-Genetic* (1989) (Fig. 5) is a modular work that can be shown both by itself and as part of an installation. In the video module (6 minutes 30 sec), images of sperm and eggs, cropped and blown up, spill out in a seemingly endless stream, accompanied by texts appropriated from technical literature and the media, for example, "Many spermatozoa may fix themselves to the membrane of an unfertilized ovum of mouse. Some may penetrate this membrane but only one will fertilize the ovum".

For an installation at L'École de Nîmes, I built a structure in which *Géo-Genetic* was installed. The video images were viewed through a 20-cm crack in the structure. I propose a larger installation comprised of a triangular structure 7 meters on each side. Spectators would enter through a hole and come face to face with coital activity.

MAHASUKHA HALO

Richard Gess

Cataloging Department
Woodruff Library
Emory University
Atlanta, Georgia 30322-2870 USA
Email: libgess@emuvm1.bitnet

Mahasukha Halo is a text with two lives. Its first incarnation, written in May–June 1990, was a block of 120 sentences in a single unindented paragraph. Most of the sentences were written in first person in several voices differentiated by italics and/or subject. One rule was set for their assembly: no sentence was allowed to continue the voice or subject of the sentence preceding it. This text was eventually published in *Lowlife* magazine[4]. In August–December 1991 I converted the print *Halo* into a Macintosh-based 376K standalone Storyspace hypertext. This electronic *Halo* consists of 308 text spaces interconnected by 759 links; the 120-sentence core has been expanded to include the working notes made before and during the writing of the print text and a substructure of samples, citations, and references detailing the web of intertexts the original work was drawn from. Each space containing one of the original sentences is captioned with the name of its speaker or subject; sentences with the same speaker or subject are linked in circular paths, as are sentences sharing images or comprising partial narratives. The Storyspace *Mahasukha Halo* animates the original.

Guy Davenport, discussing the "architectonic" films of Stan Brakhage and others, described those films as "succession[s] of images that do not tell a story but define a state of mind"[5]. This is how *Mahasukha Halo* is meant; not as a "Garden-of-Forking-Paths"–genre multiple narrative, but as a field of images for interactive exploration. Using the Storyspace Reader, it is navigable in several virtual directions, but no direction is ever privileged or denied. This means that readers may initially feel lost; this is a state the *Halo* deliberately invokes. By exploiting "lostness"—via fragmentation, repetition, digressions to notes and intertexts, and looping—the *Halo* breaks down conditioned expectations of narrative, making readers concentrate instead on individual images and their resonances in accretion. All this may sound less than reader-friendly, but readers usually find the *Halo* more seductive than forbidding, a work that invites its necessary rereading.

The *Halo*'s sentences cumulate towards a description of an extraterrestrial subculture taking mutating drugs to alter and accelerate their species' natural cycles of cross-sexual alternation. The sentences do not add up to a "story." Pieces of stories start and stop, a world is delineated, characters speak, but the "action" of the *Halo*, like a cloud after an explosion, may consist primarily of happenings never seen. Hyperfiction author Michael Joyce has called it "a story that hasn't been told yet"[6]. The word "halo" in the title alludes to the work's cloud-like structure, and also to the circular arrangement of its text pieces and the interlocking circles of its paths. The word "mahasukha" is the name for the Nepalese Bud-

---

4. Richard Gess, *Mahasukha Halo*, *Lowlife* **17**, n.p.

5. Guy Davenport, "Narrative Tone and Form." in *The Geography of the Imagination* (San Francisco: North Point Press, 1981) p. 317.

6. Michael Joyce, personal communication (1992).

dhist concept of transcendence through erotic experience.

The hypertext *Mahasukha Halo* was commissioned by *Perforations* magazine, and appeared as an on-disk supplement to *Perforations* 1, no. 2. A 2.0 version was slated for publication in an issue of Eastgate Press' hypertext quarterly; copies of the 1.1 version are available from the author. The Storyspace hypertext writing environment is published by Eastgate Systems (PO Box 1307, Cambridge, MA 02238 USA).

CHROMATISM

Francesco Giomi

Divisione Musicologica
CNUCE/C.N.R.
Conservatorio di Musica
"L.Cherubini"
Piazza Belle Arti, 2
50122 Florence, Italy
Tel: 39 55 282105
Fax: 239 6785
Email: conserva@ifiidg.fi.cnr.it

The computer music piece *Chromatism* (for tape, 1992, 12 minutes 30 seconds) takes as a starting point the author's research on electroacoustic music analysis, based on the sound object concept. It also integrates some experiences in the field of music and image interaction. The title derives from the above-mentioned reasons. In fact, the word "chromatism" has specific traits both in the musical and visual field.

Chromatism includes six studies: at first the studies should have represented six of the twelve colors of the chromatic disk, in order to re-create, at an auditory level, a sort of sound colors. But during its composition the piece partially lost this component in favor of the creation of completed narrative structures which are developed inside each of the six single fragments. I tried to link the single narrative paths through an overall structure comprising the six studies. As far as the sound material is concerned, each fragment takes into consideration particular aspects of the electronic sound world, like the alternation between sound and noise, the rhythm caused by partially random parameters and the environmental characteristics of certain timbral/harmonical textures. Many of the musical elements are repeated and amplified from one single piece to another (usually only between adjacent pieces), in order to create timbral, besides structural, bonds between the six fragments.

In the work there are both electronic sounds and sampled acoustic instruments. The first are used in order to emphasize the timbral aspects, trying to insert compound objects characterized by a tonic and/or complex mass. Sampled acoustic instruments were used to create composite events, formed by a rhythmic assemblage of simple objects or by sound "groups" with a rhythmic function.

Chromatism has been realized in Florence at the Musicological Department of CNUCE/C.N.R. (Conservatory of Music) with the automatic composition software Teletau, the Yamaha TX81Z synthesizers and the Roland S550 sampler.

NEZUMI (RAT)

Reiko Goto

1446 San Bruno Avenue
San Francisco, California 94110
USA
Fax: (415) 647-0678
Email: tmc@well.sf.ca.us

Nezumi (1989) is a result of my interest in spaces that are created by animal movement. My ideas often come from my work experiences as a volunteer at the Marin Wildlife Center. The Center takes care of injured wild animals and raises rats to feed captured predators. One of my jobs is feeding the rats and cleaning out their cages.

In summer 1989, there were about 50 rats at the center. Small towels were placed in the rat cages to provide protection and warmth for the baby rats. The rats chewed on the towels to limit the length of their teeth. Strangely, every rat chewed a different pattern on the towels. One towel looked very carefully chewed, while another was completely torn apart. I imagined that the rats must be bored in their cages, and I wondered about other things the rats might be doing in their everyday lives.

In preparation for the 1989 annual exhibition at the San Francisco Art Institute, I worked with these rats over a 3-month period, providing them with 200 white face towels. Three months later, I presented the towels as a part of my installation, which filled a gallery space. I built a human-sized rat box, 11.5-x-28.5 ft. I covered the space, including most of the ceiling and windows, with brown cardboard full of various sizes and shapes of holes and spread yellowish wood shavings on the floor. I eliminated all artificial light, allowing only natural light from a narrow ceiling window and from the holes in the cardboard. Diagonal light patterns from the holes changed with the movement of the sun.

Viewers entered the installation through an irregularly shaped hole in the cardboard wall. Because the entrance hole provided ventilation, the facade of 200 towels completely veiling one wall moved slightly in the air.

Inside the entrance, an old rat-chewed chest of drawers and metal dishes containing water and dry food could be seen. An audio tape recording of subtle rat noises played for the duration of the installation.

I had hoped to make a room for rats in which they could stay comfortably, yet leave anytime that they wanted. But since I did not want to show my rat friends as art objects for the viewers, there were no live rats in the exhibition space. Instead, the spirit of the rats was present.

SOMETHING ABOUT QUIBBLING, A HYPERFICTION

Carolyn Guyer

807 First
Jackson, Michigan 49203 USA
Email: caroway@aol.com

To write about *Quibbling* seems almost contrary to its conceptual warp. It's hardly *about* anything itself, being more like the gossip, family discussions, letters, passing fancies and daydreams that we tell ourselves every day in order to make sense of things. These are not exactly like myths, or fairy tales, or literary fiction. They are instead the quotidian stream. In this sense, then, *Quibbling* is a work that tries not to be literary. It's somewhat unsuccessful in that, but then, it's art.

As ever, we're in a transitional age, and given that as pan-generational condition, we're forever seeking ways to understand our own unique to and fro. We can't, however, claim ours has specifically to do with technology. It *always* has to do with technology, whether it's inventing a way to hold fire, write speech, or send email. We're always changing according to the changes we make, and artists concern themselves more with that flux than any kind of conclusions.

It is in that rhythmic sense of ebb and flow, of multi-directional change, of events that disappear before they're quite intelligible but somehow come to mean something, that *Quibbling* was made. In hindsight, I can see why water and its properties became one of the pervasive, propelling metaphors in the work. A lake with many coves is how I saw it. The coves being where we focus, where individuals exist, where things are at least partly comprehensible; the lake being none of that, but, naturally, more than the sum of the coves, or more than what connects them. As a metaphor, the lake and coves stand not just for the form of this hyperfiction, but hyperfictions generally, and yes, (sorry) for life itself. The thing about hyperfictions is that, for art, they tend to be extremely lifelike. They move and shift, allowing everything, and so allow only that we find our own perspective. They are so multiple they reveal what is individual, ourselves, readers of our own story.

So, if you got this far, and are thinking what a load of artsy crap, then just especially for you I'll say, it's about how women and men are together, it tends slightly toward salacious, it's broadly feminist, heh-heh, or, you could say it's the story of someone's life just before the beginning or a little after the end.

ed: Quibbling is a hyperfiction for Macintosh Computers available from Eastgate Systems.

CONFIGURABLE SPACE

Craig Harris

c/o Leonardo/ISAST
672 South Van Ness Avenue
San Francisco, California 94110
USA
Tel: (415) 431-7414
Fax: (415) 431-5737
Email: craig@well.sf.ca.us

Configurable Space is a series of multimedia works built upon the simulation of future creative environments. These works represent ongoing research and artistic explorations—probing the creative process and the relationship between artists and new technologies.

Configurable Space is directed towards the development of a balanced understanding about how we use the visual, aural, tactile and configurable capabilities of digital technologies, and how the tools developed affect ways that we think, feel, formulate and develop on intellectual, spiritual and emotional planes. The simulations incorporate representations of interactive computer-display tables, walls and holographic images, within a multidimensional sound environment. In *Configurable Space* I dynamically construct the total environment and the creative tools to suit specific requirements.

The set for the original installation (constructed in a large studio in 1989) consisted of a light table, a light wall, slide projectors, a piano bench, chair and table with accouterments. Marion Gray shot hundreds of photographs during multiple work sessions in the environment, in which I used sketches on transparencies, colored gels, slide projections and live drawing. These images capture various perspectives of room views and close images, documenting the sketching and representation process during the development of a music composition.

Configurable Space VII was a hybrid performance-presentation sponsored by Yamaha Music Technologies in Marin, California, in May of 1990. The purpose was to demonstrate the underlying concepts of *Configurable Space* in a context permitting experimentation with multimedia communication resources. The event space, appropriately located in an office presentation space intended for corporate communication, was built around a large, white wall. Three slide projectors were positioned carefully with respect to image size, angle and proximity. The multilayered sound environment included original music, prerecorded music from different cul-

Fig. 6. Craig Harris, *Configurable Space VII*, performance-presentation, San Francisco, CA, 1990. The artist writes and draws on the surface of a large wall as part of this work, which explores creative activities and communication by simulating future environments utilizing multimedia resources including sound, text and projected images. (Photo: Marion Gray)

Fig. 7. Madelon Hooykaas and Elsa Stansfield, *Point of Reference*, video installation, Foundation for Visual Arts, Amsterdam, the Netherlands, 1990. *Point of Reference* consists of 3 monitors, 3 videotapes, 108 videobooks and 5 bookcases. (Photo: White Bird Studio)

tures and styles, and prepared soundfiles of sampled and processed sound, all placed in a variety of simulated room environments. Sound from the two microphones was processed to create two distinct ambiances. I used one, the evocation of a large room with a distant dreamy character, for story-telling and indirect communications and the other, which evoked a smaller, less-reverberant environment, for declamatory and direct communication techniques.

During the event, I wrote and drew over the surface of the wall, selecting multicolored marking pens of different thicknesses, with attention towards the functional use of color, shapes and multidimensional containers (Fig. 6). The work consisted of two movements. Each movement was weighted differently with respect to direct, linear presentation techniques and indirect, nonlinear modes of communication. Michael Czeiszperger and Scott Lyons were given score directions for performing the visual and aural components. Writing and drawing on the wall reinforced main points, summarized internal sections within the presentation, followed tangential thoughts and drew links between graphic and textual material—written and projected. The performers responded to what they saw, heard and felt. Images changed and modulated in light intensities— blending, highlighting, and contrasting with the drawing on the wall.

In *Configurable Space*, I track the creative process, examining tasks and the tools designed to address several circumstances. The total environment is considered in relation to its impact on creative activities, and I explore communication on many levels.

LONGSHOT

Lynn Hershman

Hotwire Productions
545 Sutter St., #305
San Francisco, California 94108
USA

In my videotape *Longshot* (63 minutes, 1989), a troubled young girl, Lian, lives desperately on the streets, singing to escape from her 'reality'. She meets a videomaker, Dennis, who chronicles her adventures until he becomes obsessed with capturing and manipulating her 'image'. She finds a roommate to share her abandoned car in Zhu Zha, a Hungarian woman who thinks she is in touch with UFOs. Lian's fears that she is acting in a 'snuff film' increase as the desire to capture her image mounts. The camera's surveillance of the subject is constant. An anonymous detective discretely reminds the audience of the links between guns and cameras.

Longshot stars Lian Amber, Dennis Mathews, Zhuzsa Koszeggi, Velora Uhmeyer and Rinde Eckert. Shot in a verité style, this 'faux documentary' explores perspectives of illusion and truth, emphasized by 'real' therapists' ongoing analysis of the 'fictional character'. Though *Longshot* constructs a portrait of Lian's alienation and self destruction, it gradually becomes clear that the piece is really about artifice and illusions of authenticity in the electronic world, the dangers of simulating artificial media images and the potential of losing identity through reliance on external electronic image enhancers. The end result is "a skillfully woven tapestry of storytelling that brings into question the viewer's ability to fully distinguish truth from fiction, as well as the capacity of the electronic medium to manipulate that perceptual ambiguity"[7].

THE ELECTRONIC DIARY

Lynn Hershman

The diary has long been used by women as a way of understanding their private thoughts and experience. A confessional of the first order, *The Electronic Diary* (1985–1989, VHS, 63 minutes) records the struggle, transformation and transcendence of a middle-aged woman whose personal story unfolds before the camera. Though touching and unnerving, her self-revelation is not simply a personal story. The piece is divided into three segments: (1) "Confessions of a Chameleon", in which confusion of truth in personal memory and fictitious episodes form a twisted history, (2) "Binge", in which the story of a body is told by a 'talking head', the monologue becoming a comic analysis of America's obsession with slimness and of the relationship of self-love to hunger, and (3) "First Person Plural", in which the articulated silences we are told not to talk about—the hidden secrets of childhood—are explained; wild connections are made between child abuse, Hitler, the vampire and survivors of the Holocaust, as the protagonist reveals the memories that caused her repressed guilt.

POINT OF REFERENCE

Madelon Hooykaas

Grote Bickersstraat 44 C
1013 KS Amsterdam
The Netherlands
Tel: 31 020 622 1898
Fax: 31 020 420 2688

Elsa Stansfield

PO Box 61106
1005 HC Amsterdam
The Netherlands

The video installation *Point of Reference* (1990) (Fig. 7) is a three-channel video, six-channel audio installation. It consists of five triangular bookcases and 108 videotape storage books.

Point of Reference is visually like a dark rocky island in a sea of information. The work has a continually shifting point of reference that has similarities to the processes of memory. On one monitor, written psychological texts (on memory) flip to pages of early books on astronomy and the earth. A finger traces the position of our planet on a solar diagram by Copernicus (1543). Simultaneously, another channel shows composite images from a camera that scans the book-lined walls of a seventeenth-century library.

On the third video channel is a portrait of a man. His thoughts are projected into a triangular form, like a mind's eye. These images are references

---

7. Valerie Soe, "Where Truth Intersects Illusion", *Artweek* **20**, No. 19. (1989) p. 6.

to our earlier videotapes such as *The Museum of Memory* videotape series (1985–). The audio channels contain, among other things, low whispering voices that remain indecipherable from every angle around this work.

Point of Reference was shown at Foundation for Visual Arts, Amsterdam, in 1990; at Foundation Het Kijkhuis, the Hague, the Netherlands, in 1991; and at the European Media Festival, Osnabruck, Germany, in 1991. A single-channel version of *Point of Reference* (13 minutes, stereo) premiered on the Netherlands Art Channel and was a part of Le Mois de la Photographie à Montréal, Canada, in 1991.

POSTCARD CARNIVAL

Michael S. Horwood

8 Grovetree Place
Bramalea, Ontario L6S 1S8 Canada

Postcard Carnival is a live electro-acoustic piece/event, a media barrage celebrating the wonder, joy and excitement of an amusement park. *Postcard Carnival* was created for a retrospective concert of my works at the Music Gallery in Toronto, 22 February 1990.

The score for *Postcard Carnival* consists of program/descriptive notes, narration and a CUE sheet. The 'performers' include the narrator (sound/text composer, Richard Truhlar), two slide projectionists, a videocassette recorder operator, a grinder organist, a violinist, a pianist and a tape-cassette player. The first projector shows slides from postcards of amusement parks and the second projector shows amusement park photographs. Video footage of the parks is presented and the narrator (electronically processed) reads from a list of postcard texts.

Dan Wilke, a friend and amusement park enthusiast from Buffalo, NY, introduced me to the wonderful sounds of his grinder organ, which he made from a kit, and to the rolls of music that he cut from a template. I incorporated these sounds into *Postcard Carnival* and created a separate piece called *Interrupted Waltz*, in which the grinder organ's part is a stand-alone piece.

Interrupted Waltz continues my work with music based on interruptions. It consists of two ideas constantly interrupting each other: a carnival-type waltz and a more freely composed, 'noisier' part based on dissonant intervals and small clusters. The waltz reflects the nervousness and impatience of our lifetime, filled, as it is, with numerous interruptions.

All parts of *Postcard Carnival* relate to amusement parks, my life-long hobby. The only exception is the solo violin. The violinist is instructed to play excerpts from familiar classical orchestral repertoire in a manner that strongly suggests 'practicing'. Ironically, the power and beauty of classical music propelled me into a career of music, yet now the performance of my own music competes with classical music. The violin's part is an homage to this strange dichotomy.

SONIC PASS/ SOUNDSTAIR

Christopher Janney

75 Kendall Road
Lexington, Massachusetts 02173
USA
Tel: (617) 862-6413
Fax: (617) 862-6114

SONIC PASS/dc is an example of 'responsive architecture'. It is a permanent interactive sound environment located in an outdoor public passageway at Techworld Plaza, Washington, D.C.

Using a series of electronic sensing devices, a computer and sampler/synthesizer, participants moving through the space trigger melodic notes, as well as natural sounds. Reacting to these movement patterns and to the time of day, this 'environmental musical instrument' generates unique 'sound images' within the space. The result is that *SONIC PASS/dc* changes the quality and mood of the space without changing the space's physical form—creating a continuously refreshing and imaginative environment for the commuting pedestrians who pass through this area daily.

SOUNDSTAIR: Minnesota is one in a series of *Soundstair* installations that I have created in the United States and Europe. Each installation is 'sound-specific', having been composed using, among other elements, the acoustics within the space as well as the indigenous sounds of the geographical region.

Composed of a series of electronic sensing devices, a computer and a sampler/synthesizer, the permanent installation *SOUNDSTAIR: Minnesota* resides on the main stairway of the Science Museum of Minnesota in St. Paul. As participants move on the stairs, their movements are translated into sounds and amplified back onto the stairs. Both the musical scales and the timbre change throughout the day, from a major scale of African flutes, to Chinese pentatonic scale of acoustic guitars and the Minnesota bird, the loon.

BIRD DANCE

Christopher Janney

Bird Dance (1987) is a sonic bird feeder, a poem and, at night, a sound score. It is composed of eight feeding trays, each wired with an electronic sensing device that is connected to a computer, synthesizer and sound system. Written on the feeder are the following words: IN THE DAY BIRDS DANCE HERE IN THE NIGHT THEIR SOUND SHADOWS APPEAR.

As the birds peck at the food, they activate the synthesizer. Using the computer, I have programmed different notes, scale progressions and harmonies to change throughout the day. The order of triggered notes and rhythmic patterns is left up to the 'improvisation' of the birds. From dusk to midnight, the computer plays back all the activity of the day in a condensed version.

Bird Dance was exhibited at the Morris Museum in Morristown, NJ, USA, and at the Jacob's Pillow Dance Festival in Beckett, MA, USA.

SKELETONS

Jim Johnson

3350 13th Street
Boulder, Colorado 80304 USA
Tel: (303) 938-8084
Fax: (303) 492-4886
Email: johnson_j@cubldr.colorado.edu

The *Skeletons* type font (Fig. 8) was inspired by a low-tech form of media—the rubber stamp. It began with the idea of designing a typeface using the image of a skeleton in the form of each letter of the alphabet. Prints were made with the stamps of the various body parts/bones assuming the position of a letterform. These were digitized and edited (turned into silhouettes) in a paint program. They were copied and pasted into a font program, where they were traced and scaled, spaced and kerned.

The *Skeletons* font was created with the intention of using pictures (images of a different sort than letters) as letters that could be ordered to make words and pictures, both at the same time. This amounts to typing a picture and literally telling an illustrated story. The nature of the story was determined, in this case, by both the syntax of words and of images, the latter being the more difficult to describe, as it has not, for all intents and purposes, been formalized.

Two works that use the *Skeletons* font are *A Thousand Words* and *Dead Air*. *A Thousand Words* is a work in progress comprised of a book set in the *Skeletons* font and an installation of the pages of the book in the form of paper tiles. The latter was installed at the CAGE Gallery in Cincinnati in April 1991 and covered one-third of a wall 40 feet in length.

Each page/tile of *A Thousand Words* consists of one word relating to human existence in general and represented more specifically by the skel-

Fig. 8. James Johnson, *Dead Air*, artist's book, 1991. This work uses the artist's *Skeletons* type font with a series of words that complete phrases beginning with the word 'Dead'.

eton letters. The work suggests several questions. Is a picture worth a thousand words? Are a thousand words worth one picture? Where is the picture? What is the picture?

Dead Air is a book that was published in July 1991 using the same typeface to represent words completing various phrases beginning with the word 'dead', such as Dead Wrong, Dead Issue and Dead Heat. A book of three (or more) texts, it raises similar questions regarding the natures of both words and images and their prospective interchangeability, as well as those relating to text and information.

AFTERNOON, A STORY

Michael Joyce

Center for Narrative and Technology,
JCC Jackson, Michigan 49201 USA
Email:
michael.Joyce@um.cc.umich.edu

I cannot say that I have not been waiting to be asked what prompted *afternoon, a story*[8], or what it seems to me to be as an art object, an electronic construction, a constant occasion, Holzer's chasing light high above the town square of the city of text, nomadic shiftings of momentary truths like sand flitting from the stone shelf in the wind, a story that changes each time you read it, *a form for what does not yet exist*. Thus, I am happy to point to what is perhaps too obvious to be seen: that the screen gives (way) before &with &after the touch, its surface not so much mottled as smoothed in the *places that yield* (the *words with texture* as the reading *directions* say), themselves nothing less than exhibit notes: what kind of text has directions? the hypnotic, the Eventualists' stimulus framed in the mirrored eye (viz. Sergio Lombardo, *Specchio tachistoscopico con stimulazione a sognare*, 1979), the shape of the mind later seen in dreams, the text of water where Bridal Veil Falls (Basho's *Urami-no-taki*) smooths the sandstone shelf in 100 million drumming fingers of light.

---

8. Michael Joyce. *afternoon, a story* (Cambridge, MA: Eastgate Systems, 1987). *afternoon, a story* is a hypertextual novel that runs on all Macintosh Plus or more powerful computers.

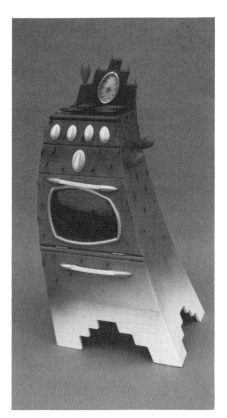

Fig. 9. Kimberly Kelzer, *Home on the Range*, jewelry box of wood, plexiglass, aluminium, plastic, silcone rubber, neon, flocking, 36-×-22-×-22 in, 1991. Kitchen technology and the Wild West converge in a sculpture made with contemporary materials. (Photo: K. Kelzer)

HOME ON THE RANGE

Kimberly Kelzer

2655 Magnolia Street
Oakland, California 94607 USA
Tel: (510) 763-8502

Print stays itself, electronic text replaces itself. If with the book we are always printing—always opening another text unreasonably composed of the same gestures—with electronic text we are always painting, each screen unreasonably washing away what was and replacing it with itself. The eye never rests upon it, though we are apt to feel the finger can touch it. The feel for electronic text is constant and plastic, the transubstantiated smear which, like silly putty, gives way to liquid or, like a painter's acrylics, forms into still encapsulated light. We are always painting. The electronic is not at all the touch of the uncertain reader who—like a child poking at a line of ants or lining up raisins—runs a finger along each cast line of print. Rather, it is touch certain, like holding moths, feeling the velvety resistance as the wing's scales slip off against the press of the fingers, dusting the whorls of the fingertip at whose root the hooked tangle of a zipper row of pincers clings, below that next to the clasped, now transparent wings, dangles the segmented leathery body, the husk of the idea dangling as palpable as Plato's dry forms, yet a worm still wet within, exploding with damp, phosphor light should you squish it open.

I wanted to create text which gave way(s) before the touch, which could be caressed into motion or repose without end. It began with a brown composition: a compact lunch (cylinder of apple juice, chevron stack of two corn beef halves on rye, tube of Dijon, rectangle of Heath bar) brought to me by a slim-hipped, taupe woman I know only as a mystery of texture. Thus the initial mystery was a problem in formal composition: "you think of me as brown not ice," the character says, texture becoming your text becoming textual yearning. (The Italian art critic Miriam Mirolla dreamed and drew herself with chocolate lipstick after the Specchio tachistoscopico and "was happy for the sweetness of it.") *afternoon* is likewise what follows from what we see in ourselves, the morning after a dark dream: "I want to say that I may have seen my son die this morning," the second screen begins.

My work is derived from things as I see 'em—a vision shaped by the life of an average (?), single, Californian "girl," born in the 1950s. I was raised by Dick and Jane, Barbie and Ken, and Roy and Dale, only to discover that I was adopted. Boy, did this burst a bubble!

Home on the Range (jewelry box, 1991) (Fig. 9) is a piece, from what I think may become my myth-busting series, about that "bubble"—that too-good-to-be-true American mom, homemaker, apple pie, happily-ever-after myth—blown away. I grew up expecting to graduate from my toy *E-Z Bake Oven* to the role of mom in the kitchen. You know, a June Cleaver. Only my reality was that of failed, less than idealistic relationships, working a 9-to-5 job (now often 8 a.m. to 10 p.m.), and p. b. and j.'s on burnt toast for dinner.

In 1986, I moved to the East Coast to attend graduate school. I missed my golden state of California so much that I began to believe the mythical state of mind that is California: the romanticized old (and new) West, progressive, cutting edge, sunny everyday, swimming pools, movie stars, riding the range through the cactus and sage brush, up the palm-studded Highway 1. Wake up and smell the cappuccino and enter yet another burst bubble: I moved back to California—San Diego—smoggy, overcrowded, unemployed surfers and exploited Mexican workers and not a

Fig. 10. Eleanor Kent, *Five Knitted Fractals: Dragon Fractal.* Knitted wool/viscose hanging mounted on padded board, 30½-×-24-×-¾ in, 1989. (Photo: Lorene Warwick)

cowpoke in sight.

All this led to *Home on the Range*, a *hot box* for the little lady to keep her *ice* in, a place to play house while the single portion frozen TV dinner is in the microwave, and the sun sets in the west amid smog over the crowded freeway.

I wanted to show both the distorted myths of my romanticized West and my romanticized view of what I thought my life (all our lives) would miraculously turn into when grown up. Sometimes in the back of my head I think a part of me is still waiting.

FIVE KNITTED FRACTALS

Eleanor Kent

544 Hill Street
San Francisco, California 94114
USA
Tel: (415) 647-8503
Email: ekent@well.sf.ca.us

Five Knitted Fractals consists of knitted hangings made of various kinds of wool and silk yarns mounted on pegboard covered with padding and cloth (Fig. 10).

When designing the work, I used a photocopier to copy and enlarge pictures of fractals from *Frontiers of Chaos* by H. O. Peitgen and P. H. Richter, then I traced them onto graph paper to make knitting patterns. I knitted the designs by hand and mounted them on padded boards.

After several years of working with computer graphics, I wanted to make something tangible that I could hold in my hands while still working with computers. I also wanted to explore the beauty of fractal designs that had been made visible only after the invention of computers. Knitting with thick wools and light silks gave me the pleasure of touching the material and also reminded me of the textile origins of computers with the Jacquard looms of the nineteenth century. By slowing down my hands, I was able to observe and think about the complexities of fractals and to make comparisons between the building of designs by stitches and of designs by pixels.

Although the correspondence of pixel to stitch is not precise in these pieces, the experience of translating the design to knitted fabric gave me an understanding of the construction of computer images, and of the connection between discrete stitches and electric pulses. It also allowed me to ruminate on fractals as boundaries, the infinite self-replications inherent in fractal makeup, and the realization of an order that I originally perceived as chaos or at least as complexity beyond comprehension. The experience made me more visually aware, and I learned how to read fractals and other kinds of complex information-laden, pixel-built images. By knitting computer designs, I enjoyed reconnecting the discoveries of computer sciences with the gentle, ancient world of making cloth.

ENGINEERS' NOTEBOOKS/ THE GEOMETRY OF COLOR

Mary Jean Kenton

Box 42
Merrittstown, Pennsylvania 15463
USA
Email: amanue!jr@vax.cs.pitt.edu

I live on Grey-brown Podzolic soil near the base of the Appalachians. The technology of firearms turned forest into farmland, but now it is seeded with broken tractor parts and the bones of our indigenous disappeared. I look for traces of the Monongahela People in the wild plants they might have used, in kinds of trees they might have loved, in the wings of the Great Horned Owl I buried in the orchard.

The apple trees in the orchard are old ones, of no commercial value. Snow Apple, Catshead, Blue Pearmain—the appeal of antique names whets urges to identify. Bred by chance, the same as us, and subject to rain, concerning which the term 'post-industrial' does not apply, they suffer from the abnormally warm winter days the past few years have offered. In spring their blossoms blow and fall like brushstrokes in my notebooks, disappearing into soil whose gridding is guarded by underpaid clerks in the county courthouse. In spring my brushstrokes mimic the need to keep on no matter what. My paints are ochre and terre verte, clays still fragrant as earth. My paints are zinc and manganese, minerals required for health. My paints are cobalt, cadmium, lead—poison in large doses. My paints are the grasses surrounding my home, and the leaf mold and the rain.

The colored geometry of cells and light imprisons as it releases. The colored geometry of light and thought releases as it imprisons. There are other intelligent creatures with vision keener than ours, but none is as

Fig. 11. Mary Jean Kenton, *The Geometry of Color: With A Sealed System Which Is Kept To Lower*, stone quarry, latex, stinging nettles, 1988–1989. This work is a detail from an ongoing installation of horticulture, naturally occurring materials and paint. (Photo: Jim Rosenberg)

Fig. 12. Lynn Kirby, *Portraits in Common Time*, film, video and sound installation, Intersection for the Arts, San Francisco, CA, 1991. The lives of three people are seen through their living room environments in this film, video and sound installation. (Photo: Rolando Dal Pezzo)

sensitive as we to nuances of color. In the unity that exists between retinas and brain, to see is to interpret. The process is poorly understood. It is conditioned by culture. I wait for the sciences of our physical being to tell me what I cannot know directly and for the sciences of society to provide the overview that links us to our past and to our future.

Paintbrushes are ancient tools, as are eyes, fingers, and neurons. Finding new uses for reliable tools is part of the artist's job.

Editor's Note: The Geometry of Color (Fig. 11) is an ongoing installation of horticulture, naturally occurring materials and paint that is limited only by the boundaries of the 49-acre farm in Fayette County, Pennsylvania, on which Mary Jean Kenton lives and works. The farm contains woods and meadow, an old stone quarry and a creek. Kenton studied catalogs and ordered hundreds of cultivars of daylilies and irises with regard to their shape and colors. She planted them in an integrated fashion with the already existing wild orange daylilies, old apple trees, pear trees, weeds and wild berries.

Most environmental installations are planned from a sculptural point of view, but, since Kenton is a painter, The Geometry of Color was planned in a 'painterly' manner. Plantings were set out with regard to color in ways that are related to Kenton's Engineers' Notebooks—notebooks containing graphed pages that have been filled with thousands of painted marks. She works on The Geometry of Color and the Engineers' Notebooks together and feels that the works are related and complementary.

PORTRAITS IN COMMON TIME

Lynn Kirby

2517 Polk Street
San Francisco, California 94109
USA

In Portraits in Common Time (1991) (Fig. 12), a film and video and sound installation, the lives of three people are seen through a living-room environment. Present in the living room are three framed film screens and three televisions, showing film and video loops for each character. Interactive sound, light and furniture complete the different spaces: auditory, cinematic/video and the actual living room. "Sitting in an enveloping easy chair or standing awkwardly as if we'd just been invited inside a strang-

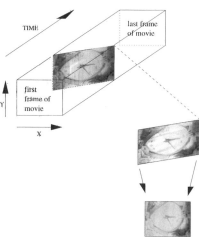

Fig. 13. Steve Mann, *DopplerDen*, 1989. *DopplerDen* is a "lightspace" and "soundspace" sculpture that allows the user to explore space and time in new ways. "TimeWarp" is one of the elements of DopplerDen.

Let us consider "lightspace". The lightspace at a given point contains all the visual information that can be obtained at that point, under all possible sources of illumination. A black and white photograph is a sampling of lightspace, and I refer to such a sampling as a "lightstroke". In this case the lightstroke is a function of two variables, say, "x" and "y". A movie (sequence of pictures) is a three-parameter lightstroke: the three parameters are "x", "y" and time, and the lightstroke can be thought of as a volume. Now if we take a slice through this lightstroke, perpendicular to the time axis, we have an ordinary picture which is a 2-D subspace (plane) from the volume, equivalent to the two-parameter lightstroke.

Suppose, however, that we now take the slice at an oblique angle. Objects that were not moving at the time the lightstroke (movie) was captured will now appear the same as in the perpendicular slice, while objects that were moving will now appear dilated or contracted along one or both of the image axes, depending on which way the slice is taken. This image of the TimeWarp sculpture is an attempt at conveying the concept of lightspace.

er's home, we experience a few revealing moments, none more important than another, in which one man and two women deliver their modern day soliloquies"[9]. The characters talk casually over the telephone of their lives and experiences, directed perhaps to each other, perhaps to an audience in the outside world. Fragments of conversation, legs of couches, bits of plants are woven in a circular pattern. "The power of these characters resides in the force of memory that allows each to create and then tell her or his own story, just as each has organized the very elements of her or his home by choosing and then arranging pieces of furniture."

Portraits in Common Time stars Paula Alexander, Lewis Gannett and Marie Senkfor. The sound composition is by Michael McNabb and is run on a NeXT computer activated by photo cells placed around the installation. *Portraits in Common Time* uses the surface textual qualities of video and the deep spatial qualities of film to deconstruct the spatial attitudes of each medium as well as fracture the spatial arrangement of the actual living room installation. This play of space mirrors a play in time in the construction of the characters' narratives. As individual stories cycle around, they combine differently with the other characters' stories (all six loops have different running times). At times all characters may talk at once. At other times the room is silent. Sound, picked up from one of the characters' environments, moves around the speakers in the room. The relationship of images and sounds and, thus, stories constantly shifts. Each narrative is told as much with fragments of furniture as with fragments of speech and memory. An elderly woman, a middle-aged woman and a young man live parallel lives. For moments their parallel histories intersect the circular time of memory as "today's Sunday is not so different from last week's." The viewer is invited to reflect as "the intersection of three voices, three bodies and three rooms creates a milieu for the flourishing of one's own contemplation."

DOPPLERDEN

Steve Mann

MIT Media Lab, 20 Ames Street
Cambridge, Massachusetts 02139 USA
Tel: (617) 253-0314
Fax: (617) 258-6264
Email: steve@media.mit.edu

One of my current works in the making, *DopplerDen*, is an interactive environment in which the speeds of light and sound are reduced in a virtual way (Fig. 13). It embodies a sort of time warp, based on stretching physical realities, such as the tendency for a train whistle to sound higher in pitch or a light source to look more blue when approached at near the

9. The quoted words are by Lynne Sachs, San Francisco Cinematheque.

Fig. 14. Benoit Maubrey, prototype for the *Poly-Phone*, 1987–1989. Seven oversize functioning telephone receivers (polyester, 13 × 2 m) equipped with 30-watt loudspeakers and microphones, plus a built-in answering system, will enable anyone to call up by means of telephone lines and talk through the sculpture to visitors at the site. Visitors will themselves be able to talk back directly at the receivers and respond to the callers.

speed of sound or light.

There are windows and various light sources in the room. When viewers walk toward one of these sources of light, the light turns bluish. When they walk away, it turns reddish. When they stand still, all the lights are their normal colors. If viewers walk north, the light sources (windows and lamps) on the north side of the room (in front of viewers) turn bluish, and those on the south side (behind the viewer) turn reddish. Those to the viewers' left and right remain the same color.

The effect is most dramatic when the viewer first enters the room. Walking down the corridor, the room is completely bathed in blue, and the sign above the door—"But SLOW, what light through yonder window breaks"—seems most appropriate to the mood.

There is also a computer with a display that looks green when the viewer stands still, but the color changes as the viewer moves. The range of colors is similar to the lights, but the computer display always maintains a much more richly saturated color than that of the lights. When the viewer moves toward it, the screen color 'blue shifts', and the fan inside the computer speeds up, making a high-pitched sound. Even the high-pitched ringing (horizontal oscillator sound), typical of video displays, and the occasional error beep from the speaker vary markedly with viewer movement.

"Radio plays that forgotten song" (Radar Love), which sounds normal when the viewer stands still but wows and flutters in speed when the viewer moves around. In fact, the song speeds up whenever the viewer moves toward it and slows down when the viewer walks away from it. The music even stops completely if the viewer walks away from it faster than about two paces per second, because the speed of sound in the *Doppler-Den* is two meters per second. If observers were to move away faster than the speed of sound, the sound would never reach them. Thus, when viewers leave *DopplerDen*, if they run quickly down the corridor, looking over their shoulders, the sound stops and the room is completely dark.

The clock in DopplerDen has a little cartoon caption over it, as if it is trying to say something to the observer. The caption reads, "The hurrier you go the aheader I get". Quite literally, as the observer moves about quickly, the clock actually speeds up, and as the observer slows down to smell the potted house plants in *DopplerDen*, the clock slows down and stops when the observer stops. Thus, just as time seems to fly when one is late for completion of a project, time in the *DopplerDen* flies if the viewer tries to hurry the visit. The idea is to slow down like the integrated media (sound, light, radar, etc.) in *DopplerDen*.

Then, suddenly, some faulty component in the clock starts making this awful buzzing noise, but when observers walk toward it to listen more closely, they realize the buzz goes up in pitch; don't forget that even seemingly unintentional sounds must not break the two-meters-per-second sound barrier.

All the elements of *DopplerDen* are currently functional modules scattered around my home and office. I am still looking for the ideal place to set them all up. The most difficult modules to install, the Doppler window panels, are adjustable in size so they can fit behind any window frame.

I hope to achieve a juxtaposition between the modern-looking computer and traditional decor in *DopplerDen*. The choice of decor will be important to set the mood for the anachronisms that enhance the twisted sense of time. Those who have visited my office have no doubt acquired a new idiomatic expression, 'time to do the red shift', meaning time to run, see you later, adios, ciao.

SPEAKERS' CORNERS

Benoît Maubrey

Die Audio Gruppe
Schulstrasse 35
100 Berlin 65 Germany
Tel: 49 30-462-2954

Since 1983, I have been creating electronic *Speakers' Corners*. These are outdoor sculptures that people can call up and talk through. The callers, using any ordinary telephone, can dial a special number and be automatically connected to these outdoor sculptures. The sculptures are usually integrated into preexisting structures on site and equipped with a public address system that enables the callers to express themselves directly to the public.

These electronically active sculptures exist in a public space and are accessible to the public on a 24-hour basis. My goal is to create, via telephone, an open forum for spontaneous oral communication (Fig. 14).

THE MUSIC FOR SUDDEN CHANGES

Michael McNabb

120 Virginia Avenue
San Francisco, California 94110
USA
Tel: (415) 695-9684
Fax: (415) 695-9629
Email: mmcnabb@next.com

Sudden Changes is a new work for five dancers by choreographer Liss Fain for the *Liss Fain Dance Company*. It premiered at the New Performance Gallery in San Francisco in May 1991. Fain commissioned me to produce an original score for the work.

Sudden Changes consists of (in her words) a series of episodes that originate in real-life events, evolving from her interest in reactions to environmental loss and diminishment. The movement idiom originates in descriptions of animal behavior and environments and the effects of land development on the species. The parallel of loss in human experiences is the perception of and adjustment to altered boundaries.

In order to fully support the depth and range of the emotional and psychological content of the work, I felt a live musical performance appropriate. It also seemed like a good opportunity to put into practice a new live performance system with which I had been experimenting. In this work, my solo instrumental performance is enlarged (by a sophisticated computer-music system) to orchestral levels of musical expression. The system is designed to allow a wide variety of configurations of musical textures, rhythms, recorded sounds, signal processing, accompaniment, etc., to be called up at will by a performer. However, none of the actual musical material is determined in advance. Everything is derived during the performance from the notes and gestures of that performance. Polyphonic accompaniment can be based strictly or loosely on the harmonic, dynamic and rhythmic structure of the performed material.

In the *Sudden Changes* performance, I performed on a soprano saxophone equipped with a pickup and an IVL pitch-to-Musical Instrument Digital Interface (MIDI) converter.

The system included a NeXT computer, Lexicon signal processors and Yamaha synthesizers. The NeXT computer controlled the configuration of the system, processed musical material, generated real-time melodic accompaniment, played back digitally recorded sounds and performed additional sound synthesis. It also displayed a graphic cue sheet and provided timing cues for me during the performance.

INVISIBLE CITIES
Michael McNabb

In 1985, the ballet *Invisible Cities* was realized as a collaboration between myself, choreographer Brenda Way and the Oberland Dance Company (ODC)/San Francisco Dance Company, and designer/engineer Gayle Curtis. Although most of the music is computer synthesized, there are also two live instrumental/electronic performers, including myself. This was a personal challenge, since I had been away from performing for a while. It was also an opportunity to try to raise the technical standards of music in dance performance, which I saw too often neglected. The music was funded by a grant from the US National Endowment of the Arts and produced at the Center for Computer Research in Music and Acoustics, Stanford University.

Italo Calvino's novel *Invisible Cities* inspired us with its beauty, its original and concise structure, and its dreamlike imagery. It is an allegorical account of a meeting between the Venetian explorer Marco Polo and the Tatar Emperor Kublai Khan. Sensing the decline of his empire, the aged Kublai Khan summons the young foreigner Marco Polo to his garden to reassure him of the greatness of his realm. Marco Polo diverts the great Khan with tales of cities he has seen within the empire. As the barrier of their different languages is overcome, the images of the cities become increasingly vivid. Kublai Khan searches for a pattern among them, concluding finally that each description is of the same place and all are within him.

The music contains both subtle and explicit stylistic elements of various popular and classical world musics, sections of pure musical fantasy, and various musical and digitally-processed environmental sounds. In this way it conveys feelings and moods similar to those created by Calvino's weaving of hyper-realistic description and veiled, dreamlike fantasy. Conversely, the literary symbolism, characters and narrative of the book provided much of the inspiration for the choreographer and designers. However, rather than follow the book explicitly, we chose to adopt something of its form, then invented our own 'invisible cities' for each of the five major movements.

At the time, Gayle Curtis was participating in work being done in machine choreography at the Veterans Administration Robotic Aid project. He wanted to see the concept carried further. For *Invisible Cities*, he directed the addition of a large robot arm as a visiting member of the ODC dance company. The powerful robot, transformed by the choreography of Way, Margo Apostolos, and Curtis, performed the role of Kublai Khan. I further enhanced its persona by amplifying the sounds of its motors and digitally processing these sounds into musical material during the performance. We deliberately treated the robotics as a proven rather than as an experimental medium, in order to avoid making any clichéd statements on 'art versus technology'. The presence of the robot garnered us worldwide publicity, often at the expense of the artistic message.

The music for *Invisible Cities* has been released on compact disc on the Wergo label, WER 2015-50, distributed in the United States by Harmonia Mundi, Los Angeles. The work was awarded a mention at the 1989 Ars Electronica. An earlier recording, *Computer Music*, which includes "Dreamsong", "Love in the Asylum" and "Mars Suite", is available on CD from Mobile Fidelity Sound Labs, MFCD-818. The "Mars Suite" formed part of the soundtrack to the NASA stereographic film *Mars in 3D*.

SEMINAL CHRONO-SCHEMA: AN ELECTRO-KINETIC WORK FOR COMPUTER SCREEN AND PRINTOUT

Stephen Moore

790 North Marine Drive, #598
Tumon, Guam 96911 USA
Tel: (671) 649-2686
Fax: (671) 649-5688

CYBER DADA MANIFESTO

Dale Nason

50 Rosamond Road
Footscray 3011 Australia

Troy Innocent

10 McCubbin Tce.
East Doncaster 3109 Australia

This work in progress, *Seminal Chrono-Schema*, is a compilation of the artists, artworks and art events that have shaped the course of art from the middle ages to the present. By marking seminal moments within the larger continuum and by separately identifying artist, artwork and content/intent, we hope to present this information from a unique perspective and to provide a personal view of art history.

Intended to display the data in literal as well as graphic formats, *Seminal Chrono-Schema* will exist both as an electronic database and a limited-edition artwork, while at the same time functioning on two distinct levels: (1) The compiled information, or database, is the basis for a schematic/analytic view of Western art, which will appear as a summary or tabulation. (2) This tabulation, in turn, becomes the structure for a strictly visual presentation of the sorted data—a kinetic image to be viewed, not read.

In its electronic state, the work will begin with tabulation and, as it scrolls across the screen, will change from a literal to a graphic form. The compiled data will become a 'visual score', the arrangement or composition being determined by the text of the tabulation. The 'hardcopy' edition, comprised of more than 100 color index cards, with a computer disk for on-screen viewing of the work, will be bound into a handcrafted limited-edition artwork.

DIGITIZE THE WORLD (a new life awaits you). KL65. TECHNOLOGY is speeding ahead : are you following the integrated golden horizons? Take technology apart and see what it really is ! REUSE EVERYTHING Make a sculpture out of polystyrene, computer plastic, metal, anything! Become a TECHNO JUNKY. Wear technology ! *ANYONE* CAN MAKE OR BE ART. Exhibit on the street. Exhibit on yourself. Glue your piece to Alan Bond's front door ! Right of access to all data. *Graffiti artists* : start CYBER-TAGGING. Don't be rude : talk to your fax machine. Work things out for yourself. Go beyond current standards and values and make your own. Master COMPUTERS and you will have HACKING POWER over banks, governments, and the military through technology. PSYCHOACTIVE DESIGNER FOODS. Subversive cultures are starting to seep from the rotten foundations of our society—CUT THEIR HYDRAULIC LINES. Civilization destroys the world so LETS DIGITIZE it and save the entire human society on MAINFRAME LASER DISK. All humans and the junk they produce will be sealed inside a huge computer. Forget the MEAT of your bodies. FULL-ON BRAIN EXPERIENCES await you inside a computer. Even have SEX with a computer. INTERFACE! Your true life aspirations are inhibited by the weal flesh of your body—YOUR BODY IS A BURDEN. It is simply meat. WETWARE can enhance it, CYBORG IMPLANTS bring you closer to true experience. JACK IN to neuro-circuits. Once all people, objects, senses, and experience are DIGITIZED onto laser disk (with backup copies) THE REAL WORLD can finally breathe a sigh of relief as man has disappeared forever. He has already tried to create his own environment, now the potential is here! Organic life is no longer a valid lifestyle. FULLY SYNTHESIZED environments where ALL PHYSICAL AND EMOTIONAL FEELINGS CAN BE CHEMICALLY SIMULATED. Soon it will be possible to

Fig. 15. Nancy Paterson, *Wringer/Washer TV*. An 11-in color monitor is encased in the wash tub of a pink, white and chrome 1950s-style wringer-washer.

INJECT A BIOLOGICAL COMPUTER to PROGRAM YOUR BRAIN, extend your life, anything. This is our FUTURE. You are your consciousness, don't let a physical existence fool you. Physical bodies are now superseded, REPLACE YOUR BODY with machine and computer components. And become superhuman! Self sufficient society. solar powered. We can now VENTURE TO THE LIMITS OF THE COSMOS because we are not bound by earthly dimensions. CYBERNETICS does not discriminate by look, race, disabilities, sex, species because it is PURE BRAIN TO BRAIN COMMUNI-CATIONS. Jack in your Neurons to complete expression and communication of self. Be free of disease, food, be totally efficient. LEARN TECHNOLOGY. MODERN MAN'S AESTHETIC is grounded in pre 20th century decorativeness and OVER INDULGENT ART theorizing. THE NEW AESTHETIC IS COMPUTER GENERATED *CYBER DADA* The NEW SPECIES are cyborgs, man/machines, precise superior flawless beings to house our consciousness and create a new world.

-= DON'T BE AFRAID : LEARN TECHNOLOGY =-

DON'T BE AFRAID. By WEARING CIRCUITRY *you* will represent the NEW AGE. Take electronics apart and see what they are. Learn electronics, computer programming : the ARTS OF THE FUTURE. Don't be intimidated by flashing lights and buzzing, and computers that look like MICROWAVE OVENS! MASTER TECHNOLOGY so it won't beat you as it RAPIDLY FILL THE WORLD. Technology controls the world so if YOU CONTROL TECH-NOLOGY..... The end of the world is coming, but it is the beginning of a PERFECT TECHNO WORLD. *STOP* REVIVING OLD CULTURES -=- MAKE NEW ONES!! -=- The YOUTH of today have become complacent and apathetic, easily controlled by ADVERTISING, the MEDIA, and UNSCRUPU-LOUS GOVERNMENTS. Let the top of this hierarchy know that they can't use TECHNOLOGY TO CONTROL US, but than we are FULLY INTEGRATED with technology and IT IS OURS. Digitize the world!! It's time to INTER-FACE WITH TECHNOLOGY AND UNDERSTAND IT. *KNOW IT* personally. Get -=tech=- out of the establishment and into the streets. LIVE IN *CYBERSPACE* WHERE ALL THE FEELINGS AND PHYSICAL REALITIES CAN BE PSYCHO-CHEMICALLY SIMULATED.

-=Don't be afraid=- : EXPOSE YOUR CIRCUITY. COME TO TERMS WITH *TODAY'S* MATERIALS. The future will come whether you like it or not so BE READY FOR IT -=Painting has died again=- : stop using purely old materials like oil and canvas. IT will not last in a CYBER WORLD (Which *will* come whether you like it or not). Art, life, and the world are becoming increasingly meaningless so—=.

-=CYBER DADA IS POPULAR CULTURE, IS TODAY'S SOCIETY, AND IT'S FUTURE!=-

THE LIGHTNING BOX

Pauline Oliveros

156 Hunter Street
Kingston, New York 12401 USA
Tel: (914) 338-5986
Email: PaulineOliveros@mci.com

The *Lightning Box* (1990) is a one-hour collaborative sound meditation with computer-controlled delay processors and lighting. It was created under my direction during a residency in the Media Arts Program at the Banff Centre in Alberta, Canada.

The *Lightning Box* calls for the players, as they are listening to the sounds that they are currently playing, to also listen for and respond to repetitions and modifications of their own sounds as well as to each other. Sound from each player is picked up by microphones and is then processed by computer-controlled digital delays. The delay times are changed by a program that results in transposition and pitch bending of each player's sound in a variety of forms and speeds ordinarily not accessible in real-time performance. Computer-controlled lighting design conducts the ensemble.

The computer programs were written by Cornelia Colyer, in collaboration with me. The digital interface that allows direct program control of the delay processors was constructed especially for this project by David Ward of PanDigital Corporation. *The Lightning Box* was performed at the Banff Centre in February 1990 with the following personnel: Pauline Oliveros, accordion; Michael Century, keyboard; Panaiotis, voice and mix; Trevor Tureski, marimba; Cornelia Colyer, programmer; Colin Griffiths, set design and technical coordinator.

BICYCLE TV: SOME INTERACTIVE EXERCISE

Nancy Paterson

475 The West Mall, #1513
Etobicoke, Ontario M9C 4Z3
Canada
Tel: (416) 621-3290
Fax: (416) 365-3332

Bicycle TV (copyrighted in Canada) consists of a 1950s-style bicycle with a color monitor mounted in front, facing the cyclist. Also included are a videodisk player, a front wheel direction-sensing device and a rear wheel motion-detector assembly. These devices are linked to the videodisk through a programmable audio/video controller.

A viewer/cyclist may cycle up to a crossroads and steer the bicycle to proceed in any direction. The videodisk player is capable of playing at half-speed, normal speed, and 2× speed. This means that the video, which was shot at approximately 17 miles per hour, can be sped up or slowed down by the rider simply by pedaling faster or slower.

In the preproduction stage, a branching system (a maze that operates within a grid) was designed and a large production grid was researched. There are a limited number of road segments that can fit on the videodisk, so the production grid was designed to keep the rider contained within a set 'world'. Cyclists cannot 'fall off the edge of the disc', no matter which way they choose to turn.

The original videotape was shot in and around the small, scenic town of Belfountain, Ontario, near the forks of the Credit River. Footage of winding country roads offers different paths to the viewer/cyclist within the 'world' offered by the videodisk.

WRINGER/WASHER TV

Nancy Paterson

The subject of this project is abortion. Rapid juxtaposition of imagery and arguments from both 'pro' and 'anti' positions are interspersed with a view of a load of wash going through the wash cycle from above. Video segments are approximately 10–20 seconds long. An 11-in color monitor is encased in the wash tub of a pink, white and chrome 1950s-style wringer-washer. In order to see the video, a viewer must look down into the machine. A control unit activates the machinery in the presence of a viewer.

The pink and chrome wringer washer represents a 1950s futuristic view of technological progress (Fig. 15). The juxtaposition of this outdated technology with the contemporary arguments of the abortion debate reveals the irony of the fact that this issue is just beginning to be publicly addressed.

A CERTAIN UNCERTAINTY

Lynn Pocock-Williams

37 Huemmer Terrace
Clifton, New Jersey 07013 USA
Tel: (201) 614-0314

A Certain Uncertainty (June, 1991) is a continuation of my exploration of the integration of sound and image. My artwork usually addresses music concepts, the emotional content of music, or a combination of the two, and I work primarily with time-variant imagery coupled with music. Incorporating the elements of time, change, and motion allows my images to exist most closely with their music counterparts.

In the past, several of my videos were automatically generated using

Fig. 16. Lynn Pocock-Williams, *A Certain Uncertainty*, video still, 1991. *A Certain Uncertainty* is an experimental music video which presents The New York Guitar Project at work.

artificial intelligence techniques. That is, I developed a computer environment that read in music data, analyzed the music, and then generated animations that correlate to the music. These videos are abstract and created according to a system.

My recent videos, on the other hand, are created according to intuition, and the imagery reflects the world around us. The method by which the videos are composed focuses on the connections between the qualities of the sounds and visuals. One of these recent videos, *A Certain Uncertainty*, is a 3 minute 40 second experimental music video featuring The New York Guitar Project, an acoustic guitar group (Fig. 16). The video takes its name from the music that accompanies it, which was written by Reinaldo Perez and R. Stuart Williams. Shot during an intensive rehearsal weekend, the images present The New York Guitar Project at work.

In the video, the musicians are presented on two overlapping visual planes—one in the foreground and one in the background. The foreground images are static and black and white, and new images are always covering over the current image. Several of these static pictures are digitally altered and reconstructed, adding to the complexity of the scene.

The background images are presented in color, and they move in a slow, dream-like manner. Abstract windows that open up into the foreground plane allow a glimpse into the background performance. Both planes of images are digitally processed resulting in an overall organic, painterly quality. The resulting video of structure and non-structure is intended to be an expression of the structure and emotional content of the music. The video was created on an Amiga 500 computer, using customized software for the presentation of images, and LIVE! by A-Squared to process the resulting video.

GHOST NETS: THE MEDICINE WHEEL GARDEN

Aviva Rahmani

Box 692
Frog Hollow
Vinalhaven Island, Maine 04863
USA
Tel/Fax: (207) 863-0925

Fig. 17. Aviva Rahmani, detail of *The Medicine Wheel Garden*, 1991. This environmental work on Vinalhaven Island, off the coast of Maine, is part of the *Ghost Nets* project. Boulders were set in place by Aviva Rahmani with Bart Hopkins to prepare for *The Medicine Wheel Garden*. Each boulder is 5–7 feet in diameter.

We enter the medicine wheel to find our places on the wheel of life and our relationship with all of life, to find hidden reservoirs of gentle strength within ourselves and find new ways of walking in harmony on the earth.

—Grandfather Thunder Cloud,
Elder of the Cherokee Nation

My work has consistently documented social questions and the recovery process since the mid-1960s. *Ghost Nets* (1991–2000) is about the trap of the familiar. The name of the project derives from the invisible monofilament fishing gill nets that get lost in the ocean, strip-mining all sea life. The first 3 years of this work address the problem of exhausting ocean resources.

The Medicine Wheel is a Native American ceremony of teaching and blessing, the purpose of which is to heal the earth and all who enter the ceremony. Because earth care is symbiotic with the sea, the air and human survival, building a *Medicine Wheel Garden* (Phase 1 of the *Ghost Nets* project) is about restoring healing energy to people and land.

Construction of the Garden (Fig. 17) is on a site that includes a promontory of manmade land that extends from a remote island off Maine. I purchased this parcel of land in 1990, in common with a local lobstering family, part of the economically-threatened fishing culture of the island. The partnership involves an overlapping work area (for commercial lobstering, social gathering, artmaking), my modest home and a sawmill in which I am producing seascape paintings in homage to the ocean.

Preparation of the *Medicine Wheel Garden* began with rebuilding the soil and reintroducing primarily indigenous trees and shrubs (such as Pin Oak, Norway Maple, Chinese Chestnut and Siberian Elm), interspersed with local granite boulders. In a series of ceremonies, the sacred rocks were gathered under the guidance of Elder Ricki Soaring Dove. The healing rituals were initiated by Grandfather Thunder Cloud, Elder of the Cherokee Nation, who conducted a traditional Medicine Wheel ceremony on 11 August 1991 in the Garden.

The living space in the *Medicine Wheel Garden* has been designed in collaboration with architect Steve Robinson, author of *The Energy Efficient Home*. The house will be a two-story 800-square-foot building that both incorporates and is included in the design and construction of the Medicine Wheel Garden. The house has unusual structural engineering that enables it to withstand the winter winds that reach 60–70 mph on the promontory. It allows maximum interaction with and minimum disruption to the microclimates of the Medicine Wheel Garden and blends stylistically with the island's town.

The sawmill-studio building includes an installation which I conceived with Ellen Zweig. On the east-facing roof of the old mill, Zweig, a performance-installation artist, will provide a *camera obscura* specifically designed for *Ghost Nets*. It will project the exterior changing moods of the sea onto a drawing surface. The projection surface will include Victorian 'quotes' in its design. Zweig (who has worked with the theme of Victorian traveling ladies) refers to it as the 'Drawing Room'.

Collaboration is essential to the *Ghost Nets* project. Each phase is marked by a cluster of planned actions that involve others. Each action is simple, performed as a humble daily housekeeping chore, such as tending a garden. The local children are particularly crucial to the evolution of the *Medicine Wheel Garden*, as is an electronic information database.

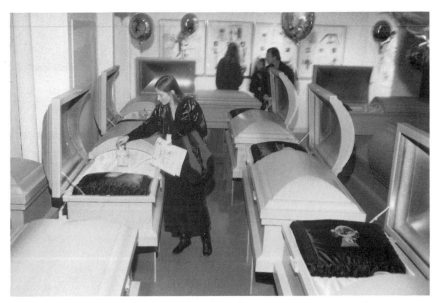

Fig. 18. Sonya Rapoport, *The Animated Soul—Gateway to Your Ka*, interactive installation, Ghia Gallery, San Francisco, CA, 1991. A participant pastes a 'words of power' label onto her printout in order to validate her 'ticket' to everlasting life. (Photo: Jay Mrozek)

THE ANIMATED SOUL— GATEWAY TO YOUR KA

Sonya Rapoport

6 Hillcrest Court
Berkeley, California 94705 USA
Tel: (510) 658-4741
Fax: (510) 642-0336
Email: actize@garnet.berkeley.edu

The *Animated Soul—Gateway to Your Ka* is an interactive installation in which viewer-participants find their ancient double (or Ka). The source and inspiration for this work is the Egyptian *Book of the Dead*, a collection of rituals and religious texts that were buried with the deceased in ancient Egypt. The rituals were intended to ensure a happy everlasting life and to enable the soul to ascend to heaven.

The procedure of selecting Western icons on a HyperCard computer program is related to the steps prescribed in the Egyptian *Book of the Dead*. However, in my installation, finding the participant's double has the added function of assigning a purpose to this life, and the double's assigned 'words of power' can expedite this purpose. Traditionally, the 'words of power' were secured with the deceased's headrest and had the magical formula of carrying out its wishes and needs for a safe journey into the next world, a place resembling life on earth.

The first venue for *The Animated Soul—Gateway to Your Ka* was in 1991 in San Francisco, California, at the Ghia Gallery, a cavernous space that specializes in selling funerary objects and is associated with nonprofit funeral societies. For this installation, the front section of the gallery had been separated from the back with scrims and large plaster portals that resembled archeological architectural remains. One wall displayed a projection of the computer program's introduction to the work. Nearby hung a printed cutout of the soul-bird, a human-headed hawk that in ancient Egypt had freedom to go anywhere. In the introduction, he is animated and plays the part of a guide who takes the viewers through the steps that they will encounter when interacting with the computer.

In another area, the high-tech tomb room, were two computers and printers on a large plaster table that resembled the architectural portals in the gallery. Here the viewers became participants when they started to take an active role by making selections on the computer.

Entering through one of three gates is the first of four phases to be experienced on the computer. A visual selection of either owl (wisdom), windmill (power) or dancers (pleasure) opens the ancient gates for further choices to be made by clicking the scarab (mouse). Each of the above choices retrieves one third of Leonardo da Vinci's *Human Figure After Vitruvius*. The participant then points with the scarab (mouse) to a specific body part 'member' in that section of the body. The deification of this 'member', necessary for an everlasting life, is achieved by choosing one of its associated icons. This selection triggers the sacred words of a Declaration of Innocence related to that body part. For instance, if the 'eyes' were selected as the body part 'member' and the choice of the icon was a door key, the Declaration would be "I have not pried into matters". Next on the screen comes the transformation, where an image of the participant's ancient Egyptian double is revealed. The image of the double is duplicated on a printout that has the format of a ticket.

The participant at the Ghia Gallery, with the printout ticket in hand, then went through the portals to the back area (Fig. 18) where 27 caskets represented each of the possible ancient Egyptian doubles in the database of the computer program. Gold balloons (souls) that had been printed with the Declarations and their corresponding doubles' images, floated above each of these sarcophagi. The images of the double on the printouts matched both the images on the balloons and the pillow masks in the sarcophagi. Near the pillows in chemical beakers were 'words of power' printed on labels. Pasting the proper label on the printout validated this 'ticket' as a 'boarding pass' to the everlasting life.

From an audiocassette player were heard excerpts of interviews that revealed contemporary attitudes about life after death. These statements, which I taped and edited with Andrew Smolle, ranged from reincarnation, pollution and gene pools, to belief in the immortal existence of the soul. Responding to each excerpt was a comment from the philosophies of the Egyptian god Shu.

Kathryn Woods designed the computer program. In 1992, *The Animated Soul* was installed at Takada Fine Arts in San Francisco, California, and at the Kuopio Museum in Finland.

FROM OSIRIS TO SINAI
Sonya Rapoport

While working on my project about Ancient Egypt and everlasting life, I came upon an interesting and remarkable chapter in the Egyptian *Book of the Dead*. "Spell 125" illustrates the lofty moral and spiritual concepts of the Egyptians in the Eighteenth Dynasty—about 1580 BC.

Described visually and verbally in the *Book of the Dead*, the deceased, after being given permission to enter the Judgment Hall of Osiris, is standing before the 42 divine ministers who help Osiris examine the souls that come before him. This dead person enumerates 38 specific sins that he or she has not committed during his or her lifetime. The declaration is called the 'Negative Confession' or, more simply, 'Declarations of Innocence'.

After the judgment has been passed successfully, a picture of the scene must be drawn in color on a new tile of earth upon which no animal has trodden. This accomplished, the living family left behind will flourish and the deceased will never be forgotten, living on the food of the gods, able to travel anywhere in the otherworld. Immediately, I was struck by the similarities between the Negative Confession and the Ten Commandments, the fundamental laws proclaimed by God on Mt. Sinai and transmitted through Moses to Israel. The tile and tablet formats also share a commonality.

The resultant artwork, *From Osiris to Sinai*, is a scroll that hangs 2 × 7 ft. It is a diazo print in which the black line has been colored over with prisma color.

The piece begins with a list of five commandments, those similar to the confessions in the Negative Confession. They are in color-coded English: Thou shalt not take the name of the Lord thy God in vain (blue lettering). Thou shalt not murder (red-orange lettering). Thou shalt not commit adultery (green lettering). Thou shalt not steal (violet lettering). Thou shalt not bear false witness against thy neighbor (yellow lettering). The Hebrew translation follows in the same color code. The similar Negative Confessions follow in hieroglyphs and English translation both in the same color code. The Egyptian section is bordered by drawings of 18 of the 42 gods to whom the confessions were addressed.

The layout of *From Osiris to Sinai* was pasted on 14 7/8-x-11-inch computer forms. This was enlarged to 2-x-7 ft on vellum by a Xerox 2080 copier. The vellum master was put through a black line blueprint process called diazo. This final print was colored with pencil crayons.

INTERACTIVE ESSAY: PORTRAITS OF PEOPLE LIVING WITH AIDS

Hazen Reed

65 South Sixth Street
Brooklyn, New York 11211 USA
Tel/Fax: (718) 782-4084
Email:
70674.507@CompuServe.com

Portraits of People Living with Aids seeks to involve users in an active understanding of the AIDS condition. This interactive documentary introduces participants to three people living with AIDS (a male painter, a woman activist, and a male inner-city AIDS councilor) via audio, video clips, and photographic essays digitally stored on a Macintosh computer. The portraits are grouped around conversations with each person, and topics, as in all conversations, are far ranging. Because the interactive documentary is non-linear, a viewer may at any time add to these conversations by leaving a digital video message for one of the three people, any of the previous viewers, as a general comment, or for the artist. In this

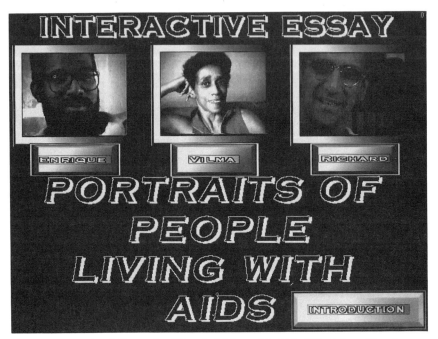

Fig. 19. Hazen Reed, *Portrait of People Living with Aids.* This interactive documentary introduces participants to three people living with AIDS.

way, each viewer continues the evolution of the documentary allowing both interviewee and end users to have a voice in a personalized, intimate atmosphere of a computer kiosk.

The interactive documentary, as I see it, is a new medium that partakes of a well-established communication mode, the dialogue. Technologically, we have a long way to go before computer interactive systems fully accomplish the randomness that make our daily conversations invigorating and lively. However, the seeds have been planted for interactive "computer conversations."

Portraits of People Living with Aids recognizes AIDS as a human condition requiring human understanding (Fig. 19). Such an understanding can come about only through repeated efforts on the part of everyone involved, which in the case of the HIV virus and AIDS, includes almost everyone in our various communities. No human being on the planet is completely immune from this condition, yet we have all seen and heard the definitions of AIDS that serve to remove certain groups from the disease's reach while focusing attention on others as more susceptible. We have come to know AIDS as a disease of "this community" or "that group." It has served to churn up the waters of prejudice and hatred. It has become the stuff of political campaign speeches, where taking a position identifies one as "bleeding heart" or "liberal." Despite these attention grabbing and often divisive public displays, one fundamental element of the disease has been missed—AIDS is a human problem. As Vilma Santiago, one of the people living with AIDS in the piece, says, "AIDS does not discriminate." Reaching the larger community via our current efforts to educate and inform poses a difficult communication event, precisely because of past and present efforts to define the disease that do discriminate. We must find ways to involve everyone in this educational task without alienating those with whom we speak. We must make it clear that people with AIDS are people who are part of our larger communities. In short, we must come to see that each of us is as much a part of this disease as are the people who suffer from its affliction.

Interaction is nothing new, it is a part of all communication. What is new is the interactive computer environment, and how it involves the care and attention of all its participants. Understanding that viewers are part of the process of meaningful creation is an important notion in all communicative acts, be they face to face conversations with other human beings, interactions with the environment, or dialogue with an interactive computer system. Communication, built on the notion of a caring self, results in a diligent acknowledgment of the contingent events that inform our lives. Computer interactive systems, designed with this human recognition, may help us to better understand ourselves and the world in which we live. While computers in and of themselves don't have the power to do this, if we can incorporate them into the process of understanding our own identity, they will have a profound effect on humanity. The interactive documentary continually reminds us of our dependent/independent nature which suggests our being as being in jeopardy among others, as powerful and as weak as our own selves.

STAKE OUT AT POST OFFICE BAY

Melynda Reid

PO Box 378
Greensboro, Florida 32330 USA
Tel: (904) 442-3300
Fax: (904) 442-6629
Email: melynda@titipu.resun.com

I live and draw near the Apalachicola River, a place where the earth still breathes beneath its vesture of wild beauty. I have drawn rare flowers here for 20 years. Six years ago I was drawing *Macbridea alba* on national forest lands. This flower is so rare that its common name was invented by botanist Daniel B. Ward for the book he edited on the rare flora of Florida[10]. Ward called this rare mint "white birds-in-a-nest." His name evokes the essential quality of this flower. The unopened buds resemble eggs in a basket of green. The unfurled flowers hover like paired birds about to take flight above this nest. This flower is breathtaking to watch in a storm: in a high wind the flowers loft whole to the sky, retaining their pristine form even after falling to the ground.

I noticed that the trees in this unique botanical paradise were marked for cutting. The actions I took are described in this letter I wrote to the Subcommittee on Forests, Family Farms and Energy of the Committee on Agriculture, US. House of Representatives, in December 1991:

> I am a local artist. I live in Sycamore, Florida. My friends and neighbors live tight on the land. I care deeply about all the creations of God, from the birds of the forest to the flowers of the fell to the children of loggers and mill operators.
>
> Five years ago I was drawing a rare white-flowering mint in the Apalachicola National Forest. I noticed that the trees in the middle of a very sensitive botanical site were splotched with blue spray paint. When I asked what these blue blazes meant I was told that the trees had been sold to Coastal Lumber Company.
>
> I pondered long and hard upon what I could do to allow the timber harvest to proceed without intruding upon the survival of these rare flowers. I talked with my neighbors about this challenge. They gave me bundles of tobacco stakes. (In my country the tobacco plantations have been planted to pine and tomatoes, leaving shade barns and stakes aside as relics of a lost economy.) I marked the rare plants with stakes topped off with neatly-tied bows of red tape. This "Stake-Out at Post Office Bay" developed into an environmental artwork which enabled the loggers to demonstrate their respect for the values of other users of the forest. Coastal Lumber Company received a national award for their actions.
>
> The timber industry, the United States Forest Service, and the environmental community achieved a sensitive resolution of the "Stake-out at Post Office Bay." We all set aside rhetoric to seek out the heart of the issue. We treated all parties as partners in the stewardship of the land. We sought a creative way which bridged many viewpoints and values and professions.
>
> This hearing today provides local people an opportunity to discuss the fragile economy of Liberty and adjacent counties. The current saw timber famine is an artifact of timber management practices which presupposed site indices for the flatwoods of Florida as though they were the same as Georgia. As a consequence much of the Apalachicola National Forest was heavily over-cut in the sixties and seventies. The regional timber quotas and guidelines did not allow for local differences.

---

10. Daniel B. Ward, ed., *Plants. Rare and Endangered Biota of Florida*, Vol. 5 (Gainesville, FL: Univ. of Florida, by Univ. Presses of Florida, n.d.)

In the 6 years since I first called the Forest Service I have taken my drawings and poetry to many meetings. I perform poems I have written to help protect the flowers and the people in my area who live tightly interlocked upon these still wild lands. I try when I speak with government officials and politicians about the rare flora and fauna of my region to mention the people whose livelihoods depend upon intact forests and clean, free-flowing water. I endeavor to seek a common future that would allow local people the economic freedom to employ their talents and resources to nurture this special land. The flowers I draw are caught on "the border of fate." I work to ensure that it is no person's "vocation to be their regret"[11].

EARLY PROGRAMMING: AN INTERACTIVE INSTALLATION

Sara Roberts

4188 Greenwood Avenue, Apt. #18
Oakland, California 94602 USA
Tel: (510) 530-2079
Email: sroberts@r2d2!pixar!ucbvax

Early Programming is an interactive character sketch which includes Margo, a talking computer compendium of maternal sayings, and a video monitor that shows segments that set up the context for a variety of typical conversations held with the computer at a kitchen table. The conversations are typical "Why do I have to?"-"Because I say you have to" exchanges, like folksongs, not written so much as arranged. They are organized around events that happen over and over in childhood: leaving the house, going to sleep at night, eating at a table. There are 18 different topics of conversation, and about 1,500 phrases spoken in different tones of voice depending on Margo's mood. There are also a number of cautionary tales. An example starts out, "Don't sit so close to the TV, it gives off rays!"

Each conversation is introduced with a short video clip of a typical childhood experience. These are shot point-of-view style from a child's perspective: a grown-up hand reaching back to take ours before crossing the street; the rubble on the floor of our rooms; watching our hands playing in the rush of air out the car window; staring into the forbidden deep end of the pool. Margo chimes in with classic remarks such as "You're not coming out of there till it's picked up", "Get your arm back in the car, do you want to lose it?" and "No swimming, you just ate!".

Each conversation gives the user a different button menu of responses ranging from cooperative to belligerent. The user's choices both directly and cumulatively effect Margo's mood, which can vary on a scale from hilarity to rage. There are other hidden factors for mood change as well, to manifest a certain unpredictability. Her mood is shown on-screen as a rectangle that changes size, shape and shade. The smaller and darker the rectangle, the grumpier are her replies.

My intention with *Early Programming* was to present a familiar, intimate, mundane relationship in a way that would allow a sort of dual focus. I wanted to shift those familiar expressions from being emotional gestures that we know without hearing to simple words with meanings. It's something that certifiably nonhuman characteristics, in a curious way, allow us to do. Margo says intimate things with a voice that is not human and has an expression that is not a face. Like text on a page, the things that Margo says are much more clearly words.

---

11. Stephen Mitchell, ed., *The Selected Poetry of Rainer Maria Rilke* (New York, NY: Vintage Books, 1984) p. 247. The quoted words are from Rilke's *The Sonnets to Orpheus*, Part Two, 14: "Look at the flowers, so faithful to what is earthly, / to whom we lend fate from the very border of fate. / And if they are sad about how they must wither and die, / perhaps it is our vocation to be their regret."

DIGITAL PROCESSING IN PERFORMANCE: REREBONG AND ELECTRICITY

Neil B. Rolnick

152 Wittenberg Road
Bearsville, New York 12409 USA
Tel/Fax: (914) 679-2869
Email: rolnick@iear.arts.rpi.edu

Early Programming runs on a Macintosh II computer with Hypercard software. Margo's voice is generated by a DecTalk voice synthesizer. A 3-videodisk player with a serial port (optimally, a Sony 1000A) and a video monitor are also needed. The installation has been exhibited at the San Francisco Arts Commission Gallery, the Richmond Art Center, and at the Works Gallery in San José as part of the 1989 NCGA Exhibits in the USA.

In the last few years, my performances with Musical Instrument Digital Interface (MIDI) equipment have gravitated towards ever more extensive use of real-time processing of instrumental and vocal performers. Somehow, it feels as though the integration of acoustic sounds with their electronic results solves two basic problems that have always hung about the edges of computer music: the acoustically-generated sources of the sounds provide a richness and variety of timbre that is always lacking in sounds that are entirely synthetic. The liveliness and unpredictability of performers add a subtlety of inflection and interpretation as well as a visual and emotive focus to performance that is necessarily lacking in taped or sequenced music.

ReRebong[12], written in 1989, is a work for four gamelan instruments which are processed through three Yamaha SPX90II processors. The work was written for and recorded by the Gamelan Son of Lion in New York City. The music is an exploration of material from the traditional piece *Rebong*, which is normally played by the *gender wayang* (a gamelan instrument played with two hammers instead of one) for Balinese shadow-puppet performances. The processors are programmed so that echoes and transpositions of the notes played by the gamelan instruments will be within the *slendro* modality (a standard gamelan tuning) of the instruments themselves. The instrumental sounds are routed through the effects sends of a mixer, and processed sound is returned at a dynamic level that competes with the unprocessed sound. Having performed the piece numerous times with several different gamelan, I have developed a real feeling for playing the mixer and processor as a kind of meta-instrument. I conduct and cue the players, while electronically shaping their ensemble sound. I find that I need to have the same kind of physical security with the controls of the mixer and the processors that I need with a keyboard when I perform my solo works.

Shortly after completing *ReRebong*, I began to think of a work that would integrate my experience performing with processors with the other computer-based techniques I have used over the last few years: the use of synthesized sounds, and the use of samples of entire musical phrases of instrumental or vocal music. The result was *ElectriCity*[13], for flute, clarinet, violin, cello, sampler, synthesizer and processing. *ElectriCity* was written for the California EAR Unit, and was recorded by the New York New Music Ensemble. In this piece the sampler plays samples of the acoustic instruments performing musical phrases from the piece, while the instruments themselves are close-mic'd and extensively processed in real time. The result in performance is a kind of strange distortion of reality in which the acoustic instruments appear to be playing electronic versions of themselves, and the sampler appears to be playing more natural versions of the instrumental parts than the instruments

---

12. *ReRebong* is available on the compact disc *Macedonian Airdrumming* (New York City, NY: Bridge Records, 1992).

13. *ElectriCity* (Bridgeport, CT: O. O. Discs, 1992).

themselves, except for strange loopings and transpositions that creep in from time to time.

Since *ElectriCity* contains three electronic parts, one of the challenges I faced in the piece was how to communicate performance information to the other players via the score and parts. When I perform on the sampler or synthesizer, I rarely think in terms of individual notes, but more often in terms of sonic gestures and events. Particularly in the case of the sampler, where a single played note results in a whole phrase of music and where a sustained chord actually unleashes a flurry of multitempo canons, a simple tablature of notes to be played seemed particularly irrelevant and unmusical. Instead, I found myself defining the kinds of gestural parameters I use in my performances, including the dynamic and textural evolution of the gesture, its coordination with other instrumental or electronic lines, the possible transpositions for the sampled phrases, etc. This meant that the parts became a combination of standard notation and instructions for different improvisational approaches to the material.

My intent in the piece, and what I hear in the recording, is a real marriage of acoustical and electronic sound worlds. This is clearly instrumental chamber music and, just as clearly, electronic music. For the moment, my ideal image for this type of performance piece includes a persistent ambiguity as to whether individual sounds are acoustically or digitally generated. And, hopefully, the result of the ambiguity is to open up both aural and expressive potential for music with an expanded set of sonic options.

PALM-SIZE PLASTIC CASE SERIES (1992)

Joe Rosen

PO Box 225
Midwood Station
Brooklyn, New York 11230 USA
Tel: (718) 377-7808
Email: joro@panix.com
joro@well.sf.ca.us applelink: joro

Skeletor, *Flyingspeck*, and *Electronic Composition No. 1* are three works which comprise the "Palm-Size Plastic Case" Series—a collection of interactive computer art projects completed between June and September of 1992. The series title is named for the 2-x-2-x-½ inch palm-size plastic cases used to house the custom designed hardware controllers that accompany each of the three projects.

All of the projects in the series were built with the intent of exploring alternative methods of hardware input to software programs. A primary goal in each was to incorporate a mind and body interplay between users and on-screen computer objects and images.

Each of the collection's three plastic cases is hand decorated with imagery that is representational of the action the individual project performs. Internal hardware was configured and assembled with parts gathered together from mail-order electronics supply catalogs and Radio Shack retail stores.

Software programs for each project were custom coded using a combination of BASIC and C or Pascal programming languages. A brief description of each project in the series follows:

Skeletor allows its user to interactively explore the yin and yang balance between life and death. By pressing a button on top of the *Skeletor* hardware controller, the program's user can repeatedly kill and bring back to life primitive on-screen representations (i.e. simple black and white geometric drawings and animations) of a skeleton-like head.

Flyingspeck is a computer simulation which gives the illusion of how a floating speck of dust might appear if observed many times magnified under a microscope lens. The program's user has the ability to move the animated dust speck around the computer screen by spinning two knobs on the *Flyingspeck* hardware controller.

Electronic Composition No. 1 gives users an opportunity to create computerized interpretations of Dutch modernist "De Stijl" paintings. Upon starting the program a stream of colored rectangles begin a continuous sweep across the computer screen. The color bias and size of the individual rectangles can be instantly changed by adjusting a slider and thumbwheel on the *Electronic Composition No. 1* hardware controller.

DIAGRAM POEMS, INTERGRAMS

Jim Rosenberg

RD. #1, Box 236
Grindstone, Pennsylvania 15442
USA
Email: amanue!jr@vax.cs.pitt.edu

As an undergraduate I was exposed to the idea of tone clusters in music. This sounded enormously exciting; I knew immediately I had to begin exploring how to do the same thing in poetry. This at once led to a difficult problem. Syntactic information is partly provided by an individual word and partly by its context. What will happen to syntactic information when 'word clusters'—words or phrases juxtaposed to occupy the same space, physically and logically—replace words as the terminal nodes in the syntax? The juxtapositions in a cluster would interfere with classical syntax. To paraphrase Cage's old objection to the 12-tone system, classical syntax is a vocabulary of structural description with no zero in it: there is no way to have elements that have no structural relationship among themselves but that participate in a higher-level structural relationship. The way out of this difficult dilemma was to separate syntax from semantics and provide a separate channel for syntax. Thus began in 1968 a long series of *Diagram Poems* that has continued to the present.

As these works evolved I became more interested in the diagram notation than in the original concept of word clusters. *Diagram Series 3* and *Diagrams Series 4* were published as ad hoc circulations, with *Diagrams Series 4* available on-line electronically on the WELL through the ACEN (ArtCom Electronic Network) conference.

After an intervening period of doing simple linear poems, I felt a strong desire to do something interactive and began working with bit-mapped graphics. (*Diagrams Series 4* and earlier works used character-mapped graphics only.) While experimenting with a drawing program I realized that with a mouse in an interactive bit-mapped graphics environment, phrases could be overlaid, rendering them mostly unintelligible. But as the mouse was moved across a cluster, all but one of the phrases could be hidden, allowing juxtaposition at the same point in logical and physical space while still preserving legibility. This has led to my current series of works called *Intergrams*. These works are implemented at the moment as HyperCard stacks. *Intergrams 1–7* have been integrated with a tutorial stack and a button menu. It can be run on any Macintosh with 1M of memory and a hard disk.

In these works the card metaphor of HyperCard is used to show a level in the syntax diagram. Navigation of levels in the syntax diagram is done through clicking buttons. As you move to a higher layer, an entire screen is replaced by a rectangular button showing a much-reduced image of that screen; return to the lower level is achieved by clicking that button. Moving the mouse cursor across a phrase cluster hides all but one of the phrases, revealing a different phrase in turn. Because the phrases of a cluster occur in the same space, they must not be constrained in time; thus *Intergrams* are not performable.

INSECT MYTHOLOGY INSECT TECHNOLOGY

Paul Rutkovsky

227 Westridge Drive
Tallahassee, Florida 32304 USA
Tel: (904) 575-3339
Fax: (904) 576-5530
Email: prutkov@cc.fsu.edu

Insect Mythology Insect Technology is a fabricated civilization created as a site-specific proposal for the Metro-Dade Art in Public Places Trust in southern Florida. To develop a pseudo-history and visual representation of insect architecture, I utilized personal computers to generate graphic images. Four locations were chosen for simulated excavation sites revealing insects and their structures. Each site represented a different geologic time in the insect civilization, beginning two million years ago and leading to its decline a million and a half years later. Digging activity, equipment and materials were still apparent on one active site.

I described the pseudo-history of *Insect Mythology Insect Technology* in this way:

> An ancient civilization of insects indigenous to Florida thrived on Key Biscayne two million years ago. They inhabited almost every square foot of the Key but dominated the area that later became Crandon Zoo. On the old zoo site, the insects built an advanced civilization that has mystified and baffled entomologists, anthropologists, archaeologists and scientists ever since remains of the civilization were first discovered in 1979, shortly before the zoo closed.

> Four major excavation sites, including one currently in progress directly beneath the main gate, are located in the old zoo. Specialists have unearthed bizarre evidence of a highly sophisticated insect civilization, with living and working environments not unlike our twentieth-century cities.

> The insects, including mites, spiders and centipedes, developed an amazing ability to harness their own physical energy and a capacity to utilize the natural resources of the Florida Keys. These insects built their own cities and constructed an empire based on a high-technology culture. It is believed that less than one million years ago they began to harness a form of energy similar to electricity. This allowed them to build extraordinarily large and complicated structures (by insect standards). At one point in their evolution it is believed that the insects metamorphosed into a resemblance of their own technological creations.

SOUND ECOLOGY

Claude Schryer

3582 Cartier
Montréal, Québec H2K 4G2 Canada
Tel: (514) 849-9534
Fax: (514) 987-1862

My work is concerned with sound ecology as expressed by the medium of electroacoustics and radio art. Through experimentation, I have come to believe in certain forms of 'soft technologies' as ecology.

I think of radio as the transmission of information that can be received as fact, fiction or fantasy, depending on the listener's attention, intention and retention, which allows artists a presence in the ear of the world. I think of radio as an ecosphere: the sum of the Earth's ecological systems (all living organisms interacting with the physical environment) with the implication of a conscious ecological stewardship of the Earth and all that is in it.

I enjoy feeling soundscapes in time and in process. The ecology of sound is in finding a balance. My recent work as a composer and producer presents the joys and pains of discovering and rediscovering the implications of environment.

In 1990, I curated a series of radio-ecology capsules for the Musique Actuelle program of Radio-Canada (the French network of the Canadian Broadcasting Company), which questioned the role of electroacoustics in the ecology movement. Later in 1990, I completed a work for cello and tape called *ABBNF*, an ecological portrait of the relationship between humankind and nature inspired by the beauty, fragility and power of Banff National Park—my home from 1987 to 1990 and the hometown of cellist Shauna Rolston, who commissioned the work.

My most recent work is called *Le Matin du Monde* (The Morning of the World). It is a 28-minute 'sound film' inspired by the philosophy of sound ecology of R. Murray Schafer and the World Soundscape Project in Vancouver, that is: respect for the ear and the natural voice, awareness of the symbolism of sounds, knowledge of the rhythms and tempi of soundscapes, fresh hearing (with clarity), soundwalking to discover our sonic environment.

MACHINEDREAMS

Jill Scott

Hochschule den Bildenden Kunst Saar
Kepplerstrasse 3-5
6600 Saarbrucken, Germany
Fax: 49 681 584 7287

MachineDreams uses video to trigger zones of individual sound samples. It is an interactive installation in which the reaction of the participant to the visual component of the space produces a soundscape.

The visual component refers to visions of technological utopia, demonstrated by four modified machines taken from the lives of four women in history. These machines are a sewing machine (1900), a typewriter (1940), a mixmaster (1960), and a telephone switchboard (1990).

Four graphics images, displayed on a wall, connect the technology on display and the human body. The sound composition reflects the utopian dreams of each era and the technology itself.

The sound for *MachineDreams* was sponsored by Perceptive Systems, Melbourne, Australia, and was created with the 3DIS System. The images were created on the Silicon Graphics 4D80GT and proprietary software, IBM PC with Lumena by Time Arts and Michelangelo V4 computerized spray printer.

EARTH SIGNALS

Paul Sermon

68 Finley Road
Reading, Berkshire RG1 3QQ
United Kingdom
Email: lqpsermn@uk.ac.rdg.am.cms

My installation in *Earth Signals* (a group show in 1991 at the Omphalos Gallery in London that included six artists working with chaos theory) consisted of a Dexion metal leaf-shaped structure, 10-x-4-x-3 ft. Six Amiga 500 computers were placed inside the leaf-shaped structure about 1 ft from the ground. A monitor was placed above each of the computers facing upwards, with the screens level with the top of the frame. Each of the monitors formed a side of an elongated hexagon/leaf shape, supported by the Dexion metal. The whole installation was covered with flex, cable, leads and wires emphasizing the veins and stem of the leaf.

This installation worked as a networking workstation. It was linked via a telephone line and modem to a computer mainframe at Reading University and, through EARN, to 11 other artists involved in an international networking exchange of Amiga image and animation files.

Martin Johnson (a student from Gwent College, Wales) and I maintained the workstation and presented the networking project on the computers of the leaf installation. Each of the computers carried out a particular function: Amiga 1 displayed exchanged IFF image files in a loop programme, Amiga 2 constantly digitized images of people entering the gallery, Amiga 3 displayed exchanged animation files in a loop programme, Amiga 4 displayed Deluxe Paint III working on images to send, Amiga 5 displayed exchanged IFF image files in a loop programme controlled by the computer's mouse, Amiga 6 displayed terminal workstation exchanging image, animation and text files.

Although the main intention of this project was the development of Amiga image file-exchange through computer networks, a large amount of the interaction that took place was text based. The other artists involved in the *Earth Signals* Amiga image exchange were Peter Bardazzi, Simon Hewison, Robert Dunn, Anne Hayes, Mathias Fuchs, Simon Rae, Jocelyn J. Paquette, Ivan Pope, Jamie Jamison and Michael Ciri. The 11 of us involved took a metaphysical journey to the Omphalos—a stone at the Delphi that marks the centre of the world, as well as being the Greek word for the navel.

REVOLUTION/ REVOLUTIONS

Jeffrey Shaw

126 Javastraat
1094 HP Amsterdam
The Netherlands

Revolution (1990) is an interactive video sculpture. The viewer can physically rotate a monitor in two directions. One direction shows the rotation of a millstone grinding flour, the other direction accesses digitally processed images of revolutionary events from 1765 to 1989. The revolution (?) in Rumania in 1989 was the referent for the idea of this monument. It is an optimistic interactive mechanism where the viewer's own effort can turn the wheel of mediated revolutions.

Imaginary Museum of Revolutions (with Tjebbe van Tijen) is a partially realized proposal for a monumental interactive videodisk installation. At its center, the viewer can explore a large database of processed images, sounds and texts concerning 200 revolutions since the French Revolution. Space, time and ideology constitute the three main interactive paths of this exploration, enabling each viewer to create a new historicity from the data.

ANAMORPHOSES OF MEMORY

Jeffrey Shaw

Anamorphoses of Memory (1987) is a videotape sculpture. A horizontal monitor, lying on a bed, has a mirrored cylinder standing vertically in the center of the screen. Scrolling concentric circles of text on the screen are anamorphically reflected and read on the mirrored surface of the cylinder. The text (like a metaphor embodied in the sculpture) evokes a constellation of erotic memories associated with that bed. In 1987, *Anamorphoses of Memory* was shown in *Kunst Over de Vloer*, Entrepotdok, Amsterdam, and in *Municipal Art Acquisitions*, Fodor Museum, Amsterdam.

SOUND-TRACKS TO REALITY

Walter Siegfried

Lindwurm Str. 74
D-8000 Munchen 2 Germany
Tel: 089 50 33 08

The Max Mueller Bhaven in Bombay organized a congress on 'SPACE' in 1991. I was invited to participate and proposed a guided tour through the congress area within the National Center of Performing Arts (NCPA).

During the 10 days that I was strolling around in the NCPA area, I allowed myself to be guided by the numerous sounds around me. They provided me with an acoustical topography of the area. I collected them during the whole time span. Out of this collection, I produced a tape with various acoustical atmosphere related to certain zones of the area. In this polyphonically structured tape, sounds of horses in the evening coexisted with motor-launches, fast cars, alarms, exhaust fans, cattle, crickets and birds at dawn.

This tape was the soundtrack to a walk that I guided. In groups of a dozen visitors, we went towards different spots in the area. During these walks each visitor had their own walkman on and listened to soundscapes, which had been composed entirely using recorded elements from the same spatial situation.

Thus, the visitors walked in a concrete space—listening to an artificial sound-track. This opposition between the concrete space and the acoustical dimension (which is removed from the concrete situation) invited the visitors to look for the source of what they heard, to see what they heard, and to imagine how certain sounds could have been linked to the specific situation.

THE NIXON BOOKMOBILE

G. P. Skratz and Bob Davis

5524 Vicente Way
Oakland, California 94609 USA

> Come on down
> take a leap & click your heels.
> It's good enough to pass for real.
> It's the Nixon Bookmobile,
> barreling into town,
> barreling into town.
> —Advertising Jingle

In *The Nixon Bookmobile* (1991), we examine the connections linking Richard Nixon as nonpartisan myth, shamanism, contemporary China, astrology, old-time medicine shows and the moon. Sheer coincidence or conspiracy? You be the judge.

Excerpt:

> Moonrise over Gushan, or "Drum Hill," east of Fuzhou: the Nixonauts—Sabina & the Dwarf—perform a chant for a spontane-ous crowd of over 50 curiosity seekers:
> & these are the things we left on the moon
> american flags
> & these are the things we left on the moon
> laser ranging device
> & these are the things we left on the moon
> a one hundred pound seismometer
> & these are the things we left on the moon
> walking boots, equipment boxes
> & these are the things we left on the moon
> aluminum poles & urine bags
> & these are the things we left on the moon
> television cameras
> & these are the things we left on the moon
> richard nixon's autograph
> & these are the things we left on the moon
> & these are the things we left on the moon

Excerpt:

> We ate popcorn & watched a slideshow at the Nixon Bookmobile. A bolt of lightening struck a manzanita tree which almost fell on the Nixon Bookmobile. We were married by the captain of the Nixon Bookmobile. It would take days to read all there was to read at the Nixon Bookmobile.

Editor's Note: The Nixon Bookmobile is a two-man performance that con-sists of spoken text, songs and audiovisual effects. Accompanied by visual illustrations, a cappella duets and sounds produced by Davis (on unusual instruments such as large water bottles), Skratz describes the progress through China of the American artifact-laden Nixon Bookmobile. In 1991, The Nixon Bookmobile was performed by Skratz and Davis at Intersection for the Arts in San Francisco and at Small Press Distribution in Berkeley.

DIVERSITY

Valerie Soe

27 Winfield Street
San Francisco, California 94110
USA

Diversity (1990) (Fig. 20) is a three-channel video installation that features footage of Chan Cheong-Toon, regularly seen at a traffic island at the corner of Broadway and Columbus in San Francisco's North Beach section, singing furiously in Chinese to whoever cares to listen. Through interviews with Chan, as well as with his many observers, the piece addresses the projection of individual desire onto single subject as each interviewee offers his or her interpretation of Chan's intentions. In addition, by focusing on this unusual personality, the piece explodes the myth of the model minority, contradicting the fallacy that Asians are quiet, well-behaved and aligned with social conventions.

The installation consists of three separate channels of video played simultaneously on individual monitors arranged in a triangular configuration with screens facing inward. The viewer, positioned at the center of the piece, chooses to view one or two monitors at once, although sound from all three is audible at all times. In this way the viewer sequences and selects the configuration of the piece, choosing the order in which the images and narrative unfold. This three-fold arrangement reflects the many aspects of the singing Chan, the focus of the piece—as he sees himself, as others see him, and as he objectively appears—suggesting the variety of perceptions and personalities found in a single individual.

Also included in the installation are a number of names on the gallery wall of various Asian Americans who in one way or another have distinguished themselves. Although several are notable for outstanding achievements, such as author Wakako Yama-guchi and singer Pat Suzuki, others, such as convicted felons Joe Fong and Wendy Yoshimura, are known for more notorious actions. This points out the complexity of Asian-American culture, emphasizing again the diversity of a community too often stereotyped as one-dimensional.

Diversity has been exhibited at the LAB Gallery, San Francisco, the San Francisco Art Institute McBean Gallery, the Woman's Building in Los Angeles, and the SUSHI Gallery in San Diego.

Fig. 20. Valerie Soe, *Diversity*, video installation, the LAB Gallery, San Francisco, CA, 1990. This three-channel video installation points out the complexity of Asian culture.

AGAR

Stephen s'Soreff

79 Mercer Street
New York City, New York 10012
USA

THE FLYING DREAM

Fred Truck

4225 University
Des Moines, Iowa 50311 USA
Tel: (515) 255-3552
Email: fjt@well.sf.ca.us

Fig. 21. Fred Truck, *The Flying Dream*, 1991, a virtual sculpture which runs on the Sense8 Virtual Reality Development System.

The aesthetic experience, illusory, elusive has taken a myriad of forms through the centuries and will continue to do so. What will be the forms to come?

I have focused my art on just this question. I seek to bind the future to the present in a single whole—my art form is *future art-forms*. The last image or word in my works is never final.....

For over four years through the mediums of slide shows, video, drawings, paintings, and print, I have speculated on art-to-come. I present my ideas in forms which heretofore have been thought of as reportage, not conventional art media. I have created an art history slide lecture from 1992, broadcast an art-event which may take place in 1991, on Dutch television; and sent an art message to the stars. My ongoing project is publication of my conceptual art magazine AGAR (AVANT GARDE ART REVIEW) which reviews art in the future.

I began *The Flying Dream* (a virtual sculpture that can only exist in virtual space and can be explored only through the techniques of virtual reality) (Fig. 21) in 1990, by building a three-dimensional (3D) computer model of a flying machine designed by Leonardo da Vinci in the early 1590s.

The particular ornithopter I rendered is a combination of several Leonardo drawings: two different fuselage and empennage ideas, and a modified version of an articulated bat wing. The focus of my model was on the underlying geometry of Leonardo's ideas, rather than on his intricate rope and pulley driving mechanisms.

I executed this work in Paracomp's (now MacroMind's Paracomp) Swivel 3D. My choice of software was later to prove key in moving Leonardo's flyer into the virtual environment. While Swivel lacks the precision found in other 3D Computer-Aided Design (CAD) programs, its chief virtue is the rapidity with which models can be built, and the immediacy of its interface, which allows the user to "grab" the objects being built with the the mouse, and rotate them around the x, y and z axes. This playful interface is due to the fact that Paracomp developed Swivel 3D for VPL, Inc., the pioneer virtual-reality firm headed by Jaron Lanier. VPL manufactures EyePhones, the stereoscopic video goggles and the DataGlove used in many virtual-reality works.

I did my animations and ran the model through my own software *ArtEngine*[14], before setting this project aside and moving on to other works. In the fall of 1991, I had the opportunity, through Carl Loeffler, to split an art-studio residency and go to the Banff Centre for the Arts in Banff, Alberta, Canada for 5 weeks. The Banff Centre has a Sense8 Virtual Reality Development System, and the Art Studio Program, headed by Lorne Falk, was conducting the *Bioapparatus* residency to allow artists to discuss and use this new technology. One of the primary activities of the *Bioapparatus* residency was dissemination of the information generated by our discussions through the Virtual Seminar on the *Bioapparatus*. For this event, which was held 28–29 October 1991, I developed a large-scale artist's flight-simulator project using Leonardo's ornithopter as the aircraft, and presented this idea in a paper called "The Great Swan." *The Flying Dream* is a portion of that project.

Without external support, in defiance of gravity, the da Vinci flying machine hangs in an array of nine telephone poles. The virtual-reality

14. Fred Truck, *Illustrated ArtEngine* (Des Moines, IA: self-published, 1991).

interface to this world can be either a headset for stereoscopic viewing or a high-resolution color monitor for normal monoscopic viewing. A mouse or bird is used for navigation. The entire virtual world represents the human experience of flying dreams, in which telephone poles or trees often appear as obstructions. The dream state is echoed and reinforced by the flying the user does in the virtual world. As such, the virtual sculpture and the user's navigation through it are a balance of the waking state and the visual experience of swimming through the air.

An artist's book, *Archaeopteryx*[15] details my artist's flight simulator, including *The Flying Dream* and how it was moved into the Sense8 Virtual Reality Development System, the cultural history of flying dreams and the social matrix from which my work springs.

ARTENGINE
Fred Truck

ArtEngine is a program, for Macintosh Plus, SE or II personal computers with 2.5 megabytes of random access memory (RAM), that embodies the processes I use in making art. To run the program, text files are loaded into the memory of the *Engine*. These files are not only processed by *ArtEngine* but also formulate its structure—visual memory and associative memory. Visual memory contains procedures that draw a graphic image on the computer monitor. The object represented graphically is also described in associative memory in the form of a brief text statement.

ArtEngine creates new images by synthesizing similarities between texts and objects—by comparing two text descriptions of objects in memory as well as by considering the geometric properties (such as size) of the graphics. The process begins when a text is loaded into the *Engine*. The text can be a novel, a critical essay or a newspaper article and can be of any length. The text is analyzed according to previously created lists, and further analysis results in recommendations concerning the size, color and medium of that described object. The analysis is stored in a special form of associative memory called a 'frame', which is accessible as a descriptive text report written by *ArtEngine*.

The application places emphasis on creating links between visual memory and associative memory, thus becoming an interactive application and giving *ArtEngine* the spark of life and the potential for surprising behavior.

DEUS EX MACHINA/ CLOSET OF ANGELS
Deborah Whitman

567 6th Street, #8
Brooklyn, New York 11215 USA
Tel: (718) 499-5573

I have made film sculptures since 1977 by looping Super-8 film on reels through a wooden structure, creating a mechanism[16]. The film projects onto screens within the structure. Running continuously, the film sculptures are like allegorical machines with whimsical features which involve the audience in poetic narratives.

The film sculptures run continuously. It is as though the audience saw a play, a mythical play, like a Greek play or a symbolic play like Shakespeare and then it continued playing in a room somewhere and occasionally the audience would open the door to that room and would immediately recognize the play whether they chose to stay for part of it or not and the audience could close the door and say, oh yes, that's Hamlet or that's Antigone and the plays would just continue playing endlessly

15. Fred Truck, *Archaeopteryx* (Des Moines, IA: self-published, 1992).

16. Such as *The Definitive's Shadow*, 1981 (installed at The Franklin Furnace, 1981) and *A Cloud is on the Top of the Box of Doors* (1982); *A Staircase with a Tree at the End* (1983); *The Upper Room* (1984) (all installed at the Whitney Museum of American Art, 1985)

and they would know that about those rooms. Except in the film sculptures, the plots continue to change and the audience becomes characters within them, even if their stay is brief.

Deus ex Machina/Closet of Angels (1992)[17]

There is a white closet (3' × 6') (Fig. 22) which is mechanized by a film loop that runs up from a film projector at the base, to a reel on the side. There are two doors on the front of the closet and a rear screen projection. A large screen (4' × 6') is hanging to the left of the closet. The film first projects onto a mirror placed nine feet behind the closet, which then reflects the images back onto the screens. The mirror is cut into two facets, the angles of which are adjustable, so as to throw the images to the two separate screens. The film format is divided in half. The left half of the image projects onto the large screen. The right half projects into the closet and is chiefly of angles ascending and descending. The projector, the mirror and the film loop establish the *Deus ex Machina*. The film runs continuously but the actual length is 2 minutes and 35 seconds.

The *Closet of Angels* is at an angle to the hanging screen so that the two screens are viewed separately from the front and together from behind. From the front where both screens are viewed separately, there is a sense of two locations. The steady ascending and descending of angels in the closet mimics the infinite expanse of the heavenly spheres. The images projected onto the large screen are of objects which contain infinity for a moment, such as a jar of air, a shadow in the corner, a door partly open. As infinity is represented by blue in both screens, from behind where the two screens are seen together, there is a sense of one continuous plane. The objects seem to be states of being which enclose eternity for awhile to then return as part of it—stones by a river, a jar of stones. The clockwork of the *Deus ex Machina* is disclosed, a conductor of the ebb and flow of infinity within and without the forms, ascending and descending the angels.

---

17. Wood, screen material, Super 8 film and projector, mirror. 8' height × 10' width × 16½" depth.

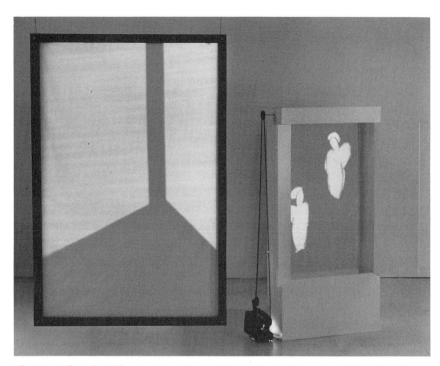

Fig. 22. Deborah Whitman, *Deus Ex Machina/Closet of Angels*, 1992. This film sculpture is an allegorical machine with Super-8 film looping and projecting within it, which involves the audience in a poetic narrative about the ebb and flow of infinity within and without form.

LEONARDO AWARD WINNERS

INTRODUCTION

Every society in every era defines a role for the arts and the relationship its artists have with the society's social, political and economic structure. Organized religion was a major component in sponsoring artistic activity in Mesopotamian art and architecture, in Zen Buddhist painting of the Kamakura period, and in European music, painting and sculpture throughout most of the second millennium a.d. The secular patronage evident in Western European art and music tradition supported painting, sculpture, architecture, composition and music performance in service of the court's social environment, as seen in the Medici family patronage of Michelangelo, and in the Esterházy family support of the composer Franz Josef Haydn.

A transformation began with the growth of the middle class throughout Europe in the eighteenth century that is now operating on a global scale. In the early stages there was a growth in popular support of art and music, legitimizing and, in some cases, popularizing artistic activity. Today the fabric for incorporating the arts into an international society includes government and private funding activities, market-driven arts proliferation, industrial cooperation and the sheer persistence of an intensely active arts community. In some countries, such as in Canada, the public endorses limited taxation by the government in support of its artists and musicians. Artistic activity is appreciated as an integral component of life in many parts of Europe, creating a vibrant contemporary art environment supported by individual, government and commercial participation. The commercialization of art on a global scale establishes a strong market-driven imprint, most evident perhaps in the contemporary United States. Government and private funding supports predominantly traditional artistic activity with decreasing resources. The full weight of an experienced and technologically rich marketing and advertising community drives the promotion of the popular arts, and many artists look towards the advertising, industrial development and academic communities for their basic survival.

A vibrant experimental arts community exists in this environment, with new art forms, venues and media springing up in many countries, supported by a variety of activities. This scenario is enlivened by a commingling among artistic, scientific and technological communities, reflecting a humanistic revolution, the full impact of which has yet to be exhibited. Contemporary artists participate directly in both scientific and technological developments, evidenced in the participation by visual artists in the development of methods for scientific visualization, and in the participation by contemporary musicians in the development of new gestural computer interfaces. Artists are incorporating science and technology with determination, as seen in the application of fractals and chaos theory in computer graphics and computer music and as evidenced by the use of artificial intelligence and connectionism in the design of interactive performance systems. The democratization of art contributes further to the redefinition of artistic activity and the role that art plays in our culture. Even the nature of art and the role of the individual artist is under serious scrutiny, reflecting a transformation in our attitudes about how art is created and experienced.

It is within this historical perspective that Leonardo/ISAST approaches its award program. In a context where subsistence is increasingly linked with visibility and recognition on an international scale, there is a need to widely acknowledge work purely for its artistic and social value and for its integrity in its relationship to society. The Leonardo/ISAST awards are dedicated to recognizing significant work by contemporary artists and to acknowledging exemplary contributions made by individuals toward the synthesis of the contemporary art, science and technology domains. The strategy is based on the funding of a series of endowments consisting of targeted private donations. Winners are selected using a combination of techniques, including nominations from the society's membership, external jurying by peers and by the Leonardo Advisory and Editorial Boards, and internal review by the society staff and by the Board of Directors. Leonardo/ISAST provides a cash award, and features the award winners in the society's publications. The amount of the cash award and the frequency of the award is based on the financial state of the endowment.

Leonardo/ISAST features current and past award winners in this premier edition of the *Leonardo Almanac*. These individuals embody the vision that the journal *Leonardo* and the International Society for the Arts, Sciences and Technology represent. This is a group of people who, both as individuals and as a group, reflect the frontiers of contemporary society and provide a view into our creative futures. Their work bridges chasms that cross artistic, technological, scientific, social and cultural boundaries, offering a perspective that is inclusive and interdisciplinary. In addition to brief biographies on each award winner, we offer examples of work and some of their personal statements regarding their perspectives on art and contemporary society. A bibliography is included highlighting articles in the journal *Leonardo* in which the award winners are represented.

LEONARDO AWARD FOR EXCELLENCE

The *Leonardo Award for Excellence* recognizes excellence in an article published in the journal *Leonardo*. Excellence is defined as originality, rigor of thought, clarity of expression, and effective presentation. The *Leonardo Award for Excellence* was originally established by chemist and inventor Myron Coler and publisher Robert Maxwell. Recipients to date include Rudolf Arnheim, Otto Piene, Charles Ames, Frieda Stahl, Donna Cox, George Gessert and Janet Saad-Cook.

1992

George Gessert

1230 W. Broadway
Eugene, Oregon 97402 USA
Tel: (503) 343-2920

George Gessert, the 1992 recipient of the *Leonardo Award for Excellence*, is an American artist who has raised the fusion of artmaking with science and technology to a new height. He addresses ethical and moral issues in his conceptual artwork involving nuclear weaponry, ecology and genetic engineering. His three award-winning articles are "Notes toward a Radioactive Art", in which he discusses his proposals for artworks made of discarded nuclear weaponry; "Flowers of Human Presence: Effects of Esthetic Values on the Evolution of Ornamental Plants", in which he discusses the influence of plant breeders on the environment; and "Notes on Genetic Art", in which he discusses his and

Fig. 1. George Gessert, *Iris Selection: Painting with DNA*, Installation, 1990. University of Oregon, Museum of Art. (Photo: J. Bauguess)

other artists' works involving DNA (Fig. 1). He has exhibited extensively in the United States and Canada and was a recipient of the New Langton Arts Interdisciplinary Grant in 1990. He is also a graphic artist for the University of Oregon and was previously an art editor for *Northwest Review*.

Gessert, George, "Notes on Genetic Art," *Leonardo* **26**, No. 3 (1993).
—, "Flowers of Human Presence: Effects of Esthetic Values on the Evolution of Ornamental Plants," *Leonardo* **26**, No. 1, 37-44 (1993).
—, "Notes toward a Radioactive Art," *Leonardo* **25**, No. 1, 37-41 (1992).

1989

Donna Cox

University of Illinois
at Urbana-Champaign
National Center
for Supercomputing Applications
152 Computing Applications Bldg.
605 East Springfield Avenue
Champaign, Illinois 61820 USA
Email: cox@ncsa.uiuc.edu

Donna Cox is one of two recipients of the 1989 *Leonardo Award for Excellence* for her article "Using the Supercomputer to Visualize Higher Dimensions: An Artist's Contribution to Scientific Visualization". She is the artist contributor to a team exploring interdisciplinary research through supercomputing. Cox recounts her role as a member of the "Renaissance Team" discovering visual representations of multidimensional computations. Supercomputing is particularly valuable for complex simulations as its speed, vector environment and parallel processing enable many equations to be solved simultaneously. These experiments are valuable in distinguishing appropriate new tools to enable scientists to find correlations in data. Scientific simulations are further evidence of the shared quest of artists and scientists—to make visible the complex, yet invisible, structures of the universe (Fig. 2).

Cox, Donna, "Caricature, Readymades and Metamorphosis: Visual Mathematics in the Context of Art," *Leonardo* **25**, No. 3/4, 295-302 (1992).
—, "The Tao of Postmodernism: Computer Art, Scientific Visualization and Other Paradoxes," *Leonardo* Supplemental Issue, *Computer Art in Context*, 7-12 (1989).

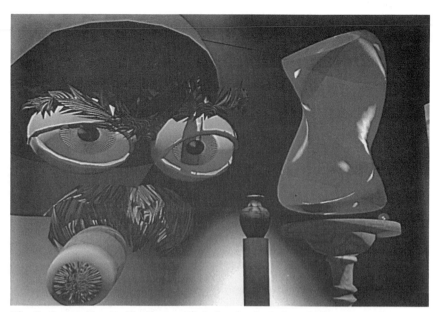

Fig. 2. Donna Cox, Robin Bargar, Chris Landreth, Robert Patterson, et al., *Venus & Milo*, computer-graphics animation, 1990. A close-up view of Milo looking at the audience, with Venus, a topological surface, floating on a pedestal behind.

—, "Using the Supercomputer to Visualize Higher Dimensions: An Artist's Contribution to Scientific Visualization," *Leonardo* **21**, No. 3, 233-242 (1988).

Janet Saad-Cook

1454 Encina Road
Santa Fe, New Mexico 87501 USA
Tel: (505) 983-2884
Fax: (505) 983-3017

Janet Saad-Cook, sculptor, is one of the two 1989 recipients of the *Leonardo Award for Excellence*. In her award-winning article, "Touching the Sky: Artworks Using Natural Phenomena, Earth, Sky and Connections to Astronomy", four artists are discussed who produce monumental works in which a larger order of space and time and of celestial bodies can be experienced. These artists' work permits the observer to personally perceive relationships with solar bodies—space, time and cycle—well outside an individual's lifetime. A sense of wonder and, observer permitting, the possibility of sharing real time with a larger order is possible.

Saad-Cook, Janet, with M.E. Warlick, "Sun Drawing Sculptures of Reflected Sunlight Connecting the Earth and Sky," *Leonardo* **22**, No. 2, 151-158 (1989).
Saad-Cook, Janet, with Charles Ross, Nancy Holt and James Turrell, "Touching the Sky: Artworks Using Natural Phenomena, Earth, Sky and Connections to Astronomy," *Leonardo* **21**, No. 2, 123-134 (1988).

1988

Charles Ames

68 Stevenson Blvd.
Eggertsville, New York 14226 USA

Charles Ames is one of the two 1988 recipients of the *Leonardo Award for Excellence*. In his article "Automated Composition in Retrospect: 1956-1986", he chronicles computer programs for automated musical composition over the last 30 years, providing musical examples from 11 computer-composed works. Examining the factors that have motivated composers to use computers, as well as the actual computer programs, Ames notes that computers are increasingly recognized as legitimate creative tools.

Ames, Charles, "A Catalog of Sequence Generators: Accounting for Proximity, Pattern, Exclusion, Balance and/or Randomness," *Leonardo Music Journal* **2**, No. 1, 55-72 (1992).

—, "A Catalog of Statistical Distributions: Techniques for Transforming Random, Determinate and Chaotic Sequences," *Leonardo Music Journal* **1**, No. 1, 55-70 (1991).

—, "The Markov Process as a Compositional Model: A Survey and Tutorial," *Leonardo* **22**, No. 2, 175-187 (1989).

—, "Automated Composition in Retrospect: 1956-1986," *Leonardo* **20**, No. 2, 169-185 (1987).

—, "Review of *Meta + Hodos: A Phenomenology of Twentieth-Century Musical Materials and an Approach to the Study of Form and Meta Meta + Hodos*," *Leonardo* **20**, No. 2, 192-204 (1987).

Frieda Stahl

Department of Physics & Astronomy
California State University
Los Angeles, California 90032 USA

Frieda Stahl, also a 1988 *Leonardo Award for Excellence* recipient, discusses relationships between language, logic and scientific explanation in her award-winning article, "Physics as Metaphor and Vice Versa". She explores the limitations inherent in Western logic for modern physics and the metaphoric nature of terminology in classic and contemporary physics. She describes non-verbal metaphors in representations of physical behavior and illustrates the reciprocal contributions from physics vocabulary to contemporary American English and the deployment of physics ideas and language in English prose and poetry.

Stahl, Frieda, "Physics as Metaphor and Vice Versa," *Leonardo* **20**, No. 1, 57-64 (1987).

1987

Rudolf Arnheim

1200 Earhart Road, #537
Ann Arbor, Michigan 48105 USA

Rudolf Arnheim is one of the two 1987 recipients of the *Leonardo Award for Excellence* for his editorial "To the Rescue of Art". He is a gestalt psychologist who is recognized as a leader in the academic field of the psychology of art. Arnheim bridges the studies of perception and thinking through careful study of art and art-making, while utilizing the tools and discipline of psychology in the interpretation of art.

In my early years in Berlin, Germany, the technology of film and radio, developing in the 1920s, offered the instruments for two new media of artistic expression. My interest in this opportunity resulted in two books, *Film as Art* (1932/1957) and *Radio, an Art of Sound* (1936/1971). The tools of art—the brush and chisel as well as the computer as it creates shape and motion—remained a necessary aspect of my concern with the arts.

After my arrival in America in 1940, I was helped by fellowships of the Rockefeller and Guggenheim Foundations to embark on an extensive investigation of visual experience and its expression in the visual arts (*Art and Visual Perception*, 1954/1974). During forty years of teaching, mostly at Sarah Lawrence College (1943 - 1968), Harvard (1968 - 1974), and after retirement at the University of Michigan (1974 - 1984), I found time to expand my research to *Visual Thinking* (1969) as the basic aspect of cognition in the sciences and in teaching and learning. Among my later books I attribute particular relevance to *The Power of the Center: A Study of Composition in the Visual Arts* (1982/1988), where I applied my analysis of the visual medium to a theory of artistic composition. Retired in Ann Arbor, Michigan, I continue to explore along the same lines by whatever remains within the more limited resources of a man in his late years.

Arnheim, Rudolf, "Review of *Rethinking the Forms of Visual Expression*", Robert Sowers, *Leonardo* **26**, No. 2, 172. (1993).

—, "Review of *Changing Images of Pictorial Space: A History of Spatial Illusion in Painting*", William Dunning, *Leonardo* **26**, No. 2, 172. (1993).

—, "Review of *Symmetrie Bauplan der Welt*," *Leonardo* **26**, No. 1, 87 (1993).

—, "Review of *Goethe's Botanical Writings*," *Leonardo* **26**, No. 1, 85 (1993).

—, "Gaugin's Homage to Honesty," *Leonardo* **25**, No. 2, 175-178 (1992).

—, "Review of *The Challenge of Art to Psychology*," *Leonardo* **25**, No. 1, 98-99 (1992).

—, "Review of *Seeing Voices: A Journey Into the World of the Deaf*," *Leonardo* **24**, No. 3, 364 (1991).

—, "Outer Space and Inner Space," *Leonardo* **24**, No. 1, 73-74 (1991).

—, "Review of *The Science of Art: Optical Themes in Western Art From Brunelleschi to Seurat*," *Leonardo* **24**, No. 1, 92-93 (1991).

—, "Language and the Early Cinema," *Leonardo* Supplemental Issue *Digital Image—Digital Cinema*, 3-4 (1990).

—, "Review of *Beauty and the Brain: Biological Aspects of Aesthetics*," *Leonardo* **23**, No. 1, 144-145 (1990).

—, "Review of *The Mind's Eye: Readings from Scientific American*," *Leonardo* **22**, No. 3/4, 445-446 (1989).

—, "Review of *Rot Gelb Blau. Die Primarfärben in Der Kunst Des 20. Jahrhunderts*," *Leonardo* **22**, No. 3/4, 452-453 (1989).

—, "Review of *Secret Teachings in the Art of Japanese Gardens: Design Principles, Artistic Values*," *Leonardo* **22**, No. 1, 126-127 (1989).

—, "Review of *Fearful Symmetry. The Search for Beauty in Modern Physics*," *Leonardo* **21**, No. 4, 457-458 (1988).

—, "Symmetry and the Organization of Form: A Review Article," *Leonardo* **21**, No. 3, 273-276 (1988).

—, Introduction to "Cubism and Relativity, with a Letter of Albert Einstein," *Leonardo* **21**, No. 3, 313-315 (1988).

—, "Review of *Arrest and Movement: An Essay on Space and Time in the Representational Art of the Near East*," *Leonardo* **21**, No. 3, 330 (1988).

—, Commentary, *Leonardo* **21**, No. 2, 226 (1988).

—, "The State of Art in Perception," *Leonardo* **20**, No. 4, 305-307 (1987).

—, "Progress in Color and Composition," *Leonardo* **20**, No. 2, 165-168 (1987).

—, Commentary, *Leonardo* **20**, No. 2, 210 (1987).

—, "Review of *World War I and the Weimar Artists: Dix, Grosz, Beckman, Schlemmer*," *Leonardo* **20**, No. 2, 199-200 (1987).

—, "Review of *Alles Veloziferisch: die Eisenbahn, vom Ungeheuer zur Asthetik der Geschwindigkeit*," *Leonardo* **20**, No. 1, 99-100 (1987).

—, "To the Rescue of Art," *Leonardo* **19**, No. 2, 95-97 (1986).

—, "Review of *Picasso, 'Guernica'* and *Picasso's 'Guernica' after Rubens' 'Horrors of War'*," *Leonardo* **18**, No. 2, 116 (1985).

—, Commentary, *Leonardo* **18**, No. 2, 126 (1985).

—, "Review of *Distortion in Art: The Eye and the Mind*," *Leonardo* **17**, No. 4, 302 (1984).

—, "Review of *Structure in Science and Art*," *Leonardo* **15**, No. 4, 316 (1982).

Arnheim, Rudolf with Monroe Beardsley, "An Exchange of Views on Gestalt Psychology and Aesthetic Explanation," *Leonardo* **14**, No. 3, 220-223 (1981).

Arnheim, Rudolf, "Some Comments on J.J. Gibson's Approach to Picture Perception," *Leonardo* **12**, No. 2, 121-122 (1979).

—, "Perception of Perspective Pictorial Space From Different Viewing Points," *Leonardo* **10**, No. 4, 283-285 (1977).

—, "On Order, Simplicity and Entropy," *Leonardo* **7**, No. 2, 139 (1974).

—, "Inverted Perspective in Art: Display and Expression," *Leonardo* **5**, 2, 125-136 (1972).

—, Commentary, *Leonardo* **4**, No. 2, 197 (1971).

* Additional Letters and Commentaries by Rudolf Arnheim are listed in the *Leonardo Cumulative Author/Subject Index 1968 -1987, Volumes 1-20*, George Agoston, indexer (Oxford: Pergamon Press, 1988).

Otto Piene

MIT, Center for Advanced
Visual Studies
40 Massachusetts Avenue
Cambridge, Massachusetts 02139
USA

Otto Piene is the other 1987 recipient of the *Leonardo Award for Excellence* for his article "Sky, Scale and Technology in Art". Piene, a painter, light sculptor, designer, writer and environmental artist, also co-founded Group Zero in 1957. He has been director of the MIT Center for Advanced Visual Studies since 1974. Piene's artwork evolved from "Light Ballet" in 1959 to helium-lifted sculptures as operatic characters. One of Piene's "Sky Art" projects was the 1972 "Olympic Rainbow" for the closing ceremony of the Munich Olympic Games. Through his artwork, Piene urges us to develop and experience a world of full existence by advancing the physical, elemental and technological features of art, rather than attempting to reduce it to a purely internal activity.

Piene, Otto, with Robert Russet, "Sky, Scale and Technology in Art," *Leonardo* **19**, No. 3, 193-200 (1986).

LEONARDO NEW HORIZONS AWARD FOR INNOVATION

Leonardo/ISAST recognizes the challenges that artists face as they strive for exposure and recognition. These challenges are amplified when artists work with new media and new techniques. At the same time, it is often these same artists who are pushing the boundaries of art and technology. The *Leonardo New Horizons Award for Innovation* recognizes new and emerging artists for innovation in new media. Evelyn Edelson-Rosenberg, Jean-Marc Philippe, Jaroslav Belik, Peter Callas, Patrick Boyd, Christian Schiess, and I Wayan Sadra have all received this award.

1991

I Wayan Sadra

Jursan Karawitan
Sekolah Tinggi Seni Indonesia
Kentingan/Jebres
Surakarta, Ja Teng 51739 Indonesia

I Wayan Sadra, an innovative young composer from Indonesia, is the 1991 recipient of the *Leonardo New Horizons Award*. Sadra combines disparate musical elements from widely ranging musical traditions, as is evident in his commissioned composition featured in the premier issue of the *Leonardo Music Journal*. He is well-known for his multimedia performances, which include pieces dealing with the interaction of music and the physical senses. Sadra composes instrumental music as well as music for dance and theater, and is a regular contributor to several Indonesian newspapers, writing reviews and commentary on the relationship between the artist and society. In his writing and teaching, he shows a concern for the social context of performance as well as the musical content. He is interested in music technology and the introduction of visual elements into musical performances. Embracing a wide range of conceptual and technological approaches to music and creativity, Sadra plays an active part in the international community of experimental artists.

Sadra, I Wayan, "Reflections on a First Experience in Electronic Music," *Leonardo Music Journal* **2**, No. 1, 105 (1992).
Sadra, I Wayan, and Jody Diamond, "Komposisi Baru: On Contemporary Composition in Indonesia," *Leonardo Music Journal* **1**, No. 1, 19-24 (1991).
Sadra, I Wayan, "Stay a Maverick," *Leonardo Music Journal* **1**, No. 1, 95 (1991).
—, "Stay a Maverick," *Anthology of Music for the 21st Century*, Compact Disc (CD) (San Francisco, CA: Leonardo/ISAST, 1991).

1990

Christian Schiess

23 Meckelenburgh Square, Flat 812
London WC1N 2AD United Kingdom

Christian Schiess, sculptor, was one of two recipients of the 1990 *Leonardo New Horizons Award* for his extension of the environments in which neon can be used as a medium. He has primarily been concerned with luminism and kineticism in his work. Schiess developed frame technology for using neon underwater. He further expanded neon as a medium by creating "light suits" custom fitted to dancers, who were then able to express the kinetic qualities of light. Through a series of time-lapse videos, Schiess has experimented with the rhythm and movement of kinetic neon with dramatic results (Fig. 3). He has also constructed a completely portable neon fabrication system on wheels that allows site-specific use.

As a sculptor I consider myself a generalist with specialties. For the past several years my specialties have been primarily concerned with luminism and kineticism. Because of my involvement with luminism, I have developed considerable expertise with electric gas discharge tubes, which are commonly referred

Fig. 3. Christian Schiess, *Flora-Borealis*, 1988. Kinetic neon, motors, aluminium and steel, $7\frac{1}{2}' \times 4\frac{1}{2}' \times 4\frac{1}{2}'$.

to as *neon*. My direct and artistically-motivated involvement with neon has resulted not only in aesthetic, but in technical innovation as well.

Some of the most dramatic directions in my work include: the submerged operation and installation of neon in natural aquatic settings such as lakes, ponds and streams; the direct contact of neon with performance artists so that they may wear and handle neon for use in several of my experimental film projects; the construction of a completely portable neon fabrication system on roller wheels that allows site-specific use; and the high speed rotation and computer sequencing of neon as represented by my *Kinetic Light* and *Cyber-Flower Series*.

My intention in developing the environmental *Fire/Water Series* is to further my study and understanding of the four archaic elements of earth, air, fire and water. I hope to achieve a harmonious interaction between the man-made light or fire and the elements of a natural environment. Man-made and natural elements can exist together in opposition to each other or when appropriately combined can exist as complimentary opposites.

In my *Ignus Series* the exploration of fire/air elements are combined utilizing luminous, inflated, colored vinyl sculptures suspended from the ceiling. Sealed within the air-tight vinyl exteriors are neon light elements. Because of the light weight and construction of the sculptures in this series, they are passively kinetic to gentle air currents.

In my *Cyber-Flower Series* kineticism is achieved with variable speed motors and dim/flasher-controlled transformers attached through high speed commutators to spinning neon elements. The sculptures in this series produce a variety of flower-like petal patterns and colors. My objective is to combine modern materials with the ancient art motif of flowers to ultimately pay homage to what nature does best.

Schiess, Christian, "Les Artistes et la Lumiere," in Gateway Section, *Leonardo* **24**, No. 5, 508-510 (1991).
—, "Transportable Neon Equipment for the Light Sculptor," *Leonardo* **24**, No. 1, 19-22 (1991).

1990

Patrick Boyd

18 Whiteley Road
Crystal Palace
London SE19 1JT United Kingdom

Patrick Boyd, a British holographer who has received international recognition for his ground-breaking work, is also a 1990 *Leonardo New Horizons Award* winner. His work is unique in that it brought holography out of a controlled environment for the first time, enabling holographers to capture the outside world in holographic images, therefore freeing them from the previous artistic restrictions of the studio (Fig. 4). Boyd uses existing photographs as the basis of his holograms, combining them with film to expand the versatility of the medium. He has further developed his mixed-media approach with the introduction of computer-manipulated photographic and video-generated images. Other awards that Boyd has received are the Shearwater Foundation Holography Award (1991), the European Holography Prize (1991) and the Fulbright Arts Fellowship in Light Transmission (1989).

I was awarded the *Leonardo New Horizons Award* in conjunction with a Fulbright Fellowship in Light Transmission from the Fulbright Commission in London. The Fulbright Fellowship allowed me to be based in New York City for one year. During that year I made a new direction in my work, leaving my back-

Fig. 4. Patrick Boyd, *Breakfast.* (Photo: P. Boyd)

ground in more traditional holographic imagery behind. Arriving in America I found that most of the people working in holography were still making rather traditional statements using the color and depth elements that holography is famous for. This did nothing for me and I thought it was time that holography was taken to the streets and used to record real life.

There is a type of hologram called a stereogram, which allows the artist to be free from the confines of the studio. You take a sequence of photographic images and montage them holographically into an image that displays depth, time and movement. When the viewer looks at the finished hologram he is basically looking at two photographic images at once, and therefore sees a 3D image. When viewing the hologram from left to right he sees all the images in sequence and experiences the image over time. What I managed to do is develop the stereographic technique so that I didn't have to rely on any heavy camera track or other registration equipment which was previously necessary, but which prevented any spontaneity in recording images.

I traveled around New York recording events I came across with a 35mm hand-held camera. The resulting photographs were used to produce stereograms which combine elements of photography and film/video. They contain more information than a photograph but are more spontaneous than film. The viewer experiences the hologram at his own pace, almost exploring it. The holographic images are presented in conjunction with regular photographs, a format which plays on the different uses of the photographic medium. Using the technique described, I have been using holography as a documentary medium, to create visual statements about people and places I come across in everyday life.

In the pictures, the relationship between the people and the architecture/landscape is very important as the difference between moving and static objects is stressed. Most of the time I recorded scenes that I stumbled on by chance. Items recorded varied a great deal from professional dog walkers to Thanksgiving Day parades, and recently diverged into cows defecating and Elvis' grave in Gracelands.

Since finishing my Fellowship in America and returning to England I have won a Shearwater Holography Award and also The European Holography Award from the Museum Fur Holographic & neue Visuelle Medien and the city of Pulheim, Germany. I was also awarded a Fellowship from the Kunsthochschule fur Medien Koln, which involved working at the KHM for a period of 6 months. During this time I have developed my technique further to begin incorporating video and mixed media into my work. Most recently I have been developing my work using photomontage and synthetically creating 3D scenes using elements from different locations.

1989

Peter Callas

3/3 Werambie Street
Woolwich 2110
Sydney, NSW Australia

Peter Callas, an Australian video and computer graphics artist, received the 1989 *Leonardo New Horizons Award*. His investigation of graphic language involves the use of low-resolution computer graphics to "write" with icons. He develops icons by delineating forms, compressing space onto flat surfaces, importing imagery and manipulating it contextually as layered foreground and background patterns. Urban images—graffiti, advertising, street signs, people, decorative fragments, logos, maps—are treated as fields of energy in that the flow or character of the video does not result so much from the images themselves as from the interruptions and connections of the images. His socially-responsible work uses sweeping themes, such as the evolution of current culture, the repression of Australian aborigines and the economic subjugation of the United States by Japan. Callas was awarded "Most Socially Relevant Video Art" at Portopia '81, International Festival of Video Art in Kobe, Japan. Social, ethnic conflict, environmental and international relations continue to pervade his work.

1988

Jaroslav Belik

1610 Mulcahy
Rosenberg, Texas 77471 USA
Tel: (713) 341-7197

Jaroslav Belik was awarded the *Leonardo New Horizons Award* for his innovative work in 1988. Born in Czechoslovakia, the Canadian kinetic sculptor and mechanical engineer describes his work as aiming to create a moving machine in which motion itself plays the most important role and the work's function as an object is minimized. Belik's artwork origi-

Fig. 5. Jaroslav Belik, *Water Sculpture VO-176.*

nated directly from technology. After studying classical sculpture in Czechoslovakia, he began to create artworks that included vibrating wires, electromagnetic vibrations and, finally, motors. In 1979, Belik expanded his investigation of the emotional effects of different kinds of motion through careful selection of musical accompaniment. Experimenting with large-scale and architectural settings for his kinetic sculpture, Belik began his fountain series (Fig. 5). These large-scale water pieces contain the same thoroughness of design and originality as his well-crafted plastic and metal works. He is a founding member of the Center for Contemporary Arts of Québec in Montréal and has received official recognition by the Czechoslovakian government as a national inventor. Belik currently resides in Texas, in the USA.

The New Horizons Award for Innovation in technological art has been a source of great encouragement to me, as I continue my practical and theoretical research in this field. I have always felt that my approach to artistic creation and expression is fundamentally different from the world of mainstream contemporary art. This is what prompted me to seriously examine some theoretical questions in art, as they relate to my own work.

In my opinion, art can be defined as an original creation which emotionally affects a person. The majority of the conventional arts that we can see today explore relatively basic instincts such as joy, fear, pleasure, pain and sexual drive. Such instincts evolve from a long-ago necessity to survive, and all animals manifest these instincts in varying degrees of sophistication. Until recent centuries, physical survival has been the strongest preoccupation of our ancestors. It is not surprising that the art that has developed so far explores these instincts. Other important roles of art throughout history were communication of message (such as biblical teachings) and recording of historical events. These roles are still current in contemporary art. There are still groups of people who see art in this way, and often see it as the only acceptable art.

With the development of technology in our civilization, life conditions have changed, so that preoccupation with day-to-day survival is not the only concern. Consequently ways of thinking have changed for people today. If we can draw an analogy between a computer program with its ability to process information and the activity of the human brain, we can say that the brain "programs" have evolved. Not only have they become more sophisticated, but they also rely on different information, since our sensibilities have shifted. Basic instincts are not the only factors today that control our behavior and perception. New powerful emotions have evolved, such as pleasure of discovery, understanding of abstract ideas, or the simple joy of thinking. These emotions (or new instincts) are the ones that differentiate us from animals, and make us human beings. For civilized, intellectual beings, they are as strong and perhaps even stronger than basic instincts.

This "instinctual" evolution brought about the development of a new art form which corresponds to the level of a modern person, with his or her higher intellectual and emotional capacity. In addition, art's ancient role to communicate and record becomes obsolete with today's efficient communicating and archiving technologies. The evolution of higher human instincts supports a strong new branch of the fine arts of the future—*Technological Art*. The simple appearance of a new technology is not necessarily what makes an art work, although it can be dazzling and innovative. The important issue is whether it appeals extraordinarily to the brain capability of a modern human being. It is an error to think that new technology will become new art. For example, to render the image of a digitized *Mona Lisa* is not technological art. The use of technology should be a means to an end, not simply the end. Technology or technique must be a well-developed skill, never a limiting factor. In the same way that ancient artists had to perfect sharpening a chisel or diluting paint, today's technological artists must understand how to calculate a mechanical force, the flow of water, electric control, or whatever else they develop in their art.

The following points declare the theoretical basis for my technological art.
- Focus on visual aesthetic purity, uncompromised by any messages.
- Incorporation of intellectual perception into visual perception. Intellectual perception occurs when the viewer discovers a principle or a logic of an art work. A greater appreciation of a technological art work may result from our understanding of its character.
- Motion becomes an integral component of the entire object, not a fashionable curiosity.
- Creation of visual and emotional experiences that are positive: pleasurable, constructive, etc.
- Perfect craftsmanship using best quality materials and parts with professional execution guarantee perfect function.

My work has been accepted well by the public, especially by young people at exhibitions such as *Light & Movement* in the Museum of Natural Sciences in Houston, Texas, as well as at my other exhibitions. Based on my experience of observing and talking to viewers, I conclude that my objects are most often perceived in three phases. First, the spectators are visually intrigued by motion, color and form. In the second phase, they discover that a motion has a principle, or that a shape has a geometrical logic. In the third phase, they return to the visual effect, and because they understand it better, they can appreciate it on an intellectual level in addition to the initial purely aesthetic one. Often, this process repeats itself over and over, resulting in the discovery of many new phenomena. I believe that due to this educational process my kinetic and water objects have become increasingly popular in public spaces such as libraries, schools and office buildings.

I observe that technological art is continually receiving more recognition in the conventional art world. It has become rightfully understood as a serious artistic direction. I think that my accomplishments testify to this. My two-dimensional work, the only kinetic object accepted, won the Manhattan Bank Prize at the 1990 Osaka Triennale international exhibition of paintings. In 1992 my three-dimensional object received a bronze prize at the Osaka Triennale exhibition for conventional sculpture. These are not only personal successes, but breakthroughs for technological art as well.

Belik, Jaroslav, "Creation Through a Machine: Kinetic Art," *Leonardo* **21**, No. 3, 243-245 (1988).

1987

Jean-Marc Philippe

65 bis Boulevard Brune
75014 Paris, France
Tel/Fax: 33 1 45 39 91 28

Jean-Marc Philippe, a Parisian artist and research engineer, received the 1987 *Leonardo New Horizons Award* for his shape-memory alloy sculptures. Nickel-titanium shape-memory alloys are alloys that retain the memory of a shape imposed on them at another temperature. Sculptures from these alloys change their shapes as the ambient temperature changes. The *Bicentennial Tree*, a commission from the French Revolution Bicentenary, is a 30-foot tree-shaped sculpture for the Jardins des Tuilleries completed in 1989. The tree's shape evolves over both the diurnal and the annual temperature cycles. Philippe's innovation demonstrates his commitment to the synthesis of art, science and technology.

Fig. 6. Jean-Marc Philippe, *Hermaphrodite*, 1985.

The *Leonardo New Horizons Award* that was presented to me in 1987 was the recompense of eight years' work in which my ambition was to enrich sculpture radically by adding a fourth dimension to its classically existing three spatial ones, the dimension of memory. Such an enriching process was in fact possible on the condition of diverting and developing certain technological expertise previously reserved for military uses to the realm of art. This technological expertise, known and developed under the heading of *substances with shape memory*, referred to the physical phenomena according to which it is possible to "teach" specific metallic alloys to assume certain shapes at certain temperatures, shapes that would form each time the alloys reached these same temperatures again.

To be more precise I was presented the award for having used this concept to produce the first prototype of *Evolutive Sculpture with Memory*. First of all, in partnership with French industry and after several months of effort and a global research and development budget of $300,000 US, I was able to finish a first prototype called *Hermaphrodite 1985*. It was an evolutive sculpture in CuZnAl with memory, which at 25 degrees Celsius was the classic Greek torso of a man, and at 55 degrees Celsius displays the classical Greek bust of a woman (Fig. 6). 55 degrees Celsius is easily attainable by exposing a metallic plate to the sun's rays. From 1986 in partnership with the American Raychem Corporation I began a research and development program with $400,000 US in funding to make other prototypes of these mid-scale sculptures in Nickel Titanium, *Tree of the New Alliance* and *Circle of Life*. Then one day I received news in the mail that I had won the *1987 Leonardo New Horizons Award*.

The approach that made it possible for me to receive such significant amounts of money first from the French, then the Americans was to propose original and patentable ideas to the industries concerned of marketable products using shape-memory alloys, the financial yield of which would eventually surpass the sums I was asking for to carry out my own evolutive-memory sculptures. With a research and development budget of more than $1,500,000 US, a team consisting of a full-time engineer and two assistants, the world's specialists in this technology and the general knowledge of the Raychem group's metal division, several new alloy variations with memory with reduced hysteresis have been perfected. They take into account the specific requirements of the new sculpture concepts for monumental dimensions. Test sessions for fatigue, meaning numerous elevated cycles, have been successfully carried out on most of these variations. However, these tests are carried out on large metal test-tubes requiring fairly long (several dozen minutes) deformation/transformation cycles (because of the transfer of heat to the test-tubes tested), which explains why not all the tests have been completed yet.

One of the most complex variations of these alloys for producing a sculpture concept likely to be placed in the Cité des Sciences et de L'Industrie of Paris—a concept intended to transform the sculpture completely in an hour's time—is still being tested for fatigue in a French laboratory. The tests have been partially financed by Anvar, a French public organization for promoting research, over the past 18 months. At present we are looking for a suitable site and financing for other, more ambitious projects, such as *The Door of the Two Infinities,* the feasibility and dependability of which have already been demonstrated. But my ultimate aim and determination in the not-too-distant future is to open an advisory service for all sculptors, artists and designers who would like to give form to their imaginative creativity with these new substances, i.e. 1) using the new metallic variations, some of which are industrial products for the general public, and 2) putting the know-how I have acquired in making my own sculptures to good use.

Philippe, Jean-Marc, "Space Art: A Call for a Space Art Ethics Committee," *Leonardo* **23**, No. 1, 129-132 (1990).
—, "Art and Shape Memory Alloys," *Leonardo* **22**, No. 1, 117-120 (1989).

1986

Evelyn Edelson-Rosenberg

4812 Madison Court NE
Albuquerque, New Mexico 87110
USA

Evelyn Edelson-Rosenberg, detonographer, received the 1986 *Leonardo New Horizons Award* for her multi-metal murals. The artist was selected for her work using explosives to create large murals. The concept of fusing the detail of printmaking and the large scale of mural-making spurred Edelson-Rosenberg to develop the new technique. The explosives create bas-relief metal murals by fusing various combinations of stainless or conventional steel, aluminum, copper, brass and bronze. Various metal oxides add color to the multidimensional metal designs. Explosives act as a giant stamping press, driving the metals into the mold where the design is reproduced, down to the last detail. Following careful polishing, the mural surface achieves a jewel-like quality. Edelson-Rosenberg is further evolving her fusion of printmaking and mural-making from her initial bas reliefs to three-dimensional columns.

Edelson-Rosenberg, Evelyn, "Detonography: The Creation of Bas-Relief Sculptures by Explosives," *Leonardo* **21**, No. 3, 251-254 (1988).

FRANK J. MALINA LEONARDO AWARD FOR LIFETIME ACHIEVEMENT

Kinetic artist and astronautical pioneer Frank J. Malina founded the journal *Leonardo* in 1968. He saw the need for a journal that would serve as an international channel of communication between artists, with emphasis on the writings of artists who use science and developing technologies in their work. The *Frank J. Malina Leonardo Award for Lifetime Achievement* recognizes eminent artists who through a lifetime of work have achieved a synthesis of contemporary art, science and technology. Winners include Gyorgy Kepes, Nicolas Schöffer, Max Bill and Takis.

Takis

Panayiotis Vassilakis
22 Rue Liancourt
Paris 14, France

Takis, Greek Sculptor and experimental artist, was the 1988 recipient of the *Frank J. Malina-Leonardo Award*. He began sculpting in 1946 without formal training and went abroad in 1954, living in London and Paris. In London, he created *Signals* (1954-1958), abstract kinetic sculptures made of steel wire that were either weighted at the top in order to put them into constant motion or else used springs as sources of energy for movement. During the 1960s he explored the field of electro-magnetism, and in his *Magnetic Ballets* and other such works he created objects that moved in controlled magnetic fields and that existed less for the sake of their intrinsic form than to reveal the operation of a natural force. In particular his work using iron filings in association with powerful magnets focused attention not on the presence of the object but on a mysterious and apparently inexplicable manifestation of natural energy. With his kinetic works he sometimes combined light effects and musical sound.

1987

Max Bill

Albulastrasse 39
8048 Zurich, Switzerland

Max Bill is a Swiss painter and sculptor who received the *Frank J. Malina-Leonardo Award* in 1987. Bill studied at the Zurich School of Arts and Crafts and, later, at the Bauhaus. His art is a form of Constructivism that relies on mathematical formulae to build up components from which the work is constructed (Fig. 7). He joined the association of modern Swiss artists, *Allianz*, and in 1941 founded the *Allianz Press*. In addition to pub-

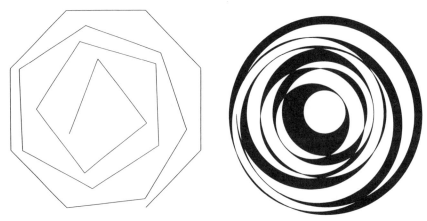

Fig. 7. Max Bill, *Quinze variations sur un même theme* (Fifteen Variations on a Single Theme), 16 lithographs with text in English, French and German, edition of 220, 30.5 x 32 cm, 1934-1938 (Paris: Editions des Chroniques du Jour, 1938). This series illustrates the creative process by starting with a single fundamental idea that leads to 15 very different developments - proof that concrete art holds an infinite number of possibilities. (Text reprinted in English in Eduard Hüttinger, *Max Bill* [Zurich: ABC Editions, 1978].)
Above left: *The Theme*, 1935. *The Theme* consists of the continuous development of an equilateral triangle to a regular octagon. The third side of the triangle, which would close it, is moved outward so as to form one of the sides of the quadrilateral (square). In this way, the area of the triangle remains open and is merely suggested. The transitions from one polygon to the next are all made in the same fashion. The resultant figure is a spiral composed of straight lines of equal length. The angles and the areas between these lines show a great variety of form and tension.
Above right: *Variation 10*, 1937. Inscribed and circumscribed circles produce thick circular rings. The parts of these rings where no overlapping takes place are shown in gray.

lishing and teaching, Bill has focused on product design. The expression of Bauhaus Functionalism is central to his art. In 1947, he founded the Institute for Progressive Culture and mounted a series of exhibitions that culminated in 1951 in an important retrospective exhibition of his work by the São Paulo Museum. That same year, Bill developed a "university" for design techniques from his appointed position as Rector of a Hochschule fur Gestaltung (Institute for Design) at Ulm. His influence has been recognized worldwide—in Brazil he was awarded the Grand Prix for sculpture at the Sao Paulo Biennale of 1951, and, in Italy, the Grand Prix for the Swiss Pavilion at the Milan Triennale in 1951. He has held more than 200 one-man exhibitions of his work.

Emmer, Michele, "Visual Art and Mathematics: The Moebius Band," *Leonardo* **13**, No. 2, 108 (1980).

1986

Nicolas Schöffer

deceased

Nicolas Schöffer received the 1986 *Frank J. Malina-Leonardo Award* for his lifetime of work as a composer of sculptures integrating visual art and sound. Schöffer studied at the École des Beaux-Arts. During the 1950s he turned toward the creation of a new art which he based on cybernetics. This led him to collaboration with artists in other media, with whom he could apply his ideas on temporal control of space and light. His three sculpture series which began in 1948—*Spatiodynamic, Luminodynamic* and *Chronodynamic Programs* (Space, Light and Time)—are environmentally responsive, interactive, multisensory structures programmed so that the artworks can be activated at any time. In 1985 he developed a system of computer graphics that he called "ordigraphics." Because he worked from a conceptual point of view, he could apply the same kind of rhythmic structures to computer graphics that he had used in the past with his sculptures, transcending media with disconcerting ease.

Schöffer, Nicolas, "Sonic and Visual Structures: Theory and Experiment," *Leonardo* **18**, No. 2, 59-68 (1985).

1985

Gyorgy Kepes

MIT, Center for Advanced Visual Studies
Cambridge, Massachusetts 02139
USA

Gyorgy Kepes, the 1985 recipient of the *Frank J. Malina-Leonardo Award*, founded the Center for Advanced Visual Studies at the Massachusetts Institute of Technology to advance new technologies and relationships among scientific discoveries and art. The Hungarian artist, a founder of the New Bauhaus and a "light artist," wrote that the revolutions that keep changing the concept of form must give way to more serious commitment. He wished to contribute to the successful reunification of man and nature. He called on other artists to break out of the claustrophobic space of the gallery and museum and tackle new ways of bringing together artwork and the public. Kepes argued that the artistic imagination belongs to the larger environmental field of nature and society and that, in this context, contemporary artists must deal with society's problems on an immense scale, from ecological disasters and social tragedies to the realities of confused and impoverished human relationships. Kepes believes that, in one and the same form, the tragedy of the environment can be dramatized while means can be provided to convert a scene of ecological regulation into a stirring focus on civic art.

Kepes, Gyorgy, "Toward Civic Art," *Leonardo* **4**, No. 1, 69-74, (1971).
—, Letter (Appreciation of *Leonardo*), *Leonardo* **1**, No. 3, 343 (1968).

THE LEONARDO SPEAKERS' NETWORK

For 25 years the journal *Leonardo* has provided a forum for people working in the realm where art, science and technology converge. The goal of the *Leonardo Speakers' Network* is to facilitate speaking and presentation engagements for artists, researchers, scholars and technology developers with interested groups and organizations. The program offers a platform from which artists, scientists and technologists can make their work known. The *Leonardo Speakers' Network* was established in 1990, and has concentrated on facilitating speaking engagements for visiting network participants in the Bay Area of California, in the United States of America. Publishing this material in the *Leonardo Almanac* makes the network more visible and accessible on an international scale, encouraging widespread use of valuable regional and international resources. The expansion of the *Leonardo Speakers' Network* addresses an increasing need for communication across cultural, social, economic, and disciplinary boundaries, reflecting the diverse needs and special capabilities of the members of a global community. On a regional level, organizations and individuals benefit by exploring human resources and presentation opportunities in their own area. On an international scale diverse groups draw upon extended resources to provide different perspectives to their communities.

Leonardo journal authors, editors, co-editors and winners of the society's awards are invited to participate in the *Leonardo Speakers' Network*. The speakers participating in the program provide sample topics, and Leonardo/ISAST publishes the information with complete contact data, including electronic mail addresses where available. A bibliography containing listings of work published in the journal *Leonardo* provides additional orientation with respect to the particular speaker's expertise and activities. Speakers are encouraged to inform Leonardo/ISAST about travel plans. Organizations planning events are invited to contact Leonardo/ISAST to inform the art, science and technology communities about their special needs. The *Leonardo Speakers' Network* is published in the journal *Leonardo*. Schedules and opportunities are announced in *Leonardo Electronic News* and in the society's newsletter, *Leonardo Currents*.

The *Leonardo Speakers' Network* provides a model for interaction which promotes effective and efficient exchange of knowledge and understanding. Arts and education groups and institutions, as well as other interested organizations, are encouraged to participate in this unique program, increasing their community's access to the latest ideas and innovations. Speakers in the program have access to Leonardo/ISAST's organizations database to assist them in developing contacts. Organizations are able to enhance their existing programs by targeting their attention directly to speakers and presenters whose expertise intersects well with their current activities.

The increasing availability of new communication technologies suggests a redefinition of the notions and mechanics of presence, communication and even economic subsistence. The frequency of telepresence contact has grown from sample test cases to a vibrant and vital communication resource in only a few years, with cyber-contact infiltrating many segments of the art, education, research and technology development communities. The design paradigm for the *Leonardo Speakers' Network* reflects these new developments by encouraging communication beyond physical presence.

Following is a listing of the speakers who are currently participating in the program. To arrange speaking or presentation engagements, contact the speakers directly at the addresses given. Financial arrangements are negotiated directly between the speakers and the host organization.

Margo Apostolos

3400 Ben Lomond Place #226
Los Angeles, CA 90027 USA
Email: margo@iris.usc.edu

Programming Robots to Dance as an Aesthetic Vehicle
Visual Perception

Apostolos, Margo, :"Robot Choreography: The Paradox of Robot Motion," Leonardo **24**, No. 5, 549-552 (1991).
—, "Robot Choreography: Moving in a New Direction," *Leonardo* **23**, No. 1, 25-30 (1990).

Sara Garden Armstrong

43 Great Jones Street
New York, NY 10012 USA

Theory and/or Execution of Installation Art incorporating any of the following: Computers, Light, Sound, Movement, Environment, Site Specificity, Paper/paper pulp

Armstrong, S. G. and R. Ross, "The Airplayer Series: Manipulation of Light, Sound and Space through Technology," *Leonardo Music Journal* **1**, No. 1, 25 (1991).

Bill Bell

56 Perry Street
Brookline, MA 02146 USA
Tel: (617) 277-4719
Fax: (617) 277-4736

Seeing in the Interstices

Bell, Bill, "Elusive Imagery of the Lightstick," *Leonardo* **19**, No. 1, 3 (1986).

Peter Beyls

Octaaf Van Dammestraat, 73
9030 Gent, Belgium
Tel: 32 91 267753
Email: peter@arti.vub.ac.be

Artificial Intelligence in the Arts (Music and Visual Art)
Artificial Life
Virtual Reality and Music
Man-Machine Interfaces
Interactive Composing
Complex Dynamics
Cellular Automata

Beyls, Peter, "Chaos and Creativity: The Dynamic Systems Approach to Musical Composition," *Leonardo Music Journal* **1**, No. 1, 31 (1991).
—, "Discovery through Interaction: A Cognitive Approach to Computer Media in the Visual Arts," *Leonardo* **24**, No. 3, 311-316 (1991).

Pierre Michel Boone

University Gent - Lab. Soete
Applied Mechanics - Workshop Holography
41 St. Pietersnieuwstraat
B9000 Gent, Belgium
Tel: 32 91 643242
Fax: 32 91 237326

Duality of Holography as a Medium—Banalization and demystification necessity

Boone, Pierre Michel, "Holographic Portraiture of Humans, Plants and Ghosts in Belgium," *Leonardo* **22**, No. 3/4, 365-368 (1989).

David Carrier

Carnegie Mellon University
Pittsburgh, PA 15213-3890 USA
Tel: (412) 268-2819
Fax: (412) 268-1440

Postmodernism and the Present Situation of Art Criticism
The History of Art History

Carrier, David, "Visual Theory and Leonardo," *Leonardo* **26**, No. 2, 93 (1993).
—, "*Artwriting* Revisited," *Leonardo* **25**, No. 2, 197 (1992).
—, Review of *The Place of Narrative: Mural Decoration in Italian Churches, 431-1600*, Marilyn Aronberg Lavin, *Leonardo* **25**, No. 1, 104 (1992).
—, Review of *Pieter Saenredam. The Painter and His Time*, Gary Schwartz and Marten Jan Bok, *Leonardo* **24**, No. 4, 492 (1991).
Carrier, David and R. Cavalier, "Theoretical and Practical Perspectives on Technology and the History of Art History," *Leonardo* **22**, No. 2, 245-250 (1989).
—, "The Arts and Science and Technology: Problems and Prospects," *Leonardo* **21**, No. 4, 341-342 (1988).
—, Review of *The Light of Early Italian Painting*, Paul Hills, *Leonardo* **21**, No. 2, 213 (1988).
—, Review of *The Psychology of Perspective and Renaissance Art*, Michael Kubovy, *Leonardo* **21**, No. 1, 103-104 (1988).
—, Letter about "Display of Art," Harry Rand and David Carrier, *Leonardo* **20**, No. 2, 209 (1987).
—, Letter about "Gestalt Psychology and the Theory of Art," Rudolf Arnheim and Roy R. Behrens, *Leonardo* **20**, No. 2, 210, (1987).
—, "The Display of Art: An Historical Perspective," *Leonardo* **20**, No. 1, 83, (1987).
—, "The Era of Post-Historical Art," *Leonardo* **20**, No. 1, 83 (1987).
—, "Artists' Intentions and Art Historians' Interpretation of the Artwork," *Leonardo* **19**, No. 4, 359 (1987).
—, Letter about Rodin's "Gates of Hell", David Carrier, *Leonardo* **19**, No. 4, 359 (1987).
—, Letter "Theory of Art," Richard Shiff, *Leonardo* **19**, No. 3, 269 (1986).
—, "Theoretical Perspectives on the Arts, Sciences and Technology Part 4: A Response to Rudolf Arnheim's 'To the Rescue of Art'," *Leonardo* **19**, No. 3, 251 (1986).
—, "Philosophical Art Criticism," *Leonardo* **19**, No. 2, 170 (1986).
—, Letter about "Theory of Art," E.H. Gombrich and Robert Dixon, *Leonardo* **19**, No. 2, 182 (1986).
—, "Theoretical Perspectives on the Arts, Sciences and Technology," *Leonardo* **19**, No. 1, 77 (1986).
—, "Theoretical Perspectives on the Arts, Sciences and Technology Part 2: Postmodernist Art Criticism," *Leonardo* **18**, No. 2, 108 (1985).
—, "On the Possibility of Aesthetic Atheism: Philosophy and the Market in Art," *Leonardo* **18**, No. 1, 35 (1985).
—, "Theoretical Perspectives on the Arts, Sciences and Technology," *Leonardo* **17**, No. 4, 288 (1984).
—, Review of *This is Not a Pipe*, Michel Foucault, *Leonardo*

17, No. 3, 218 (1984).

—, "Gombrich on Art Historical Explanations," *Leonardo* **16**, No. 2, 91, 1983.

—, Review of *Art and Philosophy: Conceptual Issues in Aesthetics*, Joseph Margolis, *Leonardo* **15**, No. 3, 242 (1982).

—, Review of *The Perception of Pictures*, Margaret A. Hagen, *Leonardo* **15**, No. 3, 250 (1982).

—, Letter about "Perspective," Nelson Goodman, E.H. Gombrich, J.J. Gibson; J.L. Ward, *Leonardo* **14**, No. 3, 262 (1981).

—, Review of *The Immortal Eight: American Painting from Eakins to the Armory Show, 1870-1913*, Bennard B. Perlman, *Leonardo* **14**, No. 2, 163 (1981).

—, Letter about "Perspective," E.H. Gombrich, J.J. Gibson, Nelson Goodman and J.L. Ward, *Leonardo* **14**, No. 1, 86 (1981).

—, "Perspective as a Convention: On the Views of Nelson Goodman and Ernst Gombrich," *Leonardo* **13**, No. 4, 283 (1980).

—, Letter about "Creativity," Michael Krausz, *Leonardo* **13**, No. 3, 262 (1980).

—, Letter about "Pictures, Perception," John F. Moffitt and Sheldon Richmond, *Leonardo* **12**, No. 4, 350 (1979).

—, "On the Depiction of Figurative Representational Pictures within Pictures," *Leonardo* **12**, No. 3, 197 (1979).

See Also:

Brook, Donald, Review of *Artwriting*, David Carrier; Response by David Carrier and a Rejoinder by Donald Brook, *Leonardo* **22**, No. 2, 197-200 (1989).

Roskill, Mark, Letter, David Carrier, *Leonardo* **19**, No. 4, 359 (1986).

Carrier, David, Letter, Richard Shiff, *Leonardo* **19**, No. 3, 269 (1986).

Poleskie, Steve, Letter, David Carrier, *Leonardo* **19**, No. 3, 255 (1986).

Shiff, Richard, Letter, David Carrier, *Leonardo* **19**, No. 3, 269 (1986).

Woodfield, Richard, Letter, David Carrier, *Leonardo* **19**, No. 3, 269 (1986).

Arnheim, Rudolf, *To the Rescue of Art*, *Leonardo* **19**, No. 2, 95 (1986).

Carrier, David, Letter, Robert Dixon, *Leonardo* **19**, No. 2, 182 (1986).

Dixon, Robert, Letter, David Carrier, *Leonardo* **19**, No. 2, 181 (1986).

Gombrich, E.H, Letter, Robert Dixon, *Leonardo* **19**, No. 2, 181 (1986).

Polansky, Larry, Letter, David Carrier, *Leonardo* **19**, No. 2, 181 (1986).

Gombrich, E.H, Letter, David Carrier, *Leonardo* **18**, No. 3, 212 (1985).

Gombrich, E.H, Letter, David Carrier, *Leonardo* **18**, No. 2, 126 (1985).

Harriet Casdin-Silver

99 Pond Avenue D403
Brookline, MA 02146 USA

The Artist and Holography

Casdin-Silver, Harriet, "My First 10 Years as Artist/Holographer (1968-1977)," *Leonardo* **22**, No. 3/4, 317-326 (1989).

Attila Csáji

Hungart
Kisgomb, 30
Budapest 1135 Hungary
Tel: 36 11 296 356
Fax: 36 11 212 982

The Application of Lasers to Compose Pictures: the Method of Superpositioning

The Pictorial Potentialities of Coherent Laser Light

Light Choreographies, Laser Animation Films, Interactive Light Mobiles

Csáji, Attila and N. Kroó, "The Application of Lasers to Compose Pictures: The Method of Superpositioning," *Leonardo* **25**, No. 1, 23-28 (1992).

Carl DeVito

University of Arizona
Department of Mathematics
Building #89
Tucson, Arizona 85721 USA
Tel: (602) 621-6893
Fax: (602) 621-8322

Problems Involved in Trying to Communicate with (Hypothetical) Extra-Terrestrial Intelligence

Languages Based on Mathematics and Physical Science

Mathematical Aspects of the Search for Extra-Terrestrial Intelligence

DeVito, Carl, "Languages, Science and the Search for Extraterrestrial Intelligence," *Leonardo* **25**, No. 1, 13-16 (1992).

Emanuel Dion

c/o Jurgen Schmidt
Niebuhrstrasse 66
D-1000 Berlin/West 12 Germany
Tel: 49-30 5291234

The Universal Concept of Symmetry: A New Philosophical and Aesthetical Theory is Changing the "Symmetrical World" of Antiquity.

The Special Concept of Symmetry: A New Social Theory Before and After the Re-established Unity of Germany.

Art as Medium: The Individuation of the Artist and the Pluralism of Society.

Autarchic Art: From Constructivism over Concrete Art to a Symbolism of Forms, Colors and Numbers on a Way to Artistic Identity.

Visual Art, Geometry and Modern Technology: From the Universe of the Spirit over the Interactions of Disciplines to the Difference Between the Beauty of Art and the Beauty of Mathematics.

Dion, Emanuel, "Weightless: The Dream of Flying in the Dream of Art," in Gateway Section, *Leonardo* **25**, 2, 115-117 (1992).

—, "Symmetry: A Social Symbol and Two Monuments," *Leonardo* **24**, No. 5, 511-518 (1992).

Gary Dwyer

444 Indian Knob Road
San Luis Obispo, CA 93401 USA

*Native American Cultural Influence on Design
    Expression*
New Opportunities in Garden Design
Humor in the Landscape, a Neglected Opportunity
Landscape Architectural Activity in a Seismic Zone
The Aesthetics of the Vast
Landscape Expression in the Nepal Himalaya

Gary Dwyer, "Mea Culpa—My Fault: A Report on an Earth-
    work in Progress," *Leonardo* **19**, No. 4, 285 (1986).

Eda Easton

90 Hillyndale Road
Storrs, CT 06268 USA

Teaching Sculpture: My Work and My Studio

Easton, Eda, "Understanding Materials as a Foundation for
    Teaching and Creating Sculpture," *Leonardo* **25**, No. 2,
    129 (1992).

Péter Érdi

Hungarian Academy of Sciences
Central Research for Physics
P.O. Box 49
Budapest H-1525 Hungary
Email: h1705erd@ella.uucp

*Structures, Forms, Patterns and Perceptions: A Brain-
    Theoretic Point of View*

Érdi, Péter, Review of "Beauty and the Brain: Biological
    Aspects of Aesthetics," David Epstein, Barbara
    Herzberger and Ingo Rentschler, eds., *Leonardo* **23**, No.
    4, 446-447 (1990).
—, ed., "Art and the New Biology: Biological Forms and Pat-
    terns," *Leonardo* **22**, No. 1 (1989).
—, "Biology and Art," *Leonardo* **22**, No. 1, 1-2 (1989).
Érdi, Péter and T.F. Farkas, "'Impossible Forms': Experimen-
    tal Graphics and Theoretical Associations," *Leonardo* **18**,
    No. 3, 179 (1985).

Dora Feïlane

2 Rue Lieutaud
13100 Aix en Provence, France

*Visual Sensations and Emotions by Projection of
    Painting on Dancers Moving in Front of Black and
    White Screen: How the Choreography Can Move the
    Painting*

Feïlane, Dora, "Image and Dance," *Leonardo* **24**, No. 4, 484
    (1991).

Herbert Franke

Puppling Haus 40
D-8195 Egling, Germany
Tel: 081 71 18329

Art/Science Connection

Franke, Herbert and H. Helbig, "Generative Mathematics:
    Mathematically Described and Calculated Visual Art,"
    Leonardo **25**, No. 3/4, 291-294 (1992).
Franke, Herbert, "Mathematics As an Artistic-Generative
    Principle," *Leonardo* Supplemental Issue *Computer Art in
    Context: SIGGRAPH '89 Art Show Catalog*, 25-26 (1989).
—, Comments on "The Expanding Medium: The Future of
    Computer Art," *Leonardo* **21**, No. 2, 223 (1988).
—, "The Expanding Medium: The Future of Computer Art,"
    Leonardo **20**, No. 4, 335 (1987).
—, Letters (Computers, Music and the Moving Image; Theo
    Goldberg, Günther Schrack, Edward Zajec), *Leonardo* **19**,
    No. 4, 356 (1986).
—, "The New Visual Age: The Influence of Computer Graph-
    ics on Art and Society," *Leonardo* **18**, No. 2, 105 (1985).
—, Comments on "Aesthetically Satisfying Order in the
    Arts," *Leonardo* **14**, No. 3, 233 (1981).
—, "A Cybernetic Approach to Aesthetics," *Leonardo* **10**, No.
    3, 203 (1977).
—, Some Remarks on "Visual Fine Art in the Age of
    Advanced Technology," *Leonardo* **8**, No. 2, 153 (1975).
—, "On Producing Graded Black and White or Color Com-
    puter Graphics in Combination with a Photographic
    Technique," *Leonardo* **7**, No. 4, 333 (1974).
—, "Computers and Visual Art," *Leonardo* **4**, No. 4, 331
    (1971).
See Also:
Dietrich, Frank, Visual Intelligence: The First Decade of
    Computer Art (19865-1975), *Leonardo* **19**, No. 2, 159
    (1986).

Stanley Gedzelman

EAS Department
City College of New York
New York, NY 10031 USA

Weather in Art
    Atmospheric Optics
    Meteorology
    Clouds

Gedzelman, Stanley, "Weather Forecasts in Art," *Leonardo*
    24, No. 4, 441-452 (1991).
—, "The Meteorological Odyssey of Vincent van Gogh,"
    Leonardo **23**, No. 1, 107-116 (1990).

Dan George

195 N. 5th Street
Brooklyn, NY 11211 USA
(718) 387-5428

Movement in Sculpture
Light in Sculpture
Public Art Installations
Social Responsibility and Art
The Visual in all Art Forms
The Artist, Science and Technology

George, Dan, "Sculpture 'Approaching the Speed of Light':
    The Use of Time as the Fourth Dimension," *Leonardo* **19**,
    No. 2, 117 (1986).

George Gessert

1230 W. Broadway
Eugene, OR 94702 USA
Tel: (503) 343-2920

Nuclear Devices as Unrecognized Monuments

The Area of Overlap Between Art and Genetics
Gessert, George. See Leonardo Award Winners Bibliography.

Elizabeth Goldring

Center for Advanced Visual Studies - MIT
40 Massachusetts Avenue
Cambridge, MA 02139 USA

Sky Art
Art and Technology
Center for Advanced Visual Studies at MIT
Poems and Eye Journals
Visualization of Vision Loss
Interactive Exhibitions

Goldring, Elizabeth, "*Desert Sun/Desert Moon* and the SKY ART Manifesto," *Leonardo* **20**, No. 4, 339 (1987).
See Also:
Piene, Otto and R. Russett, "Sky, Scale and Technology in Art," *Leonardo* **19**, No. 3, 193 (1986).

Daniel Goode

167 Spring Street #5W
New York, NY 10012 USA
Tel: (212) 925-6684

"Clarinet Songs": Microtonal Pieces and Extended Techniques as Found Sonic Objects
The Edge of Intelligibility: How to Speak Musical Thoughts
The Conservatism of Music: by Nature or by Culture?

Goode, Daniel, "From Notebooks #2," *Leonardo Music Journal* **1**, No. 1, 45-50 (1991).

Noel Gray

University of Sydney
Box 201 Holme Building A09
Sydney 2006 Australia
Tel: 2 692-0117

Philosophy of Geometry
The Mathematization of the Aesthetic: Theorizing Virtual Reality
The Kaleidoscope and the Desire for Chaos: Metaphor, Geometry and the Image
The Value of an Image: Semiotics of Paper Money, Geometric Processes and the Construction of Meaning
Fractured Futures (How the Future is Thought in Contemporary Science with Regard to the Subject and Time)
On the Wings of a Butterfly: Fractal Geometry and Critical Visual Practice

Gray, Noel, "Laughter in the Ruins: The Kaleidoscope as a Problematic—Theoretical and Visual Excess in Cultural Theory, Science and Language Theory," *Leonardo* **24**, No. 5, 621 (1992).
—, "Critique and a Science for the Sake of Art: Fractals and the Visual Arts," *Leonardo* **24**, No. 3, 317-320 (1991).

Samia Halaby

103 Franklin Street
New York, NY 10013 USA

The Development of Spatial Illusion in the History of Pictures
The Historic Steps to Abstraction and Their Revolutionary Basis
The Formal Distinctions Between the Great Paintings of the Renaissance and Modern Abstraction: the pictorial illusion of three-dimensional space as compared with that of four-dimensional abstract space
Painting in Oil and Computer Media

Halaby, Samia, Comments on "Reflecting Reality in Abstract Picturing," Leonardo **21**, No. 2, 226-227 (1988).
—, "Reflecting Reality in Abstract Picturing," *Leonardo* **20**, No. 3, 241 (1987).

David Hall

8118 Vincent Avenue S.
Bloomington, MN 55431 USA
Tel: (612) 881-5758

Pyrotechnics in 20th Century Performance Art

Hall, David, "Reviving a Forgotten Pyrotechnical Art Form: Pyrotechnics and Twentieth-Century Performance Art," *Leonardo* **24**, No. 5, 531-534 (1992).

Florence Hetzler

Chateau Rochambeau Apt. 6L
Scarsdale, NY 10583 USA

Art as Complementary to Philosophy
Art as Philosophy and More Than Philosophy
The Art of Constantin Brancusi
Ruins as Works of Art

Hetzler, Florence, "Causality: Ruin Time and Ruins," *Leonardo* **21**, No. 1, 51-55 (1988).
—, Review of "Kettle's Yard: A Way of Life," Jim Ede, *Leonardo* **17**, No. 4, 304 (1984).
—, "Art, Science, and Peace: The Proposed 'World Man Center' Project on Cyprus," *Leonardo* **17**, No. 2, 100 (1984).

Mae-Wan Ho

Biology Department
Walton Hall
Milton, Keynes MK7 6AA United Kingdom

Towards an Indigenous Western Science
Reality and Creativity in Science and Art
The New Science of Coherence and Its Implications for Society
Natural Being and Coherent Society

Ho, Mae-Wan, "Reanimating Nature: The Integration of Science with Human Experience," *Leonardo* **24**, No. 5, 607-616 (1991).

P.K. Hoenich

4 Achad Haam Street
Haifa, 33103 Israel

Sun Art—Robot Art

Hoenich, P. K., Letter about "Solar Powered Kinetic Sculpture," Andrew Stonyer et al., *Leonardo* **19**, No. 3, 272 (1986).

—, "Sun Art: Kinetic and Static Pictures Created with Sunrays," *Leonardo* **19**, No. 2, 123 (1986).

—, Review of *Readings from 'Scientific American': (1) Light and Its Uses: Making and Using Lasers, Holograms, Interferometers, and Instruments of Dispersion,* introduction by Jearl Walker; (2) *Light from the Sky,* introduction by Jearl Walker, *Leonardo* **15**, No. 4, 321 (1982).

—, "'Light Symphony, No. 1': A Kinetic Pictorial Artwork with Light," *Leonardo* **14**, No. 1, 38 (1981).

—, "An Op Art Picture on Contiguous Double-Curved Minimal Surfaces," *Leonardo* **4**, No. 1, 23 (1971).

—, Letter about "Art, Science, Technology," L. Alcopley, *Leonardo* **2**, No. 3, 328 (1969).

—, "Kinetic Art with Sunlight: Reflections on Developments in Art Needed Today," *Leonardo* **1**, No. 2, 113 (1968).

Yongping Huang

#11 Dazhong Way
Xiamen, Fujian China

The Theory and Experiment of a Turntable - Nonexpressive Art

Huang, Yongping, "Painting with Industrial Technology: Looking for New Substitutions," *Leonardo* **18**, No. 2, 91 (1985).

Tom Klinkowstein

101 Thompson Street #34
New York, NY 10012 USA
Tel: (212) 925-8213

Issues in Design and Technology
Art and Telecommunications

Klinkowstein, Tom, "Portraying Suburban America in a Global Context Using Telecommunications," *Leonardo* **19**, No. 2, 107 (1986).

Ronald P. Kostyniuk

University of Calgary
Art Department
Calgary, Alberta T3A OV2 Canada
Tel: (403) 286-1283
Fax: (403) 282-6925

The Evolution of the Constructed Relief, 1913-1988: Polychromed Constructions from Acrylic Sheet

Kostyniuk, Ron, "Polychrome Relief Constructions from Acrylic Sheet," *Leonardo* **19**, No. 4, 297 (1986).

—, "Electric Light Audio-Kinetic Artworks: 'Ecological Biomes'," *Leonardo* **12**, No. 1, 45 (1979).

Myron Krueger

Artificial Reality Corp.
P.O. Box 786
Vernon, CT 06066 USA

Artificial Reality

Krueger, Myron, "VIDEOPLACE: A Report from the ARTIFICIAL REALITY Laboratory," *Leonardo* **18**, No. 3, 145 (1985).

Craig Latta

2511 Derby Street
Berkeley, CA 94705 USA
Email: latta@xcf.berkeley.edu

Worldwide Networked Music Collaboration,
Performance and Distribution
Other Art Forms in a Distributed Context
Linking the Global Creative Communities

Latta, Craig, "Notes on the NetJam Project," *Leonardo Music Journal* **1**, No. 1, 103 (1991).

Luigi Lentini

VR Dimension
c/o Barbara Sullivan
412 South Country Hill Road
Anaheim Hills, CA 92808 USA
Tel: (714) 281-1645
Fax: (714) 921-9327

Perception and Representation of Space between
Reality and Virtual Reality

Lentini, Luigi, "Private Worlds and the Technology of the Imaginary: Effects of Science and Technology on Human Representations and Self-Conceptions," *Leonardo* **24**, No. 3, 333-340 (1991).

Arthur Loeb

Computer Center
Harvard University
Cambridge, MA 02138 USA
Tel: (617) 495-1950

Structures in Art and Science

M.C. Escher

David Drakking

Art History Review

Loeb, Arthur L., Letter, Response to David R. Topper, *Leonardo* **24**, No. 5, 635 (1991).

—, "Behaviorism, Causality and Cybernetics," *Leonardo* **24**, No. 3, 299-302 (1991).

—, Comments on "Symmetry and the Organization of Form," Rudolf Arnheim, *Leonardo* **22**, No. 2, 281-282 (1989).

—, "Symmetry of Structure: An Interdisciplinary Symposium, 13-19 August 1989," *Leonardo* **20**, No. 2/3, 321-322 (1990).

—, Review of *Synergetics Dictionary,* E.J. Applewhite, *Leonardo* **20**, No. 1, 98 (1987).

—, Letter, Linda Dalrymple Henderson, *Leonardo* **19**, No. 2, 155 (1986).

—, "Art, Science and History: On Linda Henderson's 'The Fourth Dimension and Non-Euclidean Geometry in Modern Art'," *Leonardo* **18**, No. 3, 193 (1985).

—, "On My Meetings and Correspondence between 1960 and 1971 with the Graphic Artist M.C. Escher," *Leonardo* **15**, No. 1, 23 (1982).

—, Review of *Dots and Lines*, Richard J. Trudeau, *Leonardo* **13**, No. 4, 333 (1980).

—, "Statements on the Relationships between the Natural Sciences and the Visual Fine Arts and, in Particular, On the Meaning of Order; Part 3; Some Personal Recollections of M.C. Escher," *Leonardo* **14**, No. 4, 311 (1981).

—, Comments on *Fundamental Structure: Nature's Architecture*, David L. Drabkin, *Leonardo* **10**, No. 4, 313 (1977).

—, "Structure and Patterns in Science and Art," *Leonardo* **4**, No. 4, 339 (1971).

See Also:

Danto, Arthur, Letter, Linda Dalrymple Henderson, *Leonardo* **19**, No. 2, 157 (1986).

Edgerton, Samuel Jr., Letter, Linda Dalrymple Henderson, *Leonardo* **19**, No. 2, 157 (1986).

Emmer, Michele, Comments on A.L. Loeb's "Correspondence with the Graphic Artist M.C. Escher," *Leonardo* **17**, No. 3, 200 (1984).

Judy Malloy

Box 2340, 2140 Shattuck
Berkeley, CA 94704 USA
Fax: (415) 431-5737
Email: jmalloy@well.sf.ca.us
jmalloy@garnet.berkeley.edu

Information Art
    Electronic Literature and Publishing
    Art and Telecommunications
    Artists' Books

Malloy, Judy, "Uncle Roger, an Online Narrabase," *Leonardo* **24**, No. 2, 195-202 (1991).

—, "OK Research, OK Genetic Engineering, Bad Information: Information Art Describes Technology," *Leonardo* **21**, No. 4, 371-376 (1988).

Steve Mann

Massachusetts Institute of Technology
Media Laboratory Room 325
20 Ames Street
Cambridge, MA 02139 USA
Tel: (617) 253-0314
Fax: (617) 258-6264
Email: steve@media.mit.edu

Radar or Sonar as an Art Form

Doppler Fields

Physics as Art

Structured Video (A Mixing of Graphics, Image Processing, Machine Visions and Art)

Wavelets and Chirplets: New Time Frequency Perspectives

Mann, Steve, "DopplerDanse: Some Novel Applications of Radar," *Leonardo* **25**, No. 1, 91-92 (1992).

—, "DopplerDen," in Words on Works, *Leonardo* **24**, No. 4, 487 (1991).

Benoit Maubrey

Die Audio Gruppe
Schul Strasse 35
1000 Berlin 65 Germany
Tel: 49 30 462-2954

Maubrey, Benoit, "Speakers' Corners," in Words on Works, *Leonardo* **24**, No. 1, 87 (1991).

Bruce Mazlish

11 Lowell Street
Cambridge, MA 02138 USA

The Idea of Progress, Revisited

The Frankenstein Syndrome (on Technology and Culture)

The Culture of Capitalism

A Triptych: Freud's Dream, Rider Haggard's "She", and Bulwer-Lytton's "The Coming Race"

The American Psyche

Mazlish, Bruce, "The Three and a Half Cultures," *Leonardo* **18**, No. 4, 233 (1985).

Harold McWhinnie

10111 Frederick Avenue
Kensington, MD 20895 USA

Dynamic Symmetry in Art and Design: Ideas of Jay Hambidge and Denman Ross

Spatial Abilities of Fine Arts Students

Use of Computers for Aesthetic Analysis

Aesthetic Concerns for Computer Revolution

McWhinnie, Harold, "Denman Ross: An Early Theory of Perceptual Correspondences of Sound and Visual Qualities," *Leonardo* **23**, No. 4, 444-445 (1990).

—, "The Use of Computers in the Arts: Simulation versus Abstraction," *Leonardo* **22**, No. 2, 167-170 (1989).

—, "A Biological Basis for the Golden Section in Art and Design," *Leonardo* **22**, No. 1, 61-64 (1989).

—, "Image Processing," *Leonardo Supplemental Issue on Electronic Art* (1988) pp. 119-120.

—, Commentary "An Electronic Museum?," *Leonardo* **21**, No. 2, 227 (1988).

—, Comments on "Photographic and Electronically Generated Images," *Leonardo* **21**, No. 1, 109 (1988).

—, Letter about "Evolution of Italian Painting," Colin Martindale, *Leonardo* **20**, No. 2, 211 (1987).

—, "A Review of the Use of Symmetry, the Golden Section and Dynamic Symmetry in Contemporary Art," *Leonardo* **19**, No. 3, 241 (1986).

William Melin

Lafayette College
Music Department.
Easton, PA 18042 USA

Photography and the Recording Process

Melin, William, "Photography and the Recording Process in the Age of Mechanical Reproduction," *Leonardo* **19**, No. 1, 53 (1986).

Susan Metros

University of Tennessee
Art Department
1715 Volunteer Boulevard
Knoxville, TN 37996-2410 USA
Tel: (615) 974-3208
Fax: (615) 974-3198
Email: metros@utkvx1.utk.edu

Computer-Enhanced Design

*Process = Product: An Equation for Computer-
Enhanced Creative Problem Solving*

Integrating Computers in Design Environments

*Integrating New Technology into Traditional
Education Models*

*Interactive Multimedia - the Graphic Designer's
Perspective*

Visual Attributes of Screen Design

Metros, Susan, Letter about "Electronic Thinking Cap," C.M.
Clark, *Leonardo* **19**, No. 1, 92 (1986).
—, "Electronic Thinking Cap: Microcomputer-Enhanced Cre-
ative Problem-Solving," *Leonardo* **18**, No. 2, 100 (1985).
See Also:
Clark, Christopher, Letter, *Leonardo* **19**, No. 1, 92 (1986).

Shunsuke Mitamura

Institute of Art and Design
University of Tsukuba
1-Tennodai
Tsukuba, Ibaraki 305 Japan
Tel: 81 298 53-2833
Fax: 81 298 53-6508

*High-Technology Art Activity in The School of Art and
Design, University of Tsukuba*

Mitamura, Shunsuke, "Holographic Holography," *Leonardo*
22, No. 3/4, 337-340 (1989).

Mit Mitropoulos

11 Elpidos Street
Athens 10 Greece

Mitropoulos, Mit, "The *Line of the Horizon* Fax Project: An
Example of Geopolitical Art," *Leonardo* **25**, No. 2, 135-
142 (1992).
—, "A Sequence of Video-to Video Installations Illustrating
the Together/Separate Principle, with Reference to Two-
Way Interactive Cable TV Systems," *Leonardo* **24**, No. 2,
207-212 (1991).
—, "Exploring the 'Found': A Communications Approach to
Art and Architecture," *Leonardo* **19**, No. 1, 31 (1986).

Michael Moose

3423 Manor Hill Drive
Cincinnati, OH 45270 USA

Guidelines for Constructing "Fisheye" Perspective

Moose, Michael, "Guidelines for Constructing a Fisheye Per-
spective," *Leonardo* **19**, No. 1, 61 (1986).
See Also:
Casas, Fernando, Letter, Michael Moore, *Leonardo* **19** (1986).

Robert Morgan

Rochester Institute of Technology
CIAS
1 Lomb Memorial Dr.
Rochester, NY 14623 USA
Tel: (716) 475-2674
Fax: (716) 475-6447

The New Media Arts—How Are We Communicating?

The Investment Power of Amnesia

The Catalog as a Distancing Apparatus

Morgan, Robert, "The Exhibition Catalog as a Distancing
Apparatus: Current Tendencies in the Promotion of Exhi-
bition Documents," *Leonardo* **24**, No. 3, 341-344 (1991).
—, Letter about "Computer-Aided Images," B. McCormick,
Leonardo **17**, No. 3, 225 (1984).
—, "Waterfields: Conceptual Water Drawings," *Leonardo* **17**,
No. 2, 71 (1984).
—, "Report on the Satellite Telecast Performance 'Double
Entendre' Produced by Douglas Davis," *Leonardo* **15**, No.
2, 129 (1982).
—, Letter, Appreciation of Dr. Frank J. Malina, *Leonardo* **15**,
No. 4, 334 (1982).

Rod Murray

Rose Farm
57 Moss Lane
Burscough, Lancashire, United Kingdom

Holography at the Royal College of Art in London

*Setting Up a Studio at Home and Making the Table
and Equipment*

Murray, Rod, "Holography Course, Royal College of Art,"
Leonardo **24**, No. 4, 481 (1991).
—, "Ratio-Light Meter for Holography," *Leonardo* **22**, No. 3/
4, 415 (1989).

Leo Narodny

Barbados Optics Ltd
Martins Bay
St. John, Barbados West Indies

The Time Dimension

Narodny, Leo, "A Quantum Mechanical Interpretation of
Observation," *Leonardo* **24**, No. 5, 581-582 (1991.
—, Review of *The Character of Physical Law*, Richard Feyn-
man, *Leonardo* **24**, No. 4, 493 (1991).
—, Review of *QED: The Strange Theory of Light and Matter*,
Richard Feynman, *Leonardo* **24**, No. 4, 493 (1991).
—, Review of *Ecological Communication*, Niklas Luhmann,
Leonardo **24**, No. 3, 364-365 (1991).
—, Review of *The Golden Relationship: Book 1, Universal Pat-
terns*, Martha Boles and Rochele Newman, *Leonardo* **24**,
No. 3, 365 (1991).
—, Review of *The Forms of Color*, Karl Gerstner, *Leonardo*
23, No. 4, 449-450 (1990).
—, Review of *Science, Order, and Creativity*, David Bohm and
F. David Peat, *Leonardo* **23**, No. 1, 149-150 (1990).
—, Review of *Meaning and Interpretation*, Charles Travis,
ed., *Leonardo* **22**, No. 1, 121 (1989).
—, Review of *Making Color Sing*, Jeanne Dobie, *Leonardo* **22**,
No. 1, 121-122 (1989).
—, Review of *Solid Cues*, Gerald Feinberg, *Leonardo* **20**, No.
2, 199 (1987).

—, Review of *Origins of Materials and Process*, John Delmonte, *Leonardo* **20**, No. 1, 100 (1987).

Mary Carroll Nelson

1408 Georgia NE
Albuquerque, NM 87110 USA

Layering: Approaching the 'Layer' as a Formal Element and as a Significant Metaphor in Artmaking

Nelson, Mary Carroll, "Layering: Approaching the 'Layer' As a Formal Element and a Significant Metaphor in Artmaking," *Leonardo* **19**, No. 3, 223 (1986).

Ed Osborn

P.O. Box 9121
Oakland, CA 94613 USA
Tel: (510) 763-9506
Email: edo@well.sf.ca.us

Sound Art
  Music Composition
  Sound Intelligence

Osborn, Ed, "Local Conditions and Perceptual Concerns: Notes on Several Sound Works," *Leonardo Music Journal* **1**, (1991), p. 89.

Nancy Paterson

475 The West Mall, #1513
Etobicoke, Ontario M9C 4Z3 Canada
Tel: (416) 621-3290
Fax: (416) 365-3332

Lust and Wanderlust: Sex and Tourism in a Virtual World
Feminist Aesthetics in the Age of Technological Utopianism: The Lady Luddites?

Paterson, Nancy, "Bicycle TV: Expo '92 Installation," *Leonardo* **25**, No. 2, 163-166 (1992).
—, "Bicycle TV: Some Interactive Exercise," in Words on Works, *Leonardo* **24**, No. 4, 488 (1991).
—, "Hair Salon T.V.: A Computer-Controlled Video Installation," *Leonardo* **24**, No. 1, 15-18 (1991).
—, "Wringer/Washer TV," in Words on Works, *Leonardo* **24**, No. 1, 89 (1991).

Larry Polansky

Frog Peak Music
P.O. Box 5036
Hanover, NH 03755 USA
Tel: (603) 448-1902
Email: larry.polansky@dartmouth.edu

Computer Music
Music and Technology
Artificial Intelligence and Music
Theory of Form: Composition

Polansky, Larry, "Al Het", in Interaction—New Music for Gamelan, *Leonardo Music Journal* CD Series, Volume **2** (1992).
—, "The Future of Music/The Future of Leonardo," *Leonardo Music Journal* **1**, No. 1, 1 (1991).
—, "17 Gloomy Sentences (and Commentary) at the Turn of the Millennium (in the Form of an Editorial)," *Leonardo Music Journal* **1**, No. 1, 17 (1991).
—, Review of *20th Century Microtonal Notation*, Gardner Read, *Leonardo Music Journal* **1**, No. 1, 108 (1991).
—, Review of *Electronic Cottage: International Magazine*, Hal McGee, ed., *Leonardo Music Journal* **1**, No. 1, 115 (1991).
—, Review of *Ruth Crawford Seeger: Memoirs, Memories, Music*, Matilda Guame, *Leonardo* **24**, No. 3 293-298 (1991).
—, Review of "The Sackbut Blues," Gale Young, *Leonardo* **24**, No. 1, 98 (1991).
Polansky, Larry and A. Feldman, "Collaboration: Tap Scored and Notes on the 'Three Monk Tunes' for Tap Dancer," *Leonardo* **23**, No. 4, 377-384 (1990).
Polansky, Larry, Review of *Arts/Sciences: Alloys* by Iannis Xenakis, *Leonardo* **23**, No. 4, 385-388 (1990).
—, Review of *On the Wires of Our Nerves: The Art of Electroacoustic Music*, Robin Julian Heifetz, ed., *Leonardo* **23**, No. 4, 451-452 (1990).
Polansky, Larry, R. Malina and E. Mazer, "Sounds, Musics and *Leonardo*," *Leonardo* **23**, No. 1, 1-2 (1990).
Polansky, Larry, Review of *The Music of Ben Johnston*, Heidi Von Gunden, *Leonardo* **23**, No. 1, 67-70 (1990).
—, "The Future of Music," *Leonardo* **20**, No. 4, 363 (1987).
—, "The Mills College Center for Contemporary Music's Seminar in the Formal Methods Series: A Documentary Survey," *Leonardo* **20**, No. 2, 155 (1987).
—, Letter about "Theoretical Perspectives on the Arts, Sciences and Technology," David Carrier, *Leonardo* **19**, No. 2, 181 (1986).

Ernst Pöppel

Inst. of Medical Psychology
Goethestr 31/1
8000 Munich, Germany

The Measurement of Music and the Cerebral Clock: A New Theory

Pöppel, Ernst, "The Measurement of Music and the Cerebral Clock: A New Theory," *Leonardo* **22**, No. 1, 83-90 (1989).

Long Quan

Fine Arts Institute of Sichuan Province
Chongqing, P. R. 630053 China

"My Painting and My Dream"—a Young Chinese Professional Painter's Pursuit of the Essence of Art and Its Style Under the Development of Modern Art in China

Quan, Long, "My Painting and My Dream," *Leonardo* **22**, No. 2, 165-166 (1989).

Mark Rais

Kentmanni 10-16
Tallinn EE0001 Estonia
Tel: 7-0142 684305

Sound, Space-Time and Computer Music
Electronic and Computer Music in Estonia

Rais, Mark, "Jaan Soonvald and His Musical System," *Leonardo Music Journal* **2**, No. 1, 45 (1992).
—, "The First Estonian Dance Theatre," in Gateway Section, *Leonardo* **25**, No. 2, 111-112 (1992).
—, "Some Notes about Soviet Computer Music," *Leonardo* **24**, No. 5, 535-540 (1991).

—, "Computer Music Association of the USSR," in Gateway Section, *Leonardo* **24**, No. 4, 379-340 (1991).

Sonya Rapoport
6 Hillcrest Court
Berkeley, CA 94705 USA
Tel: (510) 658-4741
Fax: (510) 642-0336
Email: actize@garnet.berkeley.edu

Interactive Installations Using Art and Technology
Incentives for Using the Computer in Art
On Becoming an Interactive Artist
Digital Dancing
Rapoport, Sonya, "The Animated Soul-Gateway to Your Ka," in Words on Works, *Leonardo* **25**, No. 2, 218-219 (1992).
—, "Process(ing) Interactive Art: Using People as Paint, Computer as Brush and Installation Site as Canvas," *Leonardo* **24**, No. 3, 285-288 (1991).
—, "From Osiris to Sinai," in Words on Works, *Leonardo* **24**, No. 1, 89-90 (1991).

Matts Roos
Physics Dept.
Siltavuorenpenger 20C
SF-00170 Helsinki Finland

Physics Semiotics
 Contemporary Abstract Painting with Pictorial Elements from Physics
Roos, Matts, "Two Observations," *Leonardo* **25**, No. 1, 89 (1992).

Paul Ryan
Video Department
Savannah College of Art and Design
201 W. Charlton Street
P.O. Box 3146
Savannah, GA 31402-3146 USA
Tel: (912) 238-2407
Fax: (912) 238-2428

Cybernetics/Semiotics/Media
Earthscore Method of Producing Videotape Interpretations of Ecological Systems
Design for Television Channel Dedicated to Ecology
The Art of Triadic Behaviors
Ryan, Paul, "The Earthscore Notational System for Orchestrating Perceptual Consensus about the Natural World," *Leonardo* **24**, No. 4, 457-466 (1991).
—, "A Genealogy of Video," *Leonardo* **21**, No. 1, 39-44 (1988).

Charles Shapiro
San Francisco State University
Department of Physics
1600 Holloway Avenue
San Francisco, CA 94132 USA

On the Relationship Between Art and Science
 Disciplinary Interdependencies
 Jacob Bronowski: Philosopher and Scientist
 Radioactivity: The Affects of Nuclear Accidents and Nuclear War
Shapiro, Charles, "Jacob Brownowski: A Retrospective," *Leonardo* **18**, No. 4, 219 (1985).

Lance Speer
60 Shepard Street
Rochester, NY 14620 USA

Before Holography: A Call for Visual Literacy
Speer, Lance, "Before Holography: A Call for Visual Literacy," *Leonardo* **22**, No. 3/4, 299-306 (1989).

Stephen s'Soreff
349 Three Mile Harbor Road
Easthampton, NY 11937 USA

Art—Tomorrow
s'Soreff, Stephen, "The Malleable Memory of Avant Garde Art Review (AGAR): A Post-Conceptual Artwork," *Leonardo* **20**, No. 4, 387 (1987).

Suzanne St. Cyr
1240 N. Ventura Avenue
Ventura, CA 93001 USA

Alignment - Treading on the Tail of the Tiger
St. Cyr, Suzanne and S. Weber, "Treading on the Tail of the Tiger: A Collaborative Effort in Large-Format Holography," *Leonardo* **22**, No. 3/4, 357-364 (1989).

Christa Sütterlin
Forschungstelle fur Human
Max-Plank-Gessellschaft von
Der Tann Str 7
D-8138 Andechs, Germany

Universals in Apotropaic Symbolism
Sütterlin, Christa, "Universals in Apotropaic Symbolism: A Behavioral and Comparative Approach to Some Medieval Sculptures," *Leonardo* **22**, No. 1, 65-74 (1989).

Dick Termes
Rt. 2 Box 435B
Spearfish, SD 57783 USA
Tel: (605) 642-4805

Slide Lecture: Twenty Plus Years of Using a Six Point Perspective and the Spherical Canvas to Express Total Environments.
Termes, Dick, "Six-Point Perspective on the Sphere: The Termesphere," *Leonardo* **24**, No. 3, 289-292 (1991).

Mark Trayle
P.O. Box 192014
San Francisco, CA 94119 USA
Email: met@well.sf.ca.us

Trayle, Mark, "Nature, Networks, Chamber Music," *Leonardo Music Journal* **1**, No. 1, 51-54 (1991).

Doris Vila

157 E. 33 Street
New York, NY 10016 USA

Holography as a Medium for Creative Expression
Architectural Applications of Holography
Light and Sculptural Installations
Vila, Doris, "Chasing Rainbows: One Holographer's
    Approach," *Leonardo* **22**, No. 3/4, 345-348 (1989).

Eugene Wachspress

1366 Orleans Drive
Knoxville, TN 37919 USA

Mathematical Basis for Design of "Polypol" Sculpture
Wachspress, Eugene, "The Rise of the Polypol Sculpture,"
    Leonardo **24**, No. 5, 525-530 (1991).

Sally Weber

1405 Callens Road
Ventura, CA 93003 USA

Art and Holography
Redirection of Light/Color/Sunlight into Architectural
    Environments
Public Art Using Holography
Light as a Mythic Metaphor in Art
Weber, Sally and S. St. Cyr, "Treading on the Tail of the
    Tiger: A Collaborative Effort in Large- Format Hologra-
    phy," *Leonardo* **22**, No. 3/4, 357-364 (1989).

Steve Wixson

University of Alabama - Birmingham
UAB Station - 420 CHSB
Birmingham, AL 35294 USA

True 3D Stereoscopic Displays: Are They for Real This
    Time?

Julie Wosk

Dept. of Humanities
State University of New York, Fort Schuyler
Bronx, NY 10465 USA

The Explosive Presence: Images of Technology in Art
Wosk, Julie, "P.U.L.S.E. Exhibit, 1987," *Leonardo* **21**, No. 3,
    318-319 (1988).
—, "The Impact of Technology on the Human Image in Art,"
    Leonardo **19**, No. 2, 145 (1986).

Horatio Zabala

10 av. du Mail
8 eme - 82
1205 Geneva, Switzerland

Theoretical Perspectives Behind the Production of Art
Relationships Between the Terms "Original" and
    "Duplicate"
Language and Image
The Massive Diffusion of Innumerable Identical Copies
The Presence of the Original

The Concept of Authenticity, Truth and Falsity.
Zabala, Horacio, "The Image of Duplication," *Leonardo* **25**,
    No. 1, 47-50 (1992).

Edward Zajec

Syracuse University
Art Media Studies Department
102 Shaffer Art Building
Syracuse, NY 13244 USA
Tel: (315) 443-1033
Email: ezajec@sunrise.acs.syr.edu

Color and Time: Digital Techniques and Aesthetic
    Principles
Computer Graphic and the Shaping of Time with
    Color (Orphics)
Zajec, Edward, "Orphics: Computer Graphics and the Shap-
    ing of Time with Color," *Leonardo* **21**, *Supplemental Issue*
    on Electronic Art, 111-116 (1988).
See Also:
    Dietrich, Frank, "Visual Intelligence: The First Decade of
    Computer Art (1965-1975)," *Leonardo* **19**, No. 2, 159
    (1986).
    Franke, Herbert, Letter, Edward Zajec, *Leonardo* **19**, No.
    4, 355 (1986).

Peter Zec

Lerchenstr. 142 a
D-4500 Osnabruck, Germany

The Aesthetic Message of Holography
Zec, Peter, "The Aesthetic Message of Holography," *Leonardo*
    22, No. 3/4, 425-430 (1989).

Opy Zouni

Vrilission 22
GR-152 36 P. Pendeli, Greece
Tel: 1/8042950

The Geometrical Structure of the Space in My Work in
    Relation to the Color, Perspective, Symmetry in
    Nature, Ecology and My Personal Aspect for the
    Contemporary Landscape
Zouni, Opy, "Space Through Colour and Illusion," *Leonardo*
    18, No. 2, 96 (1985).
See also:
    Savopoulos, Harris, Letter, Opy Zouni, *Leonardo* **19**, No.
    4, 359 (1986).

DISCIPLINES, ACTIVITIES AND RESOURCES

The goal of this chapter is to facilitate human interaction and the exchange of knowledge by providing relevant information which could effectively improve regional and international communication networks among individuals and organizations. Discipline, Activity and Resource tables identify the nature and orientation of work taking place around the world, and technological resources employed to carry out the work. These tables reveal opportunities for collaboration which would facilitate completion of existing projects and development of new projects. This process maximizes human and technological resources, and minimizes duplication of work.

Information was solicited from several sources, including 550 organizations originally in the *Leonardo FAST* Database; approximately 2000 institutional and individual subscribers to the journal *Leonardo* and members of International Society for the Arts, Sciences and Technology; over 600 subscribers to *Leonardo Electronic News*; and nearly 300 members of YLEM/Artists Using Science & Technology. Surveys were also distributed at the 1992 International Computer Music Conference, and at the 1992 CyberArts International Conference and Exposition. The total solicitation exceeded 3500 organizations and individuals in over 50 countries. Response to the solicitation was high and detailed. About 300 people returned completed surveys, with approximately one third providing information for both organizations and individuals. Approximately 250 additional organizations were categorized according to supplementary information received at the Leonardo/ISAST office, either as a result of the survey, or during the course of performing its daily operations. Where possible, noticeable gaps were enhanced through additional inquiries, with the constraint that the nature of the content necessitates timely publication. 560 organizations and 260 individuals in 28 countries have been selected for representation in the directory.

Both organizations and individuals were asked to specify primary disciplines and activities, and to clarify the nature of their work by identifying additional disciplines and activities which fall within their domain. The solicitation also sought information about technological resources, providing orientation with respect to the computer platforms used, and the functions the technology performs. The discipline categories reflect a mixture of traditional art disciplines with those which incorporate new technological resources. A broad spectrum is presented in the activity categories, reflecting many functions that organizations perform, and revealing the ways that individuals practice their disciplines. The technology section represents many contemporary computer platforms in use around the world. Selection of a primary discipline or activity was not intended to be a restrictive or arbitrary categorization. Most individuals and organizations are involved in several fields and provide a variety of services. At the same time, there is often a perspective which defines the approach brought to their work. Primary categories exist to provide insight into that perspective, where it applies. General discipline and activity categories exist for organizations and individuals that indicated that their focus did not place an emphasis on any particular discipline, and for those cases where insufficient information existed in order to categorize primary disciplines. Readers can glean the most information by perusing both organization and individual tables, viewing the information presented from a variety of perspectives.

The Disciplines, Activities and Resources (D/A/R) tables are presented by primary discipline, listing only those organizations and individuals whose main orientation is in each domain. Only the organization and full names have been used in the organization and individual tables, in order to display clusters of data in a way which could be assimilated at a glance. A directory of organizations and individuals follow each of the table sections, offering contact information. Full postal addresses, telephone and fax numbers, and electronic mail addresses are included in the directory. Contact names and positions have been included if the information was available. In some cases, only electronic mail addresses or telephone numbers were available, as was the case with the 3D Electronic BBS. The determining factor for including a listing was the availability of one secure vector to make a contact.

Future editions of the almanac will include additional scientific disciplines, and will delve deeper into aspects of technological function. Individuals and organizations are invited to provide current information about their work to be included in future editions of the *Leonardo Almanac*.

3-Dimensional Art

◆ = Primary Activity
✳ = Other Disciplines/Activities/Resources

Organization	Disciplines	Activities	Platforms
3D Book Productions	✳ Architecture; ✳ Ceramics; ✳ Environmental Art; ✳ Film; ✳ Holography; ✳ Graphic Design; ✳ Industrial Design; ✳ Installation Art; ✳ Photography; ✳ Sculpture	✳ Education; ✳ Museum; ◆ Publishing; ✳ Resource	✳ DOS/Intel
3D Electronic BBS		◆ Network Communication	
3D Foto World	✳ Photography	◆ Production	
3D International Newsletter		◆ Membership Organization	
International Stereoscopic Union		◆ Membership Organization	
National Stereoscopic Association		◆ Membership Organization	
Reel 3-D Enterprises		◆ Production	
Science-Art Research Centre	✳ Animation; ✳ Computer Graphics; ✳ Conceptual Art; ✳ Environmental Art; ✳ Holography; ✳ Robotics; ✳ Video; ✳ Virtual Reality	✳ Artist Residencies; ✳ Education; ✳ Fellowships; ◆ Gallery; ✳ Grants; ✳ Membership Organization; ✳ Publishing; ✳ Research & Development	✳ Amiga
Stereo Journal		◆ Publishing	
Stereo-Club Francais		◆ Membership Organization	
StereoScope International	✳ Animation; ✳ Computer Art; ✳ Computer Graphics; ✳ Conceptual Art; ✳ Environmental Art; ✳ Film; ✳ Holography; ✳ Graphic Design; ✳ Industrial Design; ✳ Installation Art; ✳ Interactive Art; ✳ Kinetic Art; ✳ Literary Arts; ✳ Mixed Media; ✳ Multimedia; ✳ Music and Sound; ✳ Photography; ✳ Robotics; ✳ Sculpture; ✳ Space Art; ✳ Telecommunications; ✳ Video; ✳ Virtual Reality	✳ Education; ◆ Membership Organization; ✳ Research & Development	✳ Amiga; ✳ DOS/Intel; ✳ Silicon Graphics
Stereoscopic Society		◆ Gallery; ✳ Membership Organization	
Third Dimension Arts, Inc.		◆ Publishing	
Third Dimension Society		◆ Membership Organization	

Animation

◆ = Primary Activity
✳ = Other Disciplines/Activities/Resources

Organization	Disciplines	Activities	Platforms
Ringling School of Art and Design, Computer Graphics	✳ Animation; ✳ Architecture; ✳ Computer Art; ✳ Computer Graphics; ✳ Film; ✳ Graphic Design; ✳ Video	◆ Education	✳ DOS/Intel; ✳ Macintosh; ✳ Silicon Graphics; ✳ Sun

Architecture

◆ = Primary Activity
✱ = Other Disciplines/Activities/Resources

Platforms

	Sun	Silicon Graphics	Next	Mainframe	Macintosh	Hewlett Packard	DOS/Intel	DEC	Atari	Amiga
Bureau of Architecture							✱			
Storefront for Art and Architecture										
VR Dimension							✱			

Activities

	Resource	Research & Development	Publishing	Production	Performance Space	Performance Group	Network Communication	Museum	Membership Organization	Library	Grants	Gallery	Festivals and Events	Fellowships	Education	Awards & Competitions	Artist Residencies
Bureau of Architecture	◆	✱	✱														
Storefront for Art and Architecture												◆					
VR Dimension	✱														✱		

Disciplines

(Architecture column shaded = primary discipline)

	Virtual Reality	Multimedia	Interactive Art	Installation Art	Holography	Graphic Design	Fiber Arts	Environmental Art	Computer Graphics
Bureau of Architecture				✱				✱	✱
Storefront for Art and Architecture									
VR Dimension	✱	✱	✱		✱	✱	✱		✱

Computer Art

◆ = Primary Activity
✱ = Other Disciplines/Activities/Resources

Platforms

	Sun	Silicon Graphics	Next	Mainframe	Macintosh	Hewlett Packard	DOS/Intel	DEC	Atari	Amiga
ACM Educators Newsletter, SIGGRAPH Educators Newsletter										
Abaci Gallery of Computer Art		✱			✱		✱			
Abby Joslin & Associates										
Allegheny College, Art Department										
American Journal of Computer Art in Education										
Antelope Valley College					✱					✱
Arizona State University										
Australian Network for Art and Technology (ANAT)										
Biennale des Arts Electroniques de Maiselle										
Blue Rose Studio										
California College of the Arts and Crafts, Computer Graphics Support										
Cariboo College, Digital Arts & Design										
Center for Computer Art and Technology										

Activities

	Resource	Research & Development	Publishing	Production	Performance Space	Performance Group	Network Communication	Museum	Membership Organization	Library	Grants	Gallery	Festivals and Events	Fellowships	Education	Awards & Competitions	Artist Residencies
ACM Educators Newsletter, SIGGRAPH Educators Newsletter			◆												✱		
Abaci Gallery of Computer Art												◆					
Abby Joslin & Associates														✱			
Allegheny College, Art Department															✱		
American Journal of Computer Art in Education			◆												✱		
Antelope Valley College															◆		
Arizona State University															◆		
Australian Network for Art and Technology (ANAT)	✱								◆		✱	◆	✱		✱		
Biennale des Arts Electroniques de Maiselle													◆				
Blue Rose Studio			✱									◆					
California College of the Arts and Crafts, Computer Graphics Support															✱		
Cariboo College, Digital Arts & Design		◆															
Center for Computer Art and Technology															◆		

Disciplines

(Computer Art column shaded = primary discipline)

	Virtual Reality	Video	Space Art	Performance Art	Music and Sound	Multimedia	Mixed Media	Graphic Design	Film	Environmental Art	Computer Graphics	Animation
ACM Educators Newsletter, SIGGRAPH Educators Newsletter												✱
Abaci Gallery of Computer Art	✱	✱	✱	✱	✱	✱	✱		✱		✱	
Abby Joslin & Associates												
Allegheny College, Art Department												
American Journal of Computer Art in Education												
Antelope Valley College								✱		✱		✱
Arizona State University												
Australian Network for Art and Technology (ANAT)												
Biennale des Arts Electroniques de Maiselle												
Blue Rose Studio												
California College of the Arts and Crafts, Computer Graphics Support		✱	✱					✱		✱		
Cariboo College, Digital Arts & Design												
Center for Computer Art and Technology												

128

Computer Art

◆ = Primary Activity
✳ = Other Disciplines/Activities/Resources

Columns are grouped as **DISCIPLINES** (3D Art … Visual Art), **ACTIVITIES** (Artist Residencies … Resource), and **PLATFORMS** (Amiga … Sun).

Organization	3D Art	Animation	Architecture	Ceramics	Computer Art	Computer Graphics	Conceptual Art	Copy Art	Dance	Environmental Art	Fiber Arts	Film	Graphic Design	Holography	Industrial Design	Installation Art	Interactive Art	Kinetic Art	Literary Arts	Mixed Media	Multimedia	Music and Sound	Painting	Performance Art	Photography	Robotics	Sculpture	Space Art	Telecommunications	Video	Virtual Reality	Visual Art	Artist Residencies	Awards & Competitions	Education	Fellowships	Festivals and Events	Gallery	Grants	Library	Membership Organization	Museum	Network Communication	Performance Group	Performance Space	Production	Publishing	Research & Development	Resource	Amiga	Atari	DEC	DOS/Intel	Hewlett Packard	Macintosh	Mainframe	Next	Silicon Graphics	Sun
Center for Structural Mechanics and Engineering, Technical University of Lisbon (CMEST)		✳																																	◆																								
Centre for Advanced Studies in Computer Aided Art and Design (CASCAAD), Middlesex University		✳	✳			✳																											✳		◆													✳							✳			✳	
Computer Art Contest																																		◆					✳																				
Computer Museum Boston																																										◆																	
Conceptual Design and Information Arts, San Francisco State University		✳				✳	✳						✳			✳	✳				✳	✳		✳	✳	✳				✳	✳				◆													✳							✳				
Creative Computer Exhibit, California Museum of Science and Industry																																										◆																	
Frachaos																																									◆																		
French National Institute for Research in Computer Science and Control (INRIA)																																																◆											
Galerie Eylau'5																																						◆																					
George Mason University, Art and Art History																																			◆																								
George Washington University, Fine Arts																																			◆																								
Glassboro State University, Art																																			◆																								
Institute for Computers in the Arts, School of Visual Arts																																			◆																								
Inter-Society for the Electronic Arts (ISEA)	✳	✳	✳			✳	✳		✳	✳	✳	✳	✳		✳	✳	✳	✳		✳	✳	✳		✳	✳		✳	✳	✳	✳	✳						◆				✳						✳						✳					
International Summerschool Computer and Art																																			◆													✳											
Kunsthochschule fur Medien																																			◆													◆											
Massachusetts College of Art																																			◆																								
Media Art Department, AKI Art Academy																														✳	✳				◆												✳												
Media Magic		✳				✳																																									◆						✳		✳				
Media, Electronic Art and Visual Communication Arts & Design, School of the Arts																																			◆																								
Mt. Hood Community College, Visual Art																																			◆																								
Museum Computer Network Spectra, Syracuse University, School of Infomation Studies																																										✳	✳															
Museum Computer Network																																								✳	✳	✳	✳															

129

Computer Art

◆ = Primary Activity
* = Other Disciplines/Activities/Resources

Organization	DISCIPLINES																																ACTIVITIES																	PLATFORMS									
	3D Art	Animation	Architecture	Ceramics	Computer Art	Computer Graphics	Conceptual Art	Copy Art	Dance	Environmental Art	Fiber Arts	Film	Graphic Design	Holography	Industrial Design	Installation	Interactive Art	Kinetic Art	Literary Arts	Mixed Media	Multimedia	Music and Sound	Painting	Performance Art	Photography	Robotics	Sculpture	Space Art	Telecommunications	Video	Virtual Reality	Visual Art	Artist Residencies	Awards & Competitions	Education	Fellowships	Festivals and Events	Gallery	Grants	Library	Membership Organization	Museum	Network Communication	Performance Group	Performance Space	Production	Publishing	Research & Development	Resource	Amiga	Atari	DEC	DOS/Intel	Hewlett Packard	Macintosh	Mainframe	Next	Silicon Graphics	Sun
Museum der Stadt Gladbeck		*											*	*		*	*			*	*		*	*	*	*	*			*	*				*			*				◆					*		*	*			*						
Nagano University, Department of Industrial Information																																																*							*				
Nicograph Association						*	*																																		◆																		
Northeastern Illinios University, Art Department						*																													◆																							
Northeastern University, Graphic Arts Program						*																													◆																							
Ohio State University, Advanced Computing Center for the Arts and Design																									*										◆																							
Ontario College of Art																																			◆																							
P/F Publishing BV																																															◆											
Panscan, Panpost																									*																		◆															
Porter Computer Arts		*																							*																					◆												
RISKART: The Jay Riskind Studio	*	*																																	◆			◆																				
Rutgers University, Art																*	*								*					*					*												◆												
Sarah Bendersky, Inc.	*	*																							*					*	*				*	*		*				*					◆						*		*				
School of the Art Institute of Chicago, Art and Technology Department	*	*														*	*	*		*	*	*				*				*					◆																		*		*			*	
Sheridan College, Computer Graphics Lab																																			◆												*												
Small Computers in the Arts																																			◆										◆													
St. Louis Community College - Florissant Valley																																			◆		◆																					
Sturvil Corporation																															*				◆													◆										
University of Colorado, Fine Arts Department													*																						◆																							
University of the Arts		*									*		*							*			*				*			*					◆																							
Videographic Arts		*																			*									*																												*
Visual Computer, University of Tokyo	*	*																																													◆	*										
William Patterson College, Art Department		*	*										*							*			*				*								◆													*		*			*		*			*	*
Young Electronic Arts, Atelier coArt																																									◆																		

Computer Graphics

◆ = Primary Activity

✱ = Other Disciplines/Activities/Resources

	DISCIPLINES																																ACTIVITIES																		PLATFORMS									
	3D Art	Animation	Architecture	Ceramics	Computer Art	Computer Graphics	Conceptual Art	Copy Art	Dance	Environmental Art	Fiber Arts	Film	Graphic Design	Holography	Industrial Design	Installation Art	Interactive Art	Kinetic Art	Literary Arts	Mixed Media	Multimedia	Music and Sound	Painting	Performance Art	Photography	Robotics	Sculpture	Space Art	Telecommunications	Video	Virtual Reality	Visual Art	Artist Residencies	Awards & Competitions	Education	Fellowships	Festivals and Events	Gallery	Grants	Library	Membership Organization	Museum	Network Communication	Performance Group	Performance Space	Production	Publishing	Research & Development	Resource	Amiga	Atari	DEC	DOS/Intel	Hewlett Packard	Macintosh	Mainframe	Next	Silicon Graphics	Sun
ACM SIGGRAPH	✱	✱	✱		✱											✱	✱				✱								✱		✱						✱				◆						✱													
Advanced Computing Center for Arts & Design, Ohio State University	✱	✱			✱				✱			✱	✱		✱		✱				✱	✱				✱				✱	✱	✱			◆												✱	✱		✱					✱			✱	✱
Ausgraph - Australasian Computer Graphics Association	✱	✱			✱																														◆						◆																		
Computer Arts Institute	✱	✱			✱								✱			✱	✱				✱		✱		✱			✱		✱			✱	✱	◆												✱						✱		✱				
Computer Graphics Arts Directory					✱																																										◆												
Computer Graphics Education Newsletter					✱																																										◆												
Computer Graphics Professional, Graphic Channels Inc.																																															◆												
Computer Graphics, Art Dept, Fine Arts Ctr, University of MA/Amherst																																			◆																								
Fashion Institute of Technology, Computer Graphics																																			◆																								
Graphic Arts Technical Foundation													✱																						◆																								
ICTV		✱			✱					✱			✱				✱				✱				✱					✱											◆					◆									✱				
Melbourne Computer Graphics Forum, Swinburne Institute																																																											
Pratt Institute, Computer Graphics	✱	✱	✱		✱							✱	✱		✱	✱	✱			✱	✱		✱		✱		✱		✱	✱	✱	✱	✱		◆	✱		✱									✱				✱	✱	✱	✱				✱	
Syracuse University, Art Media Studies	✱	✱	✱		✱											✱	✱				✱	✱								✱					◆	✱																	✱		✱			✱	✱
Technical and Educational Center of the Graphic Arts, Rochester Institute of Technology													✱																						◆																								

131

Copy Art

◆ = Primary Activity
✳ = Other Disciplines/Activities/Resources

Column groups: **DISCIPLINES** (3D Art, Animation, Architecture, Ceramics, Computer Art, Computer Graphics, Conceptual Art, Copy Art, Dance, Environmental Art, Fiber Arts, Film, Graphic Design, Holography, Industrial Design, Installation, Interactive Art, Kinetic Art, Literary Arts, Mixed Media, Multimedia, Music and Sound, Painting, Performance Art, Photography, Robotics, Sculpture, Space Art, Telecommunications, Video, Virtual Reality, Visual Art), **ACTIVITIES** (Artist Residencies, Awards & Competitions, Education, Fellowships, Festivals and Events, Gallery, Grants, Library, Membership Organization, Museum, Network Communication, Performance Group, Performance Space, Production, Publishing, Research & Development, Resource), **PLATFORMS** (Amiga, Atari, DEC, DOS/Intel, Hewlett Packard, Macintosh, Mainframe, Next, Silicon Graphics, Sun)

Organization	Disciplines	Activities	Platforms
Community Copyart Ltd.			
Museum fur Fotokopie		Museum ◆	Macintosh ✳
National Copier Art	Environmental Art ◆	Membership Organization ◆	

Dance

◆ = Primary Activity
✳ = Other Disciplines/Activities/Resources

Organization	Disciplines	Activities	Platforms
Canada Council - Media Projects in Dance Grants		Grants ◆	

Film

◆ = Primary Activity
* = Other Disciplines/Activities/Resources

Organization	DISCIPLINES																																ACTIVITIES																	PLATFORMS									
	3D Art	Animation	Architecture	Ceramics	Computer Art	Computer Graphics	Conceptual Art	Copy Art	Dance	Environmental Art	Fiber Arts	Film	Graphic Design	Holography	Industrial Design	Installation Art	Interactive Art	Kinetic Art	Literary Arts	Mixed Media	Multimedia	Music and Sound	Painting	Performance Art	Photography	Robotics	Sculpture	Space Art	Telecommunications	Video	Virtual Reality	Visual Art	Artist Residencies	Awards & Competitions	Education	Fellowships	Festivals and Events	Gallery	Grants	Library	Membership Organization	Museum	Network Communication	Performance Group	Performance Space	Production	Publishing	Research & Development	Resource	Amiga	Atari	DEC	DOS/Intel	Hewlett Packard	Macintosh	Mainframe	Next	Silicon Graphics	Sun
Apple Productions		*			*	*							*	*			*				*									*	*															◆							*						
Big Pond Productions, Inc.		*			*	*											*				*	*								*																◆							*						
Cinematograph, The San Francisco Cinematheque																														*																◆													
Festival International du Film par ordinateur de Montreal (FIFOM)		*																																			◆																							
Film/Video Arts, Inc																														*			*		*				*		◆									*			*						
Independent Media Distributors						*																								*					*						◆								*										
International Festival of Computer Graphics Films of Montreal																														*							◆																						
International Festival of Films on Art																														*							◆																						
Montreal International Festival of Films on Art																																		◆													*								*				
New England Film/Video Fellowship Program																														*						◆																							
Women Make Movies																														*											◆																		
Women in Film																																							◆																				

133

General

◆ = Primary Activity

※ = Other Disciplines/Activities/Resources

Column groups: **DISCIPLINES** · **ACTIVITIES** · **PLATFORMS**

Organization	3D Art	Animation	Architecture	Ceramics	Computer Art	Computer Graphics	Conceptual Art	Copy Art	Dance	Environmental Art	Fiber Arts	Film	Graphic Design	Holography	Industrial Design	Installation Art	Interactive Art	Kinetic Art	Literary Arts	Mixed Media	Multimedia	Music and Sound	Painting	Performance Art	Photography	Robotics	Sculpture	Space Art	Telecommunications	Video	Virtual Reality	Visual Art	Artist Residencies	Awards & Competitions	Education	Fellowships	Festivals and Events	Gallery	Grants	Library	Membership Organization	Museum	Network Communication	Performance Group	Performance Space	Production	Publishing	Research & Development	Resource	Amiga	Atari	DEC	DOS/Intel	Hewlett Packard	Macintosh	Mainframe	Next	Silicon Graphics	Sun
A Space	※																																									◆											※		※				
ACARTE, Fundacao Calouste Gulbenkian																																							◆																				
AN Publications			※		※	※	※			※	※	※	※	※		※	※	※		※	※		※	※	※		※	※		※	※																◆								※				
Adolph and Ester Gottleib Foundation																																							◆																				
American Academy in Rome																																				◆																							
American Association of University Women Educational Foundation, AAUW Educational Foundation																																				※																							
American Israel Cultural Foundation (AICF)												※																								※			◆																				
American Society for Aesthetics			※				※		※	※		※						※				※	※	※	※		※								※	※											◆	※					※		※				
American Studies Foundation, Inc.																																			※				◆																				
Andrew Gemant Award, American Institute of Physics																																		◆																									
Arstechnica: Center for Art and Technology, University of Massachusetts/Amherst																																			※																								
Art & Science Collaborations, Inc (ASCI)																	※	※																	※						◆																		
Art Access/Networking																												※															◆						◆										
Art Research Center	※	※	※		※	※			※	※	※	※	※	※		※		※			※	※	※	※	※		※			※			※			※		※			◆				※		※	◆					※		※				
Art+Com																																											◆																
ArtBase BBS																																									◆		◆				※												
ArtNetwork																																			※						※						※												
Artists Collective of Northern Ireland, Queen Street Studios																																	◆																										
Artists Foundation																																				※			◆																				
Artists Rights Society, Inc. (ARS)			※																	※			※		※																※								◆				※						
Arts Media Group																																														◆													
Arts Wire																																											◆				◆		◆				※						
Arts, Crafts and Theater Safety (ACTS)																																															※												
Artscience Gallery, Chicago Museum of Science																																						◆																				

General

◆ = Primary Activity
✳ = Other Disciplines/Activities/Resources

Column groups: **DISCIPLINES** (3D Art … Visual Art), **ACTIVITIES** (Artist Residencies … Resource), **PLATFORMS** (Amiga … Sun).

Organization	3D Art	Animation	Architecture	Ceramics	Computer Art	Computer Graphics	Conceptual Art	Copy Art	Dance	Environmental Art	Fiber Arts	Film	Graphic Design	Holography	Industrial Design	Installation Art	Interactive Art	Kinetic Art	Literary Arts	Mixed Media	Multimedia	Music and Sound	Painting	Performance Art	Photography	Robotics	Sculpture	Space Art	Telecommunications	Video	Virtual Reality	Visual Art	Artist Residencies	Awards & Competitions	Education	Fellowships	Festivals and Events	Gallery	Grants	Library	Membership Organization	Museum	Network Communication	Performance Group	Performance Space	Production	Publishing	Research & Development	Resource	Amiga	Atari	DEC	DOS/Intel	Hewlett Packard	Macintosh	Mainframe	Next	Silicon Graphics	Sun
Artsnet Electronic Network																																											◆				✳												
Artswatch		✳	✳				✳		✳											✳			✳	✳	✳										✳			✳			◆				✳		✳	✳	✳				✳						
Asian Cultural Council									✳																											◆																							
Association des Centres Culturels, c/o La Botanique																																			✳		✳											✳	◆				✳						
Association for Computers and the Humanities, Carnegie-Mellon University																																			✳													✳											
Balungan																																									◆						✳												
Banff Centre for the Arts, Media Arts Program					✳	✳	✳			✳						✳	✳	✳		✳	✳			✳			✳			✳	✳		◆		✳			✳							✳		✳	✳											
Barrow and Geraldine S. Cadbury Trust																																							◆																			
Bellagio Study and Conference Center, The Rockefeller Foundation																																	◆		✳		✳																						
Bilder Digital Galerie																																	◆					◆									◆												
Blue Mountain Center																																	◆																									
Brainstorms													✳							✳	✳	✳													◆																				✳				
Buckminster Fuller Institute																																			◆																							
Burning Press													✳							✳	✳	✳													◆									✳	✳		◆											
CADRE Institute: Computers in Art and Design/Research and Education, School of Art and Design	✳	✳	✳		✳	✳							✳		✳	✳	✳				✳	✳								✳	✳				◆													✳					✳		✳			✳	✳
California Institute of the Arts, Film and Video												✳																		✳	✳				◆																								
Canada Council - Integrated Media Grants					✳												✳			✳	✳	✳								✳	✳								◆									✳											
Center for Art and Technology, Carnegie-Mellon University																																			◆													✳										
Center for Art and Technology, Connecticut College	✳	✳	✳													✳	✳				✳	✳				✳	✳				✳		✳		◆			✳	✳						✳		✳	◆				✳	✳		✳			✳	
Center for International Contemporary Art (CICA)																																			◆																							
Center for Performing Arts and Technology, University of Michigan									✳													✳		✳											◆													✳							✳		✳		✳
Center for Research in Arts & Technology																																			◆													✳										
Center for Safety in the Arts, Art Hazard Info Center																				✳															◆												✳											

General
◆ = Primary Activity
✱ = Other Disciplines/Activities/Resources

The following table spans three header groups — **PLATFORMS**, **ACTIVITIES**, and **DISCIPLINES**.

Organization	Sun	Silicon Graphics	Next	Mainframe	Macintosh	Hewlett Packard	DOS/Intel	DEC	Atari	Amiga	Resource	Research & Development	Publishing	Production	Performance Space	Performance Group	Network Communication	Museum	Membership Organization	Library	Grants	Gallery	Festivals and Events	Fellowships	Education	Awards & Competitions	Artist Residencies	Visual Arts	Virtual Reality	Video	Telecommunications	Space Art	Sculpture	Robotics	Photography	Performance Art	Painting	Music and Sound	Multimedia	Mixed Media	Literary Arts	Kinetic Art	Interactive Art	Installation Art	Industrial Design	Holography	Graphic Design	Film	Fiber Arts	Environmental Art	Dance	Copy Art	Conceptual Art	Computer Graphics	Computer Art	Ceramics	Architecture	Animation	3D Art
Centre for Human Aspects of Science and Technology, University of Sydney																																																										✱	✱
Centro di Calcolo, Universita Degli Studi Di Camerino																									◆																																✱	✱	
Change, Inc																					◆																											✱											
Chapter Arts Centre Media Education Institute																									◆																																		
Checkerboard Foundation, Inc. c/o AVIF																					◆																																						
Chicago Museum of Science and Industry																		◆																																									
CompuAct	✱	✱			✱		✱	✱				◆																																															
Connemara Conservancy Foundation																					◆																																							
Cooke Foundation, c/o Beale																					◆																																							
Council for the International Bienniale in Nagoya, The Chunichi Shiumbun																										◆																																		
Creative Glass Center of America, c/o Wheaton Village																											◆																																	
Cummington Community of the Arts											◆				✱				✱		✱			✱	✱		◆			✱			✱		✱	✱	✱	✱	✱	✱		✱	✱					✱		✱			✱						
Design and Artists Copyright Society (DACS)																			✱																																								
Deutscher Akademischer Austauschdienst (DADD) - Artists in Berlin Program																											◆																																	
Directory of Exhibition Spaces											◆																																				✱												
Djerassi Resident Artists Program																											◆																																	
Do While Studio					✱		✱				◆											◆			✱		◆			✱			✱		✱	✱	✱	✱	✱	✱		✱	✱							✱			✱						
Dome Gallery																						◆																																						
Dorland Mountain Colony																								◆																																				
Dowse Art Museum																		✱																																										
European Cultural Foundation																					◆									✱																		✱											
European Network of Centers on Culture and Technology																			◆																																									
Everything Everything					✱		✱					✱	✱																										✱																				
Extensions, Aberdeen Art Gallery																						◆					✱																																	

General

◆ = Primary Activity
✱ = Other Disciplines/Activities/Resources

Feature	3D Art	Animation	Architecture	Ceramics	Computer Art	Computer Graphics	Conceptual Art	Copy Art	Dance	Environmental Art	Fiber Arts	Film	Graphic Design	Holography	Industrial Design	Installation Art	Interactive Art	Kinetic Art	Literary Arts	Mixed Media	Multimedia	Music and Sound	Painting	Performance Art	Photography	Robotics	Sculpture	Space Art	Telecommunications	Video	Virtual Reality	Visual Arts	Artist Residencies	Awards & Competitions	Education	Fellowships	Festivals and Events	Gallery	Grants	Library	Membership Organization	Museum	Network Communication	Performance Group	Performance Space	Production	Publishing	Research & Development	Resource	Amiga	Atari	DEC	DOS/Intel	Hewlett Packard	Macintosh	Mainframe	Next	Silicon Graphics	Sun
Fine Arts Interdisciplinary Computer Center, York University					✱																																	◆																					
Foundation de Lourmarin Lauret-Vibert, Chateau de Lourmarin																																	◆		◆																								
Franklin Institute of Science									✱																																	◆																	
Fund for US Artists at International Festivals and Exhibitions, National Endowment for the Arts																																	◆																										
Godlove Award																																		◆																									
Guggenheim Museum																																	✱		✱							◆					✱											
Gulbenkian Foundation, UK Branch																																							◆																			
Hambidge Center for Creative Arts and Sciences										✱																							✱		✱	✱		✱																				
Harlem Studio Museum																																										◆																	
Hartness-Schoos Galleries																																	✱					◆																					
Helena Rubenstein Fellowships, Whitney Museum Independent Study Programs																																				◆																						
Humanities Computing Facility (HCF)																																	✱		✱								✱						◆										
hypertelsaloon																																										✱																	
INTART - Society for Sciences, Arts and Pedagogy	✱	✱			✱	✱							✱				✱				✱	✱	✱	✱	✱		✱	✱		✱	✱	✱	✱		✱			✱			◆						✱	✱	✱						✱				
Indian Institute of Technology, Dept. of H.S.S																																	✱		◆													✱	✱		✱				✱			✱	✱
Institute for Art and Urban Resources, Art and Urban Resources																																	◆																										
Integrated Electronic Arts Rensselaer (iEAR), Department of the Arts																	✱				✱	✱		✱						✱					✱			✱								✱									✱				
Inter-Action Centre																																											✱							✱									
Inter/Access					✱	✱							✱			✱	✱	✱		✱	✱					✱				✱	✱		✱								✱		✱												✱				
Interface Newsletter, ACAD, Ohio State University					✱	✱							✱				✱	✱		✱	✱	✱								✱			✱		✱	✱		✱	✱								✱	✱	◆										
Intermedia Arts Minnesota												✱								✱	✱	✱		✱						✱											✱						◆								✱				
International Arts-Medicine Association (IAMA)																																									◆								✱										
International Directory of Electronic Arts (IDEA), CHAOS	✱	✱			✱	✱							✱	✱		✱	✱			✱	✱	✱				✱	✱	✱	✱	✱	✱																◆		✱						✱				

General

◆ = Primary Activity

✳ = Other Disciplines/Activities/Resources

The table below records, for each organization, its Disciplines, Activities, and Platforms. ◆ marks a Primary Activity and ✳ marks Other Disciplines/Activities/Resources.

DISCIPLINES: 3D Art · Animation · Architecture · Ceramics · Computer Art · Computer Graphics · Conceptual Art · Copy Art · Dance · Environmental Art · Fiber Arts · Film · Graphic Design · Holography · Industrial Design · Installation Art · Interactive Art · Kinetic Art · Literary Arts · Mixed Media · Multimedia · Music and Sound · Painting · Performance Art · Photography · Robotics · Sculpture · Space Art · Telecommunications · Video · Virtual Reality · Visual Art

ACTIVITIES: Artist Residencies · Awards & Competitions · Education · Fellowships · Festivals and Events · Gallery · Grants · Library · Membership Organization · Museum · Network Communication · Performance Group · Performance Space · Production · Publishing · Research & Development · Resource

PLATFORMS: Amiga · Atari · DEC · DOS/Intel · Hewlett Packard · Macintosh · Mainframe · Next · Silicon Graphics · Sun

Organization	Disciplines	Activities	Platforms
International Institute for Conservation of Historic and Artistic Works	3D Art ✳	Membership Organization ◆	
International Institute for Modern Structural Art	Animation ✳, Architecture ✳, Computer Art ✳, Conceptual Art ✳, Environmental Art ✳, Film ✳, Graphic Design ✳, Industrial Design ✳, Installation Art ✳, Interactive Art ✳, Kinetic Art ✳, Mixed Media ✳, Painting ✳, Photography ✳, Robotics ✳, Sculpture ✳, Space Art ✳, Video ✳	Education ✳, Publishing ✳, Museum ◆	DOS/Intel ✳, Macintosh ✳
International Society for the Inter-Disciplinary Study of Symmetry (ISIS-SYMMETRY)	Computer Graphics ✳	Education ✳, Fellowships ✳, Festivals and Events ✳, Gallery ✳, Membership Organization ✳, Publishing ✳, Research & Development ✳	DOS/Intel ✳
Isaac W. Bernheim Foundation		Artist Residencies ◆, Fellowships ✳	
KAOS	Computer Art ✳, Dance ✳, Film ✳, Music and Sound ✳, Performance Art ✳, Video ✳	Artist Residencies ✳, Membership Organization ✳	
Kettles Yard Gallery		Gallery ✳, Membership Organization ◆	
Kitchen		Grants ✳, Gallery ✳, Membership Organization ✳, Performance Space ✳, Production ◆	
Kulturdata			
Lehrkanzel fur Kommunikationstheorie, Hochschule fur Angewandte Kunst-Wien		Fellowships ✳	
Leonardo, the International Society for the Arts, Sciences and Technology	3D Art ✳, Architecture ✳, Computer Art ✳, Computer Graphics ✳, Conceptual Art ✳, Environmental Art ✳, Film ✳, Graphic Design ✳, Holography ✳, Industrial Design ✳, Installation Art ✳, Interactive Art ✳, Kinetic Art ✳, Literary Arts ✳, Mixed Media ✳, Multimedia ✳, Music and Sound ✳, Painting ✳, Performance Art ✳, Photography ✳, Robotics ✳, Sculpture ✳, Space Art ✳, Telecommunications ✳, Video ✳, Virtual Reality ✳, Visual Art ✳	Artist Residencies ✳, Awards & Competitions ✳, Education ✳, Membership Organization ✳, Network Communication ✳, Publishing ◆, Resource ✳	DOS/Intel ✳
Leverhulme Trust		Artist Residencies ◆, Fellowships ✳	
Lightwork		Artist Residencies ◆	
Living Art Center, Living Design International	Computer Art ✳, Computer Graphics ✳, Multimedia ✳, Music and Sound ✳, Robotics ✳, Video ✳	Festivals and Events ✳, Research & Development ◆	
Los Angeles Contemporary Exhibitions (LACE)	Installation Art ✳, Interactive Art ✳, Mixed Media ✳, Multimedia ✳, Performance Art ✳, Video ✳	Gallery ✳, Museum ◆	
Louis Vuitton Moet Hennessy Science for Art Prize, LVMH, Direction di Development		Awards & Competitions ◆	
Lugano Academy of the Electronic Arts	Computer Art ✳, Computer Graphics ✳, Holography ✳, Installation Art ✳, Interactive Art ✳, Mixed Media ✳, Multimedia ✳, Space Art ✳, Video ✳, Virtual Reality ✳, Visual Art ✳	Artist Residencies ✳, Education ✳, Publishing ◆, Research & Development ◆	
MIT Media Laboratory, MIT	Animation ✳, 3D Art ✳	Artist Residencies ✳	
MacDowell Colony, The MacDowell Colony		Artist Residencies ◆	
Martin Bequest Traveling Scholarships, Arts Management Pty. Ltd.		Fellowships ✳	
Mattress Factory		Artist Residencies ✳, Membership Organization ◆	
MedArt USA, Inc.			
Media, Culture and Society, Sage Publications, Ltd		Publishing ◆	
Michael Karolyi Memorial Foundation, Le Vieux Mas		Artist Residencies ◆	

General

◆ = Primary Activity
✳ = Other Disciplines/Activities/Resources

The following table records Disciplines, Activities, and Platforms for each listed organization.

Organization	3D Art	Animation	Architecture	Ceramics	Computer Art	Computer Graphics	Conceptual Art	Copy Art	Dance	Environmental Art	Fiber Arts	Film	Graphic Design	Holography	Industrial Design	Installation Art	Interactive Art	Kinetic Art	Literary Arts	Mixed Media	Multimedia	Music and Sound	Painting	Performance Art	Photography	Robotics	Sculpture	Space Art	Telecommunications	Video	Virtual Reality	Visual Art	Artist Residencies	Awards & Competitions	Education	Fellowships	Festivals and Events	Gallery	Grants	Library	Membership Organization	Museum	Network Communication	Performance Group	Performance Space	Production	Publishing	Research & Development	Resource	Amiga	Atari	DEC	DOS/Intel	Hewlett Packard	Macintosh	Mainframe	Next	Silicon Graphics	Sun
Millay Colony for the Arts																																	◆																										
Monbusho Scholarship, Japan Information Center																																				◆																						
N.Y. Mills Arts Retreat			✳							✳																							◆																									
NEXA, Science-Humanities Convergence Program, San Francisco State University													✳																						◆																							
Nantucket Island School of Design and the Arts, Residency Program												✳																					◆		✳																							
National Center for Science Information Systems					✳		✳																										◆			✳							✳					✳										
New Arts Program					✳		✳					✳				✳					✳	✳	✳	✳	✳		✳			✳								✳				✳					✳						✳					
New Langton Arts					✳	✳	✳									✳	✳		✳		✳	✳	✳	✳	✳		✳			✳							✳	✳	✳						✳		✳		✳						✳				
New York Experimental Glass Workshop																											✳						◆																									
New York Foundation for the Arts, Artist in Residence Program																																	◆		✳				✳									✳					✳						
Ohio State University, Department of Theatre												✳												✳						✳					◆									✳	✳										✳				
Ontario Arts Council																																			◆				◆																				
Open Channels, Long Beach Museum of Art																														✳									◆											✳									
Paramount Publishing					✳	✳							✳																						✳												◆						✳						
Pollock-Krasner Foundation																							✳				✳												◆																				
Preservation Initiative, National Endowment for the Humanities																																			✳													✳	◆										
Prix Ars Electronica		✳			✳	✳							✳								✳	✳								✳	✳	✳		◆			✳																						
Prometheus, All-union Coordinating Center for the Arts, Science and Technology																																									✳								◆										
Real Arts Way (RAW), Hartford Arts Center												✳												✳						✳					✳		✳	✳																					
Rhode Island School of Design	✳	✳	✳		✳	✳	✳				✳		✳			✳	✳				✳	✳	✳	✳	✳		✳			✳			✳		◆			✳															✳		✳				✳
Richmond Unified High School District	✳	✳			✳	✳	✳						✳			✳	✳					✳	✳	✳			✳								◆				✳																				
Ronald Feldman Fine Arts							✳									✳							✳	✳			✳											◆																	✳				
SFCA Artist Fellowships																																	✳		✳	✳	✳	✳			✳														✳				
SYMMETRION - The Institute for Advanced Symmetry Studies			✳										✳																						✳												◆	✳					✳						

139

General

◆ = Primary Activity

✳ = Other Disciplines/Activities/Resources

Disciplines

Organization	3D Art	Animation	Architecture	Ceramics	Computer Art	Computer Graphics	Conceptual Art	Copy Art	Dance	Environmental Art	Fiber Arts	Film	Graphic Design	Holography	Industrial Design	Installation Art	Interactive Art	Kinetic Art	Literary Arts	Mixed Media	Multimedia	Music and Sound	Painting	Performance Art	Photography	Robotics	Sculpture	Space Art	Telecommunications	Video	Virtual Reality	Visual Art
School of Photographic Arts and Sciences & The Technical and Education Center of the Graphic Arts, Rochester Institute of Technology												✳		✳											✳							
Science and the Arts																																
Society for the History of Technology, The University of Chicago Press, Journals Division																																
Society for the Sciences, Arts and Education, Technical University																																
Solomon R. Guggenheum Museum																									✳							
South West Arts																																
Syntex Gallery																																
Tech 2000 Ivia																																
Technology and Conservation																																
Typeworld																																
Tyrone Guthrie Center, The Tyrone Guthrie Center																			✳			✳	✳	✳	✳		✳					✳
University of Edinburgh																															✳	
University of Illinois at Champaign, Art Department	✳	✳			✳	✳											✳			✳	✳	✳								✳	✳	
University of London Audio Visual Centre, Interactive Videodisc Technology Certificate																					✳	✳										
University of Tennessee, Art Department	✳	✳			✳	✳	✳					✳	✳			✳	✳	✳		✳	✳	✳	✳	✳	✳		✳	✳		✳	✳	
V2 Organization	✳	✳														✳	✳			✳	✳						✳			✳	✳	
Verbum Gallery of Digital Art																									✳		✳					
Vermont Studio Colony																																
Winston Churchill Memorial Trust, Churchill Traveling Fellowships																																
Wolf Foundation																																
Women's Interart Center																																
Women's Studio Workshop																																
Women's Work, c/o Brixton Art Gallery																																

Activities

Organization	Artist Residencies	Awards & Competitions	Education	Fellowships	Festivals and Events	Gallery	Grants	Library	Membership Organization	Museum	Network Communication	Performance Group	Performance Space	Production	Publishing	Research & Development	Resource
School of Photographic Arts and Sciences & The Technical and Education Center of the Graphic Arts, Rochester Institute of Technology			◆														
Science and the Arts															◆		
Society for the History of Technology, The University of Chicago Press, Journals Division			◆						◆						◆		
Society for the Sciences, Arts and Education, Technical University																	
Solomon R. Guggenheum Museum										◆							
South West Arts	◆																
Syntex Gallery						◆											
Tech 2000 Ivia						◆									◆		
Technology and Conservation																	
Typeworld															◆	◆	
Tyrone Guthrie Center, The Tyrone Guthrie Center	◆		◆		✳			✳					✳				
University of Edinburgh	✳		◆														
University of Illinois at Champaign, Art Department			◆													✳	
University of London Audio Visual Centre, Interactive Videodisc Technology Certificate				✳													
University of Tennessee, Art Department	✳			✳										✳	✳		
V2 Organization						✳			◆						✳		
Verbum Gallery of Digital Art						◆									✳		
Vermont Studio Colony	◆																
Winston Churchill Memorial Trust, Churchill Traveling Fellowships				✳													
Wolf Foundation		✳		✳			✳										
Women's Interart Center	◆																
Women's Studio Workshop	✳		✳				◆										
Women's Work, c/o Brixton Art Gallery							◆										

Platforms

Organization	Amiga	Atari	DEC	DOS/Intel	Hewlett Packard	Macintosh	Mainframe	Next	Silicon Graphics	Sun
University of Tennessee, Art Department						✳				
Wolf Foundation				✳						

140

General

◆ = Primary Activity
* = Other Disciplines/Activities/Resources

Categories shown: **DISCIPLINES** · **ACTIVITIES** · **PLATFORMS**

YLEM: Artists Using Science & Technology
- Disciplines (*): 3D Art, Architecture, Ceramics, Computer Art, Computer Graphics, Conceptual Art, Copy Art, Dance, Environmental Art, Fiber Arts, Film, Graphic Design, Holography, Industrial Design, Installation Art, Interactive Art, Kinetic Art, Literary Arts, Mixed Media, Multimedia, Music and Sound, Painting, Performance Art, Photography, Robotics, Sculpture, Space Art, Telecommunications, Video, Virtual Reality, Visual Art
- Activities: Membership Organization (◆), Education (*), Festivals and Events (*), Publishing (*)
- Platforms (*): Macintosh

Yaddo Estate, Corporation of Yaddo
- Activities: Artist Residencies (◆)

Yellow Springs Institute for Contemporary Studies and the Arts
- Disciplines (*): Video
- Activities: Fellowships (◆), Artist Residencies (*), Education (*), Grants (*)

Zentrum fur Kunst Und Medientechnolgie Karlsruhe
- Disciplines (*): Computer Art, Computer Graphics, Installation Art, Interactive Art, Multimedia, Music and Sound, Virtual Reality
- Activities: Research & Development (◆), Library (*), Museum (*), Performance Space (*)

Zyzzyva
- Disciplines (*): Architecture, Photography
- Activities: Publishing (◆)
- Platforms (*): Macintosh

Graphic Design

◆ = Primary Activity
* = Other Disciplines/Activities/Resources

Categories shown: **DISCIPLINES** · **ACTIVITIES** · **PLATFORMS**

Artspace
- Activities: Gallery (◆)

College du Vieux-Montreal, Design
- Disciplines (*): Computer Art, Industrial Design
- Activities: Education (◆)

Durham College, Graphic Design
- Disciplines (*): Computer Art
- Activities: Education (◆)

Education Council of the Graphic Arts Industry, Inc.
- Activities: Education (◆), Fellowships (*), Grants (*), Publishing (*), Research & Development (*)
- Platforms (*): DOS/Intel, DEC

International Directory of Design, Penrose Press
- Activities: Publishing (◆), Membership Organization (*), Research & Development (*)
- Platforms (*): Macintosh, Sun

Ucross Foundation, Ucross Route
- Activities: Artist Residencies (◆)

Holography

◆ = Primary Activity
✳ = Other Disciplines/Activities/Resources

Organization	Sun	Silicon Graphics	Next	Mainframe	Macintosh	Hewlett Packard	DOS/Intel	DEC	Atari	Amiga	Resource	Research & Development	Publishing	Production	Performance Space	Performance Group	Network Communication	Museum	Membership Organization	Library	Grants	Gallery	Festivals and Events	Fellowships	Education	Awards & Competitions	Artist Residencies	Visual Art	Virtual Reality	Video	Telecommunications	Space Art	Sculpture	Robotics	Photography	Performance Art	Painting	Music and Sound	Multimedia	Mixed Media	Literary Arts	Kinetic Art	Interactive Art	Installation Art	Industrial Design	Holography	Graphic Design	Film	Fiber Arts	Environmental Art	Dance	Copy Art	Conceptual Art	Computer Graphics	Computer Art	Ceramics	Architecture	Animation	3D Art
Art, Science and Technology Institute											✳	✳													◆																																		
Arkitek																																																											
Atlanta Gallery of Holography																						◆																																					
Canadian Holographic Society																			✳																																								
Cherry Optical Society												◆			✳																																												
Dutch Foundation of Perception and Holography											✳																																																
Elusive Image																						◆																																					
Engineering Technology Institute												◆																																															
Fine Arts Research & Holography Center												✳										◆																																					
Fringe Research Holographics, Inc																											◆																																
Gallery for Holography																						◆																																					
Hellenic Institute of Holography																									◆																																		
Holo Media AB																		◆																																								
Holo-Gram													◆																																													
HolografieLabor Osnabruck																						◆			◆																																		
Hologramas																						◆																																					
Hologrammen Galerie																						◆																																					
Holographic Visions																						◆			◆																																		
Holography Group, Salisbury College of Art																																																											
Holography Institute					✳							✳	✳					✳			✳	✳			◆		✳		✳			✳	✳	✳	✳					✳				✳	✳		✳	✳					✳	✳	✳			✳	✳
Holography Workshop					✳		✳					✳	✳												◆																			✳										✳	✳				
Holography in Education																			✳						◆																																		
Holography Display of Artists & Engineers Club (HODIC), Central Research Institute, Toppan Printing Co.																						◆																																					
Houston Holography Center, The Anthony Foundation																									◆																																		
Integraf																																																												
Interference Hologram Gallery																						◆																																					

PLATFORMS · ACTIVITIES · DISCIPLINES

Holography

◆ = Primary Activity

* = Other Disciplines/Activities/Resources

Disciplines

Organization	3D Art	Animation	Architecture	Ceramics	Computer Art	Computer Graphics	Conceptual Art	Copy Art	Dance	Environmental Art	Fiber Arts	Film	Graphic Design	Holography	Industrial Design	Installation Art	Interactive Art	Kinetic Art	Literary Arts	Mixed Media	Multimedia	Music and Sound	Painting	Performance Art	Photography	Robotics	Sculpture	Space Art	Telecommunications	Video	Virtual Reality	Visual Art
International Society for Optical Engineering	*	*																														
Laser Arts Society for Education and Research (LASER)			*		*	*	*			*			*		*	*	*	*		*	*	*	*		*	*	*	*		*	*	
Los Angeles School of Holography																																
Lux Aeterna Lumia Theater, Lux Aeterna Lumia Teater																																
Mirage Gallery																																
Musee de l'Holographie, Forum des Halles	*																															
Museum fur Holographie & Neue Visuelle Medien																					*											
Museum of Fine Arts Research and Holography	*																															
Positive Light Holographics																*	*															
School of Holography																																
Shanghai Institute of Laser Technology																																
Shearwater Foundation																																
Southern California Laser Arts Society																																
Synchronicity Holograms	*				*	*																			*							
Third Dimension Ltd, The Israeli Gallery of Holograms																																
Universita deigli Studi di Bologna, Instituto do Comunicazione																																
University Gent - Lab. Soete, Applied Mechanics - Workshop Holography																				*	*				*			*		*	*	
University of Tsukuba, School of Art and Design																																

Activities

Organization	Artist Residencies	Awards & Competitions	Education	Fellowships	Festivals and Events	Gallery	Grants	Library	Membership Organization	Museum	Network Communication	Performance Group	Performance Space	Production	Publishing	Research & Development	Resource
International Society for Optical Engineering									*						◆		
Laser Arts Society for Education and Research (LASER)	*		*						*	*					◆		
Los Angeles School of Holography			◆														
Lux Aeterna Lumia Theater, Lux Aeterna Lumia Teater						◆											
Mirage Gallery						◆											
Musee de l'Holographie, Forum des Halles			*							◆					*		
Museum fur Holographie & Neue Visuelle Medien										◆							
Museum of Fine Arts Research and Holography										◆						◆	
Positive Light Holographics			*	*		*				*							
School of Holography			◆														
Shanghai Institute of Laser Technology			◆														
Shearwater Foundation							◆		◆								
Southern California Laser Arts Society			◆														
Synchronicity Holograms			◆													*	
Third Dimension Ltd, The Israeli Gallery of Holograms						◆											
Universita deigli Studi di Bologna, Instituto do Comunicazione			◆														
University Gent - Lab. Soete, Applied Mechanics - Workshop Holography			◆													*	
University of Tsukuba, School of Art and Design			◆														

Platforms

Organization	Amiga	Atari	DEC	DOS/Intel	Hewlett Packard	Macintosh	Mainframe	Next	Silicon Graphics	Sun
International Society for Optical Engineering										
Laser Arts Society for Education and Research (LASER)						*				
Los Angeles School of Holography										
Lux Aeterna Lumia Theater, Lux Aeterna Lumia Teater										
Mirage Gallery										
Musee de l'Holographie, Forum des Halles				*						
Museum fur Holographie & Neue Visuelle Medien										
Museum of Fine Arts Research and Holography				*						
Positive Light Holographics										
School of Holography										
Shanghai Institute of Laser Technology										
Shearwater Foundation										
Southern California Laser Arts Society										
Synchronicity Holograms						*				
Third Dimension Ltd, The Israeli Gallery of Holograms										
Universita deigli Studi di Bologna, Instituto do Comunicazione										
University Gent - Lab. Soete, Applied Mechanics - Workshop Holography				*		*				
University of Tsukuba, School of Art and Design										

Industrial Design

◆ = Primary Activity
∗ = Other Disciplines/Activities/Resources

Inventors Workshop International

Disciplines	3D Art	∗
Disciplines	Architecture	∗
Disciplines	Ceramics	∗
Disciplines	Computer Art	∗
Disciplines	Computer Graphics	∗
Disciplines	Conceptual Art	∗
Disciplines	Environmental Art	∗
Disciplines	Graphic Design	∗
Disciplines	Interactive Art	∗
Disciplines	Mixed Media	∗
Disciplines	Multimedia	∗
Disciplines	Photography	∗
Disciplines	Space Art	∗
Activities	Education	◆
Activities	Membership Organization	∗
Activities	Publishing	∗
Activities	Research & Development	∗
Platforms	DOS/Intel	∗
Platforms	Macintosh	∗

Installation Art

◆ = Primary Activity
∗ = Other Disciplines/Activities/Resources

Life On A Slice

Disciplines	3D Art	∗
Disciplines	Animation	∗
Disciplines	Computer Art	∗
Disciplines	Computer Graphics	∗
Disciplines	Literary Arts	∗
Disciplines	Mixed Media	∗
Disciplines	Multimedia	∗
Disciplines	Music and Sound	∗
Disciplines	Virtual Reality	∗
Activities	Production	◆

Interactive Art

◆ = Primary Activity
∗ = Other Disciplines/Activities/Resources

Category	Item	Coactive Aesthetics	Electronic Media Workshop - Art School in Leipzig, Werkstatt fur electronische Medien	Exploratorium
Disciplines	Computer Art	∗	∗	∗
Disciplines	Environmental Art			∗
Disciplines	Film			∗
Disciplines	Graphic Design		∗	
Disciplines	Installation Art		∗	
Disciplines	Kinetic Art	∗		∗
Disciplines	Mixed Media		∗	∗
Disciplines	Multimedia		∗	∗
Disciplines	Music and Sound	∗		∗
Disciplines	Performance Art			∗
Disciplines	Photography		∗	
Disciplines	Robotics	∗		
Disciplines	Sculpture	∗		
Disciplines	Video		∗	∗
Activities	Artist Residencies			◆
Activities	Education		◆	∗
Activities	Museum			∗
Activities	Performance Space			∗
Activities	Production	◆		
Activities	Research & Development	∗		

Literary Art

◆ = Primary Activity
✳ = Other Disciplines/Activities/Resources

DISCIPLINES / ACTIVITIES / PLATFORMS (✳ = Other, ◆ = Primary)

For all Literary Art entries the **Literary Arts** *discipline column is shaded (primary discipline area).*

Entry	Disciplines	Activities	Platforms
Artist Book Works	(Literary Arts)	Artist Residencies ◆; Publishing ✳	
D. H. Lawrence Summer Fellowship, University of New Mexico	(Literary Arts)	Fellowships ◆	
Edward F. Albee Foundation	(Literary Arts)	Artist Residencies ◆; Grants ✳	
Literary and Linguistic Computing, Institute of Advanced Studies	(Literary Arts)	Education ◆	
Society for Literature and Science (SLS), School of Interpersonal Communications	(Literary Arts)	Education ◆; Publishing ✳	DOS/Intel ✳

Mixed Media

◆ = Primary Activity
✳ = Other Disciplines/Activities/Resources

DISCIPLINES / ACTIVITIES / PLATFORMS (✳ = Other, ◆ = Primary)

For all Mixed Media entries the **Mixed Media** *discipline column is shaded (primary discipline area).*

Entry	Disciplines	Activities	Platforms
Bronx Museum of the Arts	3D Art ✳; Animation ✳; Computer Graphics ✳; Conceptual Art ✳; Graphic Design ✳; Installation Art ✳; Interactive Art ✳; Kinetic Art ✳; Multimedia ✳; Painting ✳; Performance Art ✳; Photography ✳; Sculpture ✳; Virtual Reality ✳	Artist Residencies ✳; Education ✳; Museum ◆	DOS/Intel ✳; Mainframe ✳
Capp Street Project	Installation Art ✳; Interactive Art ✳; Kinetic Art ✳; Multimedia ✳	Artist Residencies ◆; Education ✳	
Das Synthetische Mischgewebe, The Synthetic Mixture of Fabrics	Computer Art ✳; Installation Art ✳; Interactive Art ✳; Kinetic Art ✳; Music and Sound ✳; Painting ✳; Performance Art ✳; Robotics ✳	Performance Group ◆; Publishing ✳	DOS/Intel ✳
John Michael Kohler Arts Center	Computer Art ✳; Multimedia ✳; Painting ✳	Artist Residencies ✳; Education ✳; Gallery ◆	
Josh Baer Gallery	Installation Art ✳; Interactive Art ✳; Kinetic Art ✳; Multimedia ✳; Painting ✳; Sculpture ✳	Gallery ◆	

Multimedia

◆ = Primary Activity

* = Other Disciplines/Activities/Resources

Organization	Sun	Silicon Graphics	Next	Mainframe	Macintosh	Hewlett Packard	DOS/Intel	DEC	Atari	Amiga	Resource	Research & Development	Publishing	Production	Performance Space	Performance Group	Network Communication	Museum	Membership Organization	Library	Grants	Gallery	Festivals and Events	Fellowships	Education	Awards & Competitions	Artist Residencies	Visual Art	Virtual Reality	Video	Telecommunications	Space Art	Sculpture	Robotics	Photography	Performance Art	Painting	Music and Sound	Multimedia	Mixed Media	Literary Arts	Kinetic Art	Interactive Art	Installation Art	Industrial Design	Holography	Graphic Design	Film	Fiber Arts	Environmental Art	Dance	Copy Art	Conceptual Art	Computer Graphics	Computer Art	Ceramics	Architecture	Animation	3D Art
	PLATFORMS											**ACTIVITIES**																**DISCIPLINES**																																
Arts & Sciences Prod													◆	◆																																												*	*
Australia Centre for the Arts & Technology (ACAT)	*	*			*					*		*	*			*									◆		◆		*	*			*		*		*	*				*	*	*				*		*			*	*	*	*	*	*	*
Bemis - Center for Contemporary Arts							*															*			*					*			*	*	*		*			*		*		*						*			*		*		*		
Cyberspace Gallery					*											*					◆								*	*		*	*	*	*		*	*		*	*	*	*	*									*	*	*	*		*
Dynamic Showcase: A Hypermedia Journal													◆																												*																		
Eastgate Systems, Hypertext Systems and Services					*		*					◆	◆																												*		*	*										*	*			
Hooykaas/Stanfield													*			◆											*			*															*					*									
Hungart, Fine Art Section										*									*											*			*		*		*	*				*	*	*	*		*	*					*	*	*		*	*
Interactive Multimedia Association (IMA)							*					◆						*	*																																								
La Cite des Arts et des Nouvelle Technologies de Montreal					*							◆									◆						*		*	*		*	*		*	*		*				*		*			*			*			*	*	*		*	*
Mindesign	*	*			*		*						*								*				*		*		*	*					*																									
Multi Media Arts Gallery	*																					◆																																					
Muscle Fish Multimedia Engineering					*																																							*															
School of Media Art, College of Fine Arts/ University of New South Wales												◆			*							*			◆										*	*															*									
Trebas Institute					*		*		*	*															◆			*	*	*					*			*		*			*	*			*	*						*	*		*	*
UnderWorld Industries	*	*			*		*			*						*		*			*							*	*	*						*		*		*			*				*	*						*	*		*	*
Zakros InterArts														◆		*									*			*		*						*		*																*	*		*	*

Music and Sound

◆ = Primary Activity

✳ = Other Disciplines/Activities/Resources

Column groups: **DISCIPLINES** (3D Art … Visual Art), **ACTIVITIES** (Artist Residencies … Resource), **PLATFORMS** (Amiga … Sun). The "Music and Sound" discipline column is the shaded primary category for all listed organizations.

Organization	3D Art	Animation	Architecture	Ceramics	Computer Graphics	Computer Art	Conceptual Art	Copy Art	Dance	Environmental Art	Fiber Arts	Film	Graphic Design	Holography	Industrial Design	Installation	Interactive Art	Kinetic Art	Literary Arts	Mixed Media	Multimedia	Music and Sound	Painting	Performance Art	Photography	Robotics	Sculpture	Space Art	Telecommunications	Video	Virtual Reality	Visual Art	Artist Residencies	Awards & Competitions	Education	Fellowships	Festivals and Events	Gallery	Grants	Library	Membership Organization	Museum	Network Communication	Performance Group	Performance Space	Production	Publishing	Research & Development	Resource	Amiga	Atari	DEC	DOS/Intel	Hewlett Packard	Macintosh	Mainframe	Next	Silicon Graphics	Sun
ART (if) ACT					✳	✳	✳	✳				✳	✳											✳	✳					✳														◆									✳	✳	✳				
American Gamelan Institute																																			✳									✳			◆								✳				
Ampersand Productions		✳															✳				✳																									◆							✳		✳				
Association pour la Creation et la Recherche Electroacoustique du Quebec (ACREQ)																																									◆						◆	✳							✳				
Bard College, Music Program Zero									✳																										◆																								
BodySynth					✳																✳			✳							✳																	◆											
CERL Sound Group - University of Illinois					✳																✳														✳									✳				◆					✳		✳				
Canada Council - Audio Production Grants, Communications Section																																							◆							✳													
Canadian ElectroAcoustic Community (CEC)																																									◆						◆								✳				
Catalogue of Computer Programs for Music Education																																			✳												◆	◆											
Catalogue of Music Software																																															◆	◆											
Center for Computer Research in Music and Acoustics (CCRMA), Music Deptartment, Stanford University																					✳												✳		✳													◆									✳		✳
Center for Computer-Assisted Research in Humanities (CCARH)																																															◆	◆	✳										
Center for Contemporary Music, Mills College, Department of Music		✳			✳	✳				✳		✳	✳			✳	✳			✳	✳			✳						✳			✳		◆			✳						✳		✳	✳	✳		✳					✳				
Center for Experiments in Art, Information & Technology (CEAIT), California Institute of the Arts	✳	✳			✳	✳			✳	✳	✳	✳	✳			✳	✳			✳	✳		✳			✳	✳	✳	✳	✳	✳	✳	✳		◆													✳					✳		✳			✳	
Center for Music Technology, Radford University																					✳			✳											◆	✳								✳				✳				✳					✳		
Center for Research into Applications of Computers to Music, University of Lancaster					✳																														◆													✳											
Center for the Diffusion of Contemporary Music																																			◆													◆											
Centro Ricerche Musicali																																			◆													◆											
Chrysalis Foundation																																							◆																					
Computer Music & Musical Informatics Association																																			✳						◆						✳	✳					✳		✳			✳	✳

147

Music and Sound

◆ = Primary Activity
* = Other Disciplines/Activities/Resources

Organization	3D Art	Animation	Architecture	Ceramics	Computer Art	Computer Graphics	Conceptual Art	Copy Art	Dance	Environmental Art	Fiber Arts	Film	Graphic Design	Holography	Industrial Design	Installation Art	Interactive Art	Kinetic Art	Literary Arts	Mixed Media	Multimedia	Music and Sound	Painting	Performance Art	Photography	Robotics	Sculpture	Space Art	Telecommunications	Video	Virtual Reality	Visual Art	Artist Residencies	Awards & Competitions	Education	Fellowships	Festivals and Events	Gallery	Grants	Library	Membership Organization	Museum	Network Communication	Performance Group	Performance Space	Production	Publishing	Research & Development	Resource	Amiga	Atari	DEC	DOS/Intel	Hewlett Packard	Macintosh	Mainframe	Next	Silicon Graphics	Sun
Computer Music Journal	*								*			*					*	*		*	*			*		*	*			*	*	*			*						*				*		◆	*					*		*				*
Computer Music Project, University of Illinois at Urbana Champaign																																			*													*											
Computer in der Musik: Uber den Einsatz in Wissenschaft, Komposition, und Padagogik																																															◆												
Computers in Music Research, School of Music																								*																								◆						*		*				
Computers in Teaching Initiative Centre for Music, Music Department																				*															*												*	*			*		*		*		*		
Conservatory of Music, Musicological Department of CNUCE/CNR					*		*										*				*			*		*	*																		*	*		◆			*		*		*	*			
Danish Institute of Electroacoustic Music (DIEM), The Concert Hall Aarhus							*			*						*	*	*		*	*			*		*	*				*		◆		*										*	*		*							*		*		
Die Audio Gruppe						*										*	*										*																	◆				*											
Downtown Ensemble					*	*			*	*																																		◆															
East End Management																	*																													◆		*										
EthnoForum																																											◆					*											
Experimental Musical Instruments													*		*									*																							◆	*					*						
Frog Peak Music					*		*						*				*			*	*			*													*										◆	*					*				*		
Good Sound Foundation																																		*			*									◆	*	◆							*				
Groupe de Researches Musicales (GRM/IRA)																																														◆	◆	◆											
Harvestworks, Inc.																																	*						*		*				*			*											
IRCAM																																	*						*								*	◆	*										
Image and Sound Museum																																										*	◆															
Institut Fur Integrative Musikpadagogik und Polyasthetische Erziehung																																			◆																								
Instituto Nacional De Bellas Artes										*																									◆		*		*		*																		
International Computer Music Association					*		*		*	*							*	*		*	*			*		*	*	*	*	*	*	*			◆		*		*		*						*	*		*	*	*	*	*	*	*	*	*	*

Music and Sound

◆ = Primary Activity
* = Other Disciplines/Activities/Resources

	3D Art	Animation	Architecture	Ceramics	Computer Art	Computer Graphics	Conceptual Art	Copy Art	Dance	Environmental Art	Fiber Arts	Film	Graphic Design	Holography	Industrial Design	Installation Art	Interactive Art	Kinetic Art	Literary Arts	Mixed Media	Multimedia	Music and Sound	Painting	Performance Art	Photography	Robotics	Sculpture	Space Art	Telecommunications	Video	Virtual Reality	Visual Art	Artist Residencies	Awards & Competitions	Education	Fellowships	Festivals and Events	Gallery	Grants	Library	Membership Organization	Museum	Network Communication	Performance Group	Performance Space	Production	Publishing	Research & Development	Resource	Amiga	Atari	DEC	DOS/Intel	Hewlett Packard	Macintosh	Mainframe	Next	Silicon Graphics	Sun
International Digital Electroacoustic Music Archive																																								*									◆											
International Society for Contemporary Music, c/o Gaudeamus																																									◆			*									*						
Interval Magazine, Interval Foundation																																									◆						◆												
Just Intonation Network																																									◆						*												
Laboratorio de Informatica Musical, Escuela de Musica, Universidad de Guanajuato																																			*													*											
Laboratorio de Informatica Y Electronica Musical (LIEM), Centro para la Difusion de la Musica Contemporanea												*																							*											◆		*	*										
Leonardo Music Journal					*												*				*																										◆												
Liquid Crystal Music																																														◆													
Logos Foundation							*		*	*			*	*		*					*			*		*	*	*		*	*	*	*											*	◆		*												
Midi/Worldmusic, USA																																											*				◆						*						
Music Engineering Technology, Cogswell Polytechnical College																																			*														*										
Musical Microcomputer: A Resource Guide																																														◆	◆	*	*										
Musician's Music Software Catalog																																															◆												
Musicworks																																									◆						*												
NEWCOMP																																			◆																								
New England Computer Music Association																																									◆																		
Northwest Electronic Musicians (NEMUS)																																			◆						◆																		
New Music Australia (New Music Articles) (NMA)																			*	*	*			*									*											*			◆	*		*					*				
Pauline Oliveros Foundation Inc.							*												*	*	*			*																						◆	◆												
Perspectives of New Music, School of Music																					*																										◆						*						
Professional Sound Corporation																																	*	*									*	*			◆	◆					*						
Public Domain																							*			*									*												*		*				*						
Research Center for Music Iconography, City University of New York																																									◆						*	◆					*						

149

Music and Sound

◆ = Primary Activity
✳ = Other Disciplines/Activities/Resources

Organization	Sun	Silicon Graphics	Next	Mainframe	Macintosh	Hewlett Packard	DOS/Intel	DEC	Atari	Amiga	Resource	Research & Development	Publishing	Production	Performance Space	Performance Group	Network Communication	Museum	Membership Organization	Library	Grants	Gallery	Festivals and Events	Fellowships	Education	Awards & Competitions	Artist Residencies	Visual Art	Virtual Reality	Video	Telecommunications	Space Art	Sculpture	Robotics	Photography	Performance Art	Painting	Music and Sound	Multimedia	Mixed Media	Literary Arts	Kinetic Art	Interactive Art	Installation Art	Industrial Design	Holography	Graphic Design	Film	Fiber Arts	Environmental Art	Dance	Copy Art	Conceptual Art	Computer Graphics	Computer Art	Ceramics	Architecture	Animation	3D Art
Research Center for Musical Iconography (RCMI), City University of New York											◆	✳								✳																			✳																				
SGML User's Special Interest Group on Hypertext and Multimedia, c/o Techno Teacher												◆																											✳																				
Sound Basis Visual Art Festival																										✳																																	
Sound Choice																																																											
Soundings Press													◆																																														
Stockholm Electronic Art Awards																					✳					◆																																	
TIMARA (Technology in Music and Related Arts), Oberlin Conservatory																									✳																																		
Task Force and Technical Committee on Computer Generated Music, IEEE Computer Society											✳	◆													✳														✳																			
Universite de Montreal, Sector electro-acoustique																									◆					✳					✳				✳							✳													
University of Aveiro Portugual, Communication and Art Dept.					✳																				◆																																		
University of Washington, School of Music																									◆																																		
Westdeutscher Rundfunk Koeln, Studio Akustische Kunst																										◆																																	

Painting

◆ = Primary Activity
* = Other Disciplines/Activities/Resources

	Ceramics	Sculpture	Mixed Media	Video	Artist Residencies	Education	Gallery	Grants	Research & Development	Hewlett Packard	DOS/Intel	Macintosh
Elizabeth Greenshields Foundation		*			*			◆		*		
Hann Gallery	*	*	*				◆					
Micro Gallery: Computer Information Room, The National Gallery							◆					
Vasari Project, The National Gallery				*	*	*	◆		*		*	*

Photography

◆ = Primary Activity
* = Other Disciplines/Activities/Resources

	Computer Art	Computer Graphics	Conceptual Art	Film	Holography	Installation Art	Interactive Art	Mixed Media	Multimedia	Video	Virtual Reality	Artist Residencies	Education	Gallery	Grants	Library	Membership Organization	Museum	Performance Space	Publishing	Research & Development	Resource	DOS/Intel	Hewlett Packard	Macintosh
British Journal of Photography, Information Directory																				◆		*			
Creative Camera, Battersea Art Center																				◆					
De Sterreichisches Foto Archiv, Im Museum Moderner Kunst									*							*		◆		◆	*			*	*
European Photography			*			*		*	*											◆			*		
Independent Photography Directory										*										◆					
International Center of Photography									*			*	*	◆	*		*						*		
La Recherche Photographique, Paris Audiovisuel								*											*	◆	◆				
Musee de la Photographie, Charleroi			*	*		*	*		*				◆	◆			*	◆		◆	◆				
Perspetif Center for Photography	*	*		*						*		*		◆			*			*			*		
Photofile, The Australian Centre for Photography, Ltd.	*	*		*	*				*	*	*		*	◆						*			*		*
Photographic Journal, Royal Photographic Society										*						*				◆					

151

Photography

◆ = Primary Activity
* = Other Disciplines/Activities/Resources

Column groups: **DISCIPLINES**, **ACTIVITIES**, **PLATFORMS**

Disciplines: 3D Art · Animation · Architecture · Ceramics · Computer Art · Computer Graphics · Conceptual Art · Copy Art · Dance · Environmental Art · Fiber Arts · Film · Graphic Design · Holography · Industrial Design · Installation Art · Interactive Art · Kinetic Art · Literary Arts · Mixed Media · Multimedia · Music and Sound · Painting · Performance Art · Photography · Robotics · Sculpture · Space Art · Telecommunications · Video · Virtual Reality · Visual Art

Activities: Artist Residencies · Awards & Competitions · Education · Fellowships · Festivals and Events · Gallery · Grants · Library · Membership Organization · Museum · Network Communication · Performance Group · Performance Space · Production · Publishing · Research & Development · Resource

Platforms: Amiga · Atari · DEC · DOS/Intel · Hewlett Packard · Macintosh · Mainframe · Next · Silicon Graphics · Sun

Organization	Marks
Photographie Ouverte	Publishing ◆
School of Photographic Arts and Sciences	Animation *, Computer Art *, Conceptual Art *, Environmental Art *, Film *, Graphic Design *, Holography *, Mixed Media *, Photography (primary), Video *; Education *; DOS/Intel *
Society of Photographic Scientists & Engineers	Membership Organization ◆

Sculpture

◆ = Primary Activity
* = Other Disciplines/Activities/Resources

Organization	Marks
Association of Sculpture and Engineering Techniques	Sculpture (primary); Membership Organization ◆
Yorkshire Sculpture Park	Dance *, Environmental Art *, Installation Art *, Photography *; Artist Residencies *, Education *, Gallery ◆, Performance Space *, Publishing *; DOS/Intel *, Macintosh *

Space Art

◆ = Primary Activity
* = Other Disciplines/Activities/Resources

Organization	Marks
International Association for the Astronomical Arts	Space Art (primary); Membership Organization ◆
Science and Art	Film *, Installation Art *, Mixed Media *, Multimedia *, Music and Sound *, Video *; Education ◆, Performance Space *, Publishing *

Telecommunications

◆ = Primary Activity
* = Other Disciplines/Activities/Resources

	3D Art	Animation	Architecture	Ceramics	Computer Art	Computer Graphics	Conceptual Art	Copy Art	Dance	Environmental Art	Fiber Arts	Film	Graphic Design	Holography	Industrial Design	Installation Art	Interactive Art	Kinetic Art	Literary Arts	Mixed Media	Multimedia	Music and Sound	Painting	Performance Art	Photography	Robotics	Sculpture	Space Art	Telecommunications	Video	Virtual Reality	Visual Art	Artist Residencies	Awards & Competitions	Education	Fellowships	Festivals and Events	Gallery	Grants	Library	Membership Organization	Museum	Network Communication	Performance Group	Performance Space	Production	Publishing	Research & Development	Resource	Amiga	Atari	DEC	DOS/Intel	Hewlett Packard	Macintosh	Mainframe	Next	Silicon Graphics	Sun
Transit																					*			*						▓			*		*		*												*											

Video

◆ = Primary Activity
* = Other Disciplines/Activities/Resources

	3D Art	Animation	Architecture	Ceramics	Computer Art	Computer Graphics	Conceptual Art	Copy Art	Dance	Environmental Art	Fiber Arts	Film	Graphic Design	Holography	Industrial Design	Installation Art	Interactive Art	Kinetic Art	Literary Arts	Mixed Media	Multimedia	Music and Sound	Painting	Performance Art	Photography	Robotics	Sculpture	Space Art	Telecommunications	Video	Virtual Reality	Visual Art	Artist Residencies	Awards & Competitions	Education	Fellowships	Festivals and Events	Gallery	Grants	Library	Membership Organization	Museum	Network Communication	Performance Group	Performance Space	Production	Publishing	Research & Development	Resource	Amiga	Atari	DEC	DOS/Intel	Hewlett Packard	Macintosh	Mainframe	Next	Silicon Graphics	Sun
1708 East Main Gallery																														▓												◆																	
Agenda of Audiovisual Festivals in Europe												*																		▓																	◆												
Art Com		*			*		*					*					*							*						▓	*				*								◆				*	*					*						
Art and Technology Resource File - Video/Audio Installation Touring Project												*										*								▓								*										◆												
Artists Television Access (ATA)																														▓								*	*																					
Bell Canada Award in Video Art																														▓				◆																										
Center for New Television																														▓				◆							◆				*															
Deep Dish Video																														▓																◆														
Department of Art, University of Kentucky																														▓					◆																									
Directions																														▓											◆																			
Documentary Video Associates Ltd, Design, Publications						*						*	*		*					*	*	*			*					▓					*				*							◆	*								*				
European Media Art Festival																														▓											◆																			
Experimental Television Center Ltd																														▓			◆															*		*									*	
Independent Media																														▓																◆														
Le Premier Guide de L'Audiovisuel Europeen (First Guide of European Audiovisual Resources)												*																		▓																	◆												

153

Video

◆ = Primary Activity
✱ = Other Disciplines/Activities/Resources

DISCIPLINES

Organization	3D Art	Animation	Architecture	Ceramics	Computer Art	Computer Graphics	Conceptual Art	Copy Art	Dance	Environmental Art	Fiber Arts	Film	Graphic Design	Holography	Industrial Design	Installation Art	Interactive Art	Kinetic Art	Literary Arts	Mixed Media	Multimedia	Music and Sound	Painting	Performance Art	Photography	Robotics	Sculpture	Space Art	Telecommunications	Video	Virtual Reality	Visual Art
Media Investment Club																																
Mediamatic Magazine																																
Pandect, Inc.		✱			✱	✱							✱				✱				✱	✱										
Savannah College of Art and Design							✱					✱					✱				✱										✱	
Screen-L																																
Sincere Technologies																																
Society of Professional Videographers																																
Southern California Video, Video Department						✱																										
Video Art Society, University of Tasmania, Centre of the Arts																																
Video Free America																																
Visual Studies Workshop																					✱	✱			✱							

ACTIVITIES

Organization	Artist Residencies	Awards & Competitions	Education	Fellowships	Festivals and Events	Gallery	Grants	Library	Membership Organization	Museum	Network Communication	Performance Group	Performance Space	Production	Publishing	Research & Development	Resource
Media Investment Club									◆								
Mediamatic Magazine															◆		
Pandect, Inc.														◆			
Savannah College of Art and Design			◆			✱									✱	✱	
Screen-L											✱						
Sincere Technologies																	
Society of Professional Videographers			◆						◆								
Southern California Video, Video Department																	
Video Art Society, University of Tasmania, Centre of the Arts			✱						◆								
Video Free America	✱												◆				
Visual Studies Workshop	✱		◆										✱				

PLATFORMS

Organization	Amiga	Atari	DEC	DOS/Intel	Hewlett Packard	Macintosh	Mainframe	Next	Silicon Graphics	Sun
Media Investment Club										
Mediamatic Magazine										
Pandect, Inc.						✱				
Savannah College of Art and Design						✱				
Screen-L										
Sincere Technologies										
Society of Professional Videographers										
Southern California Video, Video Department				✱	✱	✱				
Video Art Society, University of Tasmania, Centre of the Arts										
Video Free America										
Visual Studies Workshop										

Virtual Reality

◆ = Primary Activity
✱ = Other Disciplines/Activities/Resources

DISCIPLINES

Organization	3D Art	Animation	Architecture	Ceramics	Computer Art	Computer Graphics	Conceptual Art	Copy Art	Dance	Environmental Art	Fiber Arts	Film	Graphic Design	Holography	Industrial Design	Installation Art	Interactive Art	Kinetic Art	Literary Arts	Mixed Media	Multimedia	Music and Sound	Painting	Performance Art	Photography	Robotics	Sculpture	Space Art	Telecommunications	Video	Virtual Reality	Visual Art
Advanced Information Methods, Inc.	✱	✱			✱	✱				✱		✱	✱			✱	✱			✱	✱	✱	✱			✱		✱	✱	✱		
CyberEdge Journal		✱			✱	✱							✱		✱					✱	✱				✱	✱				✱		
Emove, Laboratory for Virtual Musical Instrument Design									✱								✱				✱	✱										
George Coates Performance Works	✱				✱	✱			✱	✱		✱	✱		✱					✱	✱	✱		✱	✱							
Studio for Creative Inquiry																					✱											

ACTIVITIES

Organization	Artist Residencies	Awards & Competitions	Education	Fellowships	Festivals and Events	Gallery	Grants	Library	Membership Organization	Museum	Network Communication	Performance Group	Performance Space	Production	Publishing	Research & Development	Resource
Advanced Information Methods, Inc.			✱											✱	✱	◆	
CyberEdge Journal															◆		
Emove, Laboratory for Virtual Musical Instrument Design																◆	
George Coates Performance Works					✱	✱						◆	✱		✱		
Studio for Creative Inquiry			◆													✱	

PLATFORMS

Organization	Amiga	Atari	DEC	DOS/Intel	Hewlett Packard	Macintosh	Mainframe	Next	Silicon Graphics	Sun
Advanced Information Methods, Inc.	✱		✱	✱	✱	✱	✱		✱	✱
CyberEdge Journal				✱						
Emove, Laboratory for Virtual Musical Instrument Design										
George Coates Performance Works				✱		✱			✱	
Studio for Creative Inquiry										

Virtual Reality

◆ = Primary Activity

✳ = Other Disciplines/Activities/Resources

Organization	DISCIPLINES																																ACTIVITIES																	PLATFORMS									
	3D Art	Animation	Architecture	Ceramics	Computer Art	Computer Graphics	Conceptual Art	Copy Art	Dance	Environmental Art	Fiber Arts	Film	Graphic Design	Holography	Industrial Design	Installation Art	Interactive Art	Kinetic Art	Literary Arts	Mixed Media	Multimedia	Music and Sound	Painting	Performance Art	Photography	Robotics	Sculpture	Space Art	Telecommunications	Video	Virtual Reality	Visual Art	Artist Residencies	Awards & Competitions	Education	Fellowships	Festivals and Events	Gallery	Grants	Library	Membership Organization	Museum	Network Communication	Performance Group	Performance Space	Production	Publishing	Research & Development	Resource	Amiga	Atari	DEC	DOS/Intel	Hewlett Packard	Macintosh	Mainframe	Next	Silicon Graphics	Sun
Trans Data		✳			✳	✳	✳								✳		✳			✳	✳	✳				✳				✳					✳			✳	✳	✳	✳		✳					◆					✳	✳	✳				
Vivid Group, Studio 302	✳	✳			✳											✳	✳				✳	✳		✳											✳			✳			✳		✳	✳	✳			◆		✳			✳						

Visual Art

◆ = Primary Activity

✳ = Other Disciplines/Activities/Resources

Organization	DISCIPLINES																																ACTIVITIES																	PLATFORMS									
	3D Art	Animation	Architecture	Ceramics	Computer Art	Computer Graphics	Conceptual Art	Copy Art	Dance	Environmental Art	Fiber Arts	Film	Graphic Design	Holography	Industrial Design	Installation Art	Interactive Art	Kinetic Art	Literary Arts	Mixed Media	Multimedia	Music and Sound	Painting	Performance Art	Photography	Robotics	Sculpture	Space Art	Telecommunications	Video	Virtual Reality	Visual Art	Artist Residencies	Awards & Competitions	Education	Fellowships	Festivals and Events	Gallery	Grants	Library	Membership Organization	Museum	Network Communication	Performance Group	Performance Space	Production	Publishing	Research & Development	Resource	Amiga	Atari	DEC	DOS/Intel	Hewlett Packard	Macintosh	Mainframe	Next	Silicon Graphics	Sun
Afterimage, Visual Studies Workshop																																	✳		✳		✳	✳									✳	◆												
American Association for the Advancement of Science, Art of Science and Technology Program																																									◆																		
American Physician Art Association																																									◆																		
American School of Neon	✳				✳	✳							✳					✳		✳			✳		✳		✳			✳					◆																				✳				
Art Academy of Cincinnati																	✳			✳															◆																				✳				
Art Horizons																																		◆																										
Artistic License																																											◆																
Artlink, Electronic Information Center for the Visual Arts																																							✳				◆																
Betty Brazil Memorial Fund, Women Sculptor Grant																																							✳																				
Camera Austria, Forum Stadtpark																																			✳												◆												
Center for Advanced Visual Studies, MIT																						✳											✳		✳	✳																						
Center for Image and Sound Research																																																◆											
Center for the Advanced Study in the Visual Arts, National Gallery of Art																																	◆		✳			✳																		✳				
Clemson University, Art Department	✳		✳	✳		✳																	✳		✳		✳								✳																					✳				
Edizioni L'Agrifoglio																																															◆												

Visual Art

◆ = Primary Activity

✱ = Other Disciplines/Activities/Resources

Organization	3D Art	Animation	Architecture	Ceramics	Computer Art	Computer Graphics	Conceptual Art	Copy Art	Dance	Environmental Art	Fiber Arts	Film	Graphic Design	Holography	Industrial Design	Installation Art	Interactive Art	Kinetic Art	Literary Arts	Mixed Media	Multimedia	Music and Sound	Painting	Performance Art	Photography	Robotics	Sculpture	Space Art	Telecommunications	Video	Virtual Reality	Visual Art	Artist Residencies	Awards & Competitions	Education	Fellowships	Festivals and Events	Gallery	Grants	Library	Membership Organization	Museum	Network Communication	Performance Group	Performance Space	Production	Publishing	Research & Development	Resource	Amiga	Atari	DEC	DOS/Intel	Hewlett Packard	Macintosh	Mainframe	Next	Silicon Graphics	Sun
European Visual Arts Information Network (EVIAN), The Library, Suffolk Cottage																																			✱					✱									✱										
Experimental Art Foundation			✱	✱	✱	✱	✱																										◆																										
Greater London Arts Association						✱																																			✱																		
Grizedale Forest, Northern Arts																																	◆																										
IEEE Society on Social Implications of Technology, Otis/Parsons Art Institute					✱	✱																													✱						◆							✱	✱										
Image Film/Video Center												✱																		✱																			◆										
Image Technology and Art (ATI), Department of Plastic Arts, University of Paris																																									◆																		
Institute of Art and Design						✱	✱			✱		✱	✱	✱	✱	✱	✱	✱					✱		✱		✱			✱					✱													◆							✱				
International Art Horizons, Deptartment RAU												✱	✱	✱						✱	✱		✱		✱		✱			✱									◆																				
International Festival of the Image, Montage												✱		✱											✱												◆																						
International Society of Copier Artists (ISCA)								✱												✱																					✱						◆												
Kuztown University, Department of Art Ed/Crafts	✱												✱		✱	✱	✱	✱	✱	✱	✱	✱	✱	✱	✱		✱	✱	✱						◆																		✱		✱				
Lightworks Magazine																									✱																		✱				◆												
Louisiana State University			✱		✱	✱				✱																																						✱											
MIT List Visual Arts Center, Weisner Building						✱									✱																		✱		◆			◆									✱						✱		✱				
National College of Art & Design						✱							✱		✱					✱															◆																		✱		✱				
Neon News																							✱		✱										✱												◆												
Parabola Arts Foundation																																															◆												
Parachute																																															◆												
School of Visual Arts, MFA Degree Program in Computer Art	✱				✱	✱																													◆																								
Sheehan Gallery																																						◆																					
University of Illinois at Chicago, Art Department	✱				✱	✱																		✱						✱	✱				◆																				✱				
Visual Resources, James Madison University	✱	✱	✱		✱	✱							✱										✱		✱										◆				✱							✱													
Visualization Laboratory, Texas A&M University	✱	✱	✱		✱	✱																								✱					✱													◆					✱		✱	✱	✱	✱	✱
Warwick Museum																																										◆																	

Visual Art

◆ = Primary Activity

✳ = Other Disciplines/Activities/Resources

	DISCIPLINES																																ACTIVITIES																	PLATFORMS									
	3D Art	Animation	Architecture	Ceramics	Computer Art	Computer Graphics	Conceptual Art	Copy Art	Dance	Environmental Art	Fiber Arts	Film	Graphic Design	Holography	Industrial Design	Installation Art	Interactive Art	Kinetic Art	Literary Arts	Mixed Media	Multimedia	Music and Sound	Painting	Performance Art	Photography	Robotics	Sculpture	Space Art	Telecommunications	Video	Virtual Reality	Visual Art	Artist Residencies	Awards & Competitions	Education	Fellowships	Festivals and Events	Gallery	Grants	Library	Membership Organization	Museum	Network Communication	Performance Group	Performance Space	Production	Publishing	Research & Development	Resource	Amiga	Atari	DEC	DOS/Intel	Hewlett Packard	Macintosh	Mainframe	Next	Silicon Graphics	Sun
Weisses Haus Gallery																																▓				◆																								
Whitney Independent Study Program																																				◆																							

157

DIRECTORY OF ORGANIZATIONS

1708 East Main Gallery
Julyen Norman
Richmond VA 23223 USA
Tel: (804) 643-7829

3D Book Productions
Harry zur Kleinsmiede
PO Box 19
9530 AA Borger, The Netherlands
Tel: (31) 599887245
Fax: (31) 599887228

3D Foto World
Fach CH-4020
Basel, Switzerland

3D Electronic BBS
3d-request@bfmny0.BFM.COM

3D International Newsletter
Hal Thwaites
7141 Sherbrooke St. West
Montreal, Quebec H4B 1R6 Canada

A Space
Nancy Paterson
Ingrid Mayrhofer
475 The West Mall, #1513
Etobicoke, Ontario M9C 4Z3 Canada
Tel: (416) 621-3290
Fax: (416) 365-3332

ACARTE
Fundacao Calouste Gulbenkian
Maria Madalena de Azaredo Perdigao
Avenida Berne 45A
Lisbon Codex 1093 Portugal
Tel: (351 1) 734119/73

ACAT
David Worrall, Head
Australia Centre for the Arts
 & Technology
GPD Box 804
Canberra, ACT 2601 Australia
Tel: (06) 249 5640
Fax: (06) 247 0229

ACM Educators Newsletter
Jacquelyn Ford Morie
SIGGRAPH Educators Newsletter
321 Elkhorn Court
Winter Park, FL 32792 USA
Email: morie@ist.ucf.edu

ACM SIGGRAPH
Steve Cunningham, Publications Chair
Peter Pathe, Electronic Publications
Member Services Department
1515 Broadway
New York City, NY 10036 USA
Tel: (212) 626-0500
Fax: (212) 944-1318
Email: acmhelp@acmvm.bitnet

AN Publications
David Butler, Commissioning Editor
PO Box 23
Sunderland SR4 GDG United Kingdom
Tel: (041): 567 3589
Fax: (041): 564 1600

ART (if) ACT
David-John Etzen, Representative
235 East Colorado Boulevard, #292
Pasadena, CA 91101 USA
Tel: (818) 332-9577

Abaci Gallery of Computer Art
Daria Harvey Barclay
312 NW 10th
Portland, OR 97209 USA
Tel: (503) 228-8642

Abby Joslin & Associates
Abby Joslin, Principal
Justine Whitehead
Evan Ricks
2815 Bush Street
San Francisco, CA 94115 USA
Tel: (415) 885-5849
Fax: (415) 885-2805
Email: Applelink ABBY.MKTG

Adolph and Ester Gottleib Foundation
380 West Broadway
New York City, NY 10012 USA

**Advanced Computing Center
for Arts & Design**
Robert McCarthy, Jr., Assistant
 Director
Ohio State University
1224 Kinnear Road
Columbus, OH 43212-1154 USA
Tel: (614) 292-3416
Fax: (614) 292-7776
Email: accad@cgrg.ohio-state.edu

Advanced Information Methods, Inc.
Sherman Klein, Technical Director
Corporate and Technology
PO Box 5692
Mission Hills, CA 91395 USA
Tel: (818) 366-2678

Afterimage
Lance Speer
Visual Studies Workshop
31 Prince Street
Rochester, NY 14607 USA

**Agenda of Audiovisual Festivals in
Europe**
Place Flagey
Bruxelles 18-105 Belgium
Tel: (02) 640 38 15

Allegheny College
George Roland
Art Department
PO Box 85
Meadville, PA 16335 USA
Tel: (814) 724-4365

American Academy in Rome
41 East 65th Street
New York City, NY 10021 USA

**American Association
for the Advancement of Science**
Virginia Stern
Art of Science and
 Technology Program
1333 H Street NW
Washington, DC 20005 USA
Tel: (202) 326-6672

**American Association of University
Women Educational Foundation**
AAUW Educational Foundation
2401 Virginia Avenue NW
Washington, DC 20037 USA

American Gamelan Institute
Jody Diamond, Director
David Fugua, Administrative Director
Box 5036
Hanover, NH 03755 USA
Tel: (603) 448-8837
Email:
 Jody.Diamond@mac.dartmouth.edu

American Israel Cultural Foundation
32 Allenby Road
Tel Aviv, Israel

**American Journal of Computer Art
in Education**
J.F. Morie
258 Pelican Avenue
Daytona Beach, FL 32118 USA

American Physician Art Association
L.S. Rathbun, MD
76 Forest Road
Ashville, NC 28803 USA
Tel: (704) 274-0748

American School of Neon
212 Third Avenue North
Minneapolis, MN 55401 USA

American Society for Aesthetics
Roger Shiner, Secretary-Treasurer
Peggy Brackett, Business Manager
A-108 Humanities Center
University of Alberta
Edmonton, Alberta T69 2E5 Canada
Tel: (403) 492-4102
Fax: (403) 492-9160
Email: rshiner@vm.ucs.ualberta.ca

American Studies Foundation, Inc.
Yurakucho 1-Chome, Chiyoda-Ku
Dai-Ichi Seimei Bldg,13-1
Tokyo 100 Japan

Ampersand Productions
Paul J Blankinship
1661 Gateway Drive
Vallejo, CA 94589 USA
Tel: (707) 645-7448
Email: 71561.1037@compuserve.com

Andrew Gemant Award
John Rigden
American Institute of Physics
335 East 45th Street
New York City, NY 10017 USA

Antelope Valley College
Dr. White
3041 West Avenue K
Lancaster, CA 93536 USA
Tel: (805) 943-3241

Apple Productions
Jeffrey Apple, President
1230 Horn Avenue, #301
Los Angeles, CA 90069 USA
Tel: (310) 854-6182
Fax: (310) 280-1880

Arizona State University
Roberta Smith
4510 N. 37th Avenue
Phoenix, AZ 85019 USA

Arkansas Artists Council
Heritage Center, #200
225 E. Markham Street
Little Rock, AR 72001 USA

Arstechnica: Center for Art and Technology
Robert Mallary
University of Massachusetts/Amherst
Amherst, MA 01003 USA

Art & Science Collaborations, Inc (ASCI)
Cynthia Pannucci, Artistic Director
PO Box 040496
Staten Island, NY 10304-0009 USA
Tel: (718) 816-9796
Fax: (718) 273-9089

Art Academy of Cincinnati
Gary Gaffney, Professor
1125 St. Gregory Street
Cincinnati, OH 45224 USA
Tel: (513) 562-8765

Art Access/Networking
Roy Ascott
64 Upper Cheltenham Place
Bristol BS6 5HR United Kingdom

Art Business & Technology
Ed Dunn
712 100th Ave SE
Bellevue, WA 98004 USA
Tel: (206) 462-0500

Art Com
Carl Loeffler, Executive Director
Jen Tait, Distribution
Jennifer Bender, Assistant Director
PO Box 193123, Rincon Annex
San Francisco, CA 94119-3123 USA
Tel: (415) 431-7524
Fax: (415) 431-7841
Email: artcomtv@well.sf.ca.us

Art Horizons
Nora Smith
140 Prospect Avenue, Suite 16R
Hackensack, NJ 07601 USA
Tel: (201) 487-7277
Fax: (201) 343-5353

Art Research Center
Thomas Stephens, Coordinator
William Clayton Bodenhamer
Kathleen Van Voorst
PO Box 30098
4923 Walnut Street
Kansas City, MO 64112 USA
Tel: (816) 531-7799
Fax: (816) 561-1166

Art and Technology Resource File— Video/Audio Installation Touring Project
131 Spring Street
New York City, NY 10012 USA
Tel: (212) 219-9695

Art+Com
Deitrich von Hase
Hardenbergplatz 2
1000 Berlin 12 Germany

Art, Science and Technology Institute
Mary Dewatre
2018 R Street NW
Washington, DC 20009 USA

ArtBase BBS
PO Box 2154
St. Paul, MN 55102 USA
Tel: (612) 298-0123
Fax: (612) 298-0117

ArtNetwork
Constance Franklin
Genevieve Bruner, Editorial Assistant
PO Box 369
Renaissance, CA 95962 USA
Tel: (916) 692-1355

Artist Book Works
1422 West Irving Park
Chicago, IL 60613 USA
Tel: (312) 348-4469

Artistic License
Lorna Jordan
4233 Meridian Avenue N.
Seattle, WA 98103 USA

Artists Collective of Northern Ireland
Queen Street Studios
37/39 Queen Street
Belfast, BT1 6EA Ireland

Artists Foundation
110 Broad Street
Boston, MA 02110 USA

Artists Rights Society, Inc. (ARS)
Theodore Feder, President
Katia Stieglitz
Elizabeth Weisberg
65 Bleecker Street
New York City, NY 10012 USA
Tel: (212) 420-9160
Tel: (212) 420-9286

Artists Television Access (ATA)
992 Valencia Street
San Francisco, CA 94110 USA

Artkitek
Steve Anderson
122 Myrtle Ave
Cotati, CA 94931 USA
Tel: (707) 664-2330

Artlink
Alan Sandman, System Operator
Electronic Information Center
  for the Visual Arts
PO Box 5595, Station E
Atlanta, GA 30307-0595 USA

Arts & Sciences Production
George Olczak
PO Box 51777
Palo Alto, CA 94303 USA
Tel: (415) 824-7348

Arts Media Group
Adeola Solanke
90 De Beavoir Road, Hackney
London N1 4EN United Kingdom

Arts Wire
Anne Focke
Anna Couey
811 First Avenue, #403
Seattle, WA 98104 USA
Tel: (206) 343-0769
Email: afocke@tmn.com
        couey@well.sf.ca.us

Arts, Crafts and Theater Safety
Monona Rossol, President
181 Thompson Street, #23
New York City, NY 10012 USA
Tel: (212) 777-0062

Artscience Gallery
Chicago Museum of Science
Chicago, IL 60608 USA

Artsnet Electronic Network
Phillip Bannigan
PO Box 429
Eastwood, South Australia 5063
Australia
Email: suephil@peg.pegasus.oz.au

Artspace
11 Randle Street
Surry Hills, NSW 2010 Australia
Tel: 02-212-5031

Artswatch
Phyllis Free, Manager
Jan Graves, Executive Director
2337 Frankfort Avenue
Louisville, KY 40206 USA
Tel: (502) 893-9661

Asian Cultural Council
280 Madison Avenue
New York City, NY 10016 USA

Association des Centres Culturels
Paul Guisen, Director
c/o La Botanique
Rue Royale 236
Brussels 1210 Belgium
Tel: (32-2) 223 09 98
Fax: (32-2) 219 66 60

Association for Computers and the Humanities
Joseph Rudman, Treasurer
Carnegie-Mellon University
Department of English
Pittsburgh, PA 15213 USA

Association of Sculpture and Engineering Techniques
Colin Sanderson, Director
Kirktonhill, Ratho, Newbridge
Midlothian, Scotland EH28 8RU
United Kingdom

Association per Lo Studio Delle, Internazioni Tra Arte, Scienza & Technologia
Via Marmorata 169
Rome 00153 Italy

Association pour Le Creation et la Recherche Electroacoustique du Quebec (ACREQ)
Claude Schryer, Artistic Director
Lynda Clouette, Director General
4001, Berri #202
Montreal, Quebec H2L 4H2 Canada
Tel: (514) 849-9534
Fax: (514) 987-1862

Atlanta Gallery of Holography
Lisa Murray
75 Bennett Street NW
Atlanta, GA 30309 USA
Tel: (404) 352-3412

Ausgraph—Australasian Computer Graphics Association
PO Box 29
Parkville, Victoria 94107 Australia
Tel: (03) 387 9955
Fax: (03) 387 312

Australian Centre for the Arts and Technology (ACAT)
Stuart Ramsden, Lecturer in
  Computer Animation
Canberra Institute of the Arts
PO Box 804
Canberra City, ACT 2601 Australia
Tel: (61 6) 249 5640
Fax: (61 6) 247 0229

Australian Network for Art and Technology (ANAT)
PO Box 8029
Hindley Street
Adelaide 500 Australia
Tel: (61 08) 2319037
Fax: (61 08) 2117323
Email: anat@peg.pegasus.oz.au

BEEP Sounds
Robert Ceely, Director
33 Elm Street
Brookline, MA 02146-6813 USA
Tel: (617) 731-3785

Balungan
PO Box 9911
Oakland, CA 94613 USA
Tel: (510) 530-4553

Banff Centre for the Arts
Kevin Elliott, Audio
Douglas MacLeod, Computer
  Applications and Research
Sara Diamond, Television & Video
Media Arts Program
Box 1020
Banff, Alberta T0L 0C0 Canada
Tel: (403) 762-6651
Fax: (403) 762-6659
Email: kelliott@asc.ucalgary.ca

Bard College
Benjamin Boretz
Music Program Zero
Annandale-on-Hudson, NY 12504 USA
Tel: (914) 758 6822 ex 272

Barrow and Geraldine S. Cadbury Trust
2 College Walk, Selly Oak
Birmingham, United Kingdom

Bay Area Center for Art & Technology (BACAT)
1095 Market Street, Suite 209
San Francisco, CA 94103 USA
Tel: (415) 626-2979

Bell Canada Award in Video Art
Jean Gagnon
99 Metcalfe St.
PO Box 1047
Ottawa, Ontario K1P 5V8 Canada
Tel: (613) 237-3400

Bellagio Study and Conference Center
The Rockefeller Foundation
1133 Avenue of the Americas
New York City, NY 10036 USA

Bemis—Center for Contemporary Arts
Ree Schonlau, Executive Director
Joan Batson, Assistant Director
Christina Narwicz, Development
  Assistant
614 South 11 Street
Omaha, NE 68102 USA
Tel: (402) 341-7130
Fax: (402) 344-9791

Betty Brazil Memorial Fund
Women Sculptor Grant
PO Box 221
Tarrytown, NY 10591 USA

Biennale des Arts Electroniques de Maiselle
Hubert LaFont
Eurekam
77 rue de Charonne
Paris 75011 France
Tel: (1 43) 48 40 40
Tel: (1 43) 48 60 21

Big Pond Productions, Inc.
Robert Fleck, CEO
PO Box 801120
Santa Clarita, CA 91380-1120 USA
Tel: (805) 296-9083
Fax: (805) 296-3985

Bilder Digital Galerie
Tulbeckstr. 5
Munchen 2
8000 Germany
Tel: 502747 5
Fax: 503652

Blue Mountain Center
Blue Mountain, NY 12812 USA

Blue Rose Studio
Laurel Kashinn, Managing Owner
Stonecroft Village 2206
Grafton, WI 53024-9793 USA
Tel/Fax: (414) 377-1669

BodySynth
Edwin Mark Severinghaus
Chris Van Raalte
142 20th Avenue, #2
San Francisco, CA 94121-1308 USA
Tel: (415) 387-1142

Brainstorms
306 Poplar
Mill Valley, CA 94941 USA
Tel: (415) 388-3912

British Journal of Photography, Information Directory
58 Fleet Street
London EC44 1JU United Kingdom

Bronx Museum of the Arts
Jeffrey Ramirez, Deputy Director
 for Programs
1040 Grand Concourse
New York City, NY 10456-3999 USA
Tel: (718) 681-6000
Fax: (718) 681-6181

Buckminster Fuller Institute
Bonnie Goldstein
1743 S. La Cienega Blvd.
Los Angeles, CA 90035 USA
Tel: (213) 837-7710
Fax: (213) 837-7715

Bureau of Architecture
Mark Primeau, Assistant City Architect
30 Van Ness Avenue, Suite 4100
San Francisco, CA 94102 USA
Tel: (415) 557-4666

Burning Press
Luigi-Bob Drake, Editor in Chief
Kristen Ban Tepper, Editor
PO Box 585
Lakewood, OH 44107 USA
Tel: (216) 221-8940
Email: au462@cleveland.freenet.edu

CADRE Institute: Computers in Art and Design/Research and Education
Joel Slayton
School of Art and Design
San Jose State University
One Washington Square
San Jose, CA 95192 USA
Tel: (408) 924-4368
Email: slayton@sjsuvm1.bitnet.edu

CERL Sound Group
University of Illinois
Lippold Haken, Director
Carla Scaletti, Research Associate
Kurt Hebel, Research Associate
252 ERL/MC-242
103 S. Mathews
Urbana, IL 61801-2977 USA
Tel: (217) 333-0766
Fax: (217) 244-0793
Email: sound@cerl.uiuc.edu

California College of the Arts and Crafts
Harry Critchfield, Computer Graphics
 Support
Broadway
Oakland, CA 94618 USA
Tel: (510) 653-8118 ext 181

California Institute of the Arts, Film and Video
Ed Emshwiller
Valencia, CA 91355 USA
Tel: (805) 255-1050

Camera Austria
Christine Frisinghelli
Forum Stadtpark
Stadtpark 1
Graz A-8010 Austria
Tel: 316 827734
Fax: 825 3696

Canada Council
Audio Production Grants
Jean Gagnon
Communications Section
99 Metcalfe Street, Box 1047
Ottawa, Ontario K1P 5V8 Canada
Tel: (613) 598-4356

Canada Council
Media Arts Grants
Integrated Media Grants
99 Metcalf Street, Box 1047
Ottawa, Ontario K1P 5V8 Canada

Canada Council
Media Projects in Dance Grants
99 Metcalf Street, Box 1047
Ottawa, Ontario K1P 5V8 Canada
Tel: (613) 237-3400

Canadian ElectroAcoustic Community
Claude Schryer, Administrator
Daniel Leduc, President
CP 845 Succursal Place D'Armes
Montreal, Quebec H2Y 3J2 Canada
Tel: (514) 849-1564
Fax: (514) 987-1862

Canadian Holographic Society
Lorna Heaton
3998 De Bullion
Montreal, Quebec H2W 2E4 Canada

Capp Street Project
270 14th Street
San Francisco, CA 94103 USA
Tel: (415) 626-7747
Fax: (415) 626-7991

Cariboo College
Digital Arts & Design
Glenn Howard
PO Box 3010
Kamloops, British Columbia V2C 6B7
Canada

Catalogue of Computer Programs for Music Education
Charles Boody
1001 Highway 7
Hopkins, MI 49328 USA

Catalogue of Music Software
Pinetree Plaza #17, 5269 Bufor
Atlanta, GA 30340 USA

Center for Advanced Visual Studies
MIT
40 Massachusetts, Bldg W 11
Cambridge, MA 02139 USA

Center for Art and Technology, Carnegie-Mellon University
John Pane
CFA 111
Pittsburgh, PA 15213 USA

Center for Art and Technology, Connecticut College
Noel Zahler, Co-Director
David Smalley, Co-Director
270 Mohegan Avenue, Box 5632
New London, CT 06320 USA
Tel: (203) 439-2001
Fax: (203) 439-2700
Email: nbzah@mvax.cc.conncoll.edu

Center for Computer Art and Technology
Harold Hedelman
329 Bryant Street, Suite 3-D
San Francisco, CA 94107 USA
Tel: (415) 882-7063

Center for Computer Research in Music and Acoustics (CCRMA)
Patte Wood, Adminstrative Director
Chris Chafe, Technical Director
Music Deptartment,
Stanford University
The Knoll
Stanford, CA 94305 USA
Tel: (415) 723-4971
Fax: (415) 723-8468
Email: patte@ccrma.stanford.edu

Center for Computer-Assisted Research in Humanities (CCARH)
Eleanor Selfridge-Field
525 Middlefield Road, #120
Menlo Park, CA 94025 USA
Tel: (415) 322-7050
Fax: (415) 329-8365
Email: XB.L36@stanford.edu

Center for Contemporary Music
John Bischoff, CCM Studio Coordinator
Chris Brown, Co-Director
Maggi Payne, Co-Director
Mills College, Department of Music
5000 MacArthur Blvd.
Oakland, CA 94613 USA
Tel: (510) 430-2191
Fax: (510) 430-3314
Email: bischoff@mills.edu

Center for Experiments in Art, Information & Technology (CEAIT)
David Rosenboom, Dean/Professor
 of Music
Morton Subotnick, Co-Director
Mark Coniglio, Technical Assistant
California Institute of the Arts
24700 McBean Parkway
Valencia, CA 91355 USA
Tel: (805) 255-1050
Fax: (805) 254-8352
Email: davidr@calarts.edu

Center for Image and Sound Research
Jeffrey Berryman
1140 Homer Street, Suite 200
Vancouver, British Columbia V6B 2X6
Canada
Email: cisr@well.sf.ca.us

Center for International Contemporary Art (CICA)
724 Fifth Avenue
New York City, NY 10019-4106 USA

Center for Music Technology
Bruce Mahin, Director
Radford University
Box 6968
Radford, VA 24142 USA
Tel: (703) 831-6174
Email: bmahin@ruacad.ac.runet.edu

Center for New Television
Ida Jeter
1440 N. Dayton Street
Chicago, IL 60622 USA
Tel: (312) 951-6868

Center for Performing Arts and Technology
David Gregory
University of Michigan
School of Music
Ann Arbor, MI 48109-2805 USA
Tel: (313) 747-2020
Fax: (313) 763-5097

Center for Research in Arts & Technology
Bruce Marsh
USF
Tampa, FL 33620-6300 USA
Tel: (813) 974-2360
Fax: (813) 974-2091

Center for Research into Applications of Computers to Music
Alan Marsden
University of Lancaster
Lancaster LA1 4YW United Kingdom

Center for Safety in the Arts
Angela Bobin
Art Hazard Information Center
5 Beekman Street
New York City, NY 10038 USA
Tel: (212) 227-6220

Center for Structural Mechanics and Engineering, Technical University of Lisbon (CMEST)
Harold Santo
Av. Rovisco Pais
1096 Lisbon Codex, Portugal
Tel: (351 1) 80 1579/89 765

Center for the Advanced Study in the Visual Arts
National Gallery of Art
Washington, DC 20565 USA

Center for the Diffusion of Contemporary Music
Centro de Arte Reina Sofia
Santa Isabel, 52 (Atocha)
Madrid 28012 Spain
Tel: 468 2310

Centre National Art and Technologie
Serge Gaymard
1, Rue Eugene Wiet
Reims Cedex 51057 France
Tel: (33 26) 82 49 49

Centre for Advanced Studies in Computer Aided Art and Design (CASCAAD)
John Lansdown, Head
Middlesex University
Faculty of Art & Design,
Cat Hill, Barnet
Herts EN4 8HT
United Kingdom
Tel: (44 081) 362 5035
Fax: (44 081) 440 9541
Email: john17@uk.ac.mdx.clus

Centre for Human Aspects of Science and Technology
University of Sydney
Sydney, New South Wales 2006
Australia

Centro Ricerche Musicali
Laura Bianchini
via Lamarmora, 18-1
00185 Rome, Italy

Centro di Calcolo
Alberto Polzonetti
Universita Degli Studi Di Camerino
Via del Bastione 2
Camerino, Marche, Italy

Change, Inc
Michele Archambault
PO Box 705
Cooper Station
New York City, NY 10003 USA

Chapter Arts Centre Media Education Institute
Russ Allen
Market Road, Canton
Cardiff CF5 1QE United Kingdom

Checkerboard Foundation, Inc
Edgar B. Howard
c/o AVIF
625 Broadway, 9th Floor
New York City, NY 10012 USA

Cherry Optical Society
PO Box 326
Forestville, CA 95436 USA

Chicago Museum of Science and Industry
Barry Aprison
57th Street and S. Lakeshore
Chicago, IL 60637-2093 USA
Tel: (312) 684-1414 ext 2453
Fax: (312) 684-5580

Chrysalis Foundation
555 Texas Street
San Francisco, CA 94107 USA
Tel: (415) 821-6424

Cinematograph
David Gerstein
Laura Poitras
The San Francisco Cinematheque
480 Potrero Ave.
San Francisco, CA 94110 USA
Tel: (415) 558-8129

Clemson University
Sam Wang, Professor of Art
Art Department
Box 340509
Lee Hall
Clemson, SC 29634-0509 USA
Tel: (808) 656-3924
Fax: (808) 656-0204
Email: stmwang@hubcap.clemson.edu

Coactive Aesthetics
David Gaw
Ed Koch, Treasurer
Dan Hennage, Vice President
PO Box 425967
San Francisco, CA 94142 USA
Tel: (415) 626-3119
Fax: (415) 626-6320
Email: coactive@coactive.com

Cocoran School of Art
David Adamson
17th and New York Ave NW
Washington, DC 20006 USA
Tel: (301) 628-9484

College du Vieux-Montreal, Design
Francois Lamy
Beloeil, Quebec J3G 2C9 Canada

Community Copyart Ltd.
Culrose Bldgs, Battlebridge Rd.
London NW1 United Kingdom

Computer Art Contest
Donald Spencer
PO Box 1357
Ormond Beach, FL 32175 USA
Tel: (904) 672-5672

Computer Arts Institute
Richard Howard, Director
310 Townsend Street, #230
San Francisco, CA 94107 USA
Tel: (415) 546-5242
Fax: (415) 546-5237

Computer Graphics
Robert Mallary
Art Department, Fine Arts Center
University of MA/Amherst
Amherst, MA 01003 USA

Computer Graphics Arts Directory
Barbara Mones-Harttal
Fairfax, VA 22030 USA

Computer Graphics Education Newsletter
William Joel
Email: cge@maristvm.marist.edu

Computer Graphics Professional
Graphic Channels Inc.
1714 Stockton
San Francisco, CA 94133 USA

Computer Museum Boston
Lorraine Lueft
Otto Laske
300 Congress Street
Boston, MA 02210 USA
Tel: (617) 426-2800

Computer Music & Musical Informatics Association
Mark Rais
Tonismagi 7
Tallin EE0106 Estonia
Tel: (7-0142) 684305

Computer Music Journal
Stephen Travis Pope, Editor
Curtis Roads, Associate Editor
Thom Blum, Associate Editor
PO Box 60632
Palo Alto, CA 94306 USA
Tel: (415) 988-9214
Email: stp@CCRMA.Stanford.edu

Computer Music Project
James Beauchamp
Sever Tipei
University of Illinois at Urbana
  Champaign
2136 Music Bldg, MC-0561114
Urbana, IL 61801 USA
Tel: (217) 244-1207
Fax: (217) 244-4585
Email: j-beauchamp@uiuc

Computer in der Musik: Uber den Einsatz in Wissenschaft, Komposition, und Padagogik
Helmut Schaffrath
Stuttgart, Germany

Computers in Music Research
John Schaffer, Editor in Chief
School of Music
University of Wisconsin
455 N. Park Street
Madison, WI 53706 USA
Tel: (608) 263-1898
Email: jwaesss@macc.wisc.edu

Computers in Teaching Initiative Centre for Music
Lisa Whistlecroft, Research Associate
Music Department
Lancaster University
Lancaster, Lancashire LA1 4YW
United Kingdom
Tel: (44 524) 593776
Fax: (44 524) 847298
Email: CTImusic@uk.ac.lancaster

Conceptual Design and Information Arts
Steve Wilson, Professor
George Legrady
San Francisco State University
1600 Holloway Avenue
San Francisco, CA 94132 USA
Tel: (415) 338-2176
Email: swilson@sfsuvax1.sfsu.edu

Connemara Conservancy Foundation
5733 Preston Haven
Dallas, TX 75230 USA

Conservatory of Music
Francesco Giomi, Researcher/Teacher
Lelio Camilleri, Head Teacher
Musicological Department of
CNUCE/CNR
Piazza Belle Arti 2
50122 Florence, Italy
Tel: (39-55) 282105
Fax: (39-55) 239 6785
Email: conserva@ifiidg.bitnet

Cooke Foundation
c/o Beale
Route 2, Box 314
Martinsburg, WV 25401 USA

Council for the International Bienniale in Nagoya
The Chunichi Shiumbun
1-6-1 Sannomaru
Naka-Nu, Nagoya 460-11 Japan
Tel: (052) 221 0753
Fax: (052) 221 0738

Creative Camera
Battersea Art Center
The Old Townhall, Lavander Hill
London SW11 5TF United Kingdom

Creative Computer Exhibit
Joseph Deken
California Museum of Science and
Industry
Los Angeles, CA USA
Email: jdeken@agate.berkeley.edu

Creative Glass Center of America
c/o Wheaton Village
Glasstown Road
Millville, NJ 08332 USA

Cummington Community of the Arts
Rick Reiken, Assistant Director
R.R. #1
PO Box 145
Cummington, MA 01026 USA
Tel: (413) 634-2172

CyberEdge Journal
Ben Delaney, Publisher
928 Greenhill Road
Mill Valley, CA USA

Cyberspace Gallery
Patric Doherty Prince,
Co-Director/Curator
160 West Jaxine Drive
Altadena, CA 91001 USA
Tel: (818) 797-7674
Email: patric@mica.jpl.nasa.gov

D.H. Lawrence Summer Fellowship
University of New Mexico
English Dept, Humanities Bldg
Alburquerque, NM 87106 USA

Danish Institute of Electroacoustic Music (DIEM)
Wayne Siegel, Director
Steffen Brandorff, Software
Coordinator
The Concert Hall Aarhus
Thomas Jensen Alle
DK 8000 Aarhus C, Denmark
Tel: (45 86) 202133
Fax: (45 86) 194386
Email: wsiegel@daimi.aau.dk

Das Synthetische Mischgewebe
Isabelle Chemin
Guido Huebner
13 Rue Tiffonet
33000 Bordeaux, Aquitaine, France
Tel: (56) 92 00 00

David Bermant Foundation: Color, Light, Motion
David Bermant
15 Shore Road
Rye, NY 10580 USA
Tel: (914) 381-6868

De Sterreichisches Foto Archiv
Monika Faber, Chief Curator
Im Museum Moderner Kunst
Fuerstengasse 1
A-1090 Vienna, Austria
Tel: (43 1) 345-397
Fax: (43 1) 345-270

Deep Dish Video
Steve Pierce
339 Lafayette Street
New York City, NY 10012 USA
Tel: (212) 473-8933
Fax: (212) 420-8223

Department of Art, University of Kentucky
Ted Kincaid
Department of Art, 207 FAB
Lexington, KY 40506-0022 USA

Design and Artists Copyright Society
DACS Freepost
2 Whitechurch Lane
London E1 7QR United Kingdom

Deutscher Akademischer Austauschdienst (DADD) - Artists in Berlin Program
DADD Main Office
5300 Bonn 2
Kennedy-Allee 50, Germany

Die Audio Gruppe
Benoit Maubrey, Director
Sygun Schenk, Choreographer/Dancer
Gerrit de Vries, Production Manager
Schul Strasse 35
1000 Berlin 65, Germany
Tel: (49 30) 462-2954

Directions
Debbie Cawkwell
21 St. Stephen Street
London W1P 1PL United Kingdom
Tel: (071) 255 1444
Fax: (071) 436 7950

Directory of Exhibition Spaces
Ed Susan Jones
PO Box 23
Sunderland SR4 6DG United Kingdom
Tel: (091) 567 3589

Djerassi Resident Artists Program
Charles Amirkhanian, Executive
Director
2325 Bear Gulch Road
Woodside, CA 94062 USA
Tel: (415) 851-8395
Fax: (415) 747-0105

Do While Studio
Jennifer Hall
273 Summer Street
Boston, MA 02210 USA
Tel: (617) 338-9129

Documentary Video Associates Ltd.
Paul Anthony Burrows, Design
Manager
David Stewart, Director
Jeremy Burdock, Design, Publications
7 Cambell Court, Bramley
Basingstroke, Hants RG26 5EG
United Kingdom
Tel: (0256) 882032
Tel: (0256) 882024

Dome Gallery
578 Broadway
New York City, NY 10012 USA

Dorland Mountain Colony
Barbara Horton
Ruth Ehenkranz
PO Box 6
Temecula, CA 92390 USA

Downtown Ensemble
Daniel Goode, Co-Director, Founder
William Hellerman
167 Spring Street, #5W
New York City, NY 10012 USA
Tel: (212) 925-6684

Dowse Art Museum
PO Box 30-396
Lower Hutt, New Zealand

Durham College, Graphic Design
Woody Mannery
John Freeman
Oshawa, Ontario L1H 7L7 Canada

Dutch Foundation of Perception and Holography
Warenarburg 44
NL 2907 CL Capelle a/d
Ijssel, The Netherlands

Dynamic Showcase: A Hypermedia Journal
PO Box 1360
Santa Cruz, CA 95061-1360 USA
Tel: (408) 425-8619

East End Management
Alex W. Scott, Manager
8209 Melrose Avenue, 2nd Floor
Los Angeles, CA 90046 USA
Tel: (213) 653-9755
Fax: (213) 653-9663

Eastgate Systems
Mark Bernstein, Chief Scientist
Hypertext Systems and Services
PO Box 1307
Cambridge, MA 02238 USA
Tel: (617) 924-9044 (800) 562-1638
Email: EastgateS@aol.com

Edizioni L'Agrifoglio
Alberto Pivi
Via Fiori Chiari 12
Milan 20121 Italy
Tel: (02) 72001519
Fax: (02) 72001529

Education Council of the Graphic Arts Industry, Inc.
Carol J. Hurlburt, Administrator
1899 Preston White Drive
Reston, VA 22091-4367 USA
Tel: (703) 648-1768
Fax: (703) 620-0994

Edward F. Albee Foundation
14 Harrison Street
New York City, NY 10013 USA

Electronic Media Workshop—Art School in Leipzig
K.P. Ludwig John
Werkstatt fur electronische Medien
Dimitroffstr. 11
Leipzig D-701 Germany
Tel: (37 41) 391 3211
Fax: (37 41) 312 401

Elizabeth Greenshields Foundation
Patricia Graham, Treasurer
1814 Sherbrooke Street West, Suite 1
Montreal, Quebec H3H 1E4 Canada
Tel: (514) 937-9225

Elusive Image
603 Munger
Dallas, TX USA

Emove
Axel Mulder, Director
Laboratory for Virtual Musical
 Instrument Design
Koninginneweg 135-2
1075 CL Amsterdam, The Netherlands
Tel: (31 20) 673 2462
Email: a.mulder@elsevier.nl

Endangered Species Media Project
Gary Reinsch
PO Box 460567
Houston, TX 77056 USA
Tel: (713) 729-6260
Fax: (713) 729-6740

Engineering Technology Institute
PO Box 8859
Waco, TX 76714-8859 USA

EthnoForum
Karl Signell
Baltimore, MD USA
Email: listserv@umdd

European Cultural Foundation
Jan Van Goyenkade 5
NL-1075 HN Amsterdam
The Netherlands

European Media Art Festival
Postfach 1861
Hasestrasse 71
Osnabruck D-4500 Germany
Tel: (0541) 21658
Fax: (0541) 28327

European Network of Centers on Culture and Technology
PO Box 16783
1001 RG Amsterdam
The Netherlands
Tel: (31 20) 523 0404
Fax: (31 20) 238 438

European Photography
Andreas Muller-Pohle, Editor/Publisher
PO Box 3043
Gottingen 3400 Germany
Tel: (0551) 24820
Fax: (0551) 25224

European Visual Arts Information Network (EVIAN)
Jeremy Rees
The Library, Suffolk Cottage
Rope Walk
Ipswich, Suffolk IP4 1LT United
Kingdom
Tel: (44) 473 211214
Fax: (44) 473 230054

Everything Everything
Connor Freff Cochran, Partner
Jacqui Dunne, Partner
Brent Hurtig, Partner
524 San Anselmo Avenue, #229
San Anselmo, CA 94960 USA
Tel: (415) 332-6161/2
Fax: (415) 332-6163
Email: Connor.Cochran@mcimail.com

Experimental Art Foundation
Richard Grayson
PO Box 21
North Adelaide, SA 5006 Australia
Tel: (08) 211 7505
Fax: (08) 211 7323

Experimental Musical Instruments
Bart Hopkin, Editor
PO Box 784
Nicasio, CA 94946 USA
Tel: (415) 662-2182

Experimental Television Center Ltd
Ralph Hocking, Director
Sherry Miller Hocking, Assistant
 Director
RD 2 Box 235
Newark Valley, NY 13811 USA
Tel/Fax: (607) 687-4341

Exploratorium
Peter Richards, Arts Liason
3601 Lyon Street
San Francisco, CA 94123 USA
Tel: (415) 563-7337
Fax: (415) 561-0307

Extensions
Ciaran Monaghan
Aberdeen Art Gallery
Schoolhill Aberdeen, Scotland
United Kingdom

Fashion Institute of Technology, Computer Graphics
Terry Blum
New York City, NY 10001 USA
Tel: (212) 760-7938

Feature
484 Broome
New York City, NY 10013 USA

Festival International du Film par ordinateur de Montreal (FIFOM)
1276, rue Amherst
Montreal, Quebec H2L 3K8 Canada
Tel: (514) 982-9872
Fax: (514) 765-3116

Film/Video Arts, Inc
Alice Martin, Director
 of Development & PR
Rodger Larsun, Executive Director
817 Broadway (at 12th Street)
New York City, NY 10003 USA
Tel: (212) 673-9361
Fax: (212) 475-3467

Fine Arts Interdisciplinary Computer Center
Eric Bobrow
York University
4700 Keele Street
North York, Ontario M3J 1P3 Canada

Fine Arts Research & Holography Center
1134 W. Washington Blvd.
Chicago, IL 60607 USA

Foundation de Lourmarin Lauret-Vibert
Juliet Lisle, Curator
Chateau de Lourmarin
84 Lourmarin
Vaucluse, France

Frachaos
Jake Davies
Higher Trengrove
Constantine, Falmouth
Cornwall TR11 5QR United Kingdom
Tel: (0326) 40973
Fax: (0326) 316818

Franklin Institute of Science
Irene Coffey
20th Street & The Parkway
Philadelphia, PA 19103-1194 USA

French National Institute for Research in Computer Science and Control (INRIA)
Domaine de Voluceau
Rocquencourt bp 105
Chesnay 7815 France
Tel: (33 1) 39 63 55 11

Friends of Photography
PO Box 500
Carmel, CA 93921 USA

Fringe Research Holographics, Inc
Michael Sowdon, President
010-1179A King Street West
Toronto, Ontario M6K 3C5 Canada

Frog Peak Music
Larry Polansky, Director
Jody Diamond, Co-Director
PO Box 5036
Hanover, NH 03755 USA
Tel: (603) 448-1902
Email: larry.polansky@dartmouth.edu

Fund for US Artists at International Festivals and Exhibitions
Beverly Kratochvil
National Endowment for the Arts
1100 Pennsylvania Ave NW
Washington, DC 20506 USA
Tel: (202) 682-5562

Galerie Eylau'5
Eylauer Strasse 5
1000 Berlin 61, Germany

Gallery for Holography
Robert Lewison
Ken Quinn
307 South Street
Philadelphia, PA 19147 USA

George Coates Performance Works
Beau Takahara, Executive Director
David Hurd, General Manager
110 McAllister Street
San Francisco, CA 94102 USA
Tel: (415) 863-8520
Fax: (415) 863-7939

George Mason University Art and Art History
Barbara Mones-Hattan
Deborah Sokolove
4400 University Blvd
Fairfax, VA 22030 USA
Tel: (703) 323-2463

George Washington University Fine Arts
Sam Molina
2121 I Street NW
Washington, DC 20006 USA
Tel: (202) 676-6000

Glassboro State University, Art
Des Mclean
Glassboro, NJ 07083 USA
Tel: (609) 863 5000

Godlove Award
Joann Taylor
PO Box 500
M/S 50-320
Beaverton, OR 97077 USA
Tel: (503) 627-4911
Email: joann@tekirl.labs.tek.com0

Good Sound Foundation
16995 Skyline Blvd
Woodside, CA 94062 USA

Graphic Arts Technical Foundation
4615 Forbes Avenue
Pittsburgh, PA 15213-3796 USA
Tel: (412) 621-6941

Greater London Arts Association
Director of Leisure and Recreation
181 King Street
London W6 United Kingdom

Grizedale Forest
Northern Arts
Visual Arts Department
10 Osborne Terrace, Jesmond
Newcastle-upon-Tyne NE2 1NZ
United Kingdom

Groupe de Researches Musicales (GRM/IRA)
Francois Bayle
116, av du President Denney
75786 Paris 16 France
Tel: (33-1) 42 30 21 82
Fax: (33-1) 42 30 49 88

Guggenheim Museum
1071 Fifth Avenue
New York City, NY 10128 USA
Tel: (212) 360-3555

Gulbenkian Foundation, UK Branch
98 Portland Place
London WIN 4ET United Kingdom

Hambidge Center for Creative Arts a d Sciences
Judith Barber, Executive Director
PO Box 339
Rabun Gap, GA 30568 USA
Tel: (404) 746-5718
Fax: (404) 746-9933

Hann Gallery
Derek William Hann, Proprietor
2A York Street
Bath, Avon BA1 1NG United Kingdom
Tel: (44 0) 225-466904

Harlem Studio Museum
144 West 125th Street
New York City, NY 10027 USA

Hartness-Schoos Galleries
163 S. Jackson
Seattle, WA 98104 USA

Harvestworks, Inc.
Brian Karl, Director
Carl Parkinson, Director
John McGeehan, Program Coordinator
596 Broadway, #602
New York City, NY 10012 USA
Tel: (212) 431-1130
Fax: (212) 431-1134

Helena Rubenstein Fellowships
Whitney Museum Independent Study
  Programs
384 Broadway
New York City, NY 10013 USA

Hellenic Institute of Holography
Ch. Keranis
28 Dionyssou st.
GR -Chalandri 152 34
Athens, Greece
Tel: 301 68 11 803

Holo Media AB
Mona Forsberg
Box 45012
104 30 Stockholm, Sweden
Tel: 8 11 11 08
Fax: 8 10 76 38

Holo-Gram
PO Box 9035
Allentown, PA 18105 USA

HolografieLabor Osnabruck
Vito Orazem
Peter Zec
Mindener Str. 205
D-4500 Osnabruck, Germany

Hologramas
Daniel Weiss, Director
APDO 2043-15080
La Coruna, Spain

Hologrammen Galerie
Leidsestraat 30
Amsterdam, The Netherlands

Holographic Visions
300 South Grand Avenue
Los Angeles, CA 90012 USA

Holography Group
Clive Kocher
Salisbury College of Art
Southhampton Road
Salisbury, Wiltshire, United Kingdom

Holography Institute
Jeffery Murray, Owner
Patty Pink
PO Box 24-153
San Francisco, CA 94124 USA
Tel: (415) 822-7123

Holography Workshop
Frank DeFreitas, Founding Director
PO Box 9035
Allentown, PA 18105 USA
Tel: (215) 434-8236

Holography in Education
Jim MacShane
512 Braeside Drive
Arlington Heights, IL 60004 USA

**Holography Display of Artists &
Engineers Club (HODIC)**
Fujio Iwata
Central Research Institute
  Toppan Printing Co.
1-5 Taito-Ku
Tokyo 110 Japan

Hooykaas/Stanfield
Elsa Stansfield
Madelon Hooykaas
PO Box 61106
1005 HC Amsterdam, The Netherlands
Tel: (31 020) 6221898
Fax: (31 020) 4202688

Houston Holography Center
The Anthony Foundation
3202 Argonne
Houston, TX 77098 USA

Humanities Computing Facility (HCF)
University of California Santa Barbara
Santa Barbara, CA 93106-3170 USA
Tel: (805) 393-2208
Email: HCF1DAHL@ucsbuxa.ucsb.edu

Hungart
Attila Csaji, President
Fine Art Section
Kisgombu, 30
Budapest 1135 Hungary
Tel: (36 1) 12 96 356
Fax: (36 1) 131 29 82

hypertelsaloon
Carolyn F. Strauss, Director
Space 308
837 Traction Avenue
Los Angeles, CA 90013-1841 USA
Tel: (213) 621-3127
Fax: (213) 621-4187
Email: strauss@well.sf.ca.us

ICTV
Susan Weeks, Multimedia Production
  Manager
280 Martin Avenue
Santa Clara, CA 95050 USA
Tel: (408) 562-9233
Fax: (408) 986-9566
Email: Susan_Weeks@ictv.com

**IEEE Society on Social Implications of
Technology**
Nik Warren
Otis/Parsons Art Institute
134 Hast Avenue
Santa Monica, CA 90405 USA
Tel: (415) 527-2935

**INTART - Society for Sciences, Arts
and Pedagogy**
Erzsebet Tusa
Kiss Janos altb. u. 47
H 1126 Budapest, Hungary

IRCAM
Marc Battier
31, rue Saint-Merri
Paris 75004 France
Email: bam@ircam.ircam.fr

Image Film/Video Center
75 Bennet Street NW, Suite M-1
Atlanta, GA 30309 USA
Tel: (404) 352-4225

Image Technology and Art (ATI)
Department of Plastic Arts
University of Paris
University of Paris III
Paris, France

Image and Sound Museum
Sergio Martinelli
Rua Bairi 294 Alto da Lapa
Sao Paulo - SP 05059 Brazil

Independent Media
7 Cambell Court, Bramley
Basingstroke, Hants RG26 5EG
United Kingdom
Tel: (0256) 882032

Independent Media Distributors
c/o Fanlight Productions
47 Halifax Street
Boston, MA 02130 USA
Tel: (617) 524-0980
Fax: (617) 524-8838

Independent Photography Directory
Barry Lane
Ed Mike Hallett
PO Box 23
Sunderland SR4 6D United Kingdom
Tel: (091) 567 3589

Indian Institute of Technology
R.K. Bhatnagar, Assistant Professor
Dept. of H.S.S
Kanput 208016 India

**Institut Fur Integrative
Musikpadagogik und Polyasthetische
Erziehung**
Wolfgang Roscher
Mirabellplatz 1
A-5020 Salzburg, Austria

Institute for Art and Urban Resources
Art and Urban Resources
46-01 21 Street
Long Island City, NY 11101 USA

Institute for Computers in the Arts
Timothy Binkley
School of Visual Arts
209 East 23rd Street
New York City, NY 10010-3994 USA
Tel: (212) 679-7350

Institute of Art and Design
Shunsuke Mitamura, Professor
University of Tsukuba
1-Tennodai
Tsukuba, Ibaraki-ken 305 Japan
Tel: (81 298) 53-2833
Fax: (81 298) 53-508

Instituto Nacional De Bellas Artes
Francisco Nunez
Manuel Enriquez
PIS031 Eje Central Lazaro Card
06000 DF, Mexico
Tel: 518 11 18

Integraf
745 N Waukegan Road
Lake Forest, IL 60045 USA
Tel: (312) 234-3756
Fax: (312) 615-0835

**Integrated Electronic Arts Rensselaer
(iEAR)**
Neil Rolnick
Department of the Arts
Rensselaer Polytechnic Institute
DCC 135
Troy, NY 12180-3590 USA
Tel: (518) 276-4784
Fax: (518) 276-4780
Email: rolnick@iear.arts.rpi.edu

Inter-Action Centre
Robin Barson
15 Wilkin Street
London NW5 3NG United Kingdom

**Inter-Society for the Electronic Arts
(ISEA)**
Wim van der Plas
Theo Hesper
C Kouwenbergzoom 107
3065 KC Rotterdam
Tel: (31-79) 612930
Fax: (31-75) 701906
Email: isea@mbr.frg.eur.nl isea@sara.nl

Inter/Access
Dale Barrett, Program Director
Cathy Orfald, Administrative Director
96 Spadina Avenue, Suite 303
Toronto, Ontario M5V 2J6 Canada
Tel/Fax: (416) 364-1421

Interactive Multimedia Association (IMA)
Jenifer Fox
2 Church Circle, Suite 800
Annapolis, MD 21401-1933 USA
Tel: (410) 626-1380
Fax: (410) 263-0590

Interface Newsletter
ACAD, Ohio State University
1224 Kinnear Road
Columbus, OH 43212 USA
Tel: (614) 292-3416
Fax: (614) 292-7168
Email: leslie@cgrg.ohio-state.edu

Interference Hologram Gallery
008-1179 A King Street West
Toronto, Ontario M6K 3C5 Canada

Intermedia Arts Minnesota
Melanie Nyberg, Public Relations
  Manager
Tom Borrup, Executive Director
425 Ontario Street SE
Minneapolis, MN 55408 USA
Tel: (612) 627-4444
Fax: (612) 627-4430

International Art Horizons
Deptartment RAU
PO Box 1533
Ridgewood, NJ 07450 USA
Tel: (201) 487-7277

International Arts-Medicine Association (IAMA)
19 South 22nd Street
Philadelphia, PA 19103 USA

International Association for the Astronomical Arts
PO Box 354
Richford, VT 05476 USA

International Center of Photography
Timothy Druckrey
1130 Fifth Avenue
New York City, NY 10128 USA
Tel: (212) 860-1777

International Computer Music Association
Larry Austin, President
Patte Wood, Secretary
Paul Berg, Vice President
2040 Polk, Suite 330
San Francisco, CA 94109 USA
Tel: (817) 566-2235
Fax: (817) 565-2002
Email: icma@cube.cemi.unt.edu

International Digital Electroacoustic Music Archive (IDEAMA)
Marcia Bauman
Center for Computer Research in
Music & Acoustics
Stanford University
Stanford, CA 94305 USA
Tel: (415) 723-4971
Fax: (415) 723-8468

International Directory of Design
Raymond Guido Lauzzana, Publisher
Denise Penrose, Managing Editor
Penrose Press
PO Box 470925
San Francisco, CA 94147 USA
Tel: (415) 567-4157
Fax: (415) 896-1512
Email: lauzzana@netcom.com

International Directory of Electronic Arts (IDEA)
Annick Bureaud, Project Manager
CHAOS
57, Rue Falguiere
75015 Paris, France
Tel: (33 1) 43 20 92 23
Fax: (33 1) 43 22 11 24
Email: bureaud@altern.com

International Festival of Computer Graphics Films of Montreal
Yves Pilon
3708 Boulevard St-Laurent
Montreal, Quebec H2X 2V4 Canada
Tel: (514) 765-3275
Fax: (514) 842-8622

International Festival of Films on Art
Rene Rozon, Director
445 St. Francois-Xavier St., Suite 26
Montreal, Quebec H2Y 2T11 Canada
Tel: (514) 845-5233
Fax: (514) 845-5607

International Festival of the Image
Lance Speer
Montage
31 Prince Street
Rochester, NY 14607-1499 USA
Tel: (716) 442-8897
Fax: (716) 442-8931

International Institute for Conservation of Historic and Artistic Works
Ms. Perry Smith
6 Buckingham Street
London WC2N 6BA United Kingdom
Tel: (071) 839 5975
Fax: (071) 976 1564

International Institute for Modern Structural Art
T.V. Lef
PO Box 30098
Kansas City, MO 64112 USA
Tel: (816) 531-7799
Fax: (816) 231-1910

International Sculpture Center (ISC)
David Furchgott
1050 17th Street NW, Suite 250
Washington, DC 20036 USA
Tel: (202) 785-1144
Fax: (202) 785-0810

International Society for Contemporary Music
Chris Walraven, Secretary General
c/o Gaudeamus
Swammerdamstrat 38
1091 RV Amsterdam, The Netherlands
Tel: (31 20) 6947347
Fax: (31 20) 6947258

International Society for Optical Engineering
Sunny Baines
PO Box 10
Bellingham, WA 98225 USA
Tel: (206) 676-3290
Fax: (206) 647-1445

International Society for the Inter-Disciplinary Study of Symmetry (ISIS-SYMMETRY)
Gyorgy Darvas, Executive Secretary
Dene Nagy, President
Nador u. 18., PO Box 4
Budapest H-1361 Hungary
Tel: (36 1) 131-8326
Fax: (36 1) 131-3161
Email: h492dar@ella.hu

International Society of Copier Artists (ISCA)
Louise Neaderland, Director
800 West End Avenue, Suite 13B
New York City, NY 10025 USA
Tel: (212) 662-5533

International Stereoscopic Union
Guy Ventouillac
2 allee du Roule
94260 Fresnes, France
Tel: (33 1) 42 37 10 42

International Summerschool Computer and Art
Monica Balancia
Corso Elvesia 36
CH-6900 Lugano, Italy
Tel: (41 91) 228881

Interval Magazine
Jonathon Glasier
Interval Foundation
PO Box 620027
San Diego, CA 92102 USA
Tel: (619) 299-7809

Inventors Workshop International
Alan Arthur Tratner, President
3201 Corte Malpaso, Suite 304
Camarillo, CA 93012 USA
Tel: (805) 484-9786
Fax: (805) 388-3097

Isaac W. Bernheim Foundation
Charles McClure III, Executive Director
536 Starks Building
Louisville, KY 40202 USA

John Michael Kohler Arts Center
608 New York Avenue
Sheboygan, WI 53082-0489 USA
Tel: (414) 458 6144

Josh Baer Gallery
Josh Baer
476 Broome Street
New York City, NY 10013 USA

Just Intonation Network
Henry S. Rosenthal
535 Stevenson Street
San Francisco, CA 94103 USA
Tel: (415) 864-8123
Fax: (415) 864-8726

KAOS
1440 N. Dayton Street, Suite 2
Chicago, IL 60622 USA
Tel: (312) 915-0692

Kettles Yard Gallery
Castle Street
Cambridge CB3 OAQ United Kingdom

Kitchen
Amy Taubin, Video Curator
512 W. 19th Street
New York City, NY 10011 USA

Kulturdata
Richard Kriesch, Director
Trauttmansdorffg.1
Graz 8010 Austria

Kunsthochschule fur Medien
Manfred Eisenbeis
Peter-Welter-Platz 2
D-5000 Koln 1, Germany

Kuztown University
J Malenda
Department of Art Ed/Crafts
Kuztown, PA 19530 USA

La Cite des Arts et des Nouvelle Technologies de Montreal
Ginette Major, Co-Chair
Herve Fischer, Co-Chairman
15 Rue de la Commune West
Montreal, Quebec H2Y 2C6 Canada
Tel: (514) 849-1612
Fax: (514) 982-0064

La Recherche Photographique
Paris Audiovisuel
35 Rue de la Boetie
Paris 75008 France

Laboratorio de Informatica Musical
Roberto Morales-Manzanares
Escuela de Musica
Universidad de Guanajuato
Paseo de la Presa #152
Guanajuato Gto, Mexico

Laboratorio de Informatica Y Electronica Musical (LIEM)
Adolfo Nunez
Centro para la Difusion
   de la Musica Contemporanea
Santa Isabel 51
28012 Madrid, Spain 34 9
Tel: 468 23 10
Fax: 530 83 21

Laser Arts Society for Education and Research (LASER)
Jeffery Murray, President
Patty Pink, Laser News Editor
PO Box 24153
San Francisco, CA 94124 USA
Tel: (415) 822-7123

Le Botanique
Marcel de Munnynck
Rue Royale 236
1210 Bruxelles, Belgium
Tel: (32 2) 21763 86
Fax: (32 2) 21871

Le Grand Huit
Joel Boutteville
Eurekam 77, Rue de Charonne
Paris 75011 France
Tel: (33 1) 43 48 98 8

Le Premier Guide de L'Audiovisuel Europeen (First Guide of European Audiovisual Resources)
18 Place Flagey
Bruxelles 1050 Belgium

Lehrkanzel fur Kommunikationstheorie
Roy Ascott
Hochschule fur Angewandte
Kunst-Wien
Oskar-Kokoschka-Platz 2
Wien 1010 Austria

Leonardo Music Journal
Rebecca Neeley, Coordinating Editor
672 South Van Ness Avenue
San Francisco, CA 94110 USA
Tel: (415) 431-7414
Fax: (415) 431-5737
Email: isast@garnet.berkeley.edu

Leonardo, the International Society for the Arts, Sciences and Technology
Craig Harris, Executive Director
Roger Malina, Executive Editor
Pamela Grant-Ryan, Managing Editor
672 South Van Ness Avenue
San Francisco, CA 94110 USA
Tel: (415) 431-7414
Fax: (415) 431-5737
Email: isast@garnet.berkeley.edu

Leverhulme Trust
15-19 New Fetter Lane
London EX4Z 1NR United Kingdom

Life On A Slice
Hans Reiser, Hypermedia Poet
6979 Exeter Drive
Oakland, CA 94611 USA
Tel: (408) 927-1958
Fax: (408) 927-3215
Email: hansreiser@almaden.ibm.com

Lightwork
316 Waverly Avenue
Syracuse, NY 13210 USA

Lightworks Magazine
Charlton Burch
PO Box 1202
Birmingham, MI 48012-1202 USA
Tel: (313) 826-8026
Fax: (313) 370-6825

Liquid Crystal Music
Jeffrey Bova, President
8 East 77th Street, Apt. 4A
New York City, NY 10021 USA
Tel: (212) 582-8800
Fax: (212) 535-1932
Email: PAN JEFFBOVA

Literary and Linguistic Computing
Gordon Dixon
Institute of Advanced Studies
Manchester Polytechnics
Oxford Road
Manchester M15 6BH United Kingdom
Tel: (061) 247 194
Fax: (061) 236 7383
Email: g.dixon@uk.ac.manchester

Living Art Center
Igor Cronsioe, Founder
Living Design International
Viktoriagatan 15
Gothenburg 41125 Sweden
Tel: (46 31) 134550
Fax: (46 31) 1380 82

Logos Foundation
Godfried-Willem Raes, Director
Moniek Darge, Artistic Production
Kongostraat 35
9000 Gent, Flanders, Belgium
Tel: (32-91) 23 80 89
Fax: (32-91) 25 04 34

**Los Angeles Contemporary
Exhibitions (LACE)**
Anne Bray, Video Coordinator
1804 Industrial Street
Los Angeles, CA 90021 USA

Los Angeles School of Holography
PO Box 851
Woodland Hills, CA 91365 USA

**Louis Vuitton Moet Hennessy
Science for Art Prize**
LVMH, Direction di Development
30 Avenue Hoche
Paris 75008 France
Tel: (33 1) 44 12 2223

Louisiana State University
Shirlee Singer
Architecture, Interior Design,
Landscape Architecture, Art
Baton Rouge, LA 70803 USA
Tel: (504) 388-5862

**Lugano Academy
of the Electronic Arts**
Thomas Bernold
Corso Elvezia 36
CH 6900 Switzerland
Tel: (41 91) 22 88 81

Lux Aeterna Lumia Theater
Damiel Friedman
Lux Aeterna Lumia Teater
U1.l Tolstoj 12
Uzhgorod 294018 Russia

MIT List Visual Arts Center
Ron Platt, Curatorial Assistant
Katy Kline, Director
Weisner Building
20 Ames Street
Cambridge, MA 02139 USA
Tel: (617) 253-4400
Fax: (617) 258-7265

MIT Media Laboratory
40 Massachusetts Avenue
Cambridge, MA 02139 USA

MacDowell Colony
Christopher Barnes, Research Director
The MacDowell Colony
100 High Street
Peterborough, NH 03458 USA

**Martin Bequest Traveling
Scholarships**
Arts Management Pty. Ltd.
56 Kellett Street
Potts Point, NSW 2011 Australia

Massachusetts College of Art
Jeffrey Graber
621 Huntington
Boston, MA 02115 USA
Tel: (617) 232-1555 ext 311

Mattress Factory
Barbara Luderowski
500 Sampsonia Way
Pittsburgh, PA 15212 USA
Tel: (412) 231-3169

MedArt USA, Inc.
35 West Fourth Street, #876
New York City, NY 10003 USA
Tel: (212) 998-5450
Fax: (212) 995-4043

**Media Art Department, AKI Art
Academy**
Borneopstraat 16-22
AK Enschede 7512 The Netherlands
Tel: (31 53) 324057
Fax: (31 53) 328613

Media Investment Club
4, avenue de l'Europe
Bry-Sur-Marne Cedex 94366 France
Tel: (49) 83 28 63
Fax: (49) 83 25 82

Media Magic
Michael Strasmich, Owner
PO Box 598
Nicasio, CA 96946 USA
Tel: (415) 662-2426
Fax: (415) 662-2225

Media, Culture and Society
Sage Publications, Ltd
28 Banner Street
London EC1Y 8QE United Kingdom

**Media, Electronic Art and Visual
Communication Arts & Design**
John DeMao
School of the Arts
Virginia Commonwealth University
325 North Harrison Street
Richmond, VA 23284 USA
Tel: (804) 367-1709
Fax: (804) 367-6469

Mediamatic Magazine
W. Velthoven
Postbus 17490
1001 J1 Amsterdam, The Netherlands
Tel: (020) 6384534
Fax: (020) 6384534
Email: uucphp4hl!neabbs!media

Melbourne Computer Graphics Forum
Swinburne Institute
PO Box 218, John Street
Hawthorne VIC 3122 Australia

Metropolitan Arts Commission
Alan Alexander
1120 SW 5th
Portland, OR 97204 USA

Michael Karolyi Memorial Foundation
Catherine Karolyi
Le Vieux Mas
232 Boulevard de Lattre
Vence 06140 France

**Micro Gallery:
Computer Information Room**
The National Gallery
Trafalgar Square
London WC2N 5DN United Kingdom
Tel: (071) 839-3321

Midi/Worldmusic, USA
PO Box 933
Santa Monica, CA 90406-0933 USA

Millay Colony for the Arts
Steepletop
Austerlitz, NY 12017 USA

Mindesign
Mihai Nadin
35 Butts Rock Road
Little Compton, RI 02837 USA
Tel/Fax: (401) 635-1675

Mirage Gallery
Herald Centre, Herald Square
New York City, NY 10001 USA

Monbusho Scholarshhip
Japan Information Center
1 Citicorp Center 44th Floor
153 E. 53rd Street
New York City, NY 10022 USA

**Montreal International Festival of
Films on Art**
445 St. Francois-Xavier St, #26
Montreal, Quebec H2Y 2T1 Canada
Tel: (514) 845-5233
Fax: (514) 849-5929

Mt. Hood Community College Visual Art
Craig Clark
2600 SE Stark Street
Gresham, OR 97030 USA
Tel: (503) 667-7303

Multi Media Arts Gallery
5 Broadway, Suite 504
New York City, NY 10012 USA

Muscle Fish Multimedia Engineering
Thom Blum, Partner
Erling Wold, Partner
Jim Wheaton, Partner
2550 9th Street, Suite 207B
Berkeley, CA 94710 USA
Tel: (510) 486-0141
Fax: (510) 486-0868
Email: thom@musclefish.com

Musée de l'Holographie
A.M. Christakis, Director
Forum des Halles
15 à 21 Grand Balcon
75001 Paris, France
Tel: (33 1) 40399683
Fax: (33 1) 42743357

Musee de la Photographie, Charleroi
Georges Vercheval, Director
11 Avenue Paul Pastur
6032 Charleroi
Hainaut, Belgium
Tel: (32 71) 43 58 10
Fax: (32 71) 36 46 45

Museum Computer Network
Lynn Cox
5001 Baum Blvd.
Pittsburgh, PA 15213-1851 USA
Tel: (412) 681-1818
Fax: (412) 681-5758

Museum Computer Network Spectra
Syracuse University, School
  of Infomation Studies
Syracuse, NY 13244 USA

Museum der Stadt Gladbeck
Wolfgang Schneider, Director
Wasserschloss Wittringen
Burgstrasse 64
Gladbeck, NW D-4390 Germany
Tel: (49) 2043 275297

Museum fur Fotokopie
Klaus Urbons, Director/Founder
Postfach 10 12 30
Kettwiger Strasse 33
D-4330 Mulheim an der Ruhr 1,
Germany
Tel/Fax: (0049) 208 3 44 61

Museum fur Holographie & Neue Visuelle Medien
Matthias Lauk
Pletschmuhlenweg 7
Pulheim, Koln D-5024 Germany
Tel: (02238) 51052
Fax: (02238) 52158

Museum of Fine Arts Research and Holography
1134 W. Washington Blvd.
Chicago, IL 60607 USA
Tel: (312) 226-1007

Museum of the Moving Image
South Bank
London, United Kingdom

Music Engineering Technology, Cogswell Polytechnical College
Cupertino, CA 95014 USA

Musical Microcomputer: A Resource Guide
136 Madison Avenue
New York City, NY 10016 USA

Musician's Music Software Catalog
21 Glen Ridge Road
Mahopac, NY 10541 USA
Tel: (800) 332-2251

Musicworks
Wende Bartley
1087 Queen Street West
Toronto, Ontario M6J 1H3 Canada
Tel: (416) 533-0192

N.Y. Mills Arts Retreat
R.R. Box 217
New York Mills, MN 56567 USA

NEWCOMP
Lorraine Lueft
38 Dexter Road
Lexington, MA 02173 USA

NEXA, Science-Humanities Convergence Program
San Francisco State University
1600 Holloway Avenue
San Francisco, CA 94132 USA

Nagano University
Takao Shimono, Professor
Department of Industrial Information
Shimono-go
Ueda-shi, Nagano 386-12 Japan
Tel: (81-268) 38-2350
Fax: (81-268) 38-5887
Email: shimono@nagano.ac.jp

Nantucket Island School of Design and the Arts
Residency Program
PO Box 1848
Nantucket, MA 02554 USA

National Center for Science Information Systems (NACSIS)
3-29-1 Otsuka
Tokyo 112 Japan
Tel: (81-3) 3942-2351
Fax: (81-3) 3814-4931

National College of Art & Design
John Timothy Turpin, Director
Theo McNab, Professor of Fine Art
Mealla Gibbons, Registrar
100 Thomas Street
Dublin 8 Ireland
Tel: 711377
Fax: 711748

National Copier Art
1708 East Main Street
Richmond, VA 23223 USA
Tel: (804) 643-7829

National Stereoscopic Association
PO Box 14801
Columbus, OH 43214 USA

Neon News
V. L. Crawford, Publisher/Editor
T. Pirsig, Publisher/Editor
PO Box 668
Volcano, HI 96785 USA
Tel: (808) 967-7648

New Arts Program
James Carroll, Director
PO Box 82
173 West Main Street
Kutztown, PA 19530 USA
Tel: (215) 683-6440

New England Computer Music Association
Otto Laske
926 Greendale Avenue
Needham, MA 02192 USA
Tel: (617) 449-0781
Email: laske@bu-cs.bu.edu

New England Film/Video Fellowship Program
Tel: (617) 536-1540

New Langton Arts
Nancy Gonchar, Executive Director
Arnold Kemp, Office Manager
1246 Folsom Street
San Francisco, CA 94117 USA
Tel: (415) 626-5416
Fax: (415) 255-1453

New York Experimental Glass Workshop
142 Mulberry Street
New York City, NY 10013 USA

New York Foundation for the Arts
Artist in Residence Program
5 Beekman Street, Suite 600
New York City, NY 10038 USA

Nicograph Association
Ogawa Bldg, 1-2-2 Uchikanda
Chiyoda-Ku
Tokyo 101 Japan
Tel: 03 233 3475

**Northeastern Illinios University,
Art Department**
Jane Weintraub
Chicago, IL 60625 USA
Tel: (312) 583-4050

**Northeastern University, Graphic
Arts Program**
Frank Trocki
360 Huntingtin Avenue
Boston, MA 02115 USA
Tel: (617) 437-2380

**Northwest Electronic Musicians
(NEMUS)**
James Cobb
23811 132nd Ave SE, #P5
Kent, WA 98042 USA

**New Music Australia (New Music
Articles) (NMA)**
Ranier Linz
PO Box 185
Brunswick 3056 Australia
Tel: (03) 428 2405

Ohio State University
Donald Stredney
Advanced Computing Center
  for the Arts and Design
Columbus, OH 43212 USA
Tel: (614) 292-3416

Ohio State University
Collis H. Davis, Jr., Assistant Professor
Department of Theatre
Haskett Hall
156 West 19th Avenue
Columbus, OH 43210 USA
Tel: (614) 292-6637
Fax: (614) 292-3222
Email: Davis.14@osu.edu

Ontario Arts Council
Resource System F/P/V
151 Bloor Street West, #500
Toronto, Ontario M5S 1T6 Canada
Tel: (416) 961-1660

Ontario Arts Council
151 Bloor Street West, Suite 5
Toronto, Ontario M5S 1T6 Canada
Tel: (416) 387 0058

Ontario College of Art
100 McCaul Street
Toronto, Ontario Canada

Open Channels
Long Beach Museum of Art
2300 E. Ocean Blvd
Long Beach, CA 90803 USA

P/F Publishing BV
M. C. van Baasbank
Postbus 773
2700 AT Den Haag, The Netherlands
Tel: (079) 612930
Fax: (079) 611737

Pandect, Inc.
Gene Paul Lippman, President
14437 1/2 Dickens Street
Sherman Oaks, CA 91423 USA
Tel: (818) 995-4761
Fax: (818) 752-3360

Panscan
Mark Bloch
Panpost
PO Box 1500
New York City, NY 10009-8905 USA

Parabola Arts Foundation
David Donihue
131 Spring Street, #4EF
New York City, NY 10012 USA
Tel: (212) 219-9695

Parachute
Chantal Pontbriand
4060 Blvd St. Laurent, # 501
Montreal, Quebec H2W 1Y9 Canada
Tel: (514) 842-9805
Fax: (514) 287-7146

Paramount Publishing
Robert Edgar, Multimedia Designer
707 Continental Circle, Apt. 1412
Mountain View, CA 94040
Email: lull@well.sf.ca.us

Pauline Oliveros Foundation Inc.
Pauline Oliveros, Artistic Director
Karen Moak, Executive Director
Panaiotis, Director, Technical Research
156 Hunter Street
Kingston, NY 12401 USA
Tel: (914) 338-5984
Fax: (914) 338-5986
Email: PaulineOliveros@mci.com

Perspectives of New Music
Jerome H. Kohl, Managing Editor
John Rahn, Editor
School of Music DN-10
University of Washington
Seattle, WA 98195 USA
Tel: (206) 543-0196
Fax: (206) 543-9285
Email: pnm@u.washington.edu

Perspetif Center for Photography
Frits Gierstberg, Staff Member
Bas Vroege, Director
Hans Zonnevylle, Documentation
Sint-Jobsweg 30
3024 Rotterdam, The Netherlands
Tel: (31 10) 4780655
Fax: (31 10) 4772072

Photofile
Crispin Rice, Managing Editor
Deborah Euy, Director
The Australian Centre
  for Photography
Dobell House, 257 Oxford Street
Paddington, NSW 2021 Australia
Tel: (61 2) 331-6253
Fax: (61 2) 331-6887

Photographic Journal
Roy Green
Royal Photographic Society
Acorn House
74-94 Cherry Orchard Rd
Croyden CR0 6BA United Kingdom
Tel: (081) 681 8339
Fax: (081) 681 1880

Photographie Ouverte
Avenue Paul Pastur 11
B-6100 Charleroi/Montsur, Belgium

Pollock-Krasner Foundation
PO Box 4957
New York City, NY 10185 USA

Porter Computer Arts
Gene La Von Porter, President
1105 North Cardova St.
Burbank, CA 91505 USA
Tel: (818) 848-1405

Positive Light Holographics
Bernadette Olson, Artist Holographer
Ronald B. Olson, Artist Holographer
6116 Highway 9
Felton, CA 95018 USA
Tel: (408) 335-2288
Fax: (408) 335-2245

Pratt Institute
Isaac Kerlow, Chairman
Computer Graphics, P.S. 21
200 Willoughby Avenue
New York City, NY 11205 USA
Tel: (718) 636-3693
Fax: (718) 622-6174

Preservation Initiative
National Endowment
  for the Humanities
Room 802
1100 Pennsylvania Ave NW
Washington, DC 20506 USA

Prix Ars Electronica
Christine Schopf
Gottfried Hattinger
Franckstrasse 2-a
A-4010 Linz, Austria
Tel: (43 732) 53481 26
Fax: (43 732) 53481 270

Prix Ars Electronica, Linz
Rachel Carpenter, US Representative
82 Queva Vista
Novato, CA 94947 USA
Tel: (415) 892-8254
Fax: (415) 892-4469

Professional Sound Corporation
Christopher John Palmer, Production
  Manager
10643 Riverside Drive
North Hollywood, CA 91602 USA
Tel: (818) 760-6544
Fax: (818) 760-3235

**Prometheus, All-union Coordinating
Center for the Arts, Science and
Technology**
Bulat Galeyev
ul. K. Marksa
10 Kazan 420084 Russia

Public Domain
Jim Demmers
PO Box 8899
522 Harold Avenue N.E.
Atlanta, GA 30332 USA
Tel: (404) 612-7529
Fax: (404) 894-7227
Email: jd21@prism.gatech.edu
       balder@gnu.ai.mit.edu

RISKART: The Jay Riskind Studio
Jay Riskind, Owner
700 N Carpenter
Chicago, IL 60622 USA
Tel: (312) 644-0638
Fax: (312) 433-7686
Email: jayrisk@well.sf.ca.us
       73720.2375@compuserve.com

Real Arts Way (RAW)
Hartford Arts Center
PO Box 3313
Hartford, CT 01606 USA

Reel 3-D Enterprises
PO Box 2368
Culver City, CA 90231 USA

**Research Center for Music
Iconography**
Zdravko Blazekovic, Associate Director
City University of New York
33 West 42nd Street
New York City, NY 10036 USA
Tel: (212) 642-2709
Fax: (212) 642-2642
Email: 2dr@cunyvms1.gc.cuny.edu

Rhode Island School of Design
Tom Ockerse
Benefit Street
Providence, RI 02903 USA
Tel: (401) 331-3511

**Richmond Unified High School
District**
Brigid Richards, Communications
  Specialist
1250 23rd Street
Richmond, CA 94804 USA
Tel: (510) 237-8770
Email: brigid@CoCo.ca.rop.edu

Ringling School of Art and Design
Maria Palazzi, Department Head
Computer Graphics
2700 N. Tamiami Trail
Sarasota, FL 34234 USA
Tel: (813) 359-7574
Fax: (813) 359-7517

Ronald Feldman Fine Arts
Susan Yung
31 Mercer Street
New York City, NY 10013 USA
Tel: (212) 226-3232
Fax: (212) 941-1536

Rutgers University, Art
Phillip Orenstein
358 George Street
Camden, NJ 08102 USA
Tel: (201) 932-1766

SFCA Artist Fellowships
335 Merchant Street, Room 202
Honolulu, HI 96813 USA
Tel: (808) 586-0302

**SGML User's Special Interest Group
on Hypertext and Multimedia**
Steven Newcomb, Chairman
c/o Techno Teacher
1810 High Road
Tallahassee, FL 32303-4408 USA
Tel: (904) 422-3574
Fax: (904) 386-2562
Email: newcomb@techno.com

**SYMMETRION - The Institute for
Advanced Symmetry Studies**
Gyorgy Darvas, Co-Director
Denes Nagy, Co-Director
Nador u. 18., PO Box 4
Budapest H-1361 Hungary
Tel: (36 1) 131-8326
Fax: (36 1) 131-3161
Email: h492dar@ella.hu

Sarah Bendersky, Inc.
Sarah Bendersky,
  Photo Editor/Researcher
46 Eagle Street
San Francisco, CA 94114 USA
Tel: (415) 864-0766

Savannah College of Art and Design
Paul Ryan, Video Professor
John Drop, Video Chair
Video Department
201 West Charlton Street
PO Box 3146
Savannah, GA 31402-3146 USA
Tel: (912) 238-2407
Fax: (912) 238-2428

School of Holography
Sharon McCormack
550 Shotwell Street
San Francisco, CA 94110 USA

School of Media Art
Adrian Hall, Assoc Prof/Head of School
  College of Fine Arts
University of New South Wales
PO Box 259
Paddington, New South Wales 2041
Australia
Tel: (61 2) 339-9548
Fax: (61 2) 810-1614
Email: adrian.hall@unsw.edu.au

**School of Photographic Arts and
Sciences**
Elaine O'Neil, Director
Gannett Building, Room 2115
PO Box 9887
Rochester, NY 14604 USA
Tel: (716) 475-2720

**School of Photographic Arts and
Sciences & The Technical and
Education Center of the Graphic Arts**
Rochester Institute of Technology
1 Lomb Memorial Drive
Rochester, NY 14623 USA

School of Visual Arts
MFA Degree Program in Computer Art
209 East 23rd Street
New York City, NY 10010 USA
Tel: (212) 683-0600
Fax: (212) 725-3587

School of the Art Institute of Chicago
Joan Truckenbrod, Professor
Art and Technology Department
37 S. Wabash
Chicago, IL 60115 USA
Tel: (312) 899-1230
Fax: (312) 899-1232

Science and Art
Marc Van Boom, Chairman
Guy Ryckeboer, Secretary
Heldenstraat 3512
Edegem, Antwerp 2650 Belgium
Tel: (38) 03 458 26 74

Science and the Arts
PO Box 791
Davis, CA 95617 USA

Science-Art Research Centre
Chris Illert, Director of Computing &
Graphics
Robert Pope, Director/Administrator
2/3 Birch Crescent
East Corrimal, New South Wales 2518
Australia
Tel: (042) 833 009

Screen-L
Jeremy Butler
listserv@ua1vm.ua.edu

**Secretariat of the European Network
of Centres on Culture and
Technology**
Erik Veltman
Ton van Hoek
Geldersekade 101
PO Box 16783
1001 RG Amsterdam, The Netherlands
Tel: (31 20) 523 0404

**Shanghai Institute of Laser
Technology**
319 Yue Yang Road
Shanghai, China

Shearwater Foundation
423 W. 43rd Street
New York City, NY 10036 USA

Sheehan Gallery
David Lynx
Whitman College
Walla Walla, WA 99362 USA
Tel: (509) 527-5249
Email: LYNX%WHITMAN.BITNET

Sheridan College
Robin King
Computer Graphics Lab
Oakville, Ontario L6H 2L1 Canada
Tel: (416) 845-9430

Sincere Technologies
4026 Martin Luther King Way
Oakland, CA 94609 USA

Small Computers in the Arts
Mark & Misako Scott
Box 1954
Philadelphia, PA 19106 USA
Tel: (215) 472-2392

Society for Literature and Science
Judith Yaros Lee, Executive Director
School of Interpersonal
  Communications
Lesher Hall
Ohio University
Athens, OH 45701 USA
Tel: (614) 593-4844
Fax: (614) 593-4810
Email: leej@ouvaxa.ucls.ohiou.edu

Society for the History of Technology
The University of Chicago Press
Journals Division
PO Box 37005
Chicago, IL 60637 USA

**Society for the Sciences, Arts and
Education**
P. Greguss, Director
Technical University
H-111 Budapest
Krusper UTCA 2-4, Hungary

**Society of Photographic Scientists &
Engineers**
7003 Kilworth Lane
Springfield, VA 22151 USA

**Society of Professional
Videographers**
Deana Nunley
PO Box 1933
Huntsville, AL 35807 USA
Tel: (205) 534-9722

Solomon R. Guggenheum Museum
Glory Jones
1071 Fifth Avenue
New York City, NY 10128 USA
Tel: (212) 727-6200

Sound Basis Visual Art Festival
Richard Kolodziejski
PO Box 744
PL Wroclaw 2, 50-950 Poland
Tel: (44 24) 10 375 49

Sound Choice
PO Box 1251
Ojai, CA 93023 USA

Soundings Press
PO Box 8319
Santa Fe, NM 87504 USA

South West Arts
Tony Foster
Bradninch Place, Gandy Street
Exeter, Devon EX4 3LS United Kingdom

**Southern California Laser Arts
Society**
Kathy Davis
30007 Prospect
Santa Monica, CA 90405 USA

Southern California Video
Robert Gabriel, Operations Director
Video Department
1010 East Union, Suite 205
Pasadena, CA 91106 USA

**St. Louis Community College
Florissant Valley**
3400 Pershall Road
St. Louis, MO 63135 USA
Tel: (314) 595-4372

Stereo Journal
Karl-Heinz Hatle
Theodor-Hurth-Str. 3
5000 Koln, 21 FRG, Germany

Stereo-Club Francais
CCP
6491-41 U
Paris, France

StereoScope International
John Rupkalvis, Stereoscopic
  Consultant
303 East Alameda, #Q
Burbank, CA 91502-1507 USA
Tel: (818) 848-9601

Stereoscopic Society
N. Jackson
32 Orkney Close
Hinckley, Leics LE10 OTA
United Kingdom

Stockholm Electronic Art Awards
Svenska Rikskonserter
PO Box 1225
S-111 82 Stockholm, Sweden

Storefront for Art and Architecture
97 Kenmore Street
New York City, NY 10012 USA

**Studio for Creative Inquiry,
Telecommunications and Virtual
Reality**
Carl Loeffler
College of Fine Arts
Carnegie Mellon University
Forbes Avenue
Pittsburgh, PA 15213 USA
Tel: (412) 268-3452
Fax: (412) 268-2829
Email: cel@andrew.cmu.edu

Sturvil Corporation
Russell Kirsch, Director of Research
Joan L. Kirsch, Art Director
23523 Stringtown Road
PO Box 157
Clarksburg, MD 20871 USA
Tel: (301) 972-3083
Email: kirsch@cme.nist.gov

Synchronicity Holograms
Arlene Jurewicz, Founder
Box 4235
Youngtown Road
Lincolnville, ME 04849 USA
Tel: (207) 763-3182

Synergistics Institute
Yasushi Kajikawa
5-4 Nakajima-cho
Naka-ku
Hiroshima 730 Japan
Tel: (0081) 82 241 1609
Fax: (0081) 82 240 840

Syntex Gallery
Bill Cleere
3401 Hillview Avenue
Palo Alto, CA 94304 USA
Tel: (415) 855-5525

Syracuse University
Edward Zajec, Professor
Lev Manovich, Assistant Professor
Art Media Studies
102 Shaffer Art Building
Syracuse, NY 13244 USA
Tel: (315) 443-1033
Email: ezajec@sunrise.acs.syr.edu

TIMARA (Technology in Music and Related Arts)
Gary Lee Nelson
Oberlin Conservatory
Oberlin, OH 44074 USA
Email: fnelson@oberlin.bitnet

Task Force and Technical Committee on Computer Generated Music
Goffredo Haus
Denis Baggi
IEEE Computer Society
1730 Massachusetts Avenue
Washington, DC 20036-1903 USA
Email: music@imiucca.csi.unimi.it
baggi@berkeley.edu

Task Force and Technical Committee on Computer Generated Music
Goffredo Haus
Denis Baggi
IEEE Computer Society
Corso Elvezia 36
Lugano, CH-6900 Switzerland

Tech 2000 Ivia
1900 L Street NW, Suite 500
Washington, DC 20036 USA
Tel: (202) 872-8845

Technical and Educational Center of the Graphic Arts
Rochester Institute of Technology
One Lomb Memorial Drive
Rochester, NY 14623 USA

Technology and Conservation
Susan Schur, Editor
1 Emerson Place
Boston, MA 02114 USA

Third Dimension Arts, Inc.
1134 Fourth Street
San Rafael, CA 94901 USA

Third Dimension Ltd
The Israeli Gallery of Holograms
Dizengoff Center
Tel Aviv 63333 Israel

Third Dimension Society
Derek Wardle
2 Davidson Road
Darlington, Co Durham DL1 3DR
United Kingdom
Tel: (0325) 359272

Trans Data
Joachim Steingrubner, Trustee
Wendy Aft, Trustee
Roy Dittman, Advisory Board
2824 Oak Point Drivee
Hollywood Hills, CA 90068 USA
Tel: (800) 945-5433
Fax: (213) 851-4467

Transit
Wilhelm-Greil-Str-1
A-6020 Innsbruck, Austria
Tel: (0512) 58 06 01
Fax: (0512) 58 32 02

Trebas Institute
David P Leonard, President
451 St. Jean Street
Montreal, Quebec H2Y 2R5 Canada
Tel: (514) 845-4141
Fax: (514) 845-2581

Typeworld
PO Box 170
Salem, NH 03079 USA

Tyrone Guthrie Center
Bernard Loughlin, Resident Director
Tyrone Guthrie Center
at Annaghmakerrig
Newbliss, County Monaghan
Ireland
Tel: (047) 54003
Fax: (047) 54380

Ucross Foundation
Jane Cannon
Ucross Route
PO Box 19
Clearmont, WY 82834 USA

UnderWorld Industries
Jon Van Oast
PO Box 4060
Ann Arbor, MI 48106-4060 USA
Tel: (313) 936-1951
Email: kca@caen.engin.umich.edu

Universita delgli Studi di Bologna
Pier Luigi Capucci
Instituto do Comunicazione
via Fuimazzo 347
Belricetto 4801 Italy

Universite de Montreal
Myke Roy, Coordinator
Sector electro-acoustique
200, av Vincent d'Indy CP 6128
Montreal, Quebec H3C 3J7 Canada
Tel: (514) 343-6427
Fax: (514) 343-5727

University Gent - Lab. Soete
Pierre Michel Boone, Professor
Applied Mechanics - Workshop
Holography
41 St. Pietersnieuwstraat
B9000 Gent, Belgium
Tel: (32 91) 643242
Fax: (32 91) 237326

University of Aveiro Portugal
Amilcar Vasques Dias, Composer
Communication and Art Dept.
3800 Aveiro, Portugal
Tel: (351-34) 25085/22224
Fax: (351-34) 23384

University of Colorado
Charles Roitz
Fine Arts Department
Boulder, CO 80309 USA
Tel: (303) 492-6645

University of Edinburgh
Details Secrty
Old College, South Bridge
Edinburgh, Scotland, United Kingdom

University of Illinois at Champaign, Art Department
James Kauffman
Donna Cox
Champaign, IL 61820 USA
Tel: (217) 333-7713

University of Illinois at Chicago
Dan Sandin
Tom DeFanti
Art Department
Box 4348
Chicago, IL 60680 USA
Tel: (312) 996-0798

University of London Audio Visual Centre, Interactive Videodisc Technology Certificate
North Wing Studios
Senate House, Malet Street
London WC1E 73Z United Kingdom

University of Tennessee
Susan Metros, Assoc. Professor of Art
Art Department
1715 Volunteer Boulevard
Knoxville, TN 37996-2410 USA
Tel: (615) 974-3208
Fax: (615) 974-3198
Email: metros@utkvx1.utk.edu

University of Tsukuba, School of Art and Design
Tsukuba
Ibakai-ken 305 Japan

University of Washington
Richard Karpen
School of Music
Seattle, WA 98195 USA
Email:
          karpen@edu.washington.acs.blake

University of the Arts
Karen Tuohey
Broad and Pine Streets
Philadelphia, PA 19102 USA
Tel: (215) 875-2221

V2 Organization
Alex Adriaansens
Joke Brouwer
Rik Delhaas
Muntelstraat 23
5211 PT's-Hertogenbosch
The Netherlands
Tel: (31-73) 137958
Fax: (31-73) 122238

VR Dimension
Luigi Lentini, Partner
Barbara Sullivan, Partner
c/o Barbara Sullivan
412 South Country Hill Road
Anaheim Hills, CA 92808 USA
Tel: (714) 281-1645
Fax: (714) 921-9327

Various Media
PO Box 1144
Venice, CA 90294 USA
Tel: (213) 281-6778

Vasari Project
The National Gallery
Trafalgar Square
London WC2N 5DN United Kingdom
Tel: (071) 839-3321

Verbum Gallery of Digital Art
670 Seventh Avenue, Second Floor
San Diego, CA 92101 USA
Tel: (619) 233 9977

Vermont Studio Colony
PO Box 613
Johnson, VT 05656 USA

Video Art Society
University of Tasmania
Centre of the Arts
Hunter Street
Tasmania, Hobart 700 Australia
Tel: (002) 384300

Video Free America
442 Shotwell
San Francisco, CA 94110 USA

Videographic Arts
Anne Farrell
131 Huddleson
Santa Fe, NM 87501 USA
Tel: (505) 983-5126

Visual Computer
Tosiyasu L. Kunii, Editor
University of Tokyo
Department of Information Science
7-3-1 Hongo, Bunkyo-ku
Tokyo 113 Japan

Visual Resources
Christina Updike
James Madison University
Art Department
Harrisonburg, VA 22807 USA

Visual Studies Workshop
James B. Wyman
31 Prince Street
Rochester, NY 14607 USA
Tel: (716) 442-8676
Fax: (716) 442-8931

Visualization Laboratory
William Jenks, Director
Texas A&M University
Langford Architecture Center
College Station, TX 77843-3137 USA
Tel: (409) 845-3465
Fax: (409) 845-4491
Email: bdj@archone.tamu.edu

Vivid Group
Vincent John Vincent, Co-Director
Steve Warme, Production Coordinator
Studio 302
317 Adelaide St. West
Toronto, Ontario M5V 1P9 Canada
Tel: (416) 340-9290
Fax: (416) 348-9809
Email: vivid@well.sf.ca..us

Warwick Museum
Gregg A. Mierka
3259 Post Road
Warwick, RI 02886 USA
Tel: (401) 737-0010

Weisses Haus Gallery
Thomas Wegner
Herlwigstr 52
Hamburg 20, 2000 Germany

West Midlands Arts' Artists in Industry Program
West Midlands Arts
82 Granville Street
Birmingham, B1 2LH United Kingdom

Westdeutscher Rundfunk Koeln
Studio Akustische Kunst
Acustica International
Postfach 101950
D-Cologne 1, Germany

Whitney Independent Study Program
384 Broadway, 4th Floor
New York City, NY 10013 USA

William Patterson College
Leslie Farber, Assistant Professor
Art Department
300 Pompton Road
Wayne, NJ 07470 USA
Tel: (201) 595-2722

Winston Churchill Memorial Trust
Churchill Traveling Fellowships
15 Queen's Gate Terrace
London SW7 5PR United Kingdom

Wolf Foundation
Yaron E. Gruder, Director General
PO Box 398
Herzlia Bet 46103 Israel
Tel: (972 52) 557 120
Fax: (972 52) 541 253

Women Make Movies
Michello Materre
225 Lafayette St, Suite 211
New York City, NY 10012 USA
Tel: (212) 925-0606

Women in Film
6464 Sunset Blvd, # 660
Los Angeles, CA 90028 USA

Women's Interart Center
Artist-in-Residence Program
549 W. 52nd Street
New York City, NY 10019 USA

Women's Studio Workshop
PO Box V
Rosendale, NY 12472 USA

Women's Work
c/o Brixton Art Gallery
21 Atlantic Road
London SW9 8HX United Kingdom

Xeros Art Centre Documentazione
Guiseppe Enti
Via Messina 2
Milano, CAP 20143 Italy

YLEM: Artists Using Science & Technology
Trudy Myrrh Reagan, Founder
Beverly Reiser, President
Eleanor Kent, Membership Chair
PO Box 749
Orinda, CA 94563 USA
Tel: (510) 482-2483
Email: ylem@well.sf.ca.us
trudymyrrh@aol.com

Yaddo Estate
Corporation of Yaddo
PO Box 395
Saratoga Springs, NY 12866 USA

Yellow Springs Institute for Contemporary Studies and the Arts
Jennifer Borders
Vesna Todorovic
1645 Art School Road
Chester Springs, PA 19425 USA
Tel: (215) 827-9111
Fax: (215) 827-7093

Yorkshire Sculpture Park
Clare Louise Lilley, Art Coordinator
Peter Murray, Executive Director
Bretton Hall
West Bretton
Wakefield WF4 4LG United Kingdom

Young Electronic Arts
Robert Jungk
Atelier coArt
D-8383 Exing Nr.32
Eichendorf, Germany
Tel: (0049 0) 9956 753
Fax: (0049 0) 99561228

Zakros InterArts
Randall Packer, Artistic Director
Belen Garcia-Alvarado, Managing
  Director
614 York Street
San Francisco, CA 94110 USA
Tel: (415) 282-5497
Fax: (415) 282-4228

Zentrum fur Kunst Und Medientechnolgie Karlsruhe
Heinrich Klotz
Jeffrey Shaw, Director of Image Media
Johannes Goebel, Director of Music
  & Acoustics
Kaiserstr. 64
D-76 131 Karlsruhe, Germany
Tel: (49 721) 93400
Fax: (49 721) 934019
Email: info@zkm.de music@zkm.de
image@zkm.de

Zyzzyva
Howard Junker, Editor
41 Sutter Street, Suite 1400
San Francisco, CA 94104 USA
Tel: (415) 255-1282
Fax: (415) 255-1144

3-Dimensional Art

◆ = Primary Activity
✳ = Other Disciplines/Activities/Resources

Legend per column group: **DISCIPLINES** · **ACTIVITIES** · **PLATFORMS**

Brisson, Harriet
- Disciplines: Ceramics ✳, Computer Art ✳, Computer Graphics ✳, Sculpture ✳
- Activities: Educator ✳, Musician ✳, Visual Artist ◆
- Platforms: DOS/Intel ✳

Brown, Ronald
- Disciplines: Animation ✳, Computer Art ✳, Computer Graphics ✳, Environmental Art ✳, Mixed Media ✳, Music and Sound ✳, Sculpture ✳
- Activities: Composer ✳, Educator ✳, Mathematician ✳, Musician ✳, Software Developer ◆, Visual Artist ✳
- Platforms: DOS/Intel ✳

Herrick, Kennan
- Disciplines: Computer Art ✳, Computer Graphics ✳, Holography ✳, Kinetic Art ✳, Sculpture ✳
- Activities: Visual Artist ◆
- Platforms: DOS/Intel ✳

Illert, Chris
- Disciplines: Animation ✳, Conceptual Art ✳, Environmental Art ✳, Robotics ✳
- Activities: Mathematician ◆, Visual Artist ✳

Kostyniuk, Ronald P.
- Disciplines: Environmental Art ✳, Sculpture ✳, Virtual Reality ✳, Visual Art ✳
- Activities: Curator ✳, Designer ✳, Educator ✳, Multimedia Artist ✳, Researcher ✳, Scientist ✳, Software Developer ✳, Theoretician ✳, Visual Artist ◆, Writer/Editor ✳
- Platforms: Amiga ✳

Rupkalvis, John
- Disciplines: Computer Art ✳, Computer Graphics ✳, Film ✳, Graphic Design ✳, Industrial Design ✳, Installation Art ✳, Interactive Art ✳, Kinetic Art ✳, Mixed Media ✳, Multimedia ✳, Music and Sound ✳, Photography ✳, Sculpture ✳, Space Art ✳, Video ✳, Virtual Reality ✳, Visual Art ✳
- Activities: Architect ✳, Designer ✳, Educator ✳, Hardware Developer ✳, Multimedia Artist ✳, Researcher ✳, Scientist ✳, Visual Artist ✳, Writer/Editor ✳
- Platforms: Amiga ✳, DOS/Intel ✳, Silicon Graphics ✳

Van De Bogart, Willard George
- Disciplines: Computer Art ✳, Computer Graphics ✳, Graphic Design ✳, Industrial Design ✳, Mixed Media ✳, Multimedia ✳, Photography ✳, Sculpture ✳, Video ✳, Virtual Reality ✳, Visual Art ✳
- Activities: Designer ◆, Educator ✳, Multimedia Artist ✳, Visual Artist ✳, Writer/Editor ✳
- Platforms: Macintosh ✳

Animation

◆ = Primary Activity
✳ = Other Disciplines/Activities/Resources

Bishko, Leslie
- Disciplines: Computer Art ✳, Computer Graphics ✳, Dance ✳, Film ✳
- Activities: Educator ✳, Visual Artist ◆, Writer/Editor ✳
- Platforms: Silicon Graphics ✳, Sun ✳

Lippman, Gene Paul
- Disciplines: Computer Art ✳, Computer Graphics ✳, Graphic Design ✳, Interactive Art ✳, Multimedia ✳, Music and Sound ✳, Video ✳
- Activities: Designer ◆, Multimedia Artist ✳, Musician ✳
- Platforms: Macintosh ✳, Silicon Graphics ✳, Sun ✳

Palazzi, Maria
- Disciplines: Computer Graphics ✳
- Activities: Educator ◆
- Platforms: Silicon Graphics ✳, Sun ✳

Ramsden, Stuart
- Disciplines: Computer Art ✳, Computer Graphics ✳, Multimedia ✳, Music and Sound ✳, Performance Art ✳, Space Art ✳
- Activities: Architect ✳, Critic ✳, Designer ✳, Educator ✳, Hardware Developer ✳, Mathematician ✳, Multimedia Artist ✳, Performing Artist ◆, Researcher ✳, Scientist ✳, Software Developer ✳
- Platforms: DOS/Intel ✳, Macintosh ✳, Silicon Graphics ✳, Sun ✳

Sen, Amit
- Disciplines: Computer Graphics ✳
- Activities: Educator ✳, Hardware Developer ✳
- Platforms: Silicon Graphics ✳, Sun ✳

Architecture

◆ = Primary Activity
✳ = Other Disciplines/Activities/Resources

Lentini, Luigi
- Disciplines: Computer Art ✳, Computer Graphics ✳, Graphic Design ✳, Holography ✳, Installation Art ✳, Interactive Art ✳, Fiber Arts ✳, Multimedia ✳, Virtual Reality ✳
- Activities: Designer ✳, Educator ✳, Multimedia Artist ✳, Architect ◆
- Platforms: DOS/Intel ✳

Primeau, Mark
- Disciplines: Computer Art ✳, Computer Graphics ✳, Environmental Art ✳
- Activities: Researcher ✳, Architect ◆
- Platforms: DOS/Intel ✳

Strauss, Carolyn F.
- Disciplines: Conceptual Art ✳, Environmental Art ✳, Graphic Design ✳, Industrial Design ✳, Installation Art ✳, Kinetic Art ✳, Literary Arts ✳, Mixed Media ✳, Multimedia ✳, Painting ✳, Performance Art ✳, Photography ✳, Robotics ✳, Space Art ✳, Video ✳
- Activities: Arts Administrator ✳, Critic ✳, Curator ✳, Designer ◆, Performing Artist ✳, Researcher ✳, Theoretician ✳, Visual Artist ✳, Writer/Editor ✳
- Platforms: Macintosh ✳

Computer Art

◆ = Primary Activity
✱ = Other Disciplines/Activities/Resources

The following chart cross-references each artist against DISCIPLINES, ACTIVITIES, and PLATFORMS.

DISCIPLINES: 3D Art · Animation · Architecture · Ceramics · Computer Art · Computer Graphics · Conceptual Art · Copy Art · Dance · Environmental Art · Fiber Arts · Film · Graphic Design · Holography · Industrial Design · Installation Art · Interactive Art · Kinetic Art · Literary Arts · Mixed Media · Multimedia · Music and Sound · Painting · Performance Art · Photography · Robotics · Sculpture · Space Art · Telecommunications · Video · Virtual Reality · Visual Art

ACTIVITIES: Actor · Architect · Art Collector · Arts Administrator · Choreographer · Composer · Critic · Curator · Dancer · Designer · Educator · Hardware Developer · Historian · Mathematician · Multimedia Artist · Musician · Performance Artist · Performing Artist · Publisher · Researcher · Scientist · Software Developer · Student · Theoretician · Visual Artist · Writer/Editor

PLATFORMS: Amiga · Atari · DEC · DOS/Intel · Hewlett Packard · Macintosh · Mainframe · Next · Silicon Graphics · Sun

Acevedo, Victor C
Astrahan, Ilene
Batten, Trevor
Brodsky, Michael
Brown, Paul
Cash, Sydney
Casper, Stuart
Daniel, Tommie
Farber, Leslie
Farrell, Anne
Fergusson, Robert
Freeman, Nancy Jackson
Glynn, David
Hendel, Robert
Johnson, James
Joslin, Abby
Kashinn, Laurel
Kaul, Paras
Kent, Eleanor
Kirsch, Russell
Knowlton, Kenneth
Lansdown, John
Lovelett, Felicia
McSherry, Stewart
Prince, Patric Doherty
Riskind, Jay
Schneider, Wolfgang
Shimono, Takao
Smith, Edith MacNamara
Truckenbrod, Joan
Verostko, Roman
Young, Emily

Computer Graphics

◆ = Primary Activity
✳ = Other Disciplines/Activities/Resources

PLATFORMS

Name	Sun	Silicon Graphics	Next	Mainframe	Macintosh	Hewlett Packard	DOS/Intel	DEC	Atari	Amiga
Abe, Yoshiyuki							✳			
Clayson, James			✳		✳					
Edwards, Kimberly					✳					
Garrett, David							✳			
Howard, Richard					✳		✳			
Koach, Damon					✳		✳	✳		
Land, Richard					✳		✳			
Ng, George										✳
Rinehart, Marion										
Rosen, Peter H.					✳		✳			✳
Zajec, Edward	✳	✳			✳		✳	✳		

ACTIVITIES

Name	Writer/Editor	Visual Artist	Theoretician	Student	Software Developer	Scientist	Researcher	Publisher	Performing Artist	Performance Artist	Musician	Multimedia Artist	Mathematician	Historian	Hardware Developer	Educator	Designer	Dancer	Curator	Critic	Composer	Choreographer	Arts Administrator	Art Collector	Architect	Actor
Abe, Yoshiyuki	✳	◆			✳										✳											
Clayson, James	✳	✳	✳		✳		✳						✳			◆	✳									
Edwards, Kimberly		✳								◆								✳								✳
Garrett, David				✳												◆										
Howard, Richard						✳						✳			✳	◆	✳						✳			
Koach, Damon				✳	◆																					
Land, Richard		✳	✳			◆	✳		✳			✳	✳			✳	✳									✳
Ng, George		◆																								
Rinehart, Marion		◆																								
Rosen, Peter H.	✳	✳		✳			✳		✳	✳	✳	◆			✳		✳		✳		✳		✳			✳
Zajec, Edward		◆			✳		✳					✳				✳										

DISCIPLINES

Name	Visual Art	Virtual Reality	Video	Telecommunications	Space Art	Sculpture	Robotics	Photography	Performance Art	Painting	Music and Sound	Multimedia	Mixed Media	Literary Arts	Kinetic Art	Interactive Art	Installation Art	Industrial Design	Holography	Graphic Design	Film	Fiber Arts	Environmental Art	Dance	Copy Art	Conceptual Art	Computer Graphics	Computer Art	Ceramics	Architecture	Animation	3D Art
Abe, Yoshiyuki								✳													✳						▓	✳				
Clayson, James									✳	✳										✳				✳			▓					
Edwards, Kimberly																✳				✳				✳			▓	✳				
Garrett, David																										✳	▓					
Howard, Richard								✳				✳															▓	✳				
Koach, Damon			✳																								▓	✳				
Land, Richard	✳	✳	✳			✳	✳		✳	✳			✳		✳	✳	✳			✳	✳			✳			▓	✳				
Ng, George																			✳								▓					
Rinehart, Marion																											▓	✳				
Rosen, Peter H.			✳					✳	✳	✳	✳	✳	✳			✳	✳			✳	✳		✳	✳		✳	▓	✳			✳	✳
Zajec, Edward			✳									✳				✳											▓	✳				

Conceptual Art

◆ = Primary Activity
✳ = Other Disciplines/Activities/Resources

PLATFORMS

Name	Sun	Silicon Graphics	Next	Mainframe	Macintosh	Hewlett Packard	DOS/Intel	DEC	Atari	Amiga
Franklin, Marjorie					✳					✳
Hubel, Paul										
Kemp, Arnold					✳					
Malloy, Judy	✳				✳		✳			
Moore, Stephen					✳		✳			
Morgan, Robert										
Roberts, Sara		✳			✳					

ACTIVITIES

Name	Writer/Editor	Visual Artist	Theoretician	Student	Software Developer	Scientist	Researcher	Publisher	Performing Artist	Performance Artist	Musician	Multimedia Artist	Mathematician	Historian	Hardware Developer	Educator	Designer	Dancer	Curator	Critic	Composer	Choreographer	Arts Administrator	Art Collector	Architect	Actor
Franklin, Marjorie		✳										◆														
Hubel, Paul		◆			✳		✳					✳	✳													
Kemp, Arnold	◆	✳								✳									✳	✳			✳	✳		
Malloy, Judy	✳	◆			✳					✳		✳							✳							
Moore, Stephen		◆										✳														
Morgan, Robert	✳		✳													✳				◆						
Roberts, Sara	✳	✳										◆				✳										

DISCIPLINES

Name	Visual Art	Virtual Reality	Video	Telecommunications	Space Art	Sculpture	Robotics	Photography	Performance Art	Painting	Music and Sound	Multimedia	Mixed Media	Literary Arts	Kinetic Art	Interactive Art	Installation Art	Industrial Design	Holography	Graphic Design	Film	Fiber Arts	Environmental Art	Dance	Copy Art	Conceptual Art	Computer Graphics	Computer Art	Ceramics	Architecture	Animation	3D Art
Franklin, Marjorie			✳								✳	✳	✳			✳	✳										▓	✳			✳	✳
Hubel, Paul		✳				✳				✳		✳	✳		✳								✳				▓		✳			✳
Kemp, Arnold												✳					✳										▓			✳		
Malloy, Judy								✳	✳			✳	✳	✳		✳	✳										▓	✳				
Moore, Stephen								✳				✳															▓	✳				
Morgan, Robert										✳											✳						▓					
Roberts, Sara			✳			✳	✳		✳							✳	✳				✳						▓	✳				

Copy Art

◆ = Primary Activity
✳ = Other Disciplines/Activities/Resources

Name	Disciplines	Activities	Platforms
Neaderland, Louise	Graphic Design ✳, Literary Arts ✳, Mixed Media ✳, Photography ✳	Arts Administrator ✳, Educator ✳, Visual Artist ◆, Writer/Editor ✳	Macintosh ✳
Urbons, Klaus	(Copy Art)	Visual Artist ◆, Writer/Editor ✳	Macintosh ✳

Environmental Art

◆ = Primary Activity
✳ = Other Disciplines/Activities/Resources

Name	Disciplines	Activities	Platforms
Ferguson, Theodosia	3D Art ✳, Architecture ✳, Computer Graphics ✳, Conceptual Art ✳, Film ✳, Graphic Design ✳, Installation Art ✳, Interactive Art ✳, Kinetic Art ✳, Literary Arts ✳, Mixed Media ✳, Multimedia ✳, Painting ✳, Photography ✳, Sculpture ✳, Video ✳	Designer ◆, Educator ✳, Multimedia Artist ✳, Researcher ✳, Visual Artist ✳	DOS/Intel ✳, Hewlett Packard ✳, Macintosh ✳
Follis, Charles	3D Art ✳, Architecture ✳, Fiber Arts ✳, Kinetic Art ✳, Sculpture ✳	Visual Artist ◆	
Gessert, George	Conceptual Art ✳, Holography ✳, Installation Art ✳, Painting ✳, Photography ✳	Visual Artist ◆, Writer/Editor ✳	Macintosh ✳
Kepes, Gyorgy	Painting ✳	Visual Artist ◆	
Saad-Cook, Janet	Sculpture ✳, Space Art ✳	Visual Artist ◆	Macintosh ✳
Schryer, Claude	Music and Sound ✳	Musician ◆	
Schwendinger, Leni	3D Art ✳, Architecture ✳, Conceptual Art ✳, Interactive Art ✳, Multimedia ✳, Space Art ✳	Architect ✳, Educator ✳, Multimedia Artist ✳, Performance Artist ✳, Visual Artist ◆	

Film

◆ = Primary Activity
✳ = Other Disciplines/Activities/Resources

Name	Disciplines	Activities	Platforms
Apple, Jeffrey	3D Art ✳, Animation ✳, Computer Graphics ✳, Holography ✳, Installation Art ✳, Interactive Art ✳, Mixed Media ✳, Multimedia ✳, Photography ✳, Video ✳, Virtual Reality ✳	Multimedia Artist ✳, Visual Artist ✳	DOS/Intel ✳
Fox, John	Mixed Media ✳, Sculpture ✳, Video ✳	Educator ◆, Multimedia Artist ✳, Writer/Editor ◆	DOS/Intel ✳
McWhirter, Ellen Ann	3D Art ✳, Animation ✳, Architecture ✳, Computer Art ✳, Computer Graphics ✳, Installation Art ✳, Multimedia ✳, Video ✳	Educator ◆, Mathematician ✳, Multimedia Artist ✳, Theoretician ✳, Visual Artist ✳, Writer/Editor ✳	DOS/Intel ✳, Silicon Graphics ✳, Sun ✳

General

◆ = Primary Activity
✳ = Other Disciplines/Activities/Resources

DISCIPLINES

Name	3D Art	Animation	Architecture	Ceramics	Computer Art	Computer Graphics	Conceptual Art	Copy Art	Dance	Environmental Art	Fiber Arts	Film	Graphic Design	Holography	Industrial Design	Installation Art	Interactive Art	Kinetic Art	Literary Arts	Mixed Media	Multimedia	Music and Sound	Painting	Performance Art	Photography	Robotics	Sculpture	Space Art	Telecommunications	Video	Virtual Reality	Visual Art
Beers, Lisa	✳	✳			✳	✳								✳			✳			✳	✳	✳		✳		✳		✳		✳	✳	
Bureaud, Annick		✳			✳	✳	✳		✳			✳	✳			✳	✳	✳		✳	✳	✳	✳	✳	✳		✳	✳		✳	✳	✳
Cochran, Connor Freff	✳				✳	✳											✳															
Connors, John				✳	✳	✳				✳			✳				✳	✳			✳				✳	✳	✳				✳	
Crawford, V L	✳																															
Cronsioe, Igor																																
Darvas, Gyorgy		✳			✳	✳	✳						✳			✳	✳			✳	✳	✳	✳	✳				✳	✳	✳	✳	
Devito, Carl																																
Drake, Luigi-Bob					✳	✳	✳						✳		✳	✳													✳			
Klinkowstein, Tom																					✳								✳			
Loeb, Arthur																																
Major, Ginette																																
Mann, Steve	✳	✳	✳		✳	✳	✳		✳	✳	✳	✳		✳		✳	✳	✳		✳	✳	✳		✳	✳	✳		✳		✳	✳	
Nagy, Denes																																
Nishimura, Yumi																																
Perkins, Carolyn V		✳			✳	✳	✳			✳		✳	✳	✳			✳	✳		✳	✳	✳	✳	✳	✳	✳	✳			✳	✳	
Podnar, Gregg		✳																														
Reiken, Rick	✳				✳	✳						✳	✳				✳	✳			✳	✳								✳		
Richards, Brigid	✳	✳			✳	✳	✳									✳	✳				✳	✳		✳						✳	✳	
Scott, Jill	✳	✳			✳	✳	✳					✳	✳	✳							✳	✳		✳						✳	✳	
Stilley, Tucker	✳	✳																			✳	✳		✳								
Van der Plas, Wim																																
Welch, Chuck																																
Zouni, Opy																							✳				✳					

ACTIVITIES

Name	Actor	Architect	Art Collector	Arts Administrator	Choreographer	Composer	Critic	Curator	Dancer	Designer	Educator	Hardware Developer	Historian	Mathematician	Multimedia Artist	Musician	Performance Artist	Performing Artist	Publisher	Researcher	Scientist	Software Developer	Student	Theoretician	Visual Artist	Writer/Editor
Beers, Lisa							✳										✳								◆	✳
Bureaud, Annick	✳					✳	✳	◆	✳	✳	✳	✳			✳	✳	✳	✳		✳			✳	✳	✳	✳
Cochran, Connor Freff														✳	✳					✳		✳				
Connors, John			✳				✳			✳	✳	✳			✳					✳						◆
Crawford, V L								✳		◆		✳								◆	✳	✳				
Cronsioe, Igor												✳		✳						✳						
Darvas, Gyorgy				✳			✳				✳				✳	✳	✳	✳		✳		✳		✳	✳	◆
Devito, Carl										✳	✳		✳		✳	✳				✳				◆	✳	✳
Drake, Luigi-Bob															✳							✳			◆	✳
Klinkowstein, Tom															✳										✳	
Loeb, Arthur																										
Major, Ginette								◆																		✳
Malina, Roger			✳		✳				✳	✳	✳	✳		✳	✳	✳			✳	✳	✳		✳	✳	◆	✳
Mann, Steve					✳									✳						◆	✳					
Nagy, Denes											✳															✳
Nishimura, Yumi										◆													✳			
Perkins, Carolyn V			✳								✳		✳	✳	✳					✳		✳		✳	✳	✳
Podnar, Gregg						✳					✳						✳	✳		✳	✳	✳	✳		◆	✳
Reiken, Rick																										
Richards, Brigid										◆	◆				✳		✳	✳		✳			✳		◆	✳
Scott, Jill															✳	✳	✳	✳							✳	✳
Stilley, Tucker						✳	✳			✳	✳		✳		✳	✳	✳								◆	✳
Van der Plas, Wim				✳																✳	✳				◆	✳
Welch, Chuck			✳				✳				✳		✳		✳										◆	
Zouni, Opy																									◆	

PLATFORMS

Name	Amiga	Atari	DEC	DOS/Intel	Hewlett Packard	Macintosh	Mainframe	Next	Silicon Graphics	Sun
Beers, Lisa										
Bureaud, Annick						✳				
Cochran, Connor Freff			✳	✳		✳				
Connors, John			✳	✳		✳			✳	
Crawford, V L				✳						
Cronsioe, Igor				✳						
Darvas, Gyorgy						✳				
Devito, Carl						✳				
Drake, Luigi-Bob						✳				
Klinkowstein, Tom				✳						
Loeb, Arthur										
Major, Ginette										
Malina, Roger				✳		✳		✳	✳	✳
Mann, Steve				✳		✳		✳	✳	
Nagy, Denes				✳						
Nishimura, Yumi										
Perkins, Carolyn V				✳		✳			✳	✳
Podnar, Gregg			✳	✳						✳
Reiken, Rick				✳		✳			✳	
Richards, Brigid				✳		✳				
Scott, Jill										
Stilley, Tucker				✳						
Van der Plas, Wim				✳		✳				
Welch, Chuck										
Zouni, Opy										

Graphic Design

◆ = Primary Activity
※ = Other Disciplines/Activities/Resources

DISCIPLINES

Name	3D Art	Animation	Architecture	Ceramics	Computer Art	Computer Graphics	Conceptual Art	Copy Art	Dance	Environmental Art	Fiber Arts	Film	Graphic Design	Holography	Industrial Design	Installation Art	Interactive Art	Kinetic Art	Literary Arts	Mixed Media	Multimedia	Music and Sound	Painting	Performance Art	Photography	Robotics	Sculpture	Space Art	Telecommunications	Video	Virtual Reality	Visual Art
Burrows, Paul	※	※			※	※															※									※		
D'Angelo, Aldo	※	※			※	※						※		※			※	※		※	※		※		※		※			※	※	
Graham, Victoria			※																	※			※	※	※		※				※	
Hurlburt, Carol J.																								※								
Metros, Susan	※	※			※	※	※			※		※				※	※				※									※		

ACTIVITIES

Name	Actor	Architect	Art Collector	Arts Administrator	Choreographer	Composer	Critic	Curator	Dancer	Designer	Educator	Hardware Developer	Historian	Mathematician	Multimedia Artist	Musician	Performance Artist	Performing Artist	Publisher	Researcher	Scientist	Software Developer	Student	Theoretician	Visual Artist	Writer/Editor
Burrows, Paul							※			◆										※					※	※
D'Angelo, Aldo										※	※	※		※	※					※				※	◆	※
Graham, Victoria			※							◆	※	※			※										※	※
Hurlburt, Carol J.											※															◆
Metros, Susan				※						※	◆	※			※					※		※			※	※

PLATFORMS

Name	Amiga	Atari	DEC	DOS/Intel	Hewlett Packard	Macintosh	Mainframe	Next	Silicon Graphics	Sun
Burrows, Paul		※				※				
D'Angelo, Aldo				※		※				
Graham, Victoria						※				
Hurlburt, Carol J.										
Metros, Susan						※				

Holography

◆ = Primary Activity
※ = Other Disciplines/Activities/Resources

DISCIPLINES

Name	3D Art	Animation	Architecture	Ceramics	Computer Art	Computer Graphics	Conceptual Art	Copy Art	Dance	Environmental Art	Fiber Arts	Film	Graphic Design	Holography	Industrial Design	Installation Art	Interactive Art	Kinetic Art	Literary Arts	Mixed Media	Multimedia	Music and Sound	Painting	Performance Art	Photography	Robotics	Sculpture	Space Art	Telecommunications	Video	Virtual Reality	Visual Art
Berkhout, Rudie	※	※			※	※										※	※			※	※	※			※		※			※		
Boone, Pierre Michel					※	※														※	※				※			※				
Boyd, Patrick	※	※			※	※	※					※				※				※	※				※			※				
Christakis, A.M.																※																
DeFreitas, Frank	※	※			※																											
Jurewicz, Arlene					※	※	※																									
Kac, Eduardo	※																												※			
Kellner, Michael																																
Kodera, Mitsuo																										※						
Lieberman, Larry																																
Mitamura, Shunsuke																※	※			※												
Murray, Jeffery	※	※														※	※										※					
Olson, Bernadette	※															※	※															
Orazem, Vito																																
Pink, Patty					※	※	※						※			※	※	※		※	※	※	※		※					※		
Shimon, Hameiri																																
Thwaites, Hal	※																															

ACTIVITIES

Name	Actor	Architect	Art Collector	Arts Administrator	Choreographer	Composer	Critic	Curator	Dancer	Designer	Educator	Hardware Developer	Historian	Mathematician	Multimedia Artist	Musician	Performance Artist	Performing Artist	Publisher	Researcher	Scientist	Software Developer	Student	Theoretician	Visual Artist	Writer/Editor
Berkhout, Rudie						※				※	※				※	※				※					◆	
Boone, Pierre Michel										◆	◆				※					※	※					
Boyd, Patrick										※					※										◆	
Christakis, A.M.								◆																		
DeFreitas, Frank											◆														※	
Jurewicz, Arlene											◆														◆	※
Kac, Eduardo																				※				※	◆	※
Kellner, Michael																								※	◆	
Kodera, Mitsuo																									◆	
Lieberman, Larry																									◆	
Mitamura, Shunsuke											※														※	
Murray, Jeffery			※				※	※		※		※	※							※					※	※
Olson, Bernadette			※					※			◆									※					◆	
Orazem, Vito				※													※	※		※					◆	※
Pink, Patty				※							◆												※		※	
Shimon, Hameiri																									◆	
Thwaites, Hal											◆														◆	

PLATFORMS

Name	Amiga	Atari	DEC	DOS/Intel	Hewlett Packard	Macintosh	Mainframe	Next	Silicon Graphics	Sun
Berkhout, Rudie										
Boone, Pierre Michel				※	※	※				
Boyd, Patrick					※	※				
Christakis, A.M.										
DeFreitas, Frank				※		※				
Jurewicz, Arlene				※	※	※				
Kac, Eduardo					※				※	
Kellner, Michael					※					
Kodera, Mitsuo										
Lieberman, Larry										
Mitamura, Shunsuke						※				
Murray, Jeffery					※					
Olson, Bernadette				※						
Orazem, Vito										
Pink, Patty										
Shimon, Hameiri										
Thwaites, Hal					※	※				

Industrial Design

◆ = Primary Activity
✳ = Other Disciplines/Activities/Resources

DISCIPLINES

Discipline	Nathanson, Theodore Herzl	Tratner, Alan Arthur
3D Art		✳
Animation	✳	
Architecture	✳	✳
Ceramics		✳
Computer Art		✳
Computer Graphics	✳	✳
Conceptual Art		✳
Graphic Design		✳
Interactive Art		✳
Mixed Media		✳
Multimedia		✳
Painting	✳	
Photography	✳	✳
Sculpture	✳	✳

ACTIVITIES

Activity	Nathanson, Theodore Herzl	Tratner, Alan Arthur
Designer	◆	✳
Educator		◆
Hardware Developer		✳
Multimedia Artist		✳
Researcher		✳
Scientist		✳
Visual Artist		✳
Writer/Editor		✳

PLATFORMS

Platform	Nathanson, Theodore Herzl	Tratner, Alan Arthur
DOS/Intel	✳	✳
Macintosh		✳

Installation Art

◆ = Primary Activity
✳ = Other Disciplines/Activities/Resources

DISCIPLINES

Discipline	Bell, Lillian	Draznin, Wayne	George, Dan	Hall, Adrian	Kenton, Mary Jean	Siegfried, Walter
3D Art	✳	✳	✳			
Animation		✳				
Architecture			✳			
Computer Art		✳		✳		
Computer Graphics	✳	✳		✳		
Conceptual Art	✳	✳		✳	✳	
Copy Art	✳					
Dance		✳				
Environmental Art	✳	✳		✳	✳	
Fiber Arts	✳					
Film		✳				
Graphic Design		✳	✳			
Holography		✳				
Industrial Design			✳			
Interactive Art	✳	✳				✳
Kinetic Art		✳				
Literary Arts	✳					
Mixed Media	✳	✳		✳		✳
Multimedia		✳				
Music and Sound		✳		✳		✳
Painting					✳	
Performance Art				✳		✳
Photography	✳	✳		✳		
Sculpture	✳	✳	✳	✳		
Space Art						✳
Video		✳		✳		

ACTIVITIES

Activity	Bell, Lillian	Draznin, Wayne	George, Dan	Hall, Adrian	Kenton, Mary Jean	Siegfried, Walter
Critic		✳				
Educator		✳		✳		
Multimedia Artist	✳	◆		✳		◆
Musician						✳
Performance Artist				✳		
Performing Artist				✳		
Researcher						✳
Scientist						✳
Theoretician						✳
Visual Artist	◆	✳	◆	◆	◆	✳
Writer/Editor		✳		✳	✳	

PLATFORMS

Platform	Bell, Lillian	Draznin, Wayne	George, Dan	Hall, Adrian	Kenton, Mary Jean	Siegfried, Walter
Amiga		✳				
Atari				✳		
DOS/Intel	✳	✳				
Hewlett Packard						
Macintosh		✳	✳	✳	✳	

Interactive Art

◆ = Primary Activity
✳ = Other Disciplines/Activities/Resources

DISCIPLINES

Discipline	Bell, Bill	Bhatnagar, Ranjit Sahai	Capucci, Pier Luigi	Edgar, Robert	Gaw, David	John, K.P. Ludwig	Paterson, Nancy
3D Art	✳	✳					
Animation		✳	✳				
Computer Graphics		✳		✳	✳	✳	
Computer Art		✳		✳	✳	✳	✳
Copy Art		✳					
Dance		✳					
Environmental Art		✳					
Film				✳			
Graphic Design					✳		
Holography		✳					
Industrial Design		✳		✳	✳	✳	
Interactive Art							
Kinetic Art	✳			✳		✳	
Mixed Media		✳		✳	✳		
Multimedia		✳	✳	✳	✳	✳	
Music and Sound		✳		✳	✳	✳	
Performance Art					✳		✳
Robotics			✳		✳		
Sculpture	✳				✳		
Video		✳	✳	✳		✳	✳
Virtual Reality		✳	✳	✳		✳	✳

ACTIVITIES

Activity	Bell, Bill	Bhatnagar, Ranjit Sahai	Capucci, Pier Luigi	Edgar, Robert	Gaw, David	John, K.P. Ludwig	Paterson, Nancy
Composer			✳				
Critic			✳				✳
Curator			✳				✳
Designer		✳	✳		✳	✳	✳
Educator	✳	✳	✳				
Hardware Developer	✳			✳	✳		
Mathematician	✳						
Multimedia Artist		✳		◆		◆	✳
Musician			✳				
Performing Artist				✳			
Researcher		◆	◆				✳
Scientist	✳						
Software Developer	✳	✳		◆			
Theoretician			✳				
Visual Artist	◆	✳			✳		◆
Writer/Editor			✳				✳

PLATFORMS

Platform	Bell, Bill	Bhatnagar, Ranjit Sahai	Capucci, Pier Luigi	Edgar, Robert	Gaw, David	John, K.P. Ludwig	Paterson, Nancy
Amiga				✳		✳	
DOS/Intel				✳	✳	✳	✳
Hewlett Packard		✳					
Macintosh		✳		✳	✳	✳	✳
Next				✳			
Silicon Graphics		✳					
Sun		✳					

185

Interactive Art

◆ = Primary Activity
* = Other Disciplines/Activities/Resources

Column groups (left to right): **DISCIPLINES** — 3D Art, Animation, Architecture, Ceramics, Computer Art, Computer Graphics, Conceptual Art, Copy Art, Dance, Environmental Art, Fiber Arts, Film, Graphic Design, Holography, Industrial Design, Installation Art, Interactive Art, Kinetic Art, Literary Arts, Mixed Media, Multimedia, Music and Sound, Painting, Performance Art, Photography, Robotics, Sculpture, Space Art, Telecommunications, Video, Virtual Reality, Visual Art; **ACTIVITIES** — Actor, Architect, Art Collector, Arts Administrator, Choreographer, Composer, Critic, Curator, Dancer, Designer, Educator, Hardware Developer, Historian, Mathematician, Multimedia Artist, Musician, Performance Artist, Performing Artist, Publisher, Researcher, Scientist, Software Developer, Student, Theoretician, Visual Artist, Writer/Editor; **PLATFORMS** — Amiga, Atari, DEC, DOS/Intel, Hewlett Packard, Macintosh, Mainframe, Next, Silicon Graphics, Sun.

Name	Disciplines	Activities	Platforms
Rapoport, Sonya	3D Art *, Architecture *, Computer Art *, Computer Graphics *, Conceptual Art *, Graphic Design *, Installation Art *, Multimedia *, Music and Sound *	Multimedia Artist ◆, Visual Artist *, Writer/Editor *	DOS/Intel *, Macintosh *
Reed, Hazen	Animation *, Computer Art *, Computer Graphics *, Conceptual Art *, Installation Art *, Multimedia *, Music and Sound *, Video *	Multimedia Artist ◆, Visual Artist *, Writer/Editor *	Macintosh *
Reid, Melynda	Environmental Art *, Fiber Arts *, Multimedia *, Music and Sound *, Painting *, Performance Art *, Photography *, Sculpture *, Space Art *	Actor *, Composer *, Dancer *, Designer *, Educator *, Performance Artist *, Performing Artist *, Visual Artist ◆, Theoretician *, Writer/Editor *	Amiga *
Reiser, Hans	Multimedia *, Virtual Reality *	Theoretician ◆, Visual Artist *, Writer/Editor *	
Rosen, Joe	Computer Art *, Computer Graphics *, Film *, Graphic Design *, Multimedia *, Robotics *, Virtual Reality *	Designer *, Educator *, Hardware Developer *, Historian *, Mathematician *, Multimedia Artist *, Researcher *, Scientist *, Software Developer *, Student *, Visual Artist ◆, Writer/Editor *	DOS/Intel *, Macintosh *
Wilson, Steve	Kinetic Art *, Multimedia *, Robotics *, Virtual Reality *	Educator *, Multimedia Artist ◆, Researcher *, Software Developer *, Writer/Editor *	Macintosh *

Kinetic Art

◆ = Primary Activity
* = Other Disciplines/Activities/Resources

Name	Disciplines	Activities	Platforms
Belik, Jaroslav	3D Art *, Computer Graphics *, Graphic Design *, Installation Art *, Interactive Art *, Multimedia *, Music and Sound *, Painting *, Performance Art *, Robotics *, Sculpture *	Designer *, Multimedia Artist *, Visual Artist ◆	
Worthington, Nancy	Installation Art *, Interactive Art *, Multimedia *, Music and Sound *, Painting *, Performance Art *, Robotics *, Sculpture *	Actor *, Art Collector *, Curator *, Educator *, Multimedia Artist *, Visual Artist ◆, Writer/Editor *	Hewlett Packard *, Macintosh *

Literary Arts

◆ = Primary Activity
* = Other Disciplines/Activities/Resources

Name	Disciplines	Activities	Platforms
Guyer, Carolyn	Computer Art *, Conceptual Art *, Fiber Arts *, Interactive Art *, Mixed Media *, Multimedia *	Educator *, Visual Artist ◆, Writer/Editor ◆	Macintosh *
Lee, Judith Yaros	Ceramics *, Computer Graphics *	Composer *, Educator *, Historian ◆, Performing Artist *, Researcher *, Scientist *, Software Developer *, Student *, Theoretician *, Visual Artist ◆, Writer/Editor *	DOS/Intel *

Mixed Media

◆ = Primary Activity
✳ = Other Disciplines/Activities/Resources

Disciplines

Name	3D Art	Animation	Architecture	Computer Art	Computer Graphics	Conceptual Art	Graphic Design	Installation Art	Interactive Art	Kinetic Art	Literary Arts	Mixed Media	Music and Sound	Painting	Performance Art	Photography	Robotics	Sculpture	Video	Virtual Reality
Altman, Richard	✳	✳	✳	✳			✳	✳				◼				✳			✳	
Colby, Sas						✳			✳		✳	◼		✳						
Gaffney, Gary	✳							✳				◼						✳		
Hollier, Thomas	✳	✳		✳	✳		✳		✳			◼				✳			✳	✳
Huebner, Guido				✳				✳	✳			◼	✳		✳		✳		✳	
Weiss, Lenore										✳		◼								

Activities

Name	Actor	Arts Administrator	Choreographer	Composer	Critic	Designer	Educator	Hardware Developer	Mathematician	Multimedia Artist	Musician	Performance Artist	Performing Artist	Visual Artist	Writer/Editor
Altman, Richard						◆		✳		✳				✳	
Colby, Sas														◆	✳
Gaffney, Gary		✳					✳		✳					◆	
Hollier, Thomas		✳			✳	✳	✳	✳		✳				◆	✳
Huebner, Guido	✳		✳	✳						◆	✳	✳	✳	✳	
Weiss, Lenore							✳			✳					◆

Platforms

Name	Amiga	DOS/Intel	Macintosh
Altman, Richard			✳
Colby, Sas			
Gaffney, Gary			✳
Hollier, Thomas	✳	✳	✳
Huebner, Guido		✳	
Weiss, Lenore			✳

Multimedia

◆ = Primary Activity
✳ = Other Disciplines/Activities/Resources

Disciplines

Name	3D Art	Animation	Architecture	Computer Art	Computer Graphics	Conceptual Art	Environmental Art	Film	Graphic Design	Holography	Installation Art	Interactive Art	Kinetic Art	Literary Arts	Mixed Media	Music and Sound	Painting	Performance Art	Photography	Robotics	Sculpture	Space Art	Telecommunications	Video	Virtual Reality
Alexander	✳					✳		✳		✳		✳	✳	✳	◼						✳				
Bernstein, Mark				✳										✳	◼										
Davis, Jr., Collis H.	✳	✳		✳	✳		✳	✳	✳		✳	✳	✳		◼		✳	✳	✳		✳			✳	
Glaesner, Sallee		✳		✳	✳	✳	✳		✳	✳	✳		✳		◼		✳					✳		✳	
Lausten, Thorbjorn			✳												◼										
Lauzzana, Raymond Guido	✳	✳		✳	✳	✳		✳	✳	✳	✳				◼	✳	✳	✳	✳		✳				✳
Leonard, David P															◼	✳									✳
Mosher, Mike				✳											◼										
Nadin, Mihai															◼									✳	
Packer, Randall															◼	✳									
Porter, Gene Lavon	✳	✳		✳	✳	✳	✳		✳		✳				◼	✳	✳		✳		✳			✳	
Rutkovsky, Paul							✳																		
Shepard, Scott	✳			✳		✳					✳	✳			◼		✳	✳	✳		✳				
Stansfield, Elsa						✳									◼										
Whitman, Deborah		✳	✳			✳		✳			✳	✳	✳		◼		✳	✳			✳				

Activities

Name	Actor	Architect	Art Collector	Composer	Critic	Curator	Designer	Educator	Hardware Developer	Historian	Mathematician	Multimedia Artist	Musician	Performance Artist	Performing Artist	Researcher	Scientist	Software Developer	Student	Theoretician	Visual Artist	Writer/Editor
Alexander												◆									✳	✳
Bernstein, Mark					✳							✳				✳	◆	✳				✳
Davis, Jr., Collis H.	✳		✳				✳			✳		◆	✳					✳	✳		✳	✳
Glaesner, Sallee			✳				✳					◆						✳			✳	✳
Lausten, Thorbjorn		✳										◆				✳					✳	✳
Lauzzana, Raymond Guido		✳			◆			✳	✳		✳	✳				✳	✳	✳	✳	✳		
Leonard, David P							✳	◆				◆		✳	✳							
Mosher, Mike					✳		✳	✳				◆			✳					◆	✳	
Nadin, Mihai				✳								◆				✳						
Packer, Randall												◆										
Porter, Gene Lavon						✳						◆									✳	
Rutkovsky, Paul												◆				✳						
Shepard, Scott				✳								◆				✳						
Stansfield, Elsa												◆									✳	
Whitman, Deborah												✳									◆	

Platforms

Name	Amiga	Atari	DOS/Intel	Hewlett Packard	Macintosh	Silicon Graphics	Sun
Alexander					✳		
Bernstein, Mark			✳		✳		
Davis, Jr., Collis H.			✳			✳	
Glaesner, Sallee			✳		✳		✳
Lausten, Thorbjorn			✳				
Lauzzana, Raymond Guido		✳					
Leonard, David P							
Mosher, Mike			✳		✳		
Nadin, Mihai							
Packer, Randall							✳
Porter, Gene Lavon			✳				
Rutkovsky, Paul	✳						
Shepard, Scott	✳						
Stansfield, Elsa					✳		
Whitman, Deborah							

187

Music and Sound

◆ = Primary Activity
✳ = Other Disciplines/Activities/Resources

PLATFORMS: Sun · Silicon Graphics · Next · Mainframe · Macintosh · Hewlett Packard · DOS/Intel · DEC · Atari · Amiga

ACTIVITIES: Writer/Editor · Visual Artist · Theoretician · Student · Software Developer · Scientist · Researcher · Publisher · Performing Artist · Performance Artist · Musician · Multimedia Artist · Mathematician · Historian · Hardware Developer · Educator · Designer · Dancer · Curator · Critic · Composer · Choreographer · Arts Administrator · Art Collector · Architect · Actor

DISCIPLINES: Visual Art · Virtual Reality · Video · Telecommunications · Space Art · Sculpture · Robotics · Photography · Performance Art · Painting · Music and Sound · Multimedia · Mixed Media · Literary Arts · Kinetic Art · Interactive Art · Installation Art · Industrial Design · Holography · Graphic Design · Film · Fiber Arts · Environmental Art · Dance · Copy Art · Conceptual Art · Computer Graphics · Computer Art · Ceramics · Architecture · Animation · 3D Art

Name
Alves, William
Ames, Charles
Battier, Marc
Beyls, Peter
Blankinship, Paul J
Blum, Thom
Bova, Jeffrey
Burt, Warren
Ceely, Robert
Duesenberry, John
Etzen, David-John
Fogar, Alessandro
Free, Phyllis
Giomi, Francesco
Goode, Daniel
Harris, Craig
Kreger, Tim
Lippe, Cort
Mahin, Bruce
Marsanyi, Robert
Maubrey, Benoit
McNabb, Michael
Moran, Kevin R
Normandeau, Robert
Oliveros, Pauline
Osborn, Ed
Palmer, Christopher
Phillips, John
Polansky, Larry
Pope, Stephen
Raes, Godfried-Willem

Music and Sound

◆ = Primary Activity
* = Other Disciplines/Activities/Resources

Column groups: DISCIPLINES, ACTIVITIES, PLATFORMS. "Music and Sound" discipline column is shaded (primary discipline) for all listed people.

Name	Disciplines (*)	Activities	Platforms (*)
Rais, Mark	—	Mathematician*, Composer◆, Critic*	Macintosh*, DOS/Intel*, Hewlett Packard*, Silicon Graphics*
Ray, David	—	Multimedia Artist◆, Musician*, Performance Artist*, Composer*, Critic*, Researcher*, Scientist*, Software Developer*, Hardware Developer*	Macintosh*
Rolnick, Neil	Animation*, Interactive Art*, Multimedia*, Performance Art*, Virtual Reality*, Video*	Composer◆, Musician*, Performing Artist*, Educator*	Macintosh*
Rosenboom, David	Computer Art*, Computer Graphics*, Conceptual Art*, Interactive Art*, Kinetic Art*, Mixed Media*, Multimedia*, Performance Art*	Composer◆, Multimedia Artist*, Musician*, Performance Artist*, Performing Artist*, Researcher*, Software Developer*, Educator*, Scientist*, Software Developer*, Theoretician*, Visual Artist*, Writer/Editor*	Macintosh*, DEC*, Silicon Graphics*
Sadra, I Wayan	Mixed Media*, Multimedia*	Composer◆, Musician*, Dance*	Macintosh*
Scaletti, Carla	Animation*, Dance*, Multimedia*	Composer◆, Musician*, Researcher*, Software Developer*, Visual Artist*, Writer/Editor*	Macintosh*, DOS/Intel*, Sun*
Scholz, Carter	—	Composer◆, Musician*	Macintosh*
Scott, Alex W.	Computer Art*, Computer Graphics*, Graphic Design*, Interactive Art*, Virtual Reality*	Arts Administrator◆, Visual Artist*, Writer/Editor*	Macintosh*
Siegel, Wayne	Computer Art*, Dance*, Environmental Art*, Installation Art*, Interactive Art*, Performance Art*	Composer◆, Curator*, Educator*, Critic*, Arts Administrator*	Macintosh*, DOS/Intel*, Next*, Hewlett Packard*
Supper, Martin	Film*, Mixed Media*	Scientist*, Theoretician*	Macintosh*
Vasques Dias, Amilcar	Multimedia*, Photography*, Video*	Composer◆, Musician*, Performance Artist*, Hardware Developer*	Macintosh*
Worrall, David	Computer Art*, Performance Art*, Space Art*	Composer◆, Musician*, Critic*, Researcher*	Macintosh*, Amiga*, Silicon Graphics*, Sun*

Painting

◆ = Primary Activity
* = Other Disciplines/Activities/Resources

Column groups: DISCIPLINES, ACTIVITIES, PLATFORMS. "Painting" discipline column is shaded (primary discipline) for all listed people.

Name	Disciplines (*)	Activities	Platforms (*)
Bill, Max	Industrial Design*, Sculpture*	Visual Artist◆, Designer*, Educator*	—
Carrier, David	Sculpture*	Theoretician◆, Arts Administrator◆	—
Carroll, Miranda	Computer Graphics*, Environmental Art*, Holography*, Photography*, Sculpture*	Visual Artist◆, Scientist*, Researcher*, Curator*, Educator*, Choreographer*	Macintosh*
Csaji, Attila	Computer Art*, Conceptual Art*, Sculpture*	Visual Artist◆	DOS/Intel*, Macintosh*
Guzak, Karen W.	Computer Art*, Computer Graphics*, Multimedia*, Sculpture*, Video*	Visual Artist◆, Multimedia Artist*	Amiga*, DOS/Intel*
Halaby, Samia	Kinetic Art*, Mixed Media*, Multimedia*	Visual Artist◆, Multimedia Artist*	Amiga*, DOS/Intel*
Martin, Claude	Video*	Visual Artist◆	DOS/Intel*
Martin, Tony	Environmental Art*, Installation Art*, Interactive Art*, Multimedia*, Video*, Virtual Reality*	Visual Artist◆, Multimedia Artist*	DOS/Intel*
Mueller, Robert Emmer	Environmental Art*	Visual Artist◆, Theoretician*, Arts Administrator*, Multimedia Artist*	Macintosh*
Quan, Long	Multimedia*	Visual Artist◆, Multimedia Artist*	—
Reagan, Trudy Myrrh	Computer Graphics*, Conceptual Art*, Graphic Design*, Mixed Media*, Video*	Visual Artist◆, Multimedia Artist*, Curator*, Educator*	Macintosh*
Saenger, Elizabeth	Computer Graphics*, Conceptual Art*, Fiber Arts*, Mixed Media*	Visual Artist*, Theoretician◆, Researcher*, Educator*	DOS/Intel*
Shepherd, Gerald	—	Visual Artist◆	DOS/Intel*
Termes, Dick	Kinetic Art*, Photography*, Space Art*	Visual Artist◆	—

189

Photography

◆ = Primary Activity
✱ = Other Disciplines/Activities/Resources

Platforms

Name	Amiga	Atari	DEC	DOS/Intel	Hewlett Packard	Macintosh	Mainframe	Next	Silicon Graphics	Sun
Giersberg, Frits				✱						
Muller-Pohle, Andreas				✱						
O'Neil, Elaine				✱						
Wang, Sam						✱				
Wood, Patte						✱				

Activities

Name	Curator	Critic	Educator	Historian	Musician	Theoretician	Visual Artist	Writer/Editor	Arts Administrator
Giersberg, Frits	◆	✱		✱		✱			
Muller-Pohle, Andreas		✱					◆	✱	
O'Neil, Elaine			◆				✱		
Wang, Sam			◆				✱		
Wood, Patte					✱		✱		◆

Disciplines

Name	Architecture	Computer Art	Computer Graphics	Conceptual Art	Environmental Art	Fiber Arts	Film	Installation Art	Interactive Art	Mixed Media	Multimedia	Music and Sound	Painting	Performance Art	Sculpture	Video	Virtual Reality	Visual Art
Giersberg, Frits	✱	✱		✱	✱		✱	✱	✱	✱	✱		✱	✱	✱	✱	✱	✱
Muller-Pohle, Andreas				✱						✱								
O'Neil, Elaine						✱				✱								
Wang, Sam			✱															
Wood, Patte		✱										✱						

Sculpture

◆ = Primary Activity
✱ = Other Disciplines/Activities/Resources

Platforms

Name	Amiga	Atari	DEC	DOS/Intel	Hewlett Packard	Macintosh	Mainframe	Next	Silicon Graphics	Sun
Beasley, Bruce					✱	✱				
Clar, Richard				✱						
de Marchi, John Anthony						✱				
Dickson, Stewart						✱			✱	✱
Dion, Emanuel										
Lilley, Clare Louise										
Pallas, Jim						✱				
Philippe, Jean-Marc				✱						
Piene, Otto						✱	✱			
Schiess, Christian										
Takis										

Activities

Name	Architect	Art Collector	Arts Administrator	Composer	Critic	Curator	Designer	Educator	Historian	Mathematician	Multimedia Artist	Researcher	Scientist	Software Developer	Theoretician	Visual Artist	Writer/Editor
Beasley, Bruce																◆	
Clar, Richard		✱					✱					✱			✱		
de Marchi, John Anthony									✱			✱				◆	
Dickson, Stewart	✱				✱	✱	✱	✱				✱	✱	✱	✱	◆	✱
Dion, Emanuel		✱				◆			✱	✱		✱			✱	◆	✱
Lilley, Clare Louise			✱					✱									
Pallas, Jim											✱					◆	
Philippe, Jean-Marc													✱		✱	✱	
Piene, Otto							✱						✱			◆	
Schiess, Christian				✱												◆	✱
Takis																◆	

Disciplines

Name	3D Art	Animation	Architecture	Computer Art	Computer Graphics	Conceptual Art	Dance	Environmental Art	Film	Graphic Design	Holography	Industrial Design	Installation Art	Interactive Art	Kinetic Art	Literary Arts	Mixed Media	Multimedia	Music and Sound	Painting	Photography	Robotics	Space Art	Video	Virtual Reality	Visual Art
Beasley, Bruce	✱		✱	✱	✱			✱																		
Clar, Richard						✱		✱											✱	✱			✱	✱	✱	
de Marchi, John Anthony	✱		✱				✱	✱	✱		✱	✱		✱	✱		✱	✱	✱		✱					
Dickson, Stewart	✱	✱		✱	✱			✱		✱		✱	✱	✱	✱					✱						
Dion, Emanuel						✱										✱						✱				
Lilley, Clare Louise																										
Pallas, Jim	✱												✱	✱												
Philippe, Jean-Marc																										
Piene, Otto			✱			✱		✱		✱									✱	✱			✱		✱	✱
Schiess, Christian													✱		✱											
Takis																										

190

Space Art

◆ = Primary Activity
✳ = Other Disciplines/Resources/Activities

Van Boom, Marc
- Activities: Visual Artist ◆; Scientist ✳; Researcher ✳; Multimedia Artist ✳; Arts Administrator ✳
- Disciplines: Painting ✳; Space Art (primary, shaded)

Video

◆ = Primary Activity
✳ = Other Disciplines/Resources/Activities

Callas, Peter
- Activities: Visual Artist ◆
- Disciplines: Environmental Art ✳; Computer Graphics ✳; Computer Art ✳; Animation ✳; 3D Art ✳

Gabriel, Robert
- Platforms: Macintosh ✳; DOS/Intel ✳
- Activities: Writer/Editor ◆; Software Developer ✳; Researcher ✳; Multimedia Artist ✳
- Disciplines: Interactive Art ✳; Computer Graphics ✳; Computer Art ✳; Animation ✳

Hmeljak, Matjaz
- Platforms: Macintosh ✳
- Activities: Visual Artist ◆; Researcher ✳; Musician ◆; Multimedia Artist ✳; Art Collector ✳
- Disciplines: Virtual Reality ✳; Photography ✳; Music and Sound ✳; Multimedia ✳; Mixed Media ✳; Film ✳; Computer Graphics ✳; Computer Art ✳; Animation ✳

Kirksey, Daniel
- Disciplines: Multimedia ✳; Graphic Design ✳; Computer Graphics ✳; Computer Art ✳

Martin, David
- Platforms: DOS/Intel ✳
- Activities: Visual Artist ◆; Multimedia Artist ✳; Designer ✳
- Disciplines: Sculpture ✳; Painting ✳; Music and Sound ✳; Kinetic Art ✳; Interactive Art ✳; Animation ✳

Nicoloff, Alex
- Activities: Student ◆
- Disciplines: Computer Art ✳; Animation ✳

Petterd, Robin
- Activities: Theoretician ✳; Educator ✳
- Disciplines: Dance ✳; Animation ✳

Pocock-Williams, Lynn
- Platforms: Macintosh ✳; Atari ✳; Amiga ✳
- Activities: Visual Artist ◆; Software Developer ✳; Researcher ✳; Multimedia Artist ✳; Mathematician ✳; Educator ✳; Dancer ✳; Curator ✳; Critic ✳; Arts Administrator ✳
- Disciplines: Virtual Reality ✳; Performance Art ✳; Multimedia ✳; Interactive Art ✳; Installation Art ✳; Film ✳; Environmental Art ✳

Ris, Anet Margot
- Activities: Visual Artist ◆; Performance Artist ✳; Educator ◆
- Disciplines: Performance Art ✳

Ryan, Paul
- Activities: Writer/Editor ✳; Visual Artist ✳; Educator ◆; Curator ✳; Critic ✳
- Disciplines: Performance Art ✳; Music and Sound ✳; Multimedia ✳; Interactive Art ✳; Conceptual Art ✳; Computer Art ✳; Film ✳

Tamblyn, Christine
- Activities: Writer/Editor ✳; Visual Artist ◆; Performance Artist ✳; Curator ✳; Critic ✳
- Disciplines: Multimedia ✳; Mixed Media ✳; Conceptual Art ✳

Weeks, Susan
- Platforms: Macintosh ✳
- Activities: Writer/Editor ✳; Visual Artist ✳; Multimedia Artist ✳; Designer ✳; Critic ✳
- Disciplines: Photography ✳; Music and Sound ✳; Multimedia ✳; Mixed Media ✳; Graphic Design ✳; Film ✳; Conceptual Art ✳; Computer Graphics ✳; Computer Art ✳; Animation ✳; 3D Art ✳

191

Virtual Reality

◆ = Primary Activity
✳ = Other Disciplines/Activities/Resources

DISCIPLINES

Name	3D Art	Animation	Architecture	Ceramics	Computer Art	Computer Graphics	Conceptual Art	Copy Art	Dance	Environmental Art	Fiber Arts	Film	Graphic Design	Holography	Industrial Design	Installation Art	Interactive Art	Kinetic Art	Literary Arts	Mixed Media	Multimedia	Music and Sound	Painting	Performance Art	Photography	Robotics	Sculpture	Space Art	Telecommunications	Video	Virtual Reality	Visual Art
Delaney, Ben		✳				✳							✳		✳					✳					✳					✳		
Gray, Noel			✳			✳			✳																							
Klein, Sherman						✳				✳			✳							✳	✳		✳			✳				✳		
Mulder, Axel					✳	✳	✳										✳			✳	✳	✳				✳				✳		
Steingrubner, Joachim					✳	✳									✳					✳	✳	✳					✳			✳		
Truck, Frederick John					✳	✳							✳							✳	✳	✳								✳		
Vincent, Vincent John	✳	✳							✳							✳				✳	✳	✳		✳								

ACTIVITIES

Name	Actor	Architect	Art Collector	Arts Administrator	Choreographer	Composer	Critic	Curator	Dancer	Designer	Educator	Hardware Developer	Historian	Mathematician	Multimedia Artist	Musician	Performance Artist	Performing Artist	Publisher	Researcher	Scientist	Software Developer	Student	Theoretician	Visual Artist	Writer/Editor
Delaney, Ben			✳				✳			✳		✳								✳	✳	✳			✳	◆
Gray, Noel																				✳				◆		
Klein, Sherman							✳		✳	✳	✳			✳						✳	✳	◆		✳		✳
Mulder, Axel					✳				✳	✳	✳	✳				✳				◆	✳	✳			◆	
Steingrubner, Joachim										✳	✳			✳	✳	✳				✳	✳	◆			✳	✳
Truck, Frederick John			✳				✳			✳					✳							✳			◆	✳
Vincent, Vincent John					✳				✳						✳	✳	◆	✳		✳				✳	✳	✳

PLATFORMS

Name	Amiga	Atari	DEC	DOS/Intel	Hewlett Packard	Macintosh	Mainframe	Next	Silicon Graphics	Sun
Delaney, Ben				✳						
Gray, Noel						✳				
Klein, Sherman	✳		✳	✳	✳	✳	✳		✳	✳
Mulder, Axel		✳		✳		✳				
Steingrubner, Joachim				✳	✳	✳				
Truck, Frederick John				✳	✳	✳				
Vincent, Vincent John	✳			✳		✳				

Visual Art

◆ = Primary Activity
✳ = Other Disciplines/Activities/Resources

DISCIPLINES

Name	3D Art	Animation	Architecture	Ceramics	Computer Art	Computer Graphics	Conceptual Art	Copy Art	Dance	Environmental Art	Fiber Arts	Film	Graphic Design	Holography	Industrial Design	Installation Art	Interactive Art	Kinetic Art	Literary Arts	Mixed Media	Multimedia	Music and Sound	Painting	Performance Art	Photography	Robotics	Sculpture	Space Art	Telecommunications	Video	Virtual Reality	Visual Art
Arnheim, Rudolf																																
Cox, Donna						✳							✳					✳							✳		✳			✳		
Diamond, Jody	✳																															
Levy, Shab	✳			✳	✳	✳				✳	✳	✳	✳		✳	✳							✳	✳	✳		✳					
Turpin, John Timothy	✳												✳		✳	✳				✳					✳		✳			✳		

ACTIVITIES

Name	Actor	Architect	Art Collector	Arts Administrator	Choreographer	Composer	Critic	Curator	Dancer	Designer	Educator	Hardware Developer	Historian	Mathematician	Multimedia Artist	Musician	Performance Artist	Performing Artist	Publisher	Researcher	Scientist	Software Developer	Student	Theoretician	Visual Artist	Writer/Editor
Arnheim, Rudolf											✳										✳			◆		
Cox, Donna											✳					✳				✳					✳	✳
Diamond, Jody						◆				◆	✳									✳						
Levy, Shab				◆																						
Turpin, John Timothy													✳													

PLATFORMS

Name	Amiga	Atari	DEC	DOS/Intel	Hewlett Packard	Macintosh	Mainframe	Next	Silicon Graphics	Sun
Arnheim, Rudolf										
Cox, Donna							✳			
Diamond, Jody						✳				
Levy, Shab				✳		✳				
Turpin, John Timothy				✳		✳				

DIRECTORY OF INDIVIDUALS

Yoshiyuki Abe
3-20-27 Meguro
Meguro-ku, Tokyo 153 Japan
Tel/Fax: (81 3) 3793-5953
Email: y.abe@compmail.com

Victor Acevedo
956 1/2 N. Vista Street
Los Angeles, CA 90046 USA
Tel: (213) 851-7594
Fax: (213) 461-4985

Alexander
2311 4th Street, Suite 306
Santa Monica, CA 90405 USA
Tel: (310) 393-9846
Fax: (310) 395-6538

Richard Altman
Communication Design
5005 S. Ash Avenue, A-1
Tempe, AZ 85282 USA
Tel: (602) 345-1770
Fax: (602) 345-1084
Email: Applelink D3243

William Alves
813 N. Second Street
Alhambra, CA 91801 USA
Tel: (818) 284-5674
Tel: (213) 749-1221
Email: alves@usc.edu

Charles Ames
68 Stevenson Blvd.
Eggertsville, NY 14226 USA

Jeffrey Apple
Apple Productions
1230 Horn Avenue, #301
Los Angeles, CA 90069 USA
Tel: (310) 854-6182
Fax: (310) 280-1880

Rudolf Arnheim
1200 Earhart Road, #537
Ann Arbor, MI 48105 USA

Ilene Astrahan
PO Box 660, Cooper Station
New York City, NY 10276 USA
Tel: (212) 777-7609

Trevor Batten
Kanaalstraat 15-II
1054 WX Amsterdam, The Netherlands
Tel/Fax: (31 20) 6183018

Marc Battier
IRCAM
29 Avenue de Joinville
F-94130 Nogent Sur Marne, France
Tel/Fax: (33-1) 48736257
Email: bam@ircam.fr

Bruce Beasley
322 Lewis Street
Oakland, CA 94607 USA
Tel: (510) 836-1414
Fax: (510) 763-4431

Lisa Beers
American College for Applied Arts
3330 Peachtree Road
Atlanta, GA 30326 USA

Jaroslav Belik
1610 Mulcahy
Rosenberg, TX 77471 USA
Tel: (713) 341-7197
Fax: (713) 232-9007

Lillian Bell
PO Box 1235
Mcminnville, OR 97128 USA
Tel: (503) 472-3566
Fax: (503) 434-5256

Bill Bell
56 Perry Street
Brookline, MA 02146 USA
Tel: (617) 277-4719
Fax: (617) 277-4736

Rudie Berkhout
223 West 21st Street
New York City, NY 10011 USA
Tel: (212) 255-7569
Fax: (212) 727-0532

Mark Bernstein
Eastgate Systems
Hypertext Systems and Services
PO Box 1307
Cambridge, MA 02238 USA
Tel: (617) 924-9044
Email: EastgateS@aol.com

Peter Beyls
Octaaf Van Dammestraat 73
9030 Gent, Belgium
Tel: (32-91) 26 7753
Email: peter@arti.vub.ac.be

Ranjit Sahai Bhatnagar
PO Box 8166
Philadelphia, PA 19101-8166 USA
Tel: (215) 382-3342
Fax: (215) 222-6748
Email: ranjit@grandient.cis.upenn.edu

Max Bill
Albulastrasse 39
8048 Zurich, Switzerland

Leslie Bishko
Computer Graphics Research Lab
School of Computing Science
Simon Fraser University
Burnaby, BC V5A 1S6 Canada
Tel: (604) 291-3610
Fax: (604) 291-3045
Email: leslie@cs.sfu.ca

Paul J Blankinship
Ampersand Productions
1661 Gateway Drive
Vallejo, CA 94589 USA
Tel: (707) 645-7448
Email: 71561.1037@compuserve.com

Thom Blum
Muscle Fish Multimedia Engineering
2550 9th Street, Suite 207B
Berkeley, CA 94710 USA
Tel: (510) 486-0141
Fax: (510) 486-0868
Email: thom@musclefish.com

Pierre Michel Boone
University Gent—Lab. Soete
Applied Mechanics—Workshop
 Holography
41 St. Pietersnieuwstraat
B9000 Gent, Belgium
Tel: (32 91) 626384
Fax: (32 91) 237326

Jeffrey Bova
Liquid Crystal Music
8 East 77th St., Apt. 4A
New York City, NY 10021 USA
Tel: (212) 582-8800
Fax: (212) 535-1932
Email: pan jeffbova

Patrick Boyd
18 Whiteley Road
Crystal Palace
London SE19 IJT United Kingdom
Tel: (44 0) 81-670-4160
Fax: (44 0) 81-670-7810

Harriet Brisson
PO Box 85
Rehoboth, MA 02769 USA
Tel: (508) 252-3024
Fax: (508) 252-5628

Michael Brodsky
1327 S. Carmona Avenue
Los Angeles, CA 90019 USA
Tel: (213) 932-1894
Fax: (310) 338-4470
Email: mbrodsky@lmuacad.bitnet

Ronald Brown
569 Lake Warren Road
Upper Black Eddy, PA 18972 USA
Tel: (215) 847-2359

Paul Brown
Mississippi State University
PO Box 1292
Mississippi, MS 39762-1292 USA
Tel: (601) 325-2970
Fax: (601) 325-3850
Email: brown@erc.msstate.edu

Annick Bureaud
57, Rue Falguiere
75015 Paris, France
Tel: (33-1) 43 20 9223
Fax: (33-1) 43 22 11 24

Paul Burrows
Documentary Video Associates, Ltd.
Design, Publications
7 Campbell Court, Bramley
Basingstroke, Hants RG26 5EG
United Kingdom
Tel: (0256) 882032
Fax: (0256) 882024

Warren Burt
Flat 18/102 Park Street
St. Kilda West, Victoria 3182 Australia
Tel: (613) 534-4916

Peter Callas
3/3 Werambie Street
Woolwich 2110
Sydney NSW Australia

Pier Luigi Capucci
Via Fiumazzo
Belricetto, Ravenna 48010 Italy
Tel: 0545-77296

David Carrier
Carnegie Mellon University
Pittsburgh, PA 15213-3890 USA
Tel: (412) 268-2819
Fax: (412) 268-1440

Miranda Carroll
The National Gallery
Trafalgar Square
London WC2N 5DN United Kingdom
Tel: (071) 839 3321
Fax: (071) 930 4764

Sydney Cash
72 Reservoir Road
Marlboro, NY 12542 USA
Tel: (914) 236-7032

Stuart Casper
18 Penelope
Taylorsville, NC 28681 USA
Tel: (704) 495-7736

Robert Ceely
BEEP Sounds
33 Elm Street
Brookline, MA 02146-6813 USA
Tel: (617) 731-3785

A.M. Christakis
Musee de l'Holographie
Forum des Halles
15 à 21 Grand Balcon
75001 Paris, France
Tel: (33 1) 40399683
Fax: (33 1) 42743357

Richard Clar
Art Technologies
2170 Coldwater Canyon Drive
Beverly Hills, CA 90210 USA
Tel: (310) 276-5584
Fax: (310) 276-0304

James Clayson
American University of Paris
10 Square De L'Alboni
75016 Paris, France
Tel: (33 1) 42 88 89 13
Fax: (33 1) 42 30 51 12

Connor Freff Cochran
Everything Everything
524 San Anselmo Avenue, #229
San Anselmo, CA 94960 USA
Tel: (415) 332-6161/2
Fax: (415) 332-6163
Email: Connor.Cochran@mcimail.com

Sas Colby
Box 794
El Prado, NM 87529 USA
Tel: (505) 758-3966

John Connors
University of Vermont
Computer and Information Technology
238 Waterman Building
Burlington, VT 05405-0160 USA
Tel: (802) 656-2012
Fax: (802) 656-8148
Email: jmc@uvmvax.uvm.edu

Donna Cox
National Center
   for Supercomputing Applications
University of Illinois
   at Urbana-Champaign
152 Computing Applications Bldg.
605 East Springfield Avenue
Champaign, IL 61820 USA
Email: cox@ncsa.uiuc.edu

V L Crawford
Neon News
PO Box 668
Volcano, HI 96785 USA
Tel: (808) 967-7648

Igor Cronsioe
Living Art Center
Living Design International
Viktoriagatan 15
Gothenburg 41125 Sweden
Tel: (46 31) 134550
Fax: (46 31) 1380 82

Attila Csaji
Hungart
Fine Art Section
Kisgombu, 30
Budapest 1135 Hungary
Tel: (36 1) 12 96 356
Fax: (36 1) 121 29 82

Aldo D'Angelo
Casella Postale 1432
50100 Firenze, Italy
Tel: (39-55) 662362
Tel: (39-55) 2478413

Tommie Daniel
7120 Wyoming Blvd., Suite 170
Albuquerque, NM 87109 USA
Email: daniel@unmvax.cs.unm.edu

Gyorgy Darvas
International Society
   for the Inter-Disciplinary Study
   of Symmetry (ISIS-SYMMETRY)
Nador u. 18., PO Box 4
Budapest H-1361 Hungary
Tel: (36 1) 131-8326
Fax: (36 1) 131-3161
Email: h492dar@ella.hu

Collis H. Davis, Jr.
Ohio State University
Department of Theatre
Haskett Hall
156 West 19th Avenue
Columbus, OH 43210 USA
Tel: (614) 292-6637
Fax: (614) 292-3222
Email: Davis.14@osu.edu

Frank DeFreitas
Holography Workshop
PO Box 9035
Allentown, PA 18105 USA
Tel: (215) 434-8236

Ben Delaney
CyberEdge Journal
928 Greenhill Road
Mill Valley, CA 94941-3406 USA
Tel: (415) 383-2458
Fax: (415) 389-0251
Email: bdel@well.sf.ca.us
76217.3074@compuserve.com

John Anthony de Marchi
3740 Roblar Road
Petaluma, CA 94952 USA
Tel: (707) 795-5047

Carl Devito
University of Arizona
Department of Mathematics
Building #89
Tucson, Arizona 85721 USA
Tel: (602) 621-6893
Fax: (602) 621-8322

Jody Diamond
American Gamelan Institute
PO Box 5036
Hanover, NH 03755 USA
Tel: (603) 448-8837
Fax: (603) 448-8837
Email:
    Jody.Diamond@mac.dartmouth.edu

Stewart Dickson
1105 Burtonwood Ave
Thousand Oaks, CA 91360 USA
Tel: (805) 494-6713
Fax: (213) 464-1953
Email: celia!tpg!dickson@usc.edu

Emanuel Dion
c/o Jurgen Schmidt
Niebuhrstrasse 66
D-1000 Berlin/West 12 Germany
Tel: (49-30) 5291234

Luigi-Bob Drake
Burning Press
PO Box 585
Lakewood, OH 44107 USA
Tel: (216) 221-8940
Email: au462@cleveland.freenet.edu

Wayne Draznin
Cleveland Institute of Art
Computer Arts Program
11141 East Blvd
Cleveland, OH 44106 USA
Tel: (216) 421-7472
Fax: (216) 421-7438
Email:ai182@po.cwru.edu
        draznin@cwru.bitnet

John Duesenberry
514 Harvard Street, #3B
Brookline, MA 02146 USA
Tel: (617) 232-6384
Email: jouhndu@world.std.com

Robert B. Edgar
Paramount Publishing
707 Continental Circle, Apt. 1412
Mountain View, CA 94040
Email: lull@well.sf.ca.us

Kimberly Edwards
Life On A Slice
1952 Vista Del Mar Avenue
Hollywood, CA 90068 USA
Tel: (213) 462-4817

David-John Etzen
ART (if) ACT
235 East Colorado Boulevard, #292
Pasadena, CA 91101 USA
Tel: (818) 332-9577

Leslie Farber
William Patterson College
Art Department
300 Pompton Road
Wayne, NJ 07470 USA
Tel: (201) 595-2722

Anne Farrell
Videographic Arts
131 Huddleson
Santa Fe, NM 87501 USA
Tel: (505) 983-5126

Theodosia Ferguson
1642 Milvia, #4
Berkeley, CA 94709 USA
Tel: (510) 548-7490
Fax: (510) 540-1057
Email: thferguson@lbl.gov

Robert C. Fergusson
529 Page Avenue
Lyndhurst, NJ 07071 USA
Tel: (201) 438-4243

Alessandro Fogar
Via Venezia 26
34073 Grado GO Italy
Tel: (39) 431-83545
Fax: (39) 432-520360

Charles Follis
1025 Schiele Avenue
San Jose, CA 95126 USA
Tel: (408) 292-0926

John Fox
11th Hour Productions
14755 Ventura Boulevard, Suite 1562
Sherman Oaks, CA 91403 USA

Marjorie Franklin
PO Box 1638
El Cerrito, CA 94530 USA
Tel: (510) 525-2865
Email: mf@sfsuvax1.sfsu.edu

Phyllis Free
2736 Field Avenue
Louisville, KY 40206 USA
Tel: (502) 893-3304

Nancy Jackson Freeman
3600 Sprucedale Drive
Annandale, VA 22003 USA
Tel: (703) 750-0025
Fax: (703) 658-0239

Robert Gabriel
Southern California Video
Video Department
1010 East Union, Suite 205
Pasadena, CA 91106 USA

Gary Gaffney
Art Academy of Cincinnati
1125 St. Gregory Street
Cincinnati, OH 45224 USA
Tel: (513) 562-8765

David Garrett
Los Angeles High School
Computer Science
4650 West Olympic Boulevard
Los Angeles, CA 90019 USA
Tel: (213) 937-3210

David Gaw
Coactive Aesthetics
PO Box 425967
San Francisco, CA 94142 USA
Tel: (415) 626-5152
Fax: (415) 626-6320
Email: coactive@coactive.com

Dan George
195 N. 5th Street
Brooklyn, NY 11211 USA
Tel: (718) 387-5428

George Gessert
1230 W. Broadway
Eugene, OR 97402 USA
Tel: (503) 343-2920

Frits Gierstberg
Perspetif Center for Photography
Sint-Jobsweg 30
3024 Rotterdam, The Netherlands
Tel: (31 10) 4780655
Fax: (31 10) 4772072

Francesco Giomi
Conservatory of Music
Musicological Department
    of CNUCE/CNR
Piazza Belle Arti 2
50122 Florence, Italy
Tel: (39-55) 282105
Fax: (39-55) 239 6785
Email: conserva@ifiidg.bitnet

Sallee Glaesner
DigiQuest
900 Lincoln Village Circle
Larkspur, CA 94939 USA
Tel: (415) 925-0235

David Glynn
621 1/2 South Detroit Street
Los Angeles, CA 90036 USA
Tel/Fax: (213) 933-6846

Daniel Goode
167 Spring Street, #5W
New York City, NY 10012 USA
Tel: (212) 925-6684

Victoria Graham
Geary's Advertising Department
437 North Beverly Drive
Beverly Hills, CA 90291 USA
Tel: (310) 273-4741

Noel Gray
University of Sydney
Box 201, Holme Building A09
University of Sydney
New South Wales 2006 Australia
Tel: (2) 692-0117

Carolyn Guyer
807 First Street
Jackson, MI 49203 USA
Email: caroway@aol.com

Karen W. Guzak
Studio 5A
707 South Snoqualmie
Seattle, WA 98108 USA
Tel: (206) 343-0290
Fax: (206) 622-9878

Samia Halaby
103 Franklin Street
New York City, NY 10013 USA
Tel: (212) 966-3517

Adrian Hall
College of Fine Arts, University
  of New South Wales
PO Box 259
Paddington, NSW 2041 Australia
Tel: (61-2) 339-9548
Fax: (61-2) 810-1614
Email: Adrian.Hall@unsw.edu.au

Craig Harris
Leonardo, the International Society
  for the Arts, Sciences and Technology
672 South Van Ness Avenue
San Francisco, CA 94110 USA
Tel: (415) 431-7414
Fax: (415) 431-5737
Email: craig@well.sf.ca.us

Robert Hendel
1385 York Avenue, #16B
New York City, NY 10021 USA
Tel: (212) 772-9070
Fax: (212) 450-5521

Kennan C Herrick
2160 Mastlands Drive
Oakland, CA 94611 USA
Tel: (510) 531-8819

Matjaz Hmeljak
Universita' Di Trieste
DEEI
Via Valerio 10
I-34127 Trieste, Italy
Tel: (39) 40 54 581
Fax: (39) 40 676 3460
Email: hmeljakm@univ.trieste.it

Thomas Hollier
Anti Gravity Workshop
2814 Sanborn Avenue
Venice, CA 90291 USA
Tel: (310) 827-0092

Richard Howard
Computer Arts Institute
310 Townsend, #230
San Francisco, CA 94107 USA
Tel: (415) 546-5242
Fax: (415) 546-5237

Paul Hubel
Hewlett Packard Labs
PO Box 104990
Palo Alto, CA 94303-0960 USA

Guido Huebner
Das Synthetische Mischgewebe
13 Rue Tiffonet
33000 Bordeaux, Aquitaine
France
Tel: (56) 92 00 00

Carol Hurlburt
Education Council
  of the Graphic Arts Industry, Inc.
1899 Preston White Drive
Reston, VA 22091-4367 USA
Tel: (703) 648-1768
Fax: (703) 620-0994

Chris Illert
Science-Art Research Centre
2/3 Birch Crescent
East Corrimal
New South Wales 2518 Australia
Tel: (042) 833 009

K.P. Ludwig John
Scharnhorststrasse 42
Leipzig 0-7030 Germany
Tel: (49-341) 391 3211 ext 117
Fax: (49-341) 312401

James Johnson
3350 13th Street
Boulder, CO 80304 USA
Tel: (303) 938-8084
Email: Johnson-J@cubldr.colorado.edu

Abby Joslin
Abby Joslin & Associates
2815 Bush Street
San Francisco, CA 94115 USA
Tel: (415) 885-5849
Fax: (415) 885-2805
Email: Applelink abby.mktg

Arlene Jurewicz
Synchronicity Holograms
Box 4235, Youngtown Road
Lincolnville, ME 04849 USA
Tel: (207) 763-3182

Eduardo Kac
725 W Melrose, #2F
Chicago, IL 60657 USA
Tel/Fax: (312) 871-4619
Email: u12146@uicvm.bitnet

Laurel Kashinn
Blue Rose Studio
Stonecroft Village 2206
Grafton, WI 53024-9793 USA
Tel/Fax: (414) 377-1669

Paras Kaul
Cal State LA
Fine Art Department
5151 State University Drive
Los Angeles, CA 90032 USA
Tel: (818) 794-4057

Michael Kellner
HolograFx
12 Columbia Avenue
Paterson, NJ 07503 USA

Arnold J. Kemp
New Langton Arts
1246 Folsom Street
San Francisco, CA 94117 USA
Tel: (415) 626-5416
Fax: (415) 255-1454

Eleanor Kent
544 Hill Street
San Francisco, CA 94114 USA
Tel: (415) 647-8503
Email: ekent@well.sf.ca.us

Mary Jean Kenton
PO Box 42
Merrittstown, PA 15463 USA
Email: amanue!jr@vax.cs.pitt.edu

Gyorgy Kepes
MIT, Center for Advanced
  Visual Studies
40 Massachusetts Avenue
Cambridge, MA 02139 USA

Daniel Kirksey
21660 Huron River Drive
New Boston, MI 48164 USA
Tel: (313) 753-4041

Russell Kirsch
Sturvil Corporation
PO Box 157
Clarksburg, MD 20871 USA
Tel: (301) 972-3083
Email: kirsch@cme.nist.gov

Sherman Klein
Advanced Information Methods, Inc.
Corporate and Technology
PO Box 5692
Mission Hills, CA 91395 USA
Tel/Fax: (818) 366-2678

Tom Klinkowstein
101 Thompson Street, #34
New York City, NY 10012 USA
Tel: (212) 925-8213

Kenneth Knowlton
51 Pond View Drive
Merrimack, NH 03054 USA
Tel: (603) 424-2360

Damon Koach
1199 Oddstad Boulevard
Pacifica, CA 94044-3850 USA
Tel: (415) 359-9252

Mitsuo Kodera
Holocom, Division of Domus Int
Yoshiba Bldg., #301
2-17-65 Akasaka Minato-ku
Tokyo 107 Japan

Ronald Kostyniuk
University of Calgary
Art Department
Calgary, Alberta T3A OV2 Canada
Tel: (403) 286-1283
Fax: (403) 282-6925

Tim Kreger
Australian Centre for the Arts
  and Technology (ACAT)
Canberra Institute of the Arts
PO Box 804
Canberra City, ACT 2601 Australia
Tel: (06) 249-5640
Fax: (06) 247-0229
Email: TJK691@Huxley.Anu.edu.au

Gene Lavon Porter
Porter Computer Arts
1105 North Cardova St.
Burbank CA 91505 USA
Tel: (818) 848-1405

Richard Land
10 Trapelo Road
Belmont, MA 02178-4442 USA
Tel: (617) 484-4194
Email:
  LAND%cdv.decnet@mghccc.harvard.edu

John Lansdown
CASCAAD (Centre for Advanced
  Studies in Computer Aided Art
  and Design)
Middlesex University
Faculty of Art & Design, Cat Hill
Barnet, Hearts EN4 8HT
United Kingdom
Tel: (44 081) 362 5035
Fax: (44 081) 440 9541
Email: joun17@uk.ac.mdx.clus

Thorbjorn Lausten
Asger Rygs Gade 2
DK-1727 Copenhagen V Denmark
Tel: (45) 31225084

Raymond Guido Lauzzana
Penrose Press
PO Box 470925
San Francisco, CA 94147 USA
Tel: (415) 567-4157
Fax: (415) 896-1512

Judith Yaros Lee
Society for Literature and Science (SLS)
School of Interpersonal
  Communications
Lesher Hall
Ohio University
Athens, OH 45701 USA
Tel: (614) 593 4844
Fax: (614) 593-4810
Email: leej@ouvaxa.ucls.ohiou.edu

Luigi Lentini
VR Dimension
c/o Barbara Sullivan
412 South Country Hill Road
Anaheim Hills, CA 92808 USA
Tel: (714) 281-1645
Fax: (714) 921-9327

David P Leonard
Trebas Institute
451 St. Jean Street
Montreal, Quebec H2Y 2R5 Canada
Tel: (514) 845-4141
Fax: (514) 845-2581

Shab Levy
4731 SW Iowa Street
Portland, OR 97221 USA
Tel: (503) 227-2515
Fax: (503) 227-2538

Larry Lieberman
Holographic Images, Inc.
1301 Dade Boulevard
Miami Beach, FL 33139 USA
Tel: (305) 531-1621

Clare Louise Lilley
Yorkshire Sculpture Park
Bretton Hall
West Bretton, Wakefield WF4 4LG
United Kingdom
Tel: (09 24) 830579
Fax: (09 24) 830044

Cort Lippe
IRCAM
31 Rue St. Merri
75004 Paris, France

Gene Paul Lippman
Pandect, Inc.
14437 1/2 Dickens Street
Sherman Oaks, CA 91423 USA
Tel: (818) 995-4761
Fax: (818) 752-3360

Arthur Loeb
Computer Center
Harvard University
Cambridge, MA 02138 USA
Tel: (617) 495-1950

Felicia Lovelett
3400 Damascus Road
Brookeville, MD 20833 USA
Tel: (301) 774-5648
Fax: (301) 924-3714

Bruce Mahin
Center for Music Technology
Radford University
Box 6968
Radford, VA 24142 USA
Tel: (703) 831-6174
Email: bmahin@ruacad.ac.runet.edu

Ginette Major
La Cite des Arts et des Nouvelle
  Technologies de Montreal
15 Rue de la Commune West
Montreal, Quebec H2Y 2C6 Canada
Tel: (514) 849-1612
Fax: (514) 982-0064

Roger Malina
Leonardo, the International Society
  for the Arts, Sciences and Technology
672 South Van Ness Avenue
San Francisco, CA 94110 USA
Tel: (415) 431-7414
Fax: (415) 431-5737
Email: rfm@cea.berkeley.edu

Judy Malloy
Box 2340, 2140 Shattuck
Berkeley, CA 94704 USA
Email: jmalloy@well.sf.ca.us
      jmalloy@garnet.berkeley.edu

Steve Mann
Massachusetts Institute of Technology
Media Laboratory, Room 325
20 Ames Street
Cambridge, MA 02139 USA
Tel: (617) 253-0314
Fax: (617) 258-6264
Email: steve@media.mit.edu

Robert Marsanyi
1615 Green Street, #1
San Francisco, CA 94123 USA
Tel: (415) 771-9320
Fax: (415) 928-8246
Email: rnm@well.sf.ca.us

Claude Martin
8 rue Bolinar
13200 Arles, France

Tony Martin
118 North 9th Street
Brooklyn, NY 11211 USA
Tel: (718) 387-7541

David Martin
Image + Sound
4500 Whitsett Avenue, #4
Studio City, CA 91604 USA
Tel: (818) 506-1826
Fax: (818) 506-4511

Benoit Maubrey
Die Audio Gruppe
Schul Strasse 35
1000 Berlin 65 Germany
Tel: (49-30) 462 2954

Michael McNabb
120 Virginia Avenue
San Francisco, CA 94110 USA
Tel: (415) 695-9684
Fax: (415) 695-9629
Email: michael@mcnabb.com

Stewart McSherry
2321 2nd Avenue, #3-A
San Diego, CA 92101 USA
Tel/Fax: (619) 338-0972
Email: mcsherry@sdsc.edu

Ellen Ann McWhirter
Texas A&M University
Visualization Laboratory
College of Architecture
College Station, TX 77843 USA
Tel: (409) 764-7262
Email: ellen@archone.tamu.edu

Susan Metros
University of Tennessee
Art Department
1715 Volunteer Boulevard
Knoxville, TN 37996-2410 USA
Tel: (615) 974 3208
Fax: (615) 974-3198
Email: metros@utkvx1.utk.edu

Shunsuke Mitamura
Institute of Art and Design
University of Tsukuba
I-Tennodai
Tsukuba, Ibaraki-ken 305 Japan
Tel: (81 298) 53-2833
Fax: (81 298) 53-508

Stephen Moore
#598 - 790 North Marine Dr.
Tumon 96911 Guam
Tel: (671) 649-2686

Kevin R Moran
Giant Records
A & R
8900 Wilshire Boulevard, #200
Beverly Hills, CA 90211 USA
Tel: (310) 289-5525
Fax: (310) 289-7333

Robert Morgan
Rochester Institute of Technology
CIAS
1 Lomb Memorial Dr.
Rochester, NY 14623 USA
Tel: (716) 475-2674
Fax: (716) 475-6447

Mike Mosher
302 Easy Street, #19
Mountain View, CA 94043 USA
Tel: (415) 961-4104
Email: mikemosh@well.sf.ca.us

Robert Emmer Mueller
38 Homestead Lane
Roosevelt, NJ 08555 USA
Tel: (609) 448-2605
Fax: (609) 426-8779

Axel Mulder
Emove
Laboratory for
   Virtual Musical Instrument Design
Koninginneweg 135-2
1075 CL Amsterdam, The Netherlands
Tel: (31 20) 673 2462
Email: a.mulder@elsevier.nl

Andreas Muller-Pohle
European Photography
PO Box 3043
Gottingen 3400 Germany
Tel: (0551) 24820
Fax: (0551) 25224

Jeffery Murray
Holography Institute
PO Box 24-153
San Francisco, CA 94124 USA
Tel: (415) 822-7123

Mihai Nadin
Mindesign
35 Butts Rock Road
Little Compton, RI 02837 USA
Tel/Fax: (401) 635-1675

Denes Nagy
SYMMETRION—The Institute
   for Advanced Symmetry Studies
Nador u. 18.
PO Box 4
Budapest H-1361 Hungary
Tel: (36 1) 131-3975
Fax: (36 1) 131-3161
Email: nagy_d@usp.ac.fj

Theodore Herzl Nathanson
225 S. Olive Street, Suite 1004
Los Angeles, CA 90012 USA
Tel: (213) 628-8436

Louise Neaderland
International Society of Copier Artists
800 West End Avenue, Suite 13B
New York City, NY 100225 USA
Tel: (212) 662-5533

George Ng
27 Ryerson Avenue
Toronto, Ontario M5T 2P4 Canada
Email: georgen@gpu.utcs.utoronto.ca

Alex Nicoloff
1729 Virginia Street
Berkeley, CA 94703 USA
Tel: (510) 845-7967

Yumi Nishimura
Asahi News Publishing Company
Asahi PC
5-3-2 Tsukiji Chuo-Ku
104-11 Tokyo, Japan
Tel: (81) 35545-8779
Fax: (81) 35545-8780
Email: yumi@pub.asahi.com

Robert Normandeau
2994 De Soissons
Montreal, Quebec H3S 1W2 Canada
Tel: (514) 737-9484
Fax: (514) 737-0812

Elaine O'Neil
School of Photographic Arts
   and Sciences
Gannett Building, Room 2115
PO Box 9887
Rochester, NY 14604 USA
Tel: (716) 475-2720

Pauline Oliveros
Pauline Oliveros Foundation Inc.
156 Hunter Street
Kingston, NY 12401 USA
Tel: (914) 338-5984
Fax: (914) 338-5986
Eail: PaulineOliveros@mci.com

Bernadette Olson
Positive Light Holographics
6116 Highway 9
Felton, CA 95018 USA
Tel: (408) 335-2288
Fax: (408) 335-2245

Vito Orazem
Holografielabor Osnabruck
Mindener Strasse 205
D-4500 Osnabruck, Germany

Ed Osborn
PO Box 9121
Oakland, CA 94613 USA
Tel: (510) 763-9506
Email: edo@well.sf.ca.us

Randall Packer
Zakros InterArts
614 York Street
San Francisco, CA 94110 USA
Tel: (415) 282-5497
Fax: (415) 282-4228
Email: newmusic@mcimail.com

Maria Palazzi
Ringling School of Art and Design
Computer Graphics
2700 N. Tamiami Trail
Sarasota, FL 34234 USA
Tel: (813) 359-7574
Fax: (813) 359-7517

Jim Pallas
1311 Bishop
Grosse Pointe Park, MI 48230-1145
USA
Tel: (313) 885-5669

Christopher John Palmer
Professional Sound Corporation
10643 Riverside Drive
North Hollywood, CA 91602 USA
Tel: (818) 760-6544
Fax: (818) 760-3235

Nancy Paterson
475 The West Mall, #1513
Etobicoke, Ontario M9C 4Z3 Canada
Tel: (416) 621-3290
Fax: (416) 365-3332

Carolyn Perkins
Viacom Cable
Castro Valley
5924 Stoneridge Drive
Pleasanton, CA USA
Tel: (510) 463-0870

Robin Petterd
2A/8 Byron Street
Sandy Bay, Tasmania 7005 Australia
Tel: 6102 238533
Email:
    U907079@Postoffice.utas.edu.au

Jean-Marc Philippe
65 Bis Boulevard Brune
75014 Paris, France
Tel/Fax: (33 1) 45 39 91 28

John Phillips
4522 Pine Street
Philadelphia, PA 19143 USA
Tel: (215) 476-2003
Email: hengoed@well.sf.ca.us

Otto Piene
MIT, Center for
    Advanced Visual Studies
40 Massachusetts Avenue
Cambridge, MA 02139 USA

Patty Pink
The Holography Institute
PO Box 24153
San Francisco, CA 94124 USA
Tel: (415) 822-7123

Lynn Pocock-Williams
37 Huemmer Terrace
Clifton, NJ 07013 USA

Gregg Podnar
560 Wilkins Avenue
Pittsburgh, PA 15217 USA
Tel: (412) 521-9609
Fax: (412) 521-9610
Email: gwp@cmu.edu

Larry Polansky
Frog Peak Music
PO Box 5036
Hanover, NH 03755 USA
Tel: (603) 448-1902
Email: larry.polansky@dartmouth.edu

Stephen Travis Pope
Computer Music Journal
PO Box 60632
Palo Alto, CA 94306 USA
Tel: (415) 988-9214
Email: stp@ccrma.Stanford.edu

Mark Primeau
Bureau of Architecture
30 Van Ness Avenue, Suite 4100
San Francisco, CA 94102 USA
Tel: (415) 557-4666
Tel: (415) 557-4701

Patric Doherty Prince
Cyberspace Gallery
160 West Jaxine Drive
Altadena, CA 91001 USA
Tel: (818) 797-7674
Email: patric@mica.jpl.nasa.gov

Long Quan
Fine Arts Institute of Sichuan Province
Chongqing, Sichuan 630053 China

Godfried-Willem Raes
Logos Foundation
Kongostraat 35
9000 Gent, Flanders Belgium
Tel: (32-91) 23 80 89
Fax: (32-91) 25 04 34

Mark Rais
Computer Music
    & Musical Informatics Association
Tonismagi 7
Tallinn EE0106 Estonia
Tel: (7-0142) 684305

Stuart Ramsden
Australian Centre for the Arts
    and Technology (ACAT)
Canberra Institute of the Arts
PO Box 804
Canberra City, ACT 2601 Australia
Tel: (61 6) 249 5640
Fax: (61 6) 247 0229

Sonya Rapoport
6 Hillcrest Court
Berkeley, CA 94705 USA
Tel: (510) 658-4741
Fax: (510) 642-0336
Email: actize@garnet.Berkeley.Edu

David Ray
PO Box 5631
Berkeley, CA 94705 USA
Tel: (510) 527-9010
Email: daver@sunspot.ssl.berkeley.edu

Trudy Myrrh Reagan
YLEM: Artists Using Science
    & Technology
967 Moreno
Palo Alto, CA 94303 USA
Tel: (415) 856-9593
Email: trudy@well.sf.ca.us

Hazen Reed
65 South Sixth St.
Brooklyn, NY 11211 USA
Tel: (718) 782-4084
Email: 70674.507@compuserve.com

Melynda Reid
PO Box 378
Greensboro, FL 32330 USA
Tel: (902) 442-3300
Fax: (902) 442-6629
Email: melynda@titipu.resun.com

Rick Reiken
Cummington Community of the Arts
R.R. #1, PO Box 145
Cummington, MA 01026 USA
Tel: (413) 634-2172

Hans Reiser
Life On A Slice
6979 Exeter Drive
Oakland, CA 94611 USA
Tel: (408) 927-1958
Fax: (408) 927-3215
Email: hansreiser@almaden.ibm.com

Brigid Richards
Richmond Unified High School District
1250 23rd Street
Richmond, CA 94804 USA
Tel: (510) 237-8770
Email: brigid@CoCo.ca.rop.edu

Marion Rinehart
24119 Summerhill Avenue
Los Altos, CA 94024 USA

Anet Margot Ris
Electric Waltz Video
1801-1/2 Maltman Avenue
Los Angeles, CA 90026 USA
Tel: (213) 669-8164

Jay Riskind
RISKART: The Jay Riskind Studio
700 N Carpenter
Chicago, IL 60622 USA
Tel: (312) 644-0638
Fax: (312) 433-7686
Email: 73720.2375@compuserve.com
        jayrisk@well.sf.ca.us

Sara Roberts
4188 Greenwood Ave, Apt. 18
Oakland, CA 94602 USA
Tel: (510) 530-2079
Email: sroberts@kerner.com

Neil Rolnick
152 Wittenberg Road
Bearsville, NY 12409 USA
Tel: (914) 679-2869
Email: rolnick@iear.arts.rpi.edu

Joe Rosen
PO Box 225
Midwood Station
Brooklyn, NY 11230 USA
Tel: (718) 377-7808
Email: joro@panix.com
        joro@well.sf.ca.us

Peter Rosen
VARIOUS Media
Visionary Artists Resources
PO Box 2219
Kihei, HI 96753 USA
Tel: (808) 871-3615
Email: prosen@huinet.maui.hi.us

David Rosenboom
Center for Experiments in Art,
  Information & Technology (CEAIT)
California Institute of the Arts
24700 McBean Parkway
Valencia, CA 91355 USA
Tel: (805) 253-7816
Email: davidr@calarts.edu

John Rupkalvis
StereoScope International
303 East Alameda, #Q
Burbank, CA 91502-1507 USA
Tel: (818) 848-9601

Paul Rutkovsky
227 Westridge Drive
Tallahassee, FL 32304 USA
Tel: (904) 575-3339
Fax: (904) 576-5530
Email: prutkov@cc.fsu.edu

Paul Ryan
Savannah College of Art and Design
Video Department
201 West Charlton Street
PO Box 3146
Savannah, GA 31402-3146 USA
Tel: (912) 238-2407
Fax: (912) 238-2428

Janet Saad-Cook
1454 Encina Road
Santa Fe, New Mexico 87501 USA
Tel: (505) 983-2884
Fax: (505) 983-3017

I Wayan Sadra
Jursan Karawitan
Sekolah Tinggi Seni Indonesia
Kentingan/Jebres
Surakarta, Ja Teng 51739 Indonesia

Elizabeth Saenger
422 Fleming Street
Key West, FL 33040 USA
Tel: (305) 292-0395
Fax: (305) 296-4087

Carla Scaletti
Symbolic Sound Corporation/
  University of Illinois CERL Sound
Group
PO Box 2530
Champaign, IL 61825-2530 USA
Tel: (217) 355-6273
Fax: (217) 355-6562
Email: scaletti@cerl.uiuc.edu

Christian Schiess
23 Meckelenburgh Square, Flat 812
London WC1N 2AD United Kingdom

Wolfgang Schneider
Museum der Stadt Gladbeck
Wasserschloss Wittringen
Burgstrasse 64
Gladbeck, NW
D-4390 Germany
Tel: (49) 2043 275297

Carter Scholz
2665 Virginia
Berkeley, CA 94709 USA
Tel: (510) 548-3654
Email: csz@well.sf.ca.us

Claude Schryer
3582 Cartier
Montreal, Quebec H2K 4G2 Canada
Tel: (514) 528-1644
Fax: (514) 987-1862

Leni Schwendinger
448 W. 37th St., #8G
New York City, NY 10018 USA
Tel: (212) 947-6282
Fax: (212) 947-6289

Jill Scott
PO Box 1001
Darlinghurst 2010 NSW Australia

Alex Scott
East End Management
8209 Melrose Avenue, 2nd Floor
Los Angeles, CA 90046 USA
Tel: (213) 653-9755
Fax: (213) 653-9663

Amit Sen
CompuAct
248 East Palm Avenue
Monrovia, CA 91016 USA
Tel: (818) 301-0532

Scott Shepard
Imaginary Enterprises
3540 Wyoming, 1E
St. Louis, MO 63118 USA

Gerald Shepherd
18 Ham Close, Aughton
Collingbourne Kingston
Marlborough, Wiltshire SN8 3SB
United Kingdom
Tel: (00 44) 0264 850500

Hameiri Shimon
Holography Israel
21 Haromemiut Str
Herzlia 46683 Israel
Tel: (052) 572387

Takao Shimono
Nagano University
Department of Industrial Information
Shimono-go
Ueda-shi, Nagano 386-14 Japan
Tel: (81-268) 38-2350
Fax: (81-268) 38-5887
Email: shimono@nagano.ac.jp

Wayne Siegel
DIEM (Danish Institute
  of Electroacoustic Music)
The Concert Hall Aarhus
Thomas Jensens Alle
DK 8000 Aarhus C., Denmark
Tel: (45) 86202133
Tel: (45) 86194386
Email: wsiegel@daimi.dau.dk

Walter Siegfried
Faustlestr. 8
D-8000 Munchen 2 Germany
Tel: (089) 50 33 08

Edith MacNamara Smith
3732 Laguna Avenue
Palo Alto, CA 94306 USA
Tel: (415) 493-9386
Fax: (415) 856-9394

Elsa Stansfield
Hooykaas/Stanfield
PO Box 61106
1005 HC Amsterdam, The Netherlands
Tel: (31 020) 6221898
Fax: (31 020) 4202688

Joachim Steingrubner
Trans Data
2824 Oak Point Drive
Hollywood Hills, CA 90068 USA
Tel: (800) 945-5433
Fax: (213) 851-4467

Tucker Stilley
Labyrinth
Editorial Dept.
2135 Adair Street
San Marino, CA USA
Tel: (818) 282-6289

Carolyn Strauss
hypertelsaloon
Space 308
837 Traction Avenue
Los Angeles, CA 90013-1841 USA
Tel: (213) 621-3127
Fax: (213) 621-4187
Email: strauss@well.sf.ca.us

Martin Supper
Mommsenstr. 70
D-W-1000 Berlin 12 Germany
Tel: (49 30) 881 55 55
Fax: (49 30) 882 42 09

Takis
Panayiotis Vassilakis
22 Rue Liancourt
Paris 14 France

Christine Tamblyn
555 Broderick St., Apt. #9
San Francisco, CA 94117 USA
Tel: (415) 931-0150

Dick Termes
Rt. 2
Box 435B
Spearfish, SD 57783 USA
Tel: (605) 642-4805

Hal Thwaites
Concordia University
3Dmt Center
7141 Sherbrooke St. W.
Montreal, Quebec H4B IR6 Canada
Tel: (514) 489-9139
Email: hal@vax2.concordia.ca

Alan Arthur Tratner
Inventors Workshop International
3201 Corte Malpaso, Suite 304
Camarillo, CA 93012 USA
Tel: (805) 484-9786
Fax: (805) 388-3097

Frederick John Truck
4225 University
Des Moines, IA 50311 USA
Tel: (515) 255-3552
Email: fjt@well.sf.ca.us

Joan Truckenbrod
The School of the Art Institute
   of Chicago
Art and Technology Department
37 S. Wabash
Chicago, IL 60115 USA
Tel: (815) 756-2447
Fax: (815) 758-1152

John Timothy Turpin
National College of Art & Design
100 Thomas Street
Dublin 8 Ireland
Tel: 711377
Fax: 711748

Klaus Urbons
Museum fur Fotokopie
Postfach 10 12 30
Kettwiger Strasse 33
D-4330 Mulheim an der Ruhr 1
Germany
Tel/Fax: (0049) 208 34461

Marc Van Boom
Science and Art
Heldenstraat 3512
Edegem
Antwerp 2650 Belgium
Tel: (38 03) 458 26 74

Willard George Van De Bogart
1745 Beach Street, #9
San Francisco, CA 94123-1622 USA
Tel: (415) 922-3743

Wim van der Plas
Inter-Society for the Electronic
   Arts (ISEA)
C. Kouwenbergzoom 107
3065 KC Rotterdam, The Netherlands
Tel: (31-75) 701906
Email: isea@rug.nl.bitnet

Amilcar Vasques Dias
Rua da Estacao-Eirol
3800 Aveiro, Portugal
Tel: (351-34) 25085/22224
Fax: (351-34) 23384

Roman Verostko
5535 S Clinton Avenue South
Minneapolis, MN 55419 USA
Tel/Fax: (612) 822-3800
Email: roman@mcad.edu

Vincent John Vincent
The Vivid Group
Studio 302
317 Adelaide St. West
Toronto, Ontario M5V 1P9 Canada
Tel: (416) 340-9290
Fax: (416) 348-9809
Email: vjv@well.sf.ca..us

Sam Wang
Clemson University
Art Department, Box 340509
Lee Hall
Clemson, SC 29634-0509 USA
Tel: (803) 656-3924
Fax: (803) 656-0204
Email: stmwang@hubcap.clemson.edu

Susan Weeks
ICTV
280 Martin Avenue
Santa Clara, CA 95050 USA
Tel: (408) 562-9233
Fax: (408) 986-9566
Email: Susan_Weeks@ictv.com

Lenore Weiss
City of Oakland
1317 East 27th Street
Oakland, CA 94606 USA
Tel: (510) 261-7492

Chuck Welch
Eternal Network Archive
108 Blueberry Hill Drive
Hanover, NH 03755 USA
Tel: (603) 448-4797
Fax: (603) 448-9998
Email:
   Cathryn.L.Welch@dartmouth.edu

Deborah Whitman
567 6th St., #8
Brooklyn, NY 11215 USA
Tel: (718) 499-5573

Steve Wilson
San Francisco State University
Art Department
1600 Holloway Avenue
San Francisco, CA 94132 USA
Tel: (415) 338-2291
Email: swilson@sfsuvax1.sfsu.edu

Patte Wood
4137 Park Boulevard
Palo Alto, CA 94306 USA
Tel: (415) 725-3573
Fax: (415) 723-8468
Email: patte@ccrma.Stanford.edu

David Worrall
Australia Centre for the Arts
  & Technology (ACAT)
GPD Box 804
Canberra, ACT 2601 Australia
Tel: (06) 249 5640
Fax: (06) 247 0229

Nancy Worthington
PO Box 2558
Sebastopol, CA 95473 USA
Tel: (707) 823-3581

Emily Young
Art Department
Portland State University
PO Box 751
Portland, OR 97207-0751 USA
Tel: (503) 725-3353
Fax: (503) 725-3351

Edward Zajec
Syracuse University
Art Media Studies
102 Shaffer Art Building
Syracuse, NY 13244 USA
Tel: (315) 443-1033
Email: ezajec@sunrise.acs.syr.edu

Opy Zouni
Vrilission 22
GR-15236 P. Pendeli, Greece
Tel: 804 2950
Fax: 804 4264

BIBLIOGRAPHIES

The following bibliographies were cultivated from a variety of sources. Much of the content was originally developed by Judy Malloy for the *Leonardo Fine Art Science Technology (FAST)* database and archive, incorporating library database searches in the process. Additional content is derived from lists of books received at the Leonardo editorial office which have been integrated into the appropriate categories. Topics include Computer and Electronic Music; CyberCulture; Fractals; Gender, Art and Technology; Multimedia; Television and Society; Video Art and Virtual Reality. There is also a General category which includes a sampling of titles on the themes of art, science and technology. Given the intensity of activity in each of these topic areas, the titles presented here represent only a portion of the ongoing work around the world. The Gender, Art and Technology bibliography, for example, reflects the titles collected to date for a more extensive bibliography in development for a special issue of the journal *Leonardo* on this topic. While the Computer and Electronic Music bibliography represents a vast range of activity, the focus and intent of this publication does not allow for the extensive bibliographic representation that one finds in Deta Davis' extensive work *Computer Applications in Music: A Bibliography*. The bibliographies in the *Leonardo Almanac* are offered to facilitate interdisciplinary orientation in the vast and constantly evolving information realms on each of these subjects.

COMPUTER AND ELECTRONIC MUSIC

Acreman, Carlo, 6th Colloquio di Informatica Musicale, 1985, Naples, Italy, *Musica e Tecnologia: Industria e Cultura per lo Sviluppo del Mezzogiorno*, Immacolata Ortosecco, Fausto Razzi, eds. (Milano: Unicopli, 1987).

Mauro Bagella and Serena Tamburini, eds., *I Profili del Suono: Scritti Sulla Musica Elettroacustica e la Computer Music* (Galzerano: Musica Verticale, 1987).

Bahler, Peter Benjamin, *Electronic and Computer Music: an Annotated Bibliography of Writings in English* (Rochester, NY: University of Rochester, 1966).

Balaban, Mira, K. Ebcioglu and O. Laske, *Understanding Music with AI: Perspectives on Music Cognition* (Cambridge, MA: The AAAI Press/The MIT Press, 1992).

Batel, Gunther, *Synthesizermusik und Live-Elektronik: Geschichtliche, Technologische, Kompositorische und Padagogische Aspekte der Elektronischen Musik*, Gunther Batel, Dieter Salbert, eds. (Wolfenbuttel: Moseler, 1985).

Bateman, Wayne, *1951- Introduction to Computer Music* (New York, NY: J. Wiley, 1980).

Bates, John, *The Synthesizer* (Oxford: Oxford University Press, 1988).

Battier, Marc, *Le Compositeur et l'Ordinateur* (Paris: IRCAM en association avec l'Ensemble InterContemporain, 1981).

Berlind, Gary, Writings on the Use of Computers in Music (New York, NY: Institute for Computer Research in the Humanities, New York University, 1965).

Bigelow, Steven, *1951- Making Music with Personal Computers* (La Jolla, CA: Park Row Press, 1987).

Barry S. Brook, ed., *Musicology and the Computer, Musicology 1966-2000, a Practical Program*, American Musicological Society Symposia, Greater New York Chapter, 1965-1966 (New York, NY: City University of New York Press, 1970).

Chamberlin, Hal, *Musical Applications of Microprocessors* 2nd ed. (Hasbrouck Heights, NJ: Hayden Book Co, 1985).

Davis, Deta S., *Computer Applications in Music: a Bibliography* (Madison, WI: A-R Editions, 1988/1992).

De Furia, Steve and Joe Scacciaferro, *The MIDI Book: Using MIDI and Related Interfaces*, Rick Mattingly, ed. (Pompton Lakes, NJ: Third Earth Publishing, 1988).

Del Duca, Lindoro Massimo, *Musica Digitale: Sintesi, Analisi e Filtraggio Digitale nella Musica Elettronica*, 1st ed. (Padua: F. Muzzio, 1987).

Dodge, Charles, *Computer Music: Synthesis, Composition, and Performance*, Charles Dodge, Thomas A. Jerse, eds. (New York, NY: Schirmer Books, 1985).

Simon Emmerson, ed., *The Language of Electroacoustic Music* (New York, NY: Harwood Academic Publishers, 1986).

Heinz Von Foerster and James W. Beauchamp, eds., *Music by Computers* (New York, NY: J. Wiley, 1969).

Franke, Herbert W., *Dea Alba: Eine Phantastisch Klingende Geschichte*, Herbert W. Franke, Michael Weisser, mit Computermusik von Software (Frankfurt am Main: Suhrkamp, 1988).

Furlani, Paolo, *Uno Studio Musicale all'Elaboratore: Analisi e Sintesi dello Studie 1 di K. Stockhausen*, Paolo Furlani, Paolo Zavagna, eds. (Udine, Italia: Campanotto editore, 1988).

Grossi, Pietro, *Musica senza musicisti : scritti 1966/1986*, a cura di Lelio Camilleri, Francesco Carreras, Albert Mayr (Florence: CNUCE/C.N.R., 1987).

Harenberg, Michael, *Neue Musik Durch Neue Technik?: Musikcomputer als Qualitative Herausforderung fur ein Neues Denken in der Musik* (Kassel; New York, NY: Barenreiter, 1989).

Craig R. Harris and S. Pope, eds. *Computer Music Association Source Book: Activities and Resources in Computer Music* (San Francisco, CA: The International Computer Music Association, 1987).

Harrison, David B., *Computer Applications to Music and Musicology: a Bibliography* (Waterloo, Ontario: University of Waterloo, 1977).

Haus, Goffredo, *Elementi di Informatica Musicale* (Milano: Gruppo Editoriale Jackson, 1984).

Heifetz, Robin Julian, *On the Wires of Our Nerves: the Art of Electroacoustic Music* (Cranbury, NJ: Associated University Presses, 1989).

Hiller, Lejaren Arthur, *Informationstheorie und Computermusik; Zwei Vortrage Gehalten auf den Internationalen Ferienkursen fur Neue Musik, Darmstadt*, Peter Jansen, trans. (New York, NY: Schott Music Corp., 1964).

Hiller, Lejaren Arthur and Leonard M. Isaacson, *Experimental Music; Composition with an Electronic Computer* (New York, NY: McGraw-Hill, 1959).

Hofstetter, Fred Thomas, *Computer Literacy for Musicians* (Englewood Cliffs, NJ: Prentice Hall, 1988).

Holtzman, S.R., Conference held 8th-11th April, 1980, at the Department of Computer Science, University of Edinburgh, *Computer Music in Britain* (London: EMAS (Electro-Acoustic Music Association of Great Britain), 1980).

Jaxitron, *Cybernetic Music*, 1st ed. (Blue Ridge Summit, PA : Tab Books, 1985).

Kassler, Michael, *MIR: a Simple Programming Language for Musical Information Retrieval* (Princeton, NJ: Princeton University, 1964).

Editors of *Keyboard* magazine, *Synthesizers and Computers* (Milwaukee, WI: H. Leonard Pub. Corp., 1985).

Kleinen, Gunter and Dieter Salbert, *Computermusik: Theoretische Grundlagen, Kompositionsgeschichtliche, Zusammenhange Musiklernprogramme*, Herausgegeben von Gunther Batel (Laaber: Laaber-Verlag, 1987).

Koechlin, Olivier, *La station de Travail Musical 4X* (Paris: IRCAM, 1985).

Lander, Dan, *Sound by Artists* (Ontario, Canada: Art Metropole, 1990).

Laske, Otto E., *Music and Mind: an Artificial Intelligence Perspective, 1971-1981* (San Francisco, CA: International Computer Music Association, 1981).

Leve, Frederic, *La Creation Musicale par Ordinateur* (Paris: Editions Frequences, 1988).

Lincoln, Harry B., *The Computer and Music* (Ithaca, NY: Cornell University Press, 1970).

Lister, Craig, *The Musical Microcomputer: a Resource Guide* (New York, NY: Garland Pub., 1988).

Manning, Peter, *Electronic and Computer Music* (New York, NY: Oxford University Press, 1985).

Max V. Mathews and John R. Pierce, eds., *Current Directions in Computer Music Research* (Cambridge, MA: MIT Press, 1989).

McAdams, Stephen, *Fusion Spectrale et la Creation d'Images Auditives* (Paris: IRCAM, 1986).

Melby, Carol, *Computer Music Compositions of the United States*, prepared for First International Conference on Computer Music, 28-31 October, 1976, Massachusetts Institute of Technology, 2nd ed. (Urbana, IL: Melby, 1976).

Moore, F. Richard, *Elements of Computer Music* (Englewood Cliffs, NJ: Prentice Hall, 1990).

Moore, Janet L. S., *Understanding Music through Sound Exploration and Experiments* (Lanham, MD: University Press of America, 1986).

Moorer, James A., *The Use of the Linear Prediction of Speech in Computer Music Application*, Music Computation Conference (Paris: Centres Georges Pompidou, 1978, 2nd ed.).

Christopher P. Morgan, ed., *The Byte Book of Computer Music* (Peterborough, NH: Byte Books, 1979).

Nelson, Robert, *Foundations of Music: a Computer-Assisted Introduction*, Robert Nelson, Carl J. Christensen, eds. (Belmont, CA: Wadsworth Pub. Co., 1987).

Soren Nielzen and Olle Olsson, eds., *Structure and perception of electroacoustic sound and music*, Proceedings of the Marcus Wallenberg Symposium held in Lund, Sweden, on 21-28 August 1988 (New York, NY: Elsevier Science Publishing Co., 1989).

Paturzo, Bonaventura Antony, *Making Music with Microprocessors*, 1st ed. (Blue Ridge Summit, PA: TAB Books, 1984).

John Paynter, T. Howell, R. Orton and P. Seymour, eds., *Companion to Contemporary Musical Thought* (London and New York: Routledge, 1992).

Stephen Travis Pope, ed., *Computer Music Journal* (Cambridge, MA: MIT Press).

—, *The Well-Tempered Object: Musical Applications of Object-Oriented Software Technology* (Cambridge, MA: The MIT Press, 1991).

Reetze, Jan, *Musikcomputer-Computermusik: Gegenwart und Zukunft eines Neuen Mediums* (Stuttgart: J.B. Metzler, 1987).

Risset, Jean Claude, *Archivage Numerique des Sons* (Paris: IRCAM, 1979).

—, *The Development of Digital Techniques: a Turning Point for Electronic Music?* (Paris: Centre Georges Pompidou, 1978).

Curtis Roads, ed. *Composers and the computer*, (Los Altos, CA: William Kaufman, Inc., 1985).

Curtis Roads and J. Strawn, eds., *Foundations of Computer Music* (Cambridge, MA: MIT Press, 1985).

Curtis Roads, ed., *Computer Music Journal* (Cambridge, MA: MIT Press).

—, *The Music Machine* (Cambridge, MA: MIT Press 1992).

Jon Rose, compiler; Rainer Linz, ed., *The Pink Violin: A Portrait of an Australian Musical Dynasty* (Brunswick Victoria Australia: NMA Publications, 1992).

Rowe, Robert, *Interactive Music Systems* (Cambridge, MA: MIT Press, 1992).

Rudolph, Thomas E., *Music and the Apple II: Applications for Music Education, Composition and Performance*, Richard C. Merrell, ed., 1st ed. (Drexel Hill, PA: Unsinn Publications, 1984).

Segler, H. et al, *Radiophonische Musik* (Celle: Moeck, 1985).

Xavier Serra and Patte Wood, eds., *Center for Computer Research in Music and Acoustics (Recent Work)* (Stanford, CA: CCRMA, Stanford University, 1988).

John Strawn, ed., AES 5th International Conference, 1987, Los Angeles, CA, *The Proceedings of the AES 5th International Conference: Music and Digital Technology* (New York, NY: Audio Engineering Society, 1987).

Tjepkema, Sandra L., *A Bibliography of Computer Music: a Reference for Composers* (Iowa City, IA: University of Iowa Press, 1981).

Peter Todd and D. G. Loy, ed., *Music and Connectionism* (Cambridge, MA: The MIT Press, 1991).

Traister, Robert J., *Music & Speech Programs for the IBM PC*, 1st ed. (Blue Ridge Summit, PA: Tab Books, 1983).

Waters, William J., *Music and the Personal Computer: an Annotated Bibliography* (New York, NY: Greenwood Press, 1989).

Winsor, Phil, *Computer-Assisted Music Composition: A Primer in BASIC* (Princeton, NJ: Petrocelli Books, 1987).

Wittlich, Gary E., John W. Schaffer and Larry R. Babband, *Microcomputers and Music* (Englewood Cliffs, NJ: Prentice-Hall, 1986).

Yelton, Geary, *Music and the Macintosh* (Atlanta, GA: MIDI America, 1989). Abstracts of papers read at the First International Conference on Computer Music, October 28-31, 1976 (Cambridge, MA: Dept. of Humanities, Massachusetts Institute of Technology, 1976).

Proceedings Associazione di Informatica Musicale Italiana (AIMI)/Universita di Genova, Laboratorio di Informatica Musicale (DIST), 1991.

Canadian Commission for UNESCO, Computer music: report on an international project including the international workshop held at Aarhus, Denmark in 1978, *Composition Musicale Par Ordinateur: Rapport Sur un Project Internationale Y* (Ottawa, Canada: Canadian Commission for UNESCO, 1981).

Composition et environments informatiques, Les cahiers de l'IRCAM, Recherche et Musique, No. 1 (Paris: IRCAM, Centre Georges Pompidou, 1992-1993.)

Electronic and Computer Music : 1969-1976 (Holmdel, NJ: Bell Laboratories, 1977).

Informatica, Musica/Industria: Pensiero Compositivo, Ricerca, Didattica, Sviluppo Industriale,Tirrenia, Festa nazionale dell'unita, 3-10 settembre 1982 (Milan: Edizioni UNICOPLI, 1984).

Musique et Informatique: une Bibliographie Indexée en Collaboration avec Jacques Arveiller, Reedition augmentée (Paris: Elmeratto, 1978).

Musique et Authenticite. Inharmonique Series No. 7 (Paris: IRCAM, Centre Georges Pompidou, 1991).

Proceedings of the International Computer Music Conferences (San Francisco, CA: International Computer Music Association, 1975-1993).

The MIDI Implementation Book (Pompton Lakes, NJ: Third Earth Publishing, 1986).

The MIDI Resource Book (Pompton Lakes, NJ: Third Earth Publishing, 1987).

CYBERCULTURE

Bear, Greg, *Blood Music* (New York, NY: Arbor House, 1985).

Michael Benedikt, ed., *Cyberspace: First Steps* (Cambridge, MA: MIT Press, 1991).

Brunner, John, *Stand on Zanzibar* (Garden City, NY: Doubleday,1968).

—, *The Shockwave Rider*, 1st ed. (New York, NY: Harper & Row, 1975).

—, *The Sheep Look Up*, 1st ed. (New York, NY: Harper & Row, 1972).

Burgess, Anthony, *A Clockwork Orange* (New York, NY: Ballantine Books, 1965).

Busby, F. M., *The Breeds of Man* (New York, NY: Bantam Books, 1988).

Cadigan, Pat, *Mind Players* (New York, NY: Bantam Books, 1987).

Delany, Samuel R., *Nova* (New York, NY: Bantam Books, 1968).

Dick, Philip K., *Do Androids Dream of Electric Sheep?* (New York, NY: New American Library, 1968).

Effinger, George Alec, *When Gravity Fails* (New York, NY: Arbor House, 1987).

—, *A Fire in the Sun* (New York, NY: Doubleday, 1989).

Gerrold, David, *When Harlie Was One* (release 2.0). Rev. Bantam ed. (Toronto, New York: Bantam, 1988).

Gibson, William, *Neuromancer* (New York, NY: Berkley Pub. Group, 1984).

—, *Burning Chrome*, Ace ed. (New York, NY: Ace Books, 1986).

—, *Count Zero* (New York, NY: Arbor House, 1986).

—, *Mona Lisa Overdrive* (New York, NY: Bantam Books, 1988).

Linda Jacobson, ed., *CyberArts: Exploring Art and Technology* (San Francisco, CA: Miller Freeman 1992).

Jeter, K. W., *Dr. Adder* (New York, NY: Bluejay Books, 1984).

—, *The Glass Hammer* (New York, NY: Bluejay Books, 1985).

Kadrey, Richard, *Metrophage: (a Romance of the Future)* Ace ed. (New York, NY: Berkley Pub., 1988).

Littell, Jonathan, *Bad Voltage, a Fantasy in 4/4* (New York, NY: Signet, 1989).

McDonald, Ian, *Out on Blue Six* (New York, NY: Bantam Books, 1989).

Milan, Victor, *The Cybernetic Samurai* (New York, NY: Arbor House, 1985).

Pynchon, Thomas, *Gravity's Rainbow* (New York, NY: Viking Press, 1973).

Robinson, Kim Stanley, *The Gold Coast* (New York, NY: St. Martin's Press, 1988).

Rucker, Rudy, *Software* (New York, NY: Ace Books, 1982).

—, *Wetware* (New York, NY: Avon Books, 1988).

Rudy Rucker, R.U. Sirius, Queen Mu, eds., *Mondo 2000: A User's Guide to the New Edge* (San Francisco, CA: Harper Collins, 1992).

Shirley, John, *Eclipse* (New York, NY: Bluejay Books, 1985).

—, *Eclipse Penumbra*, Popular Library ed. (New York, NY: Warner Books, 1988).

Spinrad, Norman, *Little Heroes* (New York, NY: Bantam Books, 1987).

—, *Other Americas* (New York, NY: Bantam Books, 1988).

Sterling, Bruce, *The Artificial Kid*, ACE Science Fiction ed. (New York, NY: Berkley Pub., 1980).

—, *Schismatrix* (New York, NY: Arbor House, 1985).

—, *Mirrorshades : the Cyberpunk Anthology*, Ace ed. (New York, NY: Berkley, 1988).

—, *Islands in the Net*, 1st ed. (New York, NY: Arbor House, 1988).

Swanwick, Michael, *Vacuum Flowers* (New York, NY: Arbor House, 1987).

Vinge, Joan D., *Catspaw* (New York, NY: Warner Books, 1988).

Weisenburger, Steven, *A Gravity's Rainbow Companion: Sources and Contexts for Pynchon's Novel* (Athens, GA: University of Georgia Press, 1988).

Williams, Walter Jon, *Hardwired* (New York, NY: T. Doherty Associates, 1986).

—, *Voice of the Whirlwind* (New York, NY: T. Doherty, 1987).

Wilson, Robert Charles, *Memory Wire* (New York, NY: Bantam Books, 1987).

Wompack, Jack, *Terraplane: a Novel* (New York, NY: Weidenfeld & Nicholson, 1988).

Blade Runner, Videocassette, The Ladd Company (Los Angeles, CA: Embassy Home Entertainment, 1986).

Brazil, Videocassette, Embassy International Pictures (Universal City, CA: MCA Home Video, Inc., 1986).

A Clockwork Orange, videocassette, Stanley Kubrick (New York, NY: Warner Home Video, 1983).

FRACTALS

Amann, A., L. Cederbaum and W. Gans, *Fractals, Quasicrystals, Chaos, Knots, and Algebraic Quantum Mechanics* (Boston, MA: Kluwer Academic Publishers, 1988).

Barnsley, Michael, *Fractals Everywhere* (New York, NY: Academic Press, 1988).

Barnsley, Michael F. and S. G. Demko, *Chaotic Dynamics and Fractals* (Orlando, FL: Academic Press, 1986).

Batty, Michael, *Fractal-Based Description of Urban Form* (Cardiff, Wales: University of Wales, Institute of Science and Technology, 1986).

Batty, Michael and P. Longley, *Measuring and Simulating the Structure and Form of Cartographic Lines,* Series title: Papers in planning research (Cardiff, Wales: University of Wales, Institute of Science and Technology, 1986).

Briggs, J. and F.D. Peat, *Turbulent Mirror: An Illustrated Guide to Chaos Theory and the Science of Wholeness* (New York, NY: Harper and Row, 1989).

Falconer, K. J., *The Geometry of Fractal Sets* (New York, NY: Cambridge University Press, 1984).

Feder, Jens, *Fractals* (New York, NY: Plenum Press, 1988).

P. Fischer and W.R. Smith, eds., *Chaos, Fractals, and Dynamics* (New York, NY: Dekker, 1985).

Genz, Henning, *Symmetrie - Bauplan der Natur* (Munich, Germany: Piper, 1987).

Hall, Roy, *Illumination and Color in Computer Generated Imagery* (New York, NY: Springer-Verlag, 1989).

Istvan Hargittai, ed., *Fivefold Symmetry* (Singapore: World Scientific Publishing Co., 1991).

Istvan Hargittai and C.A. Pickover, eds., *Spiral Symmetry* (Singapore: World Scientific Publishing Co., 1991).

Jullien, R. and R. Botet, *Aggregation and Fractal Aggregates* (Singapore: World Scientific Publishing Co., 1987).

Kahane, J.P., *Fractals: Dimensions Non Entieres et Applications* (Paris: Masson, 1987).

Lugiato, L.A. and E.R. Pike, *Fractals* (Bristol: Hilger, 1987).

Mandelbrot, Benoit B., *Fractals: Form, Chance, and Dimension* (San Francisco: W. H. Freeman, 1977).

—, *The Fractal Geometry of Nature* (San Francisco: W.H. Freeman, 1982).

—, *Les Objets Fractals: Forme, Hasard et Dimension*, 2nd ed. (Paris: Flammarion, 1984).

Moon, F. C., *Chaotic Vibrations: an Introduction for Applied Scientists and Engineers* (New York, NY: Wiley, 1987).

Ostrowsky, Nicole and H. Eugene Stanley, *On Growth and Form: Fractal and Non-Fractal Patterns in Physics* (Boston, MA: M. Nijhoff, 1986).

Peitgen, Heinz-Otto, *The Science of Fractal Images, Dietmar Saupe, ed.* (New York, NY: Springer-Verlag, 1988).

Peitgen, Heinz-Otto and P.H. Richter, *The Beauty of Fractals: Images of Complex Dynamical Systems* (New York, NY: Springer-Verlag, 1986).

Pickover, Clifford A., *Computers, Pattern, Chaos and Beauty* (New York, NY: St. Martin's Press, 1991).

Luciano Pietronero and Erio Tosatti, eds., *Proceedings of the Sixth Trieste International Symposium on Fractals in Physics* (ICTP) held in Trieste, Italy, 9-12, July, 1985 (New York, NY: Elsevier Science, 1986).

Roger Pynn and Tormod Riste, eds., *NATO Advanced Study Institute on Time-dependent Effects in Disordered Materials* (Geilo, Norway, 1987).

Salli, Arto, *Upper Density Properties of Hausdorff Measures on Fractals* (Helsinki: Suomalainen Tiedeakatemia, 1985).

Verostko, Roman, *Derivation of the Laws* (Minneapolis, MN: St. Sebastian Press, 1990).

Wegner, Tim, *Fractals for Windows* (Corta Madera, CA: Waite Group Press, 1992).

Time-Dependent Effects in Disordered Materials (New York, NY: Plenum Press, 1987).

GENDER, ART AND TECHNOLOGY

Amann, Dick and Dick Smith, *Forgotten Women of Computer History* (Stow, MA: Programmed Studies, Inc., 1978).

Anees, Munawar A., *Islam and Biological Futures: Ethics, Gender, and Technology* (New York, NY: Mansell, 1989).

Apple, M. W. and S. Jungck, "You Don't Have to be a Teacher to Teach this Unit - Teaching, Technology, and Gender in the Classroom," *American Educational Research Journal* **27**, No. 2, 227-251 (1990 Summer).

Arthurs, J., "Technology and Gender," *Screen* **30**, No. 1-2, 40-59 (1989).

Belenky, Mary Field, et al., *Women's Ways of Knowing* (New York, NY: Basic Books, 1986).

Beier, Lucy Adams, "Artemisia: a Women's Cooperative Gallery in Chicago," *Leonardo* 11, No. 2, 115 (Oxford, UK: Pergamon Press, 1978).

Benston, Margaret Lowe, "Feminism and System Design: Questions of Control" in *The Effect of Feminist Approaches on Research Methodologies* (Waterloo, Ontario: Wilfred Laurier Univ. Press, 1989).

Borg, Anita, "The Rationale for a Closed Electronic Forum," in *The Third Conference on Computers, Freedom and Privacy*, Burlingame, CA (1993).

Canada, K. and F.Bruscas, "The Technological Gender Gap - Evidence and Recommendations for Educators and Computer-Based Instruction Designers," *ETR&D - Educational, Technology Research and Development* 39, No. 2, 43-51 (1991).

Chadwick, Whitney, *Women, Art, and Society* (London: Thames and Hudson, 1990).

Cockburn, Cynthia, "Technological Change in a Changing Europe: Does it Mean the Same for Women as for Men?" *Women's Studies International Forum* 15, No. 1, 65-91 (1992).

Contrucci, J., and B. Fischer, "Women in a Technological World - an Interdisciplinary Core Course at Emmanuel College in Boston" *Bulletin of Science Technology & Society* 10, No 4, 191-196 (1990).

Connor, J. Robert, "Springboard to the 21st Century: Opportunities for Women and Minorities," *Aviation Week & Space Technology* 136, No. 22 (1992).

Couey, Anna, "Art Works as Organic Communications Systems", *Leonardo* 24, No. 2, 127-130 (Oxford, UK: Pergamon Press, 1991).

Damarin, Suzanne K., "Women and Information Technology: Framing Some Issues for Education," *Feminist Teacher* 6, No 2, 16-21 (1992).

De Lauretis, Teresa, *Technologies of Gender: Essays on Theory, Film, and Fiction* (Basingstoke: Macmillan, 1989).

Deery, June, "Technology and Gender in Aldous Huxley's Alternative (?) Worlds," *Extrapolation* 33, No. 3, 258-64 (1992).

Dixon, Janet, "Women, Public Policy, and the Information Age" in *The Third Conference on Computers, Freedom and Privacy*, Burlingame, CA (1993).

Eisler, Riane, "Technology, Gender, and History: Toward a Nonlinear Model of Social Evolution," *World Futures* 32, No. 4, 207-226 (1991).

Eldredge, Mary, et al., *Athena meets Prometheus: Gender, Science and Technology: a Selective Bibliography of Related Books* (Davis, CA: Women's Resources and Research Center, University of California, Davis, 1988).

—, "Gender, Science, and Technology - a Selected Annotated Bibliography," *Behavioral & Social Sciences Librarian* 9, No. 1, 77-134 (1990).

Emmett, Arielle, "A Women's Institute of Technology?" *Technology Review* 95, No. 3, 16-17 (1992).

Erlich, Reese, "Sexual Harassment an Issue on the High-Tech Frontier," *MacWeek* 20-21 (December 14, 1992).

Frissen, Valerie, "Trapped in Electronic Cages? Gender and New Information Technologies in the Public and Private Domain: an Overview of Research," *Media, Culture & Society* 14, No. 1, 31-49 (1992).

Joanna Frueh, Cassandra L. Langer, and Arlene Raven, eds., *Feminist Art Criticism: An Anthology* (Ann Arbor, MI: UMI Research Press, 1988).

Guyer, Carolyn, "Introduction," in *Its Name was Penelope*, Judy Malloy, pp.3-8 (Eastgate Systems, 1992).

Guyer, Carolyn and Martha Petry, "Notes for Izme Pass Expose," *Writing on the Edge* 2, No. 2, 82-89 (Spring, 1991).

Hacker, Sally, *Doing it the Hard Way: Investigations of Gender and Technology*, Dorothy E. Smith and Susan M. Turner, eds. (Boston, MA: Unwin Hyman, 1990).

—, *Pleasure, Power, and Technology: Some Tales of Gender, Engineering, and the Cooperative Workplace* (Boston, MA: Unwin Hyman, 1989).

Halberstam, Judith, "Automating Gender: Postmodern Feminism in the Age of the Intelligent Machine," *Feminist Studies* 17, No 3, 439-459 (1991).

Hornig, S., "Gender Differences in Responses to News about Science and Technology," *Science Technology & Human Values.* 17, No. 4, 532-542 (1992).

H. Patricia Hynes, ed., *Reconstructing Babylon: Essays on Women and Technology* (Bloomington, IN: Indiana University Press, 1991).

Jones, Glyn, "The Women Who Went Back to Technology," *New Scientist* 133, No. 1811, 36-39 (1992).

Kikauka, Laura and Nancy Patterson, "Misplaced Affection: A Computer-Controlled Interactive Household Appliance Environment", *Leonardo* 20, No. 3, 247 (Oxford, UK: Pergamon Press, 1987).

Gill Kirkup and Laurie Smith Keller, eds., *Inventing Women: Science, Technology, and Gender* (Cambridge, MA: Blackwell, 1992).

Cheris Kramarae, ed., *Technology and Women's Voices: Keeping in Touch* (New York, NY: Routledge & Kegan Paul, 1988).

LeFevre, Karen Burke, *Invention as a Social Act* (Carbondale, IL: Southern Illinois Press, 1987).

Leighton, Carolyn, "Women: Scarce at the Top," *Computerworld* **26**, No. 12, 33 (March 23, 1992).

Lewis, Lisa A., *Gender Politics and MTV: Voicing the Difference* (Philadelphia, PA: Temple University Press, 1990).

Gillian Lovegrove and Barbara Segal, eds., *Women Into Computing: Selected Papers, 1988-1990* (New York, NY: Springer-Verlag, 1991).

Magenta, Muriel, "Coiffure Carnival", *Women & Art Magazine* No. 39, 4-5 (1991).

Malloy, Judy, "Its Name was Penelope: Notes," in *Its Name Was Penelope*, pp. 9-13, Judy Malloy (Eastgate Systems, 1992).

—, "OK Research/OK Genetic Engineering/Bad Information, Information Art Defines Technology," *Leonardo* **21**, No. 4, 371-375 (Oxford, UK: Pergamon Press 1988).

—, "Uncle Roger, An Online Narrabase," *Leonardo* **24**, No. 2, 195-202 (Oxford, UK: Pergamon Press, 1991).

Martin, Michele, *"Hello, Central?": Gender, Technology, and Culture in the Formation of Telephone Systems* (Buffalo, NY: McGill-Queen's University Press, 1991).

Ong, Aihwa, "Disassembling Gender in the Electronics Age," *Feminist Studies*, **13**, 609-626 (Fall, 1987).

Perry, Ruth and Lisa Greber, "Women and Computers, an Introduction," *Signs* **16**, No. 1, 74-101 (1990).

Rakow, Lana, *Impact of New Technologies on Women as Producers & Consumers of Communication in the U.S. and Canada* (Paris: UNESCO, 1991).

Rasmussen, Bente and Tove Hapnes, "Excluding Women from the Technologies of the Future? A Case Study of the Culture of Computer Science," *Futures* **23**, No. 10, 1107-1119 (1991).

Joan Rothschild, ed., *Machina Ex Dea: Feminist Perspectives on Technology* (New York, NY: Pergamon Press, 1983).

—, *Teaching Technology from a Feminist Perspective: a Practical Guide* (New York, NY: Pergamon Press, 1988).

—, "Technology and Education: a Feminist Perspective," *American Behavioral Scientist* **32**, No. 6, 708-17 (1989).

Sandhu, Ruby and Joanne Sandler *The Tech and Tools Book: a Guide to Technologies Women are Using Worldwide* (New York, NY: International Women's Tribune Centre, 1986).

Schneemann, C., "The Obscene Body/Politic (the Nude in Paintings and Performance-Art as Censored Pornography) *Art Journal* **50**, No. 4, 28-35 (1991).

Slater, Lynn, "Community College has WIT: Women in Technology," *Vocational Education Journal* **64**, No. 7, 66 (1989).

Sparks, C. and L. Vanzoonen, "Gender and Technology - Editorial," *Media Culture & Society* **14**, No. 1, 5-7.

Stamp, Patricia, *Technology, Gender, and Power in Africa*, 2nd ed. (Ottawa, Ontario: International Development Research Centre, 1990).

Steinman, Lisa M. *Making Their Mark: Women Artists Move into the Mainstream* (New York, NY: Abbeyville Press, 1989).

Swaminathan, P., "Science and Technology for Women - a Critique of Policy," *Economic and Political Weekly* **26**, Nos. 1-2, 59-63 (1991).

Tamblyn, C, "Hershman, Lynn," *Artnews* **89,** 185 (Summer, 1990).

Tannen, Deborah, *You Just Don't Understand* (New York, NY: Ballantine Books, 1990).

Toole, Betty Alexandra, *ADA, The Enchantress of Numbers* (Critical Connection, 1993).

Truong, Hoai-An, "Gender Issues in Online Communications," in *The Third Conference on Computers, Freedom and Privacy*, Burlingame, CA (1993).

Turkle, Sherry *The Second Self: Computers and the Human Spirit* (New York, NY: Simon and Schuster, 1984).

Whitney-Smith, Elin, "Figure and Ground: Information Technology and the Economic Marginalization of Women," *Whole Earth Review* **73**, 70-72 (Winter, 1991).

Barriers to Equality in Academia: Women in Computer Science at M.I.T, Prepared by female graduate students and research staff in the Laboratory for Computer Science and the Artificial Intelligence Laboratory (Cambridge, MA: MIT, 1983).

GENERAL: ART, SCIENCE AND TECHNOLOGY

Aleksandrov, V.V. and V.S. Shneyderov, *Sketching, Drawing and Visualization with the Computer* (Moscow: Mashinostroyenie Publishing House, 1988).

E. Bisiach and A. J. Marcel, eds., *Consciousness in Contemporary Science* (New York, NY: Oxford Univ. Press, 1989).

Bohm-Duchen, Monica and Janet Cook, *Understanding Modern Art* (London: Usborne Publishing, 1992).

Bolle, E., et al, *Book for the Unstable Media/Boek voor de Instabiele Media* (Stichting, The Netherlands: V2, 1992).

Catherine C. Brawer and Randy Rosen, eds., *Made in America: Science, Technology and American Modernist Poets* (New Haven, CT: Yale Univ. Press, 1987).

Annick Bureaud, ed., *International Directory of Electronic Arts 1992/1993* (Paris, France: Chaos, 1992).

Calatrava, Santiago, *Engineering Architecture* (New York, NY: Rizzoli 1989).

Culler, Jonathan, *Framing the Sign: Criticism and Its Institutions* (Norman, OK: Univ. of Oklahoma Press, 1989).

Herman E. Daly and Kenneth N. Townsend, eds., *Valuing the Earth* (Cambridge, MA: MIT Press, 1992).

Dauben, Joseph W., *The Art of Renaissance Science: Galileo and Perspective* (New York, NY: Department of History, Lehman College and CUNY Graduate Center, Science Television, 1991).

Davis, Douglas, *Art and the Future: a History-Prophecy of the Collaboration Between Science, Technology and Art* (London, UK: Thames and Hudson, 1973).

—, *Artculture: Essays on the Post-Modern*, 1st ed. (New York, NY: Harper & Row, 1977).

Deregowski, J.B.and D.M. Parker, *Perception and Artistic Style* (Amsterdam: Elsevier Science Publishers, 1990).

Dreyfus, Hubert L., *What Computers Still Can't Do* (Cambridge, MA: MIT Press, 1992).

Earmes, Charles and Ray, *A Computer Perspective: Background to the Computer Age* (Cambridge, MA: Harvard University Press, 1990).

Farago, Claire J., *Leonardo Da Vinci's "Paragone": A Critical Interpretation with a New Edition of the Next in the Codex Urbinas*, (E.J. Brill).

Fine, Arthur, *The Shaky Game: Einstein, Realism and the Quantum Theory* (Chicago, IL: Univ. of Chicago Press, 1986).

Focillon, Henri, *The Life of Forms in Art* (New York, NY: Zone Books, 1992).

Forester, Tom and Perry Morrison, *Computer Ethics: Cautionary Tales and Ethical Dilemmas in Computing* (Cambridge, MA: MIT Press, 1992).

Gilder, George F., *Life After Television* (Knoxville, TN: Whittle Direct Books, 1990).

Goethe, Johann Wolfgang, *Goethe's Botanical Writings* (Woodbridge, CT: Ox Bow Press, 1990).

Grove, J.W., *In Defence of Science: Science, Technology and Politics in Modern Society* (Toronto, Canada: Univ. of Toronto Press, 1989).

Harding, Sandra, *The Science Question in Feminism* (Ithaca, NY: Cornell Univ. Press, 1990).

Philip Hayward, ed., *Culture, Technology & Creativity in the Late Twentieth Century* (London: John Libbey & Co Ltd.).

Hersey, George and Richard Freedman, *Possible Palladian Villas* (Cambridge, MA: MIT Press, 1992).

Kahn-Magomedov, *Pioneers of Soviet Architecture* (New York, NY: Rizzoli, 1988).

Kemp, Martin., *The Science of Art: Optical Themes in Western Art from Brunnelleschi to Seurat* (New Haven, CT: Yale University Press, 1990).

Klotz, Heinrich, *The History of Postmodern Architecture*, Radka Donnel, trans. (Cambridge, MA: MIT Press, 1990).

—, *New York Architecture 1970-1990* (New York, NY: Rizzoli, 1990).

Kosuth, Joseph, *Art After Philosophy and After: Collected Writings, 1966-1990* (Cambridge, MA: MIT Press).

Kriesche, Richard, *ARTSAT* (Graz, Austria: Kriesche, 1992).

John Lansdown, ed., *Computers in Art, Design and Animation* (New York, NY: Springer-Verlag, 1989).

Levi, Albert William and Ralph A. Smith, *Art Education, A Critical Necessity* (Urbana, IL: University of Illinois Press).

Lin, Mike W., *Architectural Rendering Techniques: A Color Reference*, American Institute of Architects (AIA), (Washington, DC: Mitchell, William Que Corp., 1990).

Maiorino, Giancarlo, *Leonardo da Vinci: The Daedalian Mythmaker* (University Park, PA: Penn State Press, 1992).

Marzouk, Tobey, *High-Technology Industries* (Washington, DC: Computer Society Press, 1988).

McTear, Michael, *The Articulate Computer* (New York, NY: Basil Blackwell, 1987).

Mendez, Raul H., *Visualization in Supercomputing* (New York, NY: Springer-Verlag, 1989).

Miller, Richard W., *Fact and Method: Explanation, Confirmation and Reality in the Natural and the Social Sciences* (Princeton, NJ: Princeton Univ. Press, 1988).

Jack Nasar, ed., *Environmental Aesthetics: Theory, Research and Application* (New York, NY: Cambridge Univ. Press, 1988).

Pickover, Clifford A., *Mazes of the Mind: Computers and the Unexpected* (New York, NY: St. Martin's Press, 1992).

Roskill, Mark, *The Interpretation of Pictures* (Amherst, MA: Univ. of Massachusetts Press, 1989).

Sarason, Seymour B., *The Challenge of Art to Psychology* (New Haven, CT: Yale University Press, 1990).

Schelling, Joseph and Friedrick Wilhelm, *The Philosophy of Art and Trans*, Douglas W. Stott, ed. (Minneapolis, MN: Univ. of Minnesota Press, 1989).

Schwartz, Lillian F., *The Computer Artist's Handbook: Concepts, Techniques and Applications* (New York, NY: W.W. Norton & Co., 1991).

Jeffrey I. Seeman, ed., *Profiles, Pathways and Dreams: Autobiographies of Eminent Chemists*, 22 Vols. (Washington, DC: American Chemical Society, 1990).

Siler, Todd, *Breaking the Mind Barrier, The Artscience of Neurocosmology* (New York, NY: Simon & Schuster, 1990).

Joseph W. Slade and Yaross Lee, eds., *Beyond the Two Cultures, Essays on Science, Technology and Literature*, Based on a conference in Brooklyn, NY in February, 1990 (Ames, IA: Iowa State University Press, 1990).

Termes, Dick A. *Termespheres,* video (Spearfish, SD: Termes, 1992).

Weiss, Sholom and Casimir Kulikowski, *Computer Systems That Learn: Classification and Prediction Methods from Stastics, Neural Nets, Machine Learning and Expert Systems* (San Mateo, CA: Morgan Kaufmann Publishers, 1990).

R. A. Zwaa and D. Meutsch, eds., *Computer Models and Technology in Media Research* (Amsterdam: Elsevier Science Publishers, 1990).

Zentrum fur Kunst und Medientehnologie Karlsruhe (Kaiserstrasse, Karlsruhe, Germany: ZKM, 1992).

MULTIMEDIA

Ambron, Sueann and Kristina Hooper, *Learning with Interactive Multimedia: Developing and Using Multimedia Tools in Education* (Redmond, WA: Microsoft Press, 1990).

Anderson, Carol J., *Creating Interactive Multimedia: a Practical Guide* (Glenview, IL: Scott, Foresman, 1990).

C.J. Armstrong and J.A. Large, eds., *CD-ROM Information Products: an Evaluative Guide and Directory* (Aldershot, Hants, England: Brookfield, VT, USA, Gower, 1990-1991).

John Barker and Richard N. Tucker, eds., *The Interactive Learning Revolution : Multimedia in Education and Training* (New York, NY: Nichols Pub., 1990).

Barker, Philip, *Multi-media Computer Assisted Learning* (New York, NY: Nichols Pub., 1989).

Edward Barrett, ed., *Sociomedia: Multimedia, Hypermedia and the Social Construction of Knowledge* (Cambridge, MA: MIT Press, 1992).

Bergman, Robert E., *Managing Interactive Video/Multimedia Projects*, Robert E. Bergman and Thomas V. Moore, eds. (Englewood Cliffs, NJ: Educational Technology Publications, 1990).

Borenstein, Nathaniel S., *Multimedia Applications Development with the Andrew Toolkit* (Englewood Cliffs, NJ: Prentice Hall, 1990).

Bove, Tony, *Que's Macintosh Multimedia Handbook*, Tony Bove and Cheryl Rhodes, eds. (Carmel, IN: Que Corp., 1990).

Cabeceiras, James, *The Multimedia Library: Materials Selection and Use*, 3rd Ed. (San Diego, CA: Academic Press, 1991).

—, *CD-ROM Applications and Markets*, Judith Paris Roth, ed. (Westport, CT: Meckler, 1988).

Chen, Ching-Chih, *HyperSource on Multimedia/Hypermedia Technologies* (Chicago, IL: Library and Information Technology Association, 1989).

Cox, John, *Keyguide to Information Sources in Online and CD-ROM Database Searching* (New York, NY: Mansell Pub., 1991).

Crowell, Peter, *Authoring Systems : a Guide for Interactive Videodisc Authors* (Westport, CT: Meckler, 1988).

Norman Desmarais, ed., *CD-ROM Local Area Networks: a User's Guide* (Westport, CT: Meckler, 1991).

Elshami, Ahmed M., *CD-ROM Technology for Information Managers* (Chicago, IL: American Library Association, 1990).

Erlbaum, L., *Cognition, Education, and Multimedia* (Hillsdale, NJ: Erlbaum, 1990).

Fraase, Michael, *Farallon's MediaTracks: the Ultimate Training Tool* (Homewood, IL: Business One Irwin, 1991).

Gabriel, Michael R., *A Guide to the Literature of Electronic Publishing: CD-ROM, Desktop Publishing, and Electronic Mail, Books, and Journals* (Greenwich, CT: Jai Press, 1989).

Gilder, George F., *Life After Television* (Knoxville, TN: Whittle Direct Books, 1990).

Haynes, George R., *Opening Minds: the Evolution of Videodiscs & Interactive Learning* (Dubuque, IA: Kendall/Hunt Pub. Co., 1989).

Iuppa, Nicholas V. and Karl Anderson, *Advanced Interactive Video Design: New Techniques and Applications* (White Plains, NY: Knowledge Industry Publications, 1988).

Douglas Kahn and Gregory Whitehead, eds, *Wireless Imagination: Sound, Radio and the Avant-Garde* (Cambridge, MA: MIT Press, 1992).

Luther, Arch C., *Digital Video in the PC Environment*, 2nd ed. (New York, NY: Intertext Publications, McGraw-Hill Book Co., 1991).

McCormick, John A., *A Guide to Optical Storage Technology: Using CD-ROM, WORM, Erasable, Digital Paper, and Other High-density Opto-magnetic Storage Devices* (Homewood, IL: Dow Jones-Irwin, 1990).

Nicholls, Paul, *CD-ROM Collection Builder's Toolkit: the Complete Handbook of Tools for Evaluating CD-ROMs* (Weston, CT: Pemberton Press, 1990).

Meta Nissley and Nancy Melin Nelson, eds., *CD-ROM Licensing and Copyright Issues for Libraries* (Westport, CT: Meckler, 1990).

Oberhauser, O.C., *Multimedia Information Storage and Retrieval Using Optical Disc Technology: Potential for Library and Information Services* (Wien, Osterreichisches Institut fur Bibliotheksforschung, Dokumentations und Informationswesen, 1990).

Charles Oppenheim, ed., *CD-ROM: Fundamentals to Applications* (Boston, MA: Butterworths, 1988).

Parisi, Lynn, *Directory of Online Databases and CD-ROM Resources for High Schools*, Lynn S. Parisi and Virginia L. Jones, eds. (Santa Barbara, CA: ABC-Clio, 1988).

Royce, Catherine, *CD-ROM: Usage and Prospects*, Catherine Royce, John Akeroyd and Liz May, eds. (London: British Library R & D Dept., 1989).

Schamber, Linda, *The Novice User and CD-ROM Database Services* (Syracuse, NY: ERIC Clearinghouse on Information Resources, Syracuse University, 1988).

Shaddock, Philip, *Multimedia Creations* (Corta Madera, CA: Waite Group Press, 1992).

Chris Sherman, ed., *The CD ROM Handbook* (New York, NY: Intertext Publications, McGraw-Hill Book Co., 1988).

Souter, Gerry, *The Disconnection: How to Interface Computers and Video* (White Plains, NY: Knowledge Industry Publications, 1988).

Thiel, Thomas, *CD-ROM Mastering for Information and Image Management*, Thomas Thiel, Scott Gielda and Ann Lancaster, eds. (Silver Spring, MD: Association for Information and Image Management, 1990).

John A. Waterworth, ed., *Multimedia: Technology and Applications* (New York, NY: Ellis Horwood, 1990).

Wegner, Tim, *Image Lab* (Corta Madera, CA: Waite Group Press, 1992).

Wilson, Stephen, *Multimedia Design with HyperCard* (Englewood Cliffs, NJ: Prentice Hall, 1991).

Compact Optical Disc Technology, CD ROM (Apr 89-Feb 90): Citations from the Information Services for the Physics and Engineering Communities (Springfield, VA: NTIS, 1990).

Interactive Multimedia (Redmond, WA: Microsoft Press, 1988).

Interactive Video (Englewood Cliffs, NJ: Educational Technology Publications, 1989).

Microsoft Windows Multimedia Authoring and Tools Guide (Redmond, WA: Microsoft Press, 1991).

SCIL 1989: the Fourth Annual Software/Computer/Database/CD-ROM Conference and Exposition for Librarians and Information Managers, Conference proceedings (Westport, CT: Meckler, 1989).

The Second Generation of CD-ROM: Proceedings of an Information Industry Association Seminar (Washington, DC: Information Industry Association, 1990).

TELEVISION AND SOCIETY

Agrawal, Binod C., *Television Comes to Village: an Evaluation of SITE* (Ahmedabad: Govt. of India, Space Applications Centre, Software Systems Group, Research and Evaluation Cell, 1978).

Agrawal, Binod C., M.R. Malek and Madhu Patel, *Television in Kheda : a social evaluation of SITE* (Ahmedabad: Govt. of India, Space Applications Centre, Software Systems Group, Research and Evaluation Cell, Indian Space Research Organisation, 1981).

Altamirano, Juan Carlos, *Los Desafios de la Television Chilena del Manana* (Santiago, Chile: Centro de Estudios del Desarrollo, 1985).

Anderson, Chuck, *Video Power: Grass Roots Television* (New York, NY: Praeger, 1975).

Arenas, Pedro Jose, *La Television y Nuestra Conducta Cotidiana: Sus Efectos Sobre Ninos, Adolescentes y Adultos* (Buenos Aires: Editorial Cuarto Mundo, 1975).

Baran, Stanley J., *The Viewer's Television Book: a Personal Guide to Understanding Television and its Influence* (Cleveland, Ohio: Penrith Pub. Co., 1980).

Barnouw, Erik, *The Sponsor: Notes on a Modern Potentate* (New York, NY: Oxford University Press, 1978).

Barwise, T. P. and Andrew Ehrenberg, *Television and its Audience* (Newbury Park, UK: Sage, 1988).

Batra, N. D., *A Self-Renewing Society: the Role of Television and Communications Technology* (Lanham, MD: University Press of America, 1990).

Belson, William A., *The Impact of Television: Methods and Findings in Program Research* (Hamden, CT: Archon Books, 1967).

Berger, Arthur Asa, *The TV-guided American* (New York, NY: Walker, 1976).

—, *Television in Society* (New Brunswick, NJ: Transaction Books, 1987).

Brown, Les, *Keeping your Eye on Television* (New York, NY: Pilgrim Press, 1979).

Les Brown and S. W. Walker, eds., *Fast Forward: the New Television and American Society: Essays from Channels of Communications* (Kansas City, MO: Andrews and McMeel, 1983).

Buddemeier, Heinz, *Illusion und Manipulation: die Wirkung von Film und Fernsehen auf Individuum und Gesellschaft* (Stuttgart: Urachhaus, 1987).

Cantor, Muriel G., *Prime-time Television: Content and Control* (Beverly Hills: Sage Publications, 1980).

Caparelli, Sergio, *Televisao e Capitalismo no Brasil: Com Dados da Pesquisa da ABEPEC* (Porto Alegre, Rio Grande do Sul: L&PM Editores, 1982).

Douglass Cater, ed., *Television as a Social Force: New Approaches to TV Criticism*, Sponsored by the Aspen Institute on Communications and Society (New York, NY: Praeger, 1975).

Charren, Peggy and Martin W. Sandler, *Changing Channels: Living (Sensibly) with Television* (Reading, MA: Addison-Wesley, 1983).

Cheney, Glenn Alan, *Television in American Society* (New York, NY: F. Watts, 1983).

Collins, Richard, *Culture, Communication, and National Identity: the Case of Canadian Television* (Buffalo, NY: University of Toronto Press, 1990).

Comstock, George A., *Effects of Television on Children: What is the Evidence?* The Rand Paper Series No. 5412 (Santa Monica, CA: Rand Corporation, 1975).

Comstock, George A. and Marilyn Fisher, *Television and Human Behavior: a Guide to the Pertinent Scientific Literature*, Report No. R-1746-CF prepared under a grant from the Edna McConnell Clark Foundation (Santa Monica, CA: Rand Corporation, 1975).

Comstock, George A., Georg Lindsey and Marilyn Fisher, *Television and Human Behavior: the Research Horizon, Future and Present*, Report No. R-1748-CF prepared under a grant from the Edna McConnell Clark Foundation (Santa Monica, CA: Rand Corporation, 1975).

Contreras Arellano, J. Asdrubal, *Influencia de la Television en la Formacion del Hombre Latinoamericano* (Caracas: Universidad Central de Venezuela, Ediciones de la Biblioteca, 1987).

Frank J. Coppa, ed., *Screen and Society: the Impact of Television Upon Aspects of Contemporary Civilization* (Chicago: Nelson-Hall, 1979).

Cumberbatch, Guy and Dennis Howitt, *A Measure of Uncertainty: the Effects of the Mass Media* (London: John Libbey, 1989).

Dahlmuller, Gotz and Wulf D. Hund and Helmut Kommer, *Kritik des Fernsehens, Handbuch gegen Manipulation* (Darmstadt: Luchterhand 1973).

Davis, Richard H. and James A. Davis, *TV's Image of the Elderly: a Practical Guide for Change* (Lexington, MA: Lexington Books, 1985).

Esslin, Martin, *The Age of Television* (San Francisco, CA: Freeman, 1982).

Fiske, John and John Hartley, *Reading television* (London: Methuen, 1978).

Fowles, Jib, *Television Viewers vs. Media Snobs: What TV Does for People* (New York, NY: Stein and Day, 1982).

Goethals, Gregor T., *The TV Ritual: Worship at the Video Altar* (Boston: Beacon Press, 1981).

Goldsen, Rose Kohn, *The Show and Tell Machine: How Television Works and Works You Over* (New York, NY: Dial Press, 1977).

Gary Granzberg and Jack Steinbring, eds., *Television and the Canadian Indians: Impact and Meaning Among Algonkians of Central Canada* (Winnipeg, Manitoba: University of Winnipeg, 1980).

Groombridge, Brian, *Television and the People: a Programme for Democratic Participation* (Harmondsworth: Penguin, 1972).

Gunter, Barrie, *Television and Sex Role Stereotyping* (London: J. Libbey: IBA, 1986).

—, *Television and the Fear of Crime* (London: Libbey, 1987).

Gunter, Barrie and Mallory Wober, *Violence on Television: What the Viewers Think* (London: J. Libbey: IBA, 1988).

Halloran, James D., *The Effects of Mass Communication, with Special Reference to Television; a Survey* (Leicester, UK: Leicester University Press, 1964).

—, *The Effects of Television* (London, UK: Panther, 1970).

Hamamoto, Darrell Y., *Nervous Laughter: Television Situation Comedy and Liberal Democratic Ideology* (New York, NY: Praeger, 1989).

Hedinsson, Elais, *TV, Family and Society: the Social Origins and Effects of Adolescent's TV Use* (Stockholm: Almqvist & Wiksell, 1981).

Hefzallah, Ibrahim M., *Critical Viewing of Television: a Book for Parents and Teachers* (Lanham, MD: University Press of America, 1987).

Hill, George H., Lorraine Raglin, and Chas Floyd Johnson, *Black Women in Television: an Illustrated History and Bibliography* (New York, NY: Garland Pub., 1990).

Horton, Robert W., *To Pay or Not to Pay; a Report on Subscription Television* (Santa Barbara, CA: Center for the Study of Democratic Institutions, 1960).

Hunt, Albert, *The Language of Television: Uses and Abuses*, 2nd International Television Studies Conference held in London, 1986 (London, UK: E. Methuen, 1981).

Jacobs, Jerry, *Changing Channels: Issues and Realities in Television News* (Mountain View, CA: Mayfield Pub. Co., 1990).

Kottak, Conrad Phillip, *Prime-time Society: an Anthropological Analysis of Television and Culture* (Belmont, CA: Wadsworth Pub. Co., 1990).

Kubin, Jerzy, *Czy Telewizja Wychowuje?* (Warszawa: Nasza Księgarnia, 1969).

Le Duc, Jean, *Au Royaume du Son et de L'Image: Cinema, Radio, Television* (Paris: Hachette, 1965).

Li, Chin-ch'uan, *Media Imperialism Reconsidered: the Homogenizing of Television Culture* (Beverly Hills, CA: Sage Publications, 1980).

Lodziak, Conrad, *The Power of Television: a Critical Appraisal* (New York, NY: St. Martin's Press, 1986).

Carl Lowe, ed., *Television and American Culture* (New York, NY: H.W. Wilson Co., 1981).

Lowe, Vincent and Jaafar Kamin, *TV Programme Management in a Plural Society : Decision-making Processes in Radio and Television Malaysia* (Singapore: Asian Mass Communication Research and Information Centre, 1982).

Colin MacCabe, ed., *High Theory/Low Culture: Analysing Popular Television and Film* (Manchester, UK: Manchester University Press, 1986).

Mander, Jerry, *Four Arguments for the Elimination of Television* (New York, NY: Morrow, 1978).

Mankiewicz, Frank and Joel Swerdlow, *Remote Control: Television and the Manipulation of American Life* (New York, NY: Times Books, 1978).

Martinez Pardo, Hernando, *Que es la Television?: Television, Televidente, y Sociedad: Su Historia, Su Lenguaje y la Ideologia, Metodologia de Analisis* (Bogota: Centro de Investigacion y Educacion Popular, 1978).

Mattelart, Michele and Armand Mattelart, *The Carnival of Images: Brazilian Television Fiction*, transl. David Buxton (New York, NY: Bergin & Garvey, 1990).

McCrohan, Donna, *Prime Time, Our Time: America's Life and Times Through the Prism of Television* (New York, NY: St. Martin's Press, 1990).

Martin McLoone and John MacMahon, eds., *Television and Irish Society: 21 Years of Irish Television* (Dublin, Ireland: Radio Telefis Eireann, 1984).

Patricia Mellencamp, ed., *Logics of Television: Essays in Cultural Criticism* (Bloomington, IN: Indiana University Press, 1990).

Mickiewicz, Ellen Propper, *Split signals: Television and Politics in the Soviet Union* (New York, NY: Oxford University Press, 1988).

Milavsky, J. Ronald [et al.], *Television and Aggression: a Panel Study* (New York, NY: Academic Press, 1982).

Milgram, Stanley and R. Lance Shotland, *Television and Antisocial Behavior: Field Experiments* (New York, NY: Academic Press, 1973).

Miller, D. Thomas, *Television; the Only Truly Mass Medium Remaining Today: its Role in Our Society*, New York State College of Agriculture and Life Sciences. Dept. of Communication Arts Bulletin 12 (Ithaca, NY: New York State College of Agriculture and Life Sciences, 1971).

Missika, Jean Louis and Dominique Wolton, *La Folle du Logis: la Television dans les Societes Democratiques* (Paris: Gallimard, 1983).

Montgomery, Kathryn C., *Target, Prime Time: Advocacy Groups and the Struggle over Entertainment Television* (New York, NY: Oxford University Press, 1989).

Morley, David, *Family television: Cultural Power and Domestic Leisure* (London, UK: Comedia Pub. Group, 1986).

Morris, Colin M., *God-in-a-Box: Christian Strategy in the Television Age* (London, UK: Hodder and Stoughton, 1984).

John P. Murray, ed., *Television and Social Behavior*, A technical report to the Surgeon General's Scientific Advisory Committee on Television and Social Behavior; Rockville, Md., National Institute of Mental Health (Washington, DC: U.S. Govt. Print. Office, 1972).

Nelson, Joyce, *The Perfect Machine: TV in the Nuclear Age* (Toronto, Ontario: Between-the-Lines, 1987).

Newcomb, Horace, *TV: the Most Popular Art*, 1st ed. (Garden City, NY: Anchor Press, 1974).

Alan M. Olson, Christopher Parr, and Debra Parr, eds. *Video Icons & Values* (Albany, NY: State University of New York Press, 1991).

Paisner, Daniel, *The Imperfect Mirror: Inside Stories of Television Newswomen*, 1st ed. (New York, NY: Morrow, 1989).

Piepe, Anthony, Miles Emerson, and Judy Lannon, *Television and the Working Class* (Lexington, MA: Lexington Books, 1975).

Milton E. Ploghoft and James A. Anderson, eds., *Education for the Television Age: the Proceedings of a National Conference on the Subject of Children and Television* (Springfield, IL: C.C. Thomas, 1981).

Primeau, Ronald, *The Rhetoric of Television* (New York, NY: Longman, 1979).

Provenzo, Eugene F., *Video Kids, Making Sense of Nintendo* (Cambridge,MA: Harvard University Press).

Quester, George H., *The International Politics of Television* (Lexington, MA: Lexington Books, 1990).

Rapping, Elayne, *The Looking Glass World of Nonfiction TV*, 1st ed. (Boston, MA: South End Press, 1987).

Ellen Seiter, ed., *Remote control: Television, Audiences, and Cultural Power* (New York, NY: Routledge, 1989).

Root, Jane, *Open the Box: About Television* (London, UK: Comedia Pub. Group, 1986).

Rowland, Willard D., *The Politics of TV Violence: Policy Uses of Communication Research* (Beverly Hills, CA: Sage, 1983).

Cynthia Schneider and Brian Wallis, eds., *Global Television* (New York, NY: Wedge Press, 1988).

Shaheen, Jack G., *The TV Arab* (Bowling Green, OH: Bowling Green State University Popular Press, 1984).

Shulman, Milton, *The Ravenous Eye: the Impact of the Fifth Factor* (London, UK: Cassell, 1973).

Siepmann, Charles Arthur, *Radio, Television and Society* (New York, NY: Oxford University Press, 1950).

Nancy Signorielli, ed., *Role portrayal and Stereotyping on Television: an Annotated Bibliography of Studies Relating to Women, Minorities, Aging, Sexual Behavior, Health, and Handicaps* (Westport, CT: Greenwood Press, 1985).

Silverstone, Roger, *The Message of Television: Myth and Narrative in Contemporary Culture* (London, UK: Heinemann Educational, 1981).

Simonson, Solomon S., *Crisis in Television; a Study of the Private Judgment and the Public Interest* (New York, NY: Living Books, 1966).

Sklar, Robert, *Prime-time America: Life On and Behind the Television Screen* (New York, NY: Oxford University Press, 1980).

Skornia, Harry Jay, *Television and Society: an Inquest and Agenda for Improvement*, 1st ed. (New York, NY: McGraw-Hill, 1965).

Stanley, William David and William P. Kuvlesky, *The Impact of the TV Event "Roots": a Case Study of East Texas Nonmetropolitan Black Women*, Departmental information report, Texas Agricultural Experiment Station (College Station, TX: Texas A & M University, 1979).

Stein, Benjamin, *The View from Sunset Boulevard: America as Brought to You by the People who Make Television* (New York, NY: Basic Books, 1979).

Sternberg, Beno and Evelyne Sullerot, *Aspects Sociaux de la Radio et de la Television; Revue des Recherches Significatives 1950-1964* (Paris: Mouton, 1966).

Taylor, Laurie and Bob Mullan, *Uninvited Guests: the Intimate Secrets of Television and Radio* (London, UK: Chatto & Windus, 1986).

John Tulloch and Graeme Turner, eds., *Australian Television: Programs, Pleasures and Politics* (Boston, MA: Allen & Unwin, 1989).

Ulmer, Gregory L., *Teletheory: Grammatology in the Age of Video* (New York, NY: Routledge, 1989).

United States Commission on Civil Rights, *Window Dressing on the Set: Women and Minorities in Television*, A report of the United States Commission on Civil Rights, Washington, DC (1977).

United States National Business Council for Consumer Affairs Sub-Council on Advertising and Promotion, *Violence & the Media* (Washington, DC: U.S. Govt. Print. Office, 1972).

David Manning White and Richard Averson, eds., *Sight, Sound, and Society; Motion Pictures and Television in America* (Boston, MA: Beacon Press, 1968).

Stephen B. Withey and Ronald P. Abeles, *Television and Social Behavior: Beyond Violence and Children*, A report of the Committee on Television and Social Behavior Social Science Research Council (Hillsdale, NJ).

Willener, Alfred, Guy Milliard and Alex Ganty, *Videology and Utopia: Explorations in a New Medium*, transl. Diana Burfield (Boston, MA: Routledge and Kegan Paul, 1976).

Wober, J. M., *Television and Social Control* (New York, NY: St. Martin's Press, 1988).

—, *The Use and Abuse of Television: a Social Psychological Analysis of the Changing Screen* (Hillsdale, NJ: L. Erlbaum Associates, 1988).

Wolfe, Morris, *Jolts: the TV Wasteland and the Canadian Oasis* (Toronto, Canada: J. Lorimer, 1985).

The Bounds of Freedom, a series of six Granada Television programmes in which top level communicators show how they respond to moments of crisis —how they decide what gets published, what doesn't and why, *Communication and Society* **14**

(London: Constable, in collaboration with Granada Television, 1980).

Discrimination in Television: Program and Legal Background for its Elimination by the Federal Communications Commission, a report of the Committee on Legal Problems in the Integrated Society (New York, NY: The Guild, 1965).

Television and Conflict, report of a conference at which the conduct of TV in today's controversial situations at the Institute for the Study of Conflict (London, 1978).

Television Looks at Aging (New York, NY: Television Information Office, 1985).

VIDEO ART

Bader, Norman, Brian A. Barsky and David Zeltzer, *Making Them Move: Mechanics, Control and Animation of Articulated Figures* (San Mateo, CA: Morgan Kaufmann Publishers 1989).

Ballester, Fernando, *Immagine Elettronica* (Bologna, Italy: 1986) Install-video-side, a cura di Lola Bonora (Bologna, Italy: Grafis, 1986).

Battcock, Gregory, *New Artists Video: a Critical Anthology*, 1st ed. (New York, NY: Dutton, 1978).

Birnbaum, Dara, *Rough Edits: Popular Image Video Works 1977-1980*, Benjamin H.D. Buchloh, ed. (Halifax, Nova Scotia: Press of the Nova Scotia College of Art and Design, 1987).

Cubitt, Sean, *Timeshift: On Video Culture* (New York, NY: Routledge, 1991).

Davis, Douglas. *Douglas Davis : Arbeiten = Works 1970-1977 (Berlin: Neuer Berliner Kunstverein, 1978).*

Debbaut, Jan, *Modus Vivendi: Ulay & Marina Abramovic, 1980-1985*, exhibition and catalogue (Eindhoven: Stedelijk Van Abbemuseum, 1985).

Duchaine, Andree. *Video du Quebec,* une Exposition Organisee par le Service des Expositions Itinerantes du Musee d'Art Contemporain, exhibit (Quebec, Canada: Gouvernement du Quebec, Ministere des Affaires Culturelles, Musee d'Art Contemporain, 1982).

Gayle, Thorsen, *A Cooperative Workshop/Exhibitions Program, 1978-79* (Minneapolis, MN: College of Art and Design, 1979).

Bettina Gruber and Maria Vedder, eds. *Kunst und Video: Internationale Entwicklung und Kunstler*, Dokumenten und grundsatzlichen Arbeiten zur Kunstgeschichte, Archaologie, Musikgeschichte und Geisteswissenschaft (Koln: DuMont, 1983).

Peggy Gale, ed., *Video by Artists* (Toronto, Canada: Art Metropole, 1976).

Gadney, Alan, *How to Enter & Win Video/Audio Contests* (New York, NY: Facts on File Publications, 1981).

Gill, Johanna, *Video: State of the Art* (New York, NY: Rockefeller Foundation, 1976).

Graham, Dan, *Video, Architecture, Television: Writings on Video and Video Works, 1970-1978*, Benjamin H. D. Buchloh, ed. (Halifax, NS: Judson, 1988).

John G. Hanhardt, ed., *Video Culture: a Critical Investigation* (Layton, UT: Visual Studies Workshop Press, 1986).

Herzogenrath, Wulf, Ulrike Rosenbach, Marcel Odenbach, Jochen Gerz, and Klaus vom Bruch, *German Video and Performance*, design layout, David Buchan (Toronto, Canada: A Space, 1980).

Herzogenrath, Wulf and Nam June Paik, *Fluxus, Video* (Munich, Germany: S. Schreiber, 1983).

Himmelstein, Hal, *On the Small Screen: New Approaches in Television and Video Criticism* (New York, NY: Praeger, 1981).

Huffman, Kathy Rae, *A Retrospective: Long Beach Museum of Art, 1974-1984*, Video (Long Beach, CA: Long Beach Museum of Art, 1984).

Jonas, Joan, *He Saw Her Burning*, Video installation (Berlin, Germany: Berliner Kunstlerprogramm des DAAD, 1984).

Kalba, Kas, *The Video Implosion: Models for Reinventing Television* (Palo Alto, CA: Aspen Institute Program on Communications and Society, 1974).

Katz, John Stuart, *Elliten Autobiography: Film/Video/Photography* (Toronto: Art Gallery of Ontario, Education Branch, Media Programmes Division, 1978).

Kitchen Center for Video and Music, *The Kitchen, 1974-1975* (New York, NY: Haleakala, 1975).

Loeffler, Carl, *Performance Anthology, Source Book for a Decade of California Performance Art*, Darlene Tong, associate ed. (San Francisco, CA: Contemporary Arts Press, 1988).

London, Barbara J., *Video from Tokyo to Fukui and Kyoto*, exhibit (New York, NY: The Museum of Modern Art, 1979).

Marsh, Ken, *Independent Video* (San Francisco, CA: Straight Arrow Press, 1974).

Michaels, Eric, *Long Beach, Calif. Museum of Art Videthos: Cross Cultural Video by Artists* (Long Beach, CA: the Museum, 1979).

Muir, Anne Ross Muir, *A Woman's Guide to Jobs in Film and Television* (London, UK: Pandora Press, 1988).

Pavon Sarrelangue, Raul, *La Electronica en la Musica - y en el Arte*, 1st ed. (Mexico City, Mexico: INBA:SEP, 1981).

Pellegrino, Ronald, *The Electronic Arts of Sound and Light* (New York, NY: Van Nostrand Reinhold, 1983).

Quart, Barbara Koenig, *Women Directors: The Emergence of a New Cinema* (New York, NY: Praeger, 1988).

Roncarelli, Robi, *The Computer Animation Dictionary* (New York, NY: Springer-Verlag, 1989).

Rosenbach, Ulrike, *Performance Art*, exhibition (Boston, MA: Institute of Contemporary Art, 1983).

Schneider, Ira and Beryl Korot, *Video Art: an Anthology*, 1st ed., Mary Lucier, ed. (New York, NY: Harcourt Brace Jovanovich, 1976).

Smead, James Douglas, *Conceptual Texts: Redefining Intermedia Translation* (1984).

Steele, Lisa, *The Ballad of Dan Peoples* (New York, NY: New York University Press, 1979).

Daniel Thalman and Nadia Magnenat-Thalmann, eds., *State-of-the-art in Computer Animation: Proceedings of Computer Animation '89* (New York, NY: Springer-Verlag, 1989).

Town, Elke, *Video by Artists 2* (Toronto, Canada: Art Metropole, 1986).

Ulmer, Gregory, *Teletheory: Grammatology in the Age of Video* (New York, NY: Routledge, 1989).

Viola, Bill, *Bill Viola, Installations and Videotapes,* Barbara London, ed. (New York, NY: Museum of Modern Art, 1987).

—, *Bill Viola: Survey of a Decade,* Marilyn Zeitlin, ed. (Houston, TX).

Williams, Alan, *Republic of Images, A History of French Filmmaking* (Cambridge, MA: Harvard University Press).

The New Television: a Public/Private Art, essays, statements, and videotapes based on "Open Circuits: an International Conference on the Future of Television" organized by Fred Barzyk and Douglas Davis (Cambridge, MA: MIT Press, 1977).

Video Visions, a Medium Discovers Itself (New York, NY: New American Library, 1977).

Videokunst, Foto, Aktion/Performance, Feministische Kunst (Frankfurt, Germany: U. Rosenbach, 1982).

Contemporary Arts Press Distribution Catalog, Winter 1990 (San Francisco, CA: Contemporary Arts Press, 1990).

VIRTUAL REALITY

Bhargava, Sunita Wadekar "In 'The Virtual Last Supper' You Can Almost Sit at the Table" *Business Week* vol. 3243: 90J (Dec. 9, 1991).

Bylinsky, Gene, "The marvels of 'virtual reality.'" *Fortune* **123**, No. 11, 138-42 (June 3, 1991).

Carrabine, Laura, "Plugging into the Computer to Sense Virtual Reality," *Computer-Aided Engineering* **9**, No. 6, 16-21 (1990).

Ceteras, Seth, "Through the Virtual Looking Glass," *ETC.: A Review of General Semantics* **47**, No. 1, 67-71 (Spring, 1990).

Crabb, Don, "Mac Realities," *Byte* **16**, No. 9, 347-48 (Sept., 1991).

Davis, Bennett, "Grand Ilusions," *Discover* **11**, No. 6, 36-41 (June, 1990).

De Groot, Marc, "Virtual Reality," *UNIX Review* **8**, No. 8, 32-36 (1990).

Ditlea, Steve, "Computerized Tour Guides: Virtual Reality for Day Trippers - the Safer, Easier Way to Travel," *Omni* **13**, No. 1, 26 (Oct., 1990).

Doherty, Richard, "CyberSpace Travel; CAD Voyages through 'Virtual Reality,'" *Electronic Engineering Times* **547**, No. 31 (July 17, 1991).

Fisher, Scott S. and Jane Morril Tazelaar, "Living in a Virtual World," *BYTE* **15**, No. 7, 215-221 (1990).

Gillespie, T., "Computer Currents - Virtual Reality," *Library Journal* **116**, No. 18, 128 (1991).

Goldstein, Harry, "Virtual Reality: Computers May Soon Allow Us to Experience Worlds We Cannot Enter," *Utne Reader* **38**, 41-42 (March-April, 1990).

Grimes, J., "Virtual Reality 91 Anticipates Future Reality," *IEEE Computer Graphics and Applications* **11**, No. 6, 81-83 (1991).

Haggerty, M., "The Art of Artificial Reality," *IEEE Computer Graphics and Applications* **11**, No. 1, 8-14 (1991).

—, "Virtual Reality Dominates SIGGRAPH," *IEEE Computer Graphics and Applications* **11**, No. 5, 14-15 (1991).

Hamit, Francis, *Virtual Reality: Adventures in Cyberspace* (San Francisco, CA: Meckler, 1991).

Jacobson, Linda, "Virtual Reality: a Status Report," *AI Expert* **6**, No. 8, 26-33 (1991).

Josephson, Hal, "Virtual Reality is Virtually Around the Corner," *New Scientist* **127**, No. 1735, 30 (Sept. 22, 1990).

Kadrey, Richard, "Cyberthon 1.0," *Whole Earth Review* **70**, 54-57 (Spring, 1991).

Keizer, Gregg, "Virtual Reality," *Compute!* **13**, No. 6, 30-32 (1991).

Kelly, Kevin, "Virtual Reality; an Interview with Jaron Lanier," *Whole Earth Review* **64**, 108-19 (1989).

Kovsky, Steven, "Virtual Reality Technology Inspires Solid Research," *Digital Review* **7**, No. 27, 9-10 (July 16, 1990).

Krueger, Myron W., *Artificial Reality II* (Reading, MA: Addison-Wesley, 1991).

LaRue, James, "The Virtual Library: What You See is. What is Real?," *Wilson Library Bulletin* **65**, No. 7, 100-102 (1991).

Laurel, Brenda, *Computer as Theatre* (Reading, MA: Addison-Wesley, 1991).

—, "Strange New Worlds of Entertainment," *Compute!* **13**, No. 11, 102 (1991).

Lavroff, Nicholas, *Virtual Reality Playhouse* (Corte Madera, CA: Waite Group Press, 1992).

Levy, Steven, "Brave New World," *Rolling Stone* **580**, 92-97 (June 14, 1990).

Lidz, Franz, "It's the Real Thing, Virtually," *Sports Illustrated* **75** No. 15, 10-11 (Oct. 7, 1991).

MacNicol, Gregory, "What's Wrong with Reality? A Realist Reflects on Virtual Reality: Is it a Virtual Boon or a Boondoggle?" *Computer Graphics World* **13**, No. 11, 102-5 (1990).

Marks, Paul, "An Extra Dimension of Realism for Games Arcades," *New Scientist* **130**, No. 1763, 23 (April 6, 1991).

Newquist, Harvey P., III, "A Computer-Generated Suspension of Disbelief," *AI Expert* **6**, No. 8, 34-39 (1991).

Nugent W. R., "Virtual Reality - Advanced Imaging Special Effects Let You Roam in Cyberspace," *Journal of the American Society for Information Science* **42**, No. 8, 609-617 (1991).

Peli E., "Visual Issues in the Use of a Head-Mounted Monocular Display," *Optical Engineering* **29**, No. 8, 883-892 (1990).

Ponting, Bob, "Virtual Reality System Readied," *InfoWorld* **11**, No. 30, 17-18 (July 24, 1989).

Puttre, M., "Virtual Reality Comes into Focus," *Mechanical Engineering* **113**, No. 4, 56-59 (April, 1991).

Raitt D., "The Electronic Library Managers Guide to Virtual Reality," *Electronic Library* **9**, No. 1, 3-5 (1991).

Rheingold, Howard, "Travels in Virtual Reality," *Whole Earth Review* **67**, 80-87 (Summer, 1990).

—, "Virtual Reality: Is it Real Yet?" *Publish!* **6**, No. 8, 42-44 (August, 1991).

—, *Virtual Reality* (New York, NY: Summit Books, 1991).

Robinett, Warren, "Electronic Expansion of Human Perception," *Whole Earth Review* **72**, 16-21 (1991).

Saffo, Paul, "Virtual Reality is Almost Real," *Personal Computing* **14**, No. 6, 99-101 (1990).

Segura J. and D. Chouchan, "Virtual Reality, or Diving Into an Image," *Recherche* **22**, No. 229, 232-235 (Feb., 1991).

SIGGRAPH 91, *Tomorrow's Realities, Virtual Reality, Hypermedia* exhibition catalog (Las Vegas, NV: ASM, 1991).

Sobchack V., "New-Age Mutant Ninja Hackers," *ArtForum* **9**, No. 8, 24-26 (1991).

Stickrod, R. A., "Multimedia, Virtual Reality and All That Babble," *Leonardo* **24**, No. 1, 3 (1991).

Stix, Gary, "Reach Out: Touch is Added to Virtual Reality Simulations," *Scientific American* **264**, No. 2, 134 (1991).

Stone, Judith, "Turn On, Tune In, Boot Up; Timothy Leary, Drug Guru of the Sixties, Has Found a New Way to Hawk Hallucinations," *Discover* **12**, No. 6, 32-35 (1991).

Suprenant, Thomas, "Libraries, Information, and Virtual Reality," *Wilson Library Bulletin* **66**, No. 2, 95-99 (Oct., 1991).

Tisdale, Sallie, "It's Been Real," *Esquire* **115**, No. 4, 34-39 (April, 1991).

Truck, F, "The Prompt and Virtual Reality," *Leonardo*, **24**, No. 2, 171-173 (1991).

Wang, J., V. Chi, and H. Fuchs, "A Real-time Optical 3D Tracker for Head-Mounted Display Systems," *Computer Graphics* **24**, No. 2 (1990).

Wells M.J., and M. Venturino, "Performance and Head Movements Using a Helmet-Mounted Display with Different Sized Fields-of-View," *Optical Engineering* **29**, No. 8, 870-877 (1990).

Wheeler, David L., "Computer-created World of 'Virtual Reality' Opening New Vistas to Scientists," *Chronicle of Higher Education* **37**, No. 26, A6-A9 (1991).

Wolley, Benjamin, "Larger than Life," *New Statesman & Society* **4**, No. 166, 36-38 (1991).

Woolnough, Roger, "Box Combines Virtual Reality · Functions," *Electronic Engineering Times* **611**, 20-22 (Oct. 8, 1990).

Wright, Jeff, "Altered States: a Software Developer's Vision of the Future of Virtual Reality," *Computer Graphics World* **12**, No. 12, 77-81 (1989).

"Altered States," *Wilson Quarterly* **15**, No. 3, 124-25 (1991).

"Being and Believing: the Ethics of Virtual Reality," *Lancet* **338**, No. 8762, 283-84 (Aug. 3, 1991).

Virtual Reality Market Place, 1991-92 (Westport, CT: Meckler, 1991).

Virtual Reality '91, Proceedings of the Second Annual Conference on Virtual Reality, Artificial Reality, and Cyberspace Technology (Westport, CT: Meckler, 1991).

APPENDIX I: Organization Demographics

AUSTRALIA

Artsnet Electronic Network

Artspace

Ausgraph—Australasian Computer
Graphics Association

Australian Centre for the Arts and
Technology (ACAT),
Canberra Institute of the Arts

Australian Network for Art and
Technology (ANAT)

Centre for Human Aspects of Science
and Technology,
University of Sydney

College of Fine Arts,
University of New South Wales

Experimental Art Foundation

Martin Bequest Traveling
Scholarships, Arts Management
Pty. Ltd.

Melbourne Computer Graphics Forum,
Swinburne Institute

New Music Australia
(New Music Articles) (NMA)

Photofile, The Australian Centre
for Photography, Ltd.

School of Media Art, College of Fine
Arts/University of New South Wales

Science-Art Research Centre

Video Art Society, University of
Tasmania, Centre of the Arts

AUSTRIA

Camera Austria, Forum Stadtpark

De Sterreichisches Foto Archiv,
Im Museum Moderner Kunst

Institut Fur Integrative
Musikpadagogik und
Polyasthetische Erziehung

Kulturdata

Lehrkanzel fur
Kommunikationstheorie,
Hochschule fur Angewandte
Kunst-Wien

Prix Ars Electronica

Transit

BELGIUM

Agenda of Audiovisual Festivals
in Europe

Association des Centres Culturels,
La Botanique

Le Premier Guide de L'Audiovisuel
Europeen (First Guide of European
Audiovisual Resources)

Logos Foundation

Musee de la Photographie, Charleroi

Photographie Ouverte

Science and Art

University Gent—Lab. Soete, Applied
Mechanics—Workshop Holography

BRAZIL

Image and Sound Museum

CANADA

Alberta

American Society for Aesthetics

Banff Centre for the Arts,
Media Arts Program

University of Calgary, Art Department

British Columbia

Center for Image and Sound Research

Computer Graphics Research Lab,
School of Computing Science

Cariboo College, Digital Arts & Design

Ontario

A Space

Bell Canada Award in Video Art

Canada Council—Audio Production
Grants, Communications Section

Canada Council—Integrated Media
Grants

Canada Council—Media Projects in
Dance Grants

Durham College, Graphic Design

Fine Arts Interdisciplinary Computer
Center, York University

Fringe Research Holographics, Inc

Inter/Access

Interference Hologram Gallery

Musicworks

Ontario Arts Council

Ontario College of Art

Sheridan College,
Computer Graphics Lab

Vivid Group

Quebec

3D International Newsletter

Association pour la Creation et la
Recherche Electroacoustique du
Quebec (ACREQ)

Canadian ElectroAcoustic Community
(CEC)

Canadian Holographic Society

College du Vieux-Montreal, Design

Concordia University, 3Dmt Center

Elizabeth Greenshields Foundation
Festival International du Film par
ordinateur de Montreal (FIFOM)

International Festival of Computer
Graphics Films of Montreal

International Festival of Films on Art

La Cite des Arts et des Nouvelle
Technologies de Montreal

Parachute

Trebas Institute

Universite de Montreal,
Sector electro-acoustique

DENMARK

Danish Institute of Electroacoustic
Music (DIEM), The Concert Hall
Aarhus

ESTONIA

Computer Music & Musical
Informatics Association

FRANCE

American University of Paris,
Mathematics

Biennale des Arts Electroniques de
Maiselle, Eurekam

Centre National Art and Technologie

Das Synthetische Mischgewebe,
The Synthetic Mixture of Fabrics

Foundation de Lourmarin
Lauret-Vibert, Chateau de
Lourmarin

French National Institute for Research
in Computer Science and Control
(INRIA)

Groupe de Researches Musicales
(GRM/IRA)

IRCAM

Image Technology and Art (ATI),
Department of Plastic Arts,
University of Paris

International Directory of Electronic
Arts (IDEA), CHAOS

International Stereoscopic Union

La Recherche Photographique, Paris
Audiovisuel

Louis Vuitton Moet Hennessy Science
for Art Prize, LVMH,
Direction di Development

Media Investment Club

Michael Karolyi Memorial Foundation,
Le Vieux Mas

Musee de l'Holographie,
Forum des Halles

Panayiotis Vassilakis

Stereo-Club Francais

GERMANY

Art+Com

Bilder Digital Galerie

Computer in der Musik: Uber den Einsatz in Wissenschaft, Komposition, und Padagogik

Deutscher Akademischer Austauschdienst (DADD)—Artists in Berlin Program

Die Audio Gruppe

Electronic Media Workshop—Art School in Leipzig, Werkstatt fur electronische Medien

European Media Art Festival

European Photography

Forschungstelle fur Human

Galerie Eylau'5

HolografieLabor Osnabruck

Institute of Medical Psychology

Kunsthochschule fur Medien

Museum der Stadt Gladbeck

Museum fur Fotokopie

Museum fur Holographie & Neue Visuelle Medien

Stereo Journal

Weisses Haus Gallery

Westdeutscher Rundfunk Koeln, Studio Akustische Kunst

Young Electronic Arts, Atelier coArt

Zentrum fur Kunst Und Medientechnolgie Karlsruhe

GREECE

Hellenic Institute of Holography

HUNGARY

Hungarian Academy of Sciences, Central Research for Physics

Hungart, Fine Art Section

INTART—Society for Sciences, Arts and Pedagogy

International Society for the Inter-Disciplinary Study of Symmetry (ISIS-SYMMETRY)

SYMMETRION—The Institute for Advanced Symmetry Studies

Society for the Sciences, Arts and Education, Technical University

INDIA

Indian Institute of Technology

IRELAND

Artists Collective of Northern Ireland, Queen Street Studios

National College of Art & Design

Tyrone Guthrie Center

ISRAEL

American Israel Cultural Foundation (AICF)

Holography Israel

Third Dimension Ltd, The Israeli Gallery of Holograms

Wolf Foundation

ITALY

Association per Lo Studio Delle, Internazioni Tra Arte, Scienza & Technologia

Centro Ricerche Musicali

Centro di Calcolo, Universita Degli Studi Di Camerino

Conservatory of Music, Musicological Department of CNUCE/CNR

Edizioni L'Agrifoglio

International Summerschool Computer and Art

Universita delgli Studi di Bologna, Instituto do Comunicazione

Universita' Di Trieste, DEEI

Xeros Art Centre Documentazione

JAPAN

American Studies Foundation, Inc.

Asahi News Publishing Company, Asahi PC

Council for the International Bienniale in Nagoya, The Chunichi Shiumbun

Holocom, Division of Domus Int

Holograpohy Display of Artists & Engineers Club (HODIC), Central Research Institute, Toppan Printing Co.

Institute of Art and Design

Nagano University, Department of Industrial Information

National Center for Science Information Systems (NACSIS)

Nicograph Association

Synergistics Institute

University of Tsukuba, School of Art and Design

Visual Computer, University of Tokyo

MEXICO

Instituto Nacional De Bellas Artes

Laboratorio de Informatica Musical, Escuela de Musica, Universidad de Guanajuato

NEW ZEALAND

Dowse Art Museum

POLAND

Sound Basis Visual Art Festival

PORTUGAL

ACARTE, Fundacao Calouste Gulbenkian

Center for Structural Mechanics and Engineering, Technical University of Lisbon (CMEST)

University of Aveiro Portugal, Communication and Art Dept.

RUSSIA

Lux Aeterna Lumia Theater, Lux Aeterna Lumia Teater

Prometheus, All-union Coordinating Center for the Arts, Science and Technology

SPAIN

Center for the Diffusion of Contemporary Music

Hologramas

Laboratorio de Informatica Y Electronica Musical (LIEM), Centro para la Difusion de la Musica Contemporanea

SWEDEN

Holo Media AB

Living Art Center, Living Design International

Stockholm Electronic Art Awards

SWITZERLAND

3-D Foto World

Lugano Academy of the Electronic Arts

Task Force on Computer Generated Music, IEEE Computer Society

THE NETHERLANDS

3-D Book Productions

Dutch Foundation of Perception and Holography

Emove, Laboratory for Virtual Musical Instrument Design

European Cultural Foundation

European Network of Centers on Culture and Technology

Hologrammen Galerie

Hooykaas/Stanfield

Inter-Society for the Electronic Arts (ISEA)

International Society
    for Contemporary Music,
    c/o Gaudeamus

Media Art Department,
    AKI Art Academy

Mediamatic Magazine

P/F Publishing BV

Perspetif Center for Photography

Secretariat of the European Network
    of Centres on Culture
    and Technology

V2 Organization

USA

3D Electronic BBS

Computer Graphics Education
    Newsletter

Screen-L

Alabama

Society of Professional Videographers

University of Alabama—Birmingham

Arkansas

Arkansas Artists Council,
    Heritage Center

Arizona

Arizona State University

Communication Design

University of Arizona,
    Department of Mathematics

California

11th Hour Productions

ART (if) ACT

Abby Joslin & Associates

Advanced Information Methods, Inc.,
    Corporate and Technology

Ampersand Productions

Antelope Valley College

Anti Gravity Workshop

Apple Productions

Art Com

Art Technologies

ArtNetwork

Artists Television Access (ATA)

Artkitek

Arts & Sciences Production

Balungan

Bay Area Center for Art & Technology
    (BACAT)

Big Pond Productions, Inc.

BodySynth

Brainstorms

Buckminster Fuller Institute

Bureau of Architecture

CADRE Institute: Computers in Art
    and Design/Research and
    Education, School of Art and Design

Cal State LA, Fine Art Department

California College of the Arts and
    Crafts, Computer Graphics Support

California Institute of the Arts, Film
    and Video

Capp Street Project

Center for Computer Art and
    Technology

Center for Computer Research in
    Music and Acoustics (CCRMA),
    Music Deptartment, Stanford
    University

Center for Computer-Assisted
    Research in Humanities (CCARH)

Center for Contemporary Music,
    Mills College, Department of Music

Center for Experiments in Art,
    Information & Technology (CEAIT),
    California Institute of the Arts

Cherry.Optical Society

Chrysalis Foundation

Cinematograph, The San Francisco
    Cinematheque

City of Oakland

Coactive Aesthetics

CompuAct

Computer Arts Institute

Computer Graphics Professional,
    Graphic Channels Inc.

Computer Music Journal

Conceptual Design and Information
    Arts, San Francisco State University

Creative Computer Exhibit, California
    Museum of Science and Industry

CyberEdge Journal

Cyberspace Gallery

Department of Physics & Astronomy,
    California State University

DigiQuest

Djerassi Resident Artists Program

Dorland Mountain Colony

Dynamic Showcase: A Hypermedia
    Journal

East End Management

Electric Waltz Video

Everything Everything

Experimental Musical Instruments

Exploratorium

Friends of Photography

Geary's Advertising Department

George Coates Performance Works

Giant Records, A & R

Good Sound Foundation

Hewlett Packard Labs

Holographic Visions

Holography Institute

Hotwire Productions

Humanities Computing Facility (HCF)

Hypertelsaloon

ICTV

IEEE Society on Social Implications
    of Technology,
    Otis/Parsons Art Institute

Image + Sound

International Computer Music
    Association

International Digital Electroacoustic
    Music Archive (IDEAMA),
    Center for Computer Research
    in Music & Acoustics

International Directory of Design,
    Penrose Press

Interval Magazine, Interval Foundation

Inventors Workshop International

Just Intonation Network

Labyrinth, Editorial Dept.

Laser Arts Society for Education and
    Research (LASER)

Leonardo Music Journal

Leonardo, the International Society for
    the Arts, Sciences and Technology

Life On A Slice

Los Angeles Contemporary
    Exhibitions (LACE)

Los Angeles High School, Computer
    Science

Los Angeles School of Holography

Media Magic

Midi/Worldmusic, USA

Muscle Fish Multimedia Engineering

Music Engineering Technology,
    Cogswell Polytechnical College

NEXA, Science-Humanities
    Convergence Program,
    San Francisco State University

New Langton Arts

Open Channels, Long Beach Museum
    of Art

Pandect, Inc.

Paramount Publishing

Penrose Press

Porter Computer Arts

Positive Light Holographics

Prix Ars Electronica

Professional Sound Corporation

Reel 3-D Enterprises

Richmond Unified High School District

San Francisco State University, Art
    Department

San Francisco State University, Physics
    Department

Sarah Bendersky, Inc.

School of Holography

Science and the Arts

Sincere Technologies

Sound Choice

Southern California Laser Arts Society

Southern California Video

StereoScope International

Syntex Gallery

Third Dimension Arts, Inc.

Trans Data

VDB Designs

VR Dimension

Various Media

Verbum Gallery of Digital Art

Viacom Cable

Video Free America

Women in Film

YLEM: Artists Using Science & Technology

Zakros InterArts

Zyzzyva

Colorado

University of Colorado, Fine Arts Department

Connecticut

Artificial Reality Corp.

Center for Art and Technology, Connecticut College

Real Arts Way (RAW), Hartford Arts Center

District of Columbia

American Association for the Advancement of Science, Art of Science and Technology Program

American Association of University Women Educational Foundation, AAUW Educational Foundation

Art, Science and Technology Institute

Center for the Advanced Study in the Visual Arts, National Gallery of Art

Cocoran School of Art

Fund for US Artists at International Festivals and Exhibitions, National Endowment for the Arts

George Washington University, Fine Arts

International Sculpture Center (ISC)

Preservation Initiative, National Endowment for the Humanities

Task Force and Technical Committee on Computer Generated Music, IEEE Computer Society

Tech 2000 Ivia

Florida

ACM Educators Newsletter, SIGGRAPH Educators Newsletter

American Journal of Computer Art in Education

Center for Research in Arts & Technology

Computer Art Contest

Holographic Images, Inc.

Ringling School of Art and Design, Computer Graphics

SGML User's Special Interest Group on Hypertext and Multimedia

Georgia

American College for Applied Arts

Artlink, Electronic Information Center for the Visual Arts

Atlanta Gallery of Holography

Catalogue of Music Software

Emory University, Cataloguing Dept.— Woodruff Library

Hambidge Center for Creative Arts and Sciences

Image Film/Video Center

Public Domain

Savannah College of Art and Design, Video Department

Hawaii

Neon News

SFCA Artist Fellowships

VARIOUS Media, Visionary Artists Resources

Illinois

Artist Book Works

Artscience Gallery, Chicago Museum of Science

CERL Sound Group—University of Illinois

Center for New Television

Chicago Museum of Science and Industry

Computer Music Project, University of Illinois at Urbana Champaign

Fine Arts Research & Holography Center

Holography in Education

Integraf

KAOS

Museum of Fine Arts Research and Holography

National Center for Supercomputing Applications, University of Illinois at Urbana-Champaign

Northeastern Illinios University, Art Department

RISKART: The Jay Riskind Studio

School of the Art Institute of Chicago, Art and Technology Department

Society for the History of Technology, The University of Chicago Press, Journals Division

Symbolic Sound Corporation/University of Illinois CERL Sound Group

University of Illinois at Champaign, Art Department

University of Illinois at Chicago, Art Department

Kentucky

Artswatch

Department of Art, University of Kentucky

Isaac W. Bernheim Foundation

Louisiana

Louisiana State University— Architecture, Interior Design, Landscape Architecture and Art

Massachusetts

Arstechnica: Center for Art and Technology, University of Massachusetts/Amherst

Artists Foundation

BEEP Sounds

Computer Center, Harvard University

Computer Graphics, Art Dept, Fine Arts Center, University of MA/Amherst

Computer Museum Boston

Cummington Community of the Arts

Do While Studio

Eastgate Systems, Hypertext Systems and Services

Independent Media Distributors

Massachusetts Institute of Technology (MIT), Media Laboratory

MIT List Visual Arts Center, Weisner Building

MIT Media Laboratory

MIT Center for Advanced Visual Studies

Massachusetts College of Art

NEWCOMP

Nantucket Island School of Design and the Arts, Residency Program

New England Computer Music Association

New England Film/Video Fellowship Program

Northeastern University, Graphic Arts Program

Technology and Conservation

Maryland

EthnoForum

Interactive Multimedia Association (IMA)

Sturvil Corporation

Maine

Synchronicity Holograms

Michigan

Catalogue of Computer Programs for Music Education

Center for Narrative and Technology

Center for Performing Arts and Technology, University of Michigan

Lightworks Magazine

UnderWorld Industries

Minnesota

American School of Neon

ArtBase BBS
Intermedia Arts Minnesota
N.Y. Mills Arts Retreat

Missouri
Art Research Center
Imaginary Enterprises
International Institute for Modern
  Structural Art
St. Louis Community College—
  Florissant Valley

Mississippi
Mississippi State University

North Carolina
American Physician Art Association

Nebraska
Bemis—Center for Contemporary Arts

New Hampshire
American Gamelan Institute
Eternal Network Archive
Frog Peak Music
MacDowell Colony
Typeworld
New Jersey
Art Horizons
Creative Glass Center of America
Glassboro State University, Art
HolograFx
International Art Horizons,
  Deptartment RAU
Rutgers University, Art
William Patterson College, Art
  Department

New Mexico
D.H. Lawrence Summer Fellowship,
  University of New Mexico
Soundings Press
Videographic Arts

New York
ACM SIGGRAPH, Member Services
  Department
Adolph and Ester Gottleib Foundation
Afterimage, Visual Studies Workshop
American Academy in Rome
Andrew Gemant Award, American
  Institute of Physics
Art & Science Collaborations, Inc (ASCI)
Art and Technology Resource File—
  Video/Audio Installation Touring
  Project
Artists Rights Society, Inc. (ARS)
Arts, Crafts and Theater Safety (ACTS)
Asian Cultural Council
Bard College, Music Program Zero
Bellagio Study and Conference Center,
  The Rockefeller Foundation

Betty Brazil Memorial Fund,
  Women Sculptor Grant
Blue Mountain Center
Bronx Museum of the Arts
Center for International
  Contemporary Art
Center for Safety in the Arts,
  Art Hazard Info Center
Change, Inc
Checkerboard Foundation, Inc.
David Bermant Foundation: Color,
  Light, Motion
Deep Dish Video
Deptartment of Humanities,
  State University of New York
Dome Gallery
Downtown Ensemble
EAS Department
Edward F. Albee Foundation
Experimental Television Center Ltd.
Fashion Institute of Technology,
  Computer Graphics
Feature
Film/Video Arts, Inc.
Guggenheim Museum
Harlem Studio Museum
Harvestworks, Inc.
Helena Rubenstein Fellowships,
  Whitney Museum Independent
  Study Programs
Institute for Art and Urban Resources,
  Art and Urban Resources
Institute for Computers in the Arts,
  School of Visual Arts
Integrated Electronic Arts Rensselaer
  (iEAR), Department of the Arts
International Center of Photography
International Festival of the Image,
  Montage
International Society of Copier Artists
  (ISCA)
Josh Baer Gallery
Kitchen
Lightwork
Liquid Crystal Music
MedArt USA, Inc.
Millay Colony for the Arts
Mirage Gallery
Monbusho Scholarshhip,
  Japan Information Center
Multi Media Arts Gallery
Museum Computer Network Spectra,
  Syracuse University, School of
  Infomation Studies
Musical Microcomputer: A Resource
  Guide
Musician's Music Software Catalog
New York Experimental Glass
  Workshop

New York Foundation for the Arts,
  Artist in Residence Program
Panscan, Panpost
Parabola Arts Foundation
Pauline Oliveros Foundation Inc.
Pollock-Krasner Foundation
Pratt Institute, Computer Graphics
Research Center for Music
  Iconography, City University of
  New York
Research Center for Musical
  Iconography (RCMI), City University
  of New York
Rochester Institute of Technology,
  CIAS
Ronald Feldman Fine Arts
School of Photographic Arts and
  Sciences & The Technical and
  Education Center of the Graphic
  Arts, Rochester Institute of
  Technology
School of Photographic Arts and
  Sciences
School of Visual Arts, MFA Degree
  Program in Computer Art
Shearwater Foundation
Solomon R. Guggenheum Museum
Sonic Architecture
Storefront for Art and Architecture
Syracuse University, Art Media Studies
Technical and Educational Center of
  the Graphic Arts, Rochester
  Institute of Technology
Visual Studies Workshop
Whitney Independent Study Program
Women Make Movies
Women's Interart Center,
  Artist-in-Residence Program
Women's Studio Workshop
Yaddo Estate, Corporation of Yaddo

Ohio
Art Academy of Cincinnati
Burning Press
Cleveland Institute of Art,
  Computer Arts Program
Interface Newsletter, ACAD,
  Ohio State University
National Stereoscopic Association
Ohio State University, Advanced
  Computing Center for the Arts
  and Design
Ohio State University, Department of
  Theatre
Society for Literature and Science
  (SLS), School of Interpersonal
  Communications
TIMARA (Technology in Music and
  Related Arts), Oberlin Conservatory

Oregon
Abaci Gallery of Computer Art

Art Department, Portland State
University

Godlove Award

Metropolitan Arts Commission

Mt. Hood Community College,
Visual Art

Pennsylvania

Allegheny College, Art Department

Association for Computers
and the Humanities,
Carnegie-Mellon University,
Center for Art and Technology

Carnegie Mellon University,
Studio for Creative Inquiry

Franklin Institute of Science

Gallery for Holography

Graphic Arts Technical Foundation

Holo-Gram

Holography Workshop

International Arts-Medicine
Association (IAMA)

Kuztown University, Department of
Art Ed/Crafts

Mattress Factory

Museum Computer Network

New Arts Program

Small Computers in the Arts

University of the Arts

Yellow Springs Institute for
Contemporary Studies and the Arts

Rhode Island

Mindesign

Rhode Island School of Design

Warwick Museum

South Carolina

Clemson University, Art Department

Tennessee

University of Tennessee,
Art Department

Texas

Connemara Conservancy Foundation

Elusive Image

Endangered Species Media Project

Engineering Technology Institute

Houston Holography Center,
The Anthony Foundation

Texas A&M University, Visualization
Laboratory

Virginia

1708 East Main Gallery

Center for Music Technology,
Radford University

Computer Graphics Arts Directory

Education Council of the Graphic Arts
Industry, Inc.

George Mason University, Art and Art
History

Media, Electronic Art and Visual
Communication Arts & Design,
School of the Arts

National Copier Art

Society of Photographic Scientists &
Engineers

Visual Resources, James Madison
University

Vermont

International Association
for the Astronomical Arts

University of Vermont, Computer and
Information Technology

Vermont Studio Colony

Washington

Art Business & Technology

Artistic License

Arts Wire

Hartness-Schoos Galleries

International Society for Optical
Engineering

Northwest Electronic Musicians
(NEMUS)

Perspectives of New Music

Sheehan Gallery

University of Washington,
School of Music

Wisconsin

Blue Rose Studio

Computers in Music Research,
School of Music

John Michael Kohler Arts Center

West Virginia

Cooke Foundation

Wyoming

Ucross Foundation, Ucross Route

UNITED KINGDOM

AN Publications

Art Access/Networking

Arts Media Group

Association of Sculpture and
Engineering Techniques

Barrow and Geraldine S. Cadbury Trust

Biology Department

British Journal of Photography,
Information Directory

Center for Research into Applications
of Computers to Music,
University of Lancaster

Centre for Advanced Studies in
Computer Aided Art and Design
(CASCAAD), Middlesex University

Chapter Arts Centre Media Education
Institute

Community Copyart Ltd.

Computers in Teaching Initiative
Centre for Music

Creative Camera, Battersea Art Center

Design and Artists Copyright Society
(DACS)

Directions

Directory of Exhibition Spaces

Documentary Video Associates, Ltd.

European Visual Arts Information
Network (EVIAN), The Library,
Suffolk Cottage

Extensions, Aberdeen Art Gallery

Frachaos

Greater London Arts Association,
Director of Leisure and Recreation

Grizedale Forest, Northern Arts

Gulbenkian Foundation, UK Branch

Hann Gallery

Holography Group, Salisbury College
of Art

Independent Media

Independent Photography Directory

Inter-Action Centre

International Institute for
Conservation of Historic
and Artistic Works

Kettles Yard Gallery

Leverhulme Trust

Literary and Linguistic Computing,
Institute of Advanced Studies

Media, Culture and Society, Sage
Publications, Ltd

Micro Gallery: Computer Information
Room, The National Gallery

Museum of the Moving Image

National Gallery

Photographic Journal, Royal
Photographic Society

Rose Farm

South West Arts

Stereoscopic Society

Third Dimension Society

University of Edinburgh

University of London Audio Visual
Centre, Interactive Videodisc
Technology Certificate,
North Wing Studios

Vasari Project, The National Gallery

West Midlands Arts' Artists
in Industry Program,
West Midlands Arts

Winston Churchill Memorial Trust,
Churchill Traveling Fellowships

Women's Work

Yorkshire Sculpture Park

WEST INDIES

Barbados Optics Ltd.

APPENDIX II: Individual Demographics

AUSTRALIA

Bannigan, Phillip
Burt, Warren
Caines, Chris
Callas, Peter
Euy, Deborah
Gray, Noel
Grayson, Richard
Hall, Adrian
Illert, Chris
Kreger, Tim
Linz, Ranier
Nason, Dale
Petterd, Robin
Pope, Robert
Ramsden, Stuart
Rice, Crispin
Scott, Jill
Worrall, David

AUSTRIA

Ascott, Roy
Faber, Monika
Frisinghelli, Christine
Hattinger, Gottfried
Kriesch, Richard
Roscher, Wolfgang
Schopf, Christine

BELGIUM

Beyls, Peter
Boone, Pierre Michel
Darge, Moniek
De Bievre Blondeel, Maria
   and Guy
Guisen, Paul
Raes, Godfried-Willem
Ryckeboer, Guy
Van Boom, Marc
Vercheval, Georges

BRAZIL

Martinelli, Sergio

CANADA

Alberta
Brackett, Peggy
Diamond, Sara
Elliott, Kevin

Kostyniuk, Ronald
MacLeod, Douglas
Shiner, Roger
British Columbia
Berryman, Jeffrey
Bishko, Leslie
Howard, Glenn
Ontario
Barrett, Dale
Bartley, Wende
Bobrow, Eric
Freeman, John
Gagnon, Jean
Horwood, Michael
King, Robin
Mannery, Woody
Mayrhofer, Ingrid
Ng, George
Orfald, Cathy
Paterson, Nancy
Sowdon, Michael
Vincent, Vincent John
Warme, Steve
Quebec
Anderson, Fortner
Clouette, Lynda
Fischer, Herve
Graham, Patricia
Heaton, Lorna
Lamy, Francois
Leduc, Daniel
Leonard, David
Major, Ginette
Normandeau, Robert
Pilon, Yves
Pontbriand, Chantal
Roy, Myke
Rozon, Rene
Schryer, Claude
Thwaites, Hal

CHINA

Huang, Yongping
Quan, Long

DENMARK

Lausten, Thorbjorn
Brandorff, Steffen
Siegel, Wayne

ESTONIA

Rais, Mark

FINLAND

Roos, Matts

FRANCE

Battier, Marc
Bayle, Francois
Bureaud, Annick
Chemin, Isabelle
Christakis, A.M.
Clayson, James
Feilane, Dora
Forest, Fred
Geoffroy, Christiane
Huebner, Guido
Karolyi, Catherine
LaFont, Hubert
Lippe, Cort
Lisle, Juliet
Martin, Claude
Philippe, Jean-Marc
Takis
Ventouillac, Guy

GERMANY

De Vries, Gerrit
Dion, Emanuel
Eisenbeis, Manfred
Franke, Herbert
Goebel, Johannes
Hatle, Karl-Heinz
John, K.P. Ludwig
Jungk, Robert
Klotz, Heinrich
Lauk, Matthias
Maubrey, Benoit
Muller-Pohle, Andreas
Orazem, Vito
Poppel, Ernst
Schaffrath, Helmut
Schenk, Sygun
Schneider, Wolfgang
Shaw, Jeffrey
Siegfried, Walter
Supper, Martin
Sutterlin, Christa
Urbons, Klaus

von Hase, Deitrich
Wegner, Thomas
Zec, Peter

GREECE

Keranis, Ch.
Mitropoulos, Mit
Zouni, Opy

GUAM

Moore, Stephen

HUNGARY

Csaji, Attila
Darvas, Gyorgy
Erdi, Peter
Greguss, P.
Nagy, Denes
Tusa, Erzsebet

INDIA

Bhatnagar, R.K.

INDONESIA

Sadra, I Wayan

IRELAND

Gibbons, Mealla
Loughlin, Bernard
McNab, Theo
Turpin, John Timothy

ISRAEL

Gruder, Yaron E.
Hoenich, P.K.
Shimon, Hameiri

ITALY

Balancia, Monica
Bianchini, Laura
Camilleri, Lelio
Capucci, Pier Luigi
D'Angelo, Aldo
Fogar, Alessandro
Giomi, Francesco
Hmeljak, Matjaz

Pivi, Alberto
Polzonetti, Alberto

JAPAN

Abe, Yoshiyuki
Iwata, Fujio
Kodera, Mitsuo
Kunii, Tosiyasu
Mitamura, Shunsuke
Nishimura, Yumi
Shimono, Takao

MEXICO

Enriquez, Manuel
Morales-Manzanares,
  Roberto
Nunez, Francisco

POLAND

Kolodziejski, Richard

PORTUGAL

Santo, Harold
Vasques Dias, Amilcar
de Azaredo Perdigao, Maria
  Madalena

RUSSIA

Friedman, Damiel
Galeyev, Bulat

SPAIN

Nunez, Adolfo
Weiss, Daniel

SWEDEN

Cronsioe, Igor
Forsberg, Mona
Rikskonserter, Svenska

SWITZERLAND

Baggi, Denis
Bernold, Thomas
Bill, Max
Zabala, Horatio

THE NETHERLANDS

Adriaansens, Alex
Batten, Trevor
Brouwer, Joke

Delhaas, Rik
Gierstberg, Frits
Hesper, Theo
Hooykaas, Madelon
Kleinsmiede, Harry zur
Mulder, Axel
Shaw, Jeffrey
Stansfield, Elsa
van Baasbank, M. C.
van der Plas, Wim
Velthoven, W.
Vroege, Bas
Walraven, Chris
Zonnevylle, Hans

USA

Alabama
Nunley, Deana
Wixson, Steve
Arizona
Altman, Richard
Smith, Roberta
Devito, Carl

California
Acevedo, Victor
Aft, Wendy
Alexander
Alves, William
Amirkhanian, Charles
Anderson, Steve
Apostolos, Margo
Apple, Jeffrey
Austin, Larry
Bacher, Lutz
Bauman, Marcia
Beasley, Bruce
Bender, Jennifer
Bendersky, Sarah
Berg, Paul
Bischoff, John
Blankinship, Paul
Blum, Thom
Bray, Anne
Britton, Ben
Brodsky, Michael
Brown, Chris
Bruner, Genevieve
Carpenter, Rachel
Chafe, Chris
Clar, Richard
Cleere, Bill
Cochran, Connor Freff
Coniglio, Mark
Cox, Martin

Critchfield, Harry
Davis, Bob
Davis, Kathy
de Marchi, John Anthony
Deken, Joseph
Delaney, Ben
Dickson, Stewart
Dittman, Roy
Dunne, Jacqui
Dwyer, Gary
Edgar, Robert
Edwards, Kimberly
Ehenkranz, Ruth
Emshwiller, Ed
Etzen, David-John
Ferguson, Theodosia
Fleck, Robert
Follis, Charles
Fox, John
Franklin, Constance
Franklin, Marjorie
Gabriel, Robert
Garcia-Alvarado, Belen
Garrett, David
Gaw, David
Gerstein, David
Glaesner, Sallee
Glasier, Jonathon
Glynn, David
Goldstein, Bonnie
Gonchar, Nancy
Goto, Reiko
Graham, Victoria
Grant-Ryan, Pamela
Harris, Craig
Hedelman, Harold
Hennage, Dan
Herrick, Kennan
Hershman, Lynn
Hollier, Thomas
Hopkin, Bart
Horton, Barbara
Howard, Richard
Hubel, Paul
Hurd, David
Hurtig, Brent
Joslin, Abby
Junker, Howard
Kaul, Paras
Kelzer, Kimberly
Kemp, Arnold
Kent, Eleanor
Kirby, Lynn
Klein, Sherman
Koach, Damon

Koch, Ed
Latta, Craig
Lauzzana, Raymond Guido
Legrady, George
Lentini, Luigi
Lewis, Annie
Lippman, Gene Paul
Loeffler, Carl
Malina, Roger
Malloy, Judy
Marsanyi, Robert
Martin, David
McCormack, Sharon
McNabb, Michael
McSherry, Stewart
Moran, Kevin
Mosher, Mike
Murray, Jeffery
Nathanson, Theodore Herzl
Neeley, Rebecca
Nicoloff, Alex
Olczak, George
Olson, Bernadette
Olson, Ronald
Osborn, Ed
Packer, Randall
Palmer, Christopher John
Payne, Maggi
Penrose, Denise
Perkins, Carolyn
Pink, Patty
Poitras, Laura
Pope, Stephen
Porter, Gene Lavon
Primeau, Mark
Prince, Patric Doherty
Rapoport, Sonya
Ray, David
Reagan, Trudy Myrhh
Reiser, Beverly
Reiser, Hans
Richards, Brigid
Richards, Peter
Ricks, Evan
Rinehart, Marion
Ris, Anet Margot
Roads, Curtis
Roberts, Sara
Rosenboom, David
Rosenthal, Henry
Rupkalvis, John
Scholz, Carter
Scott, Alex
Selfridge-Field, Eleanor
Sen, Amit

Severinghaus, Edwin
Shapiro, Charles
Skratz, G. P.
Slayton, Joel
Smith, Edith MacNamara
Soe, Valerie
St. Cyr, Suzanne
Stahl, Frieda
Steingrubner, Joachim
Stilley, Tucker
Strasmich, Michael
Strauss, Carolyn
Subotnick, Morton
Sullivan, Barbara
Tait, Jen
Takahara, Beau
Tamblyn, Christine
Tratner, Alan Arthur
Trayle, Mark
Van De Bogart, Willard
Van Raalte, Chris
Warren, Nik
Weber, Sally
Weeks, Susan
Weiss, Lenore
Wheaton, Jim
White, Dr.
Whitehead, Justine
Wilson, Steve
Wold, Erling
Wood, Patte
Worthington, Nancy

Colorado
Johnson, James
Roitz, Charles

Connecticut
Easton, Eda
Krueger, Myron
Smalley, David
Zahler, Noel

District of Columbia
Baggi, Denis
Dewatre, Mary
Furchgott, David
Haus, Goffredo
Kratochvil, Beverly
Molina, Sam
Stern, Virginia

Florida
Lieberman, Larry
Marsh, Bruce
Morie, Ford Jacquelyn
Newcomb, Steven
Palazzi, Maria

Reid, Melynda
Rutkovsky, Paul
Saenger, Elizabeth
Spencer, Donald

Georgia
Barber, Judith
Beers, Lisa
Demmers, Jim
Drop, John
Gess, Richard
Murray, Lisa
Ryan, Paul
Sandman, Alan

Hawaii
Crawford, V L
Pirsig, T
Rosen, Peter

Iowa
Truck, Frederick John

Illinois
Aprison, Barry
Beauchamp, James
Cox, Donna
DeFanti, Tom
Haken, Lippold
Hebel, Kurt
Jeter, Ida
Kac, Eduardo
Kauffman, James
MacShane, Jim
Riskind, Jay
Sandin, Dan
Scaletti, Carla
Tipei, Sever
Truckenbrod, Joan
Weintraub, Jane

Kentucky
Free, Phyllis
Graves, Jan
Kincaid, Ted
McClure III, Charles

Louisiana
Singer, Shirlee

Massachusetts
Bell, Bill
Bernstein, Mark
Brisson, Harriet
Casdin-Silver, Harriet
Ceely, Robert
Don, Abbe
Duesenberry, John
Goldring, Elizabeth
Graber, Jeffrey

Hall, Jennifer
Janney, Christopher
Kepes, Gyorgy
Kline, Katy
Land, Richard
Laske, Otto
Loeb, Arthur
Lueft, Lorraine
Mallary, Robert
Mann, Steve
Mazlish, Bruce
Piene, Otto
Platt, Ron
Reiken, Rick
Schur, Susan
Trocki, Frank

Maryland
Fox, Jenifer
Kirsch, Russell
Kirsch, Joan
Lovelett, Felicia
McWhinnie, Harold
Signell, Karl

Maine
Jurewicz, Arlene

Michigan
Arnheim, Rudolf
Boody, Charles
Burch, Charlton
Gregory, David
Guyer, Carolyn
Joyce, Michael
Kirksey, Daniel
Pallas, Jim
Van Oast, Jon

Minnesota
Borrup, Tom
Hall, David
Nyberg, Melanie
Verostko, Roman

Missouri
Bodenhamer, William
Lef, T.V.
Shepard, Scott
Stephens, Thomas
Van Voorst, Kathleen

Mississippi
Brown, Paul

North Carolina
Casper, Stuart
Rathbun, MD

Nebraska
Schonlau, Ree
Batson, Joan
Narwicz, Christina

New Hampshire
Barnes, Christopher
Diamond, Jody
Fugua, David
Knowlton, Kenneth
Polansky, Larry
Welch, Chuck

New Jersey
Farber, Leslie
David Haxton
Fergusson, Robert
Kellner, Michael
Mclean, Des
Mueller, Robert Emmer
Orenstein, Phillip
Pocock-Williams, Lynn
Smith, Nora

New Mexico
Colby, Sas
Daniel, Tommie
Edelson-Rosenberg, Evelyn
Farrell, Anne
Nelson, Mary Carroll
Saad-Cook, Janet

New York
Ames, Charles
Archambault, Michele
Armstrong, Sara Garden
Astrahan, Ilene
Baer, Josh
Berkhout, Rudie
Binkley, Timothy
Blazekovic, Zdravko
Bloch, Mark
Blum, Terry
Bobin, Angela
Boretz, Benjamin
Bova, Jeffrey
Buchen, Bill and Mary
Cash, Sydney
Cunningham, Steve
Donihue, David
Druckrey, Timothy
Feder, Theodore
Gedzelman, Stanley
George, Dan
Goode, Daniel
Halaby, Samia
Hellerman, William
Hendel, Robert

Hetzler, Florence
Hocking, Ralph
Hocking, Sherry Miller
Howard, Edgar
Jones, Glory
Karl, Brian
Kerlow, Isaac
Klinkowstein, Tom
Larsun, Rodger
Manovich, Lev
Martin, Alice
Martin, Tony
Materre, Michello
McGeehan, John
Moak, Karen
Morgan, Robert
Neaderland, Louise
O'Neil, Elaine
Oliveros, Pauline
Panaiotis
Pannucci, Cynthia
Parkinson, Carl
Pathe, Peter
Pierce, Steve
Rahmani, Aviva
Ramirez, Jeffrey
Reed, Hazen
Rigden, John
Rolnick, Neil
Rosen, Joe
Rossol, Monona
s'Soreff, Stephen
Schwendinger, Leni
Speer, Lance
Stieglitz, Katia
Taubin, Amy
Vila, Doris
Weisberg, Elizabeth
Whitman, Deborah
Wosk, Julie
Wyman, James
Yung, Susan
Zajec, Edward

Ohio
Ban Tepper, Kristen
Davis, Jr., Collis
Drake, Luigi-Bob
Draznin, Wayne
Gaffney, Gary
Lee, Judith Yaros
McCarthy, Jr., Robert
Moose, Michael
Nelson, Gary Lee
Stredney, Donald

Oregon
Barclay, Daria Harvey
Bell, Lillian
Clark, Craig
Gessert, George
Levy, Shab
Taylor, Joann
Young, Emily

Pennsylvania
Bhatnagar, Ranjit Sahai
Borders, Jennifer
Brown, Ronald
Carrier, David
Carroll, James
Coffey, Irene
Cox, Lynn
DeFreitas, Frank
Kenton, Mary Jean
Lewison, Robert
Loeffler, Carl
Luderowski, Barbara
Malenda, J
Melin, William
Pane, John
Phillips, John
Podnar, Gregg
Quinn, Ken
Roland, George
Rosenberg, Jim
Rudman, Joseph
Scott, Mark & Misako
Todorovic, Vesna
Tuohey, Karen

Rhode Island
Mierka, Gregg
Nadin, Mihai
Ockerse, Tom

South Carolina
Wang, Sam

South Dakota
Termes, Dick

Tennessee
Metros, Susan
Wachspress, Eugene

Texas
Belik, Jaroslav
Jenks, William
McWhirter, Ellen Ann

Virginia
DeMao, John
Freeman, Nancy Jackson
Hurlburt, Carol
Mahin, Bruce

Mones-Harttal, Barbara
Norman, Julyen
Sokolove, Deborah
Updike, Christina

Vermont
Connors, John

Washington
Baines, Sunny
Cobb, James
Focke, Anne
Guzak, Karen
Jordan, Lorna
Karpen, Richard
Kohl, Jerome
Lynx, David
Rahn, John

Wisconsin
Kashinn, Laurel
Schaffer, John

Wyoming
Cannon, Jane

UNITED KINGDOM
Allen, Russ
Ascott, Roy
Barson, Robin
Boyd, Patrick
Burdock, Jeremy
Burrows, Paul
Butler, David
Carroll, Miranda
Cawkwell, Debbie
Davies, Jake
Dixon, Gordon
Foster, Tony
Green, Roy
Hallett, Ed
Hann, Derek
Ho, Mae-Wan
Jackson, N.
Jones, Ed Susan
Kocher, Clive
Lane, Barry
Lansdown, John
Lilley, Clare Louise
Marsden, Alan
Monaghan, Ciaran
Murray, Peter
Murray, Rod
Rees, Jeremy
Sanderson, Colin
Schiess, Christian

Sermon, Paul
Shepherd, Gerald
Smith, Ms. Perry
Solanke, Adeola
Stewart, David
Wardle, Derek
Whistlecroft, Lisa

WEST INDIES
Narodny, Leo

INDEX OF ORGANIZATIONS

INDEX OF INDIVIDUALS